Personal Names in Asia
History, Culture and Identity

T0345514

Personal Names in Asia

History, Culture and Identity

Edited by

Zheng Yangwen and Charles J-H Macdonald

NUS PRESS
SINGAPORE

© 2010 NUS Press
National University of Singapore
AS3-01-02, 3 Arts Link
Singapore 117569

Fax: (65) 6774-0652
E-mail: nusbooks@nus.edu.sg
Website: http://www.nus.edu.sg/nuspress

ISBN 978-9971-69-380-0 (Paper)

All rights reserved. This book, or parts thereof, may not be reproduced in any form or by any means, electronic or mechanical, including photocopying, recording or any information storage and retrieval system now known or to be invented, without written permission from the Publisher.

National Library Board Singapore Cataloguing in Publication Data

Personal names in Asia: history, culture and identity / edited by Zheng Yangwen
   and Charles J-H Macdonald. – Singapore: NUS Press, c2010.
   p. cm.
   Includes bibliographical references and index.
   ISBN-13: 978-9971-69-380-0 (pbk.)

   1. Names, Personal – Asia – History. 2. Names, Personal – Social aspects –
Asia. I. Zheng, Yangwen. II. Macdonald, Charles J-H.

GN468.45
929.4095 — dc22   OCN191658764

Typeset by: Scientifik Graphics (Singapore) Pte Ltd
Printed by: Print Dynamics (S) Pte Ltd

CONTENTS

PREFACE

James C. Scott

The social use of personal names is as close to a cultural universe as one can find — even if, in some cases, that name is avoided as in a teknonym (for example, when someone is, say, identified as "x's mother's brother." In fact, it is hard to imagine social life at all without naming systems for designating or addressing a particular, unique individual. Precisely because of the universality of the practice, the form it takes in different cultures and times offers a valuable window for social analysis. And such an analysis is exactly what this exceptional collection of essays provides in abundance. Rather than summarize these essays, I intend to highlight in this preface a few of the larger issues that a study of names can illuminate.

For people who *inhabit* a culture and its naming practices, it is easy, perhaps unavoidable, to naturalize those practices, to assume that they have existed from time immemorial and that they are the most obvious techniques for navigating the social world. They thus take on a spurious historical depth and a spurious social autonomy. However, in fact, many naming practices are luxuriantly variable from place to place and have shifted dramatically from time to time. Neither they nor their close cousin, "kinship systems," are unmoved movers. They are best seen not as "givens" but as social constructions very much affected by power relations, cultural contact, and formal institutions.

Perhaps the most fundamental distinction between different naming practices is that between *vernacular* naming practices, on the one hand, and *official* (i.e., state-inflected) naming practices on the other. Long ago there were *only* vernacular naming practices. In the modern world they jostle for recognition with official, state-created forms of naming. The cultural superabundance of vernacular naming practices is illustrated by their plurality and their instability. It is common for non-state (or pre-state) peoples to have many personal names for different situations and interlocutors (e.g., with parents, various siblings, age-mates, inferiors, superiors, teachers, spirits, strangers). A child named in utero may be renamed during a difficult labor to change its (and its mother's) luck, named again after an illness or noteworthy event, or to take the name of a recently deceased person to appease his or her spirit. Such systems work perfectly well at the vernacular level. No one is in doubt about who is who.

Vernacular naming systems do not, however, have the necessary discriminating power for the most important state activities: taxation, land registration, conscription, corvée, and police work. Vernacular practices are, in a word, *illegible*. How can officials find a particular individual in a world, until recently, without photo-identification, national registration systems, birth certificates, serial numbers, fingerprints, and now, iris scans and DNA profiles? In rural, early modern England, for example, it would have been common for 90 per cent of the men in a village to carry one of only eight names (typically kings' names like William, Henry, Edward, Charles, James, or John). How to find a particular William? At the time such a man would usually have a second name — a by-name, *not* a permanent patronym. Thus a William who lived on the hill might be locally known as William Hill, and a lazy William as William Doolittle, and a William who was the son of John as William Johnson. Such names, however, changed with each generation. They were local nicknames, unknown outside the small face-to-face community. Only later did they become fixed, legal, inherited patronyms.

Gradually, from the thirteenth to the nineteenth century, the populations of Western Europe acquired permanent patronyms that tracked *male* (the taxpaying population!) genealogy, structured the official life of the nuclear family, and made the administration of taxes, conscription, land tenure, and criminal law that much easier. The proliferation of the permanent patronym closely mimics the geography of increasing contact and interaction with officials and their institutions. Prussia's Jews only got permanent patronyms in the mid-nineteenth century, following the Revolution of 1848, as a condition of full citizenship. For many people, however, vernacular names were the currency of daily life and official names might have only a "paper" existence in the tax records and deeds.

The point of this brief sketch is to emphasize that permanent patronyms were, everywhere, a state (and church) project, pursued with the goal of administrative legibility in mind. Where the state was precocious and ancient, as in Han Dynasty China, the specified clan/lineage names appear very early indeed. Where the state is historically un-precocious and of recent vintage, no permanent patronyms have yet to be established — for example, Indonesia, Burma, Laos, or Malaysia. Elsewhere, the creation of permanent patronyms is comparatively recent. The Spaniards imposed (mostly) Spanish surnames on the population of Luzon in the Philippines in the mid-nineteenth century and the Thai state mandated them after World War II. In Thailand, as in the case of Turkey under Ataturk, the new patronyms were so little known, even among friends, that the telephone book alphabetized the names beginning with the better known first name. The history of European and Chinese colonialism has been one of trying (often with indifferent success) to impose metropolitan naming systems both as a measure of administrative convenience and as a mark of cultural assimilation to the colonizer's family system.

As an administrative technique of legibility and identification, naming practices have been superseded by more effective techniques such as photo-IDs, bar codes, personal serial numbers, military "dog-tags," and internal passports. Since the bearer can discard or refuse to deliver such identification, states have preferred to move, when possible, to techniques that make evasion impossible — for example, fingerprints, DNA profiles, iris scans, or, in some cases, both traditional and modern tattoos. One senses that vernacular systems of naming might begin to enjoy a new heyday now that the pressures on state-mandated personal naming practices to serve the purpose of legibility have eased. It is in this sense that the comparative and historical study of naming systems is rich with implications for both social and political analysis.

ACKNOWLEDGEMENTS

We would like to thank Anthony Reid, Director of the Asia Research Institute (ARI) at the National University of Singapore, for initiating a roundtable on the subject of Asian naming practices on 15 February 2005 and bringing the three of us together for a common goal. We would like to thank ARI for financing and hosting the conference, "Naming Asia: Local Identities and Global Change," on 23 and 24 February 2006 that has now produced this volume. We thank ARI's Events Team: Rina Yap, Valerie Yeo, Alyson Rozells, and Henry Kwan for facilitating the conference. Their devotion to the success of ARI's events often went beyond the call of duty. Valerie Yeo continued to help long after the conference; she and ARI's Theodora Lam helped us put the manuscript together in December 2006. Our heartfelt thanks go to Geoff Wade, Binod Khadria, and Maribeth Erb who chaired the sessions, and to Geoffrey Benjamin, Wang Gungwu, Roxana Waterson, Renaldo Ileto, and Chua Beng Huat who acted as discussants. We are grateful to James Scott for the brilliant concluding remarks he delivered at the conference and for the perfect preface he wrote for this volume. Finally our thanks go to NUS Press, to Lena Qua, Eunice Low and above all Paul Kratoska who have labored hard for the publication of this volume.

We dedicate this volume to the memory of Ananda Rajah, our dear and respected colleague who died unexpectedly in January 2007. His picture (Plate 2 in Chapter 6) "Pha Dek Chaj and Pha Saw Di Enjoying a Cheroot" made us laugh at the conference and will undoubtedly entertain readers for years to come.

Zheng Yangwen, Manchester, England
Charles J-H Macdonald, Marseilles, France

August 2009

Introduction[1]

Anthony Reid and Charles J-H Macdonald

> The first time I went to get a visa from the Dutch embassy, they asked me my surname.
> "My name is Shakuntala. Javanese don't have surnames."
> "You have a father, don't you?"
> "If only I didn't."
> "Use your father's name," said the woman at the counter.
> "And why should I?"
> "The whole form must be filled in."
> I was livid. "Madam, you're Christian, aren't you? I'm not, but I learned at a Catholic school that Jesus didn't have a father. Why does a person have to use her father's name?"
> So I didn't go ahead with the visa application. (Ayu Utami)[2]

Most denizens of what passes for the "International Community" presume that there is a normative global system, comprising a family name and one or more given names. Most countries and international organizations require new members to fill out a form on that basis. We know that important national systems in Asia list the family name first, and those of European derivation list it last, but that is understood as a variation of a fundamental system, "natural" in its universality.

The reality is that the great majority of the world's population negotiates between a multiplicity of naming systems, the deployment of which depend on audience and context. Some are compatible with the "normative" system of the world of passports and identity cards, but most are not. Children growing up in Chinese families often do not know the "official" names of those around them until they go to school and see their playmates transformed from an often demeaning family name (Little Pig) to the more euphonious official name (Intellectual Orchid) used by the school. Like a great many Asians, they operate a different system within the family from the one deployed outside.

At one extreme of possibilities is a universal readability by God, such as was imagined in the apocalyptic literature of the Hebrews or early Christians. Only those would be saved whose names were "written in the book," "written in heaven," or "written in the Lamb's book of life."[3] In today's world of another kind of universality, we are known as unique individuals not by names as such but by machine-readable codes that identify us electronically in contemporary passports, and in the identity cards of many countries. This is a system which places us uniquely as the only such individual in the universe, but which we ourselves can neither pronounce nor comprehend. At the other extreme is a private system of names which two individuals give each other exclusively in their direct interactions, which is of no use to outsiders. In between is the world we inhabit, in which everybody carries multiple names meaningful to different audiences. Some are used only in family relations, like the nicknames most Chinese children are given at birth, or the relational titles particularly rich in Asian kin systems. Others locate us in terms of gender, ethnicity, religion, caste, class, and nation within larger plural societies.

This book constitutes an initial attempt at describing the systems that underlie naming practices, with examples taken primarily from Southeast Asia, where such systems are particularly abundant and fluid. The centrality of names to many of the crucial debates and preoccupations of our time — identity, hybridity, migration, nationalism, multiculturalism, globalization — makes it surprising that there has been so little systematic comparative exploration of Asian names and naming systems. The two authors of this introduction had been separately convinced of this lack for some time, but from different directions. The historian (Reid) was increasingly convinced that changes in naming systems are not only the consequences of great social shifts in history, but also influence those shifts. The anthropologist (Macdonald) was searching for patterns in Austronesian naming systems, seeing them as crucial markers of the social structure. Only our coming together, and the support of a third partner in Zheng Yangwen, made it possible to conceptualize a conference at the Asia Research Institute in Singapore, and then to bring together this book.

For Reid the fascination with this subject was stirred by the study of Southeast Asian history, but came much more to the surface when living in Los Angeles. There he taught students most of whose lineages were Asian but whose contemporary need was to negotiate the stern US naming system in ways that retained some older coherence, either by hiding a vernacular system in a private or mono-ethnic domain, or developing a hybrid name pattern which looked American but was not quite.

More recently in Singapore it became an even stronger concern as a constant problem of negotiations and missed signals in a world of overlapping and contradictory naming systems, none of which is clearly normative (unlike the US or China). Within many of the systems, kinship or relational terms dominate in family usage, but in the public domain systems overlap in confusing ways. The telephone directory, for example, does not recognize commas but lists names in the order they are written. For Chinese, Korean, and Japanese names this usually puts an inherited family name first, while for Malays, Javanese, Thais, and some Indians this would be the personal name by which they are usually known. For those operating in some variation of a European or Indian system there is no predictability in what order the name would have been registered, and hence alphabetized. For example, there are 337 people listed under John in the 2006–7 Singapore directory, representing a range of ethnicities including at least European, south Indian, Chinese, Filipino, Japanese, and Eurasian. Occasionally this John appeared to be father's name or a family name but usually a personal name.

Chinese and Korean names are on the surface the most straight-forward, always having a family name as government forms require and frequently marking the family, generation, and individual with a highly standard three-character name. Yet few people seem wholly comfortable using this official name in everyday parlance, unless some relational marker accompanies it. Koreans generally consider it impolite to use the given name in addressing anyone of the same or higher status. Official forms expect Chinese to have at least one "alias." Different romanization and dialect pronunciations create great variety in what is the same Chinese-character name. The discomfort with using the personal name in an international context has led many (especially women) to adopt a European name, and others (especially men) to resort to initials. On the Singapore tennis court, university colleagues would say "nice shot Prof" to each other, apparently unclear about what register is appropriate. As so often, surprise is the mother of analysis, and more rigorous investigation of these negotiations seemed essential.

East Asian Names and Their Translation

As Zheng Yangwen points out below, Northeast Asian names are inherently characters, expressing a meaning much more specific than the sound. How are such names to be rendered to outsiders who cannot read the characters — an issue increasingly salient in modern globalized conditions? Without the tones that distinguish monosyllables from each other, a rendering into a phonetic system such as a roman or Arabic alphabet risks restricting even more the limitations of the established "100 surnames" of Chinese tradition. On the other hand when uttered in Cantonese or Hokkien, let alone Vietnamese or Korean, these characters sound completely different and are romanized very differently. Among the most common *xing*, for example, the character romanized as Zhang in the pinyin romanization of the PRC would be Chong in the Wade-Giles system followed in Taiwan, Cheung in Cantonese, Teo in Hokkien, Truong in Vietnamese and Jang in Korean. Zhao in pinyin would be transformed into Chao, Chiu, Chew, Trieu, and Cho in the same sequence. For genealogical purposes of honoring (male) ancestors, however, the true name is held to be the Chinese character.

The order of Northeast Asian and European names is significant, with the more fundamental coming first in each case. The basic European name is the personal given name, as opposed to an extra historical accretion, the surname (derived from French *surnom* "added name," although that term in modern French refers to a nickname), which came to be inherited. In Northeast Asia the family name (*xing*) is ancient and fundamental, determining a loyalty that extends across generations. Although women keep their own *xing* at marriage, they are absorbed into that of their husband in terms of honored bloodlines. Because of their fundamental character, the family names are not something that can be readily changed, and they remain relatively few in number. Although Chinese speak of the 100 *xing*, there are in reality as many as 700 Chinese characters accepted as family names, though the majority of the population carries one of the 20 most popular. The recent trend for two-character names in the PRC has led to what one newspaper called "a serious social problem in China," of identical names. *The Youth Daily of Shanghai* reported that there were 3,937 people in 1996 named Zhang Jie in Shanghai alone, and 3,751 named Zhang Min.[4]

In Korea the total number is about 250, with Kim alone accounting for 21 per cent of the population. In Vietnam 38 per cent of the population carries the family name Nguyen (equivalent to the less common Ruan in pinyin), which together with the Tran name accounts for half the population.[5] Perhaps for this reason the family name is seldom used to address people in Vietnam, and the last given name serves as both formal and informal means of address in what is a common Southeast Asian pattern. In the diaspora where there were fewer Nguyens and Trans and an expectation that family and personal names had to differ, the Chinese pattern tends to be adopted. Nguyen Vu Dong would usually be Mr. Dong in Vietnam but Mr. Nguyen in the US, while fuller assimilation into the US naming system might lead to Dong V. Nguyen.

Family Names, Western Names, and Contemporary Identity

Although both Islam and Christianity favored the use of the names of their respective saints and prophets, they made little impression on the East Asian system of naming in Chinese characters. Because the character-based system can only with difficulty render these alien names, Muslims and Christians operating in Chinese, Korean, or Japanese have maintained the standard system of Northeast Asian names. Even European missionaries fitted into this pattern in Chinese. In translation for an international audience, however, many of the earliest Christian converts added a Christian personal name to a Northeast Asian family name, like the Cantonese Jesuit convert John Hu (1681–1741) and the prolific Vietnamese Christian writer Philiphê Binh (1759–1832).[6] These were early cases of the hybrid name, enabling its owner to operate in two different speech worlds.

In the twentieth century this hybrid pattern extended far beyond the ranks of Christians. The status of European-style schools for modernizing elites ensured that many young Asians were taught by European teachers who had difficulties with their names. As early as the first years of the twentieth century, the elite *peranakan* (local-born Chinese) girls of Java who were tutored by European private tutors were allocated pretty European names. The fashion may have been led by the family of the westernizing sugar magnate Oei Tiong Ham, whose two multilingual daughters adopted such names in their teens, and publicly performed songs by Bizet and Gounod as Gwendoline and Angèle Oeitiongham, the father's name being run together as if a surname. Not to be outdone, the leading Chinese families of Surabaya had their own Dutch tutor to train them to perform in the European mode, sporting names like Anna, Antonia, Rosa, and Josephine.[7] European "Christian" names, along with European languages and manners, proved increasingly acceptable and even fashionable for diasporic Chinese girls as the century wore on. Chinese men followed the trend to a more moderate degree, though many preferred the anonymity of initials. This pattern was certainly encouraged by missionary schools, especially convent schools, where some European teachers preferred names they could remember and pronounce, whether or not their bearers were Christian. The practice of adding a European name in front of a standard three-character Chinese one began in the diaspora but spread even to westernized circles in China itself.

It has not been sufficiently examined why this hybrid trend became so common among Chinese in multicultural situations, in contrast with other Asians. The preparation for such a development may have been a long-standing habit among diasporic Chinese of assuming aliases for use in different languages and contexts. The Chinese name made little sense if pronounced tonelessly and removed from the world of Chinese characters. Moreover Chinese seldom used their formal given names among themselves, and adopting a name for use by multicultural outsiders always involved some invention, whether by running the two given names together (Tianpoh) to sound like a Southeast Asian name, or by adopting a local one. Bilingual Chinese had to adopt naming patterns that sounded local for use among Thai, Malay, Javanese, English, or Dutch-speakers, while retaining the appropriate Chinese lineage name for ritual and other "Chinese" purposes and the usual kinship markers (even in translation) for use within extended family. For such multicultural purposes an emotionally neutral name was necessary that could be used regardless of status and intimacy.

In the era of globalization since the 1980s the trend toward hybrid western-Chinese naming has become much more prevalent in Singapore and Malaysia, despite the absence of European teachers as a causal factor. A brief survey of the "official" names of Chinese graduating from the National University of Singapore over the past 20 years reveals that about 30 per cent carried a "western" given name in addition to their Chinese name. A marked majority (around 60 per cent) of those taking western additional names were female. While the overall proportion is stable over time, a strong trend toward western names (from 29 per cent in 1986 to 39 per cent in 2006) emerges if pinyin romanizations are excluded. Since PRC students are a growing minority of the total, and all romanize in pinyin, this may deliver a more "Singaporean" sample. In reality however there has also been a trend to pinyin spelling among Singapore children born in the decade after the government's "Speak Mandarin" drive began in 1979,[8] and the importance of this cohort in the 2006 sample (26 per cent) may simply show that the more localized Chinese resistant to pinyinization are also strongly inclined to take western names.[9]

A sampling of individuals and offices in Singapore suggests a much higher proportion of young working women (especially) and men use western names in practice than those officially recorded with them in the sample above. The difference occurs in the self-attribution of western names in high school or in the workplace, thenceforth generally used by work colleagues though not carried through to a change in the official identity card. This process is described by a perspicuous colleague as being in large part a factor of the upward social and educational mobility which has been such a feature of this period. While Chinese dialect-speaking parents endowed children with auspicious or cute-sounding names romanized in Hokkien pronunciation, the English- and Mandarin-speaking children often found them embarrassingly "Chinese-y" (*cina*). "For the

upwardly mobile, the 'gold,' 'jade,' 'prosper' that are their parents' preferences become all too crass and blatant significations of desire for wealth,
and in that way very 'uncool.'"[10]

The pairing of an ancestral family name with a western given name
is one way to negotiate between private and public, vernacular and global.
It is a contemporary example of the phenomenon evident throughout this
book, of using different names for different audiences and combining
some of them in the formal name required for written records. A religious
identity, or frequently a simplified acceptable name for use by outsiders
in school or workplace, is most often used as a given name, while the
inherited name typically proclaims an ethnic and clan lineage.

South Asia

Indian names have not been given adequate weight in this book, nor
indeed in the existing literature, although they are particularly complex
and tightly bound up with identity and gender issues. It has been noted
that South and Southeast Asia together form the area of the world most
resistant to accepting a normative or global arrangement of family name
and personal name. The reasons however are quite different in the two
cases. If Southeast Asian societies typically have bilateral kinship and a
comparatively low emphasis on patrilineal descent groups, Indian society
is firmly built on the salience of just such groups.

The most basic unit of Indian society above the family has for centuries
been the *jati*, or patrilineal endogamous descent group. In rural India
each village has two or more *jati*, each of which have "certain assigned
attributes — among them a specialized occupation — according to which
the group is ranked in the local hierarchy."[11] It also has a collective name,
essential for purposes of internal recognition as the group within which
one should marry. Above this however is a cluster of related *jati*, often
in the same or related occupations, which may also have a name and a
habit of cooperation especially when outside the homeland. While all
such *jati* can be categorized as belonging to one of the four classic castes
of Hindu tradition or the "outcaste" Dalits, it was the named *jati* that
bound people and enabled them to work closely together and to trust one
another.[12] More than in other societies these names were likely to signal
the occupation appropriate to the *jati*. Patel or Chaudhari were once
headmen, Joshi astrologers, Mehta clerks, and Gandhi perfume merchants.
Even more than Chinese surname lineages, the *jati* groups were essential
to commercial activity and the growth of capital in India. Commercial *jati*
like the Agarwals in northern India or the Natukotai Chettiars in Tamilnad
were extremely important to the way commerce was organized.[13] The role

of *jati* names, therefore, made most South Asian naming patterns quite distinct from the Southeast Asian ones which constitute the majority of this book.

Reform movements in India tended to take a hostile view of caste. Because caste placed everybody in a prescribed social rank in accordance with birth, it was offensive to any liberal world-view of the brotherhood of all mankind; it was shameful in relations with outsiders, particularly the colonial British; it was divisive for those who wanted to unite society in the name of nationalism or religion; and it constrained the upwardly mobile groups who were often the leading advocates of reform. In the southern Indian states of Tamilnadu and Kerala, the widespread resentment of Brahmin domination gave rise to a particularly strident anti-caste movement in the twentieth century that encouraged the suppression of caste-identifying inherited names. The naming systems of the south were varied and complex, but patronymics were generally more favored, typically the father's name following the given name.[14] Everywhere lower-caste Hindus avoided using the *jati* names, or changed them, as they fought their way up the social system — as chronicled in Dr. de Silva's chapter in the case of Sri Lanka. Modernizing elites associated with the nationalist movement were particularly likely to oppose using caste-related names because they were seeking to escape from the caste system. Nevertheless, large and increasing numbers of Indians entering the cosmopolitan world where surnames are required, especially those in the diaspora, have used *jati* names as family names for this purpose.

The Sikh religion is interesting here in having required a change of naming practice as part of its opposition to caste. The Gurus of Sikhdom opposed the use of caste or clan markers, and instead required that all males should be surnamed Singh (Lion) and all females Kaur (Princess), making everybody theoretically equal. A personal name should in addition be chosen, beginning with the first letter of a page of the *Guru Granth Sahib* opened at random. Requiring women to take the name of neither father nor husband can be seen as resistance to patriarchy, though in some rural areas this effaced the names of married women altogether, becoming "mother of X" or "wife of Y." Faced with international pressure for a family name, however, a growing minority of Sikhs appear to be adopting the caste or clan names, particularly in diaspora where caste associations are less likely to be remembered. In Singapore, where family names are required on every manner of form, 93.5 per cent of the Sikh children registered in a Punjabi language program in 1990 used their gender-marker name (Singh or Kaur) as if it were a family name. By 1999, however, 34 per cent of such children were registered with their clan/caste names (Sidhu, Gill, Dhillon, Bandal, etc) as family names.[15] The Singapore telephone directory, representing an older generation, in 2006/7 had 96 names listed under Singh as a surname, still more numerous than those who self-registered using one of the common Punjabi *jati* names.

Southeast Asian Names and Modern Identities

> This has been the century of the great immigrant experiment. It is only this late in the day that you can walk into a playground and find Isaac Leung by the fishpond, Danny Rahman in the football cage, Quang O'Rourke bouncing a basketball, and Irie Jones humming a tune. Children with first and last names on a direct collision course. Names that secrete within them mass exodus, cramped boats and planes, cold arrivals, medical checks (Zadie Smith).[16]

In the bilateral societies of Southeast Asia outside Vietnam, inherited family names have been slow to develop. The two exceptions, where the state successfully imposed surnames in the Philippines and Thailand, are discussed in two chapters below. Four chapters discuss Austronesian societies in Indonesia and Taiwan which demonstrate the theoretical possibilities explored by Charles Macdonald. This book can by no means explore all the diversity of Southeast Asian names, but these chapters, and the others exploring Karen and Wa naming patterns faced with national (Burmese and Chinese respectively) as well as international norms, demonstrate most of the theoretical possibilities of naming systems.

In modern cosmopolitan societies, names have become the most fundamental marker of group identity. Every adolescent trying to fit in at school knows the burden of a minority name. Name choice among converts and migrants is a crucial means of negotiating the new identity and either confirming or rejecting the old.

On entry to either Islam or Christianity, Southeast Asian converts usually receive an identifiably Muslim (usually Arabic) or Christian (saint's name) designation. They do not always use it in everyday transactions, and if not particularly connected to religious institutions, they might not impose such a name on their children. The overwhelming tendency of the past century, however, has been toward increasing use of Arabic names by Muslims. Malay speakers have probably led this trend, and the proportion of Malay names like Putih, Jantan or Awang in the Singapore phone book is now vastly overwhelmed by the Arabic personal names of prophets or companions of the Prophet. One way to mark the trend may be the extent of shift from father to son as recorded, for example, in the 2003–4 Singapore phone book. Of the 340 names listed under "Ibrahim," for example, 68 (20 per cent) have fathers with Malay or Javanese names. There is much less slippage back the other way, and what there is appears to be primarily of girls with names like Puteh or Putri, whose fathers have Arabic names (but whose mothers may have indigenous ones).

Increasingly, therefore, the Arabic personal name conveys a Muslim identity. In some past times and places this was true of saints' names for Christians, though this never took hold within the name-world of Chinese characters. There has also been a definite pattern, perhaps increasing, for Vietnamese, Thai, Javanese, and Batak Christians also to use their indigenous name rather than their Christian, baptismal one.

The fact of the personal name becoming a "Christian name" in the European tradition left open the option for surnames to convey different national, clan or class identities. Aristocrats led the trend to combine the humility of a Christian name (the only one encouraged for the Catholic clergy) with the proud self-assertion of their lineage in a surname. In Islam the *nisbah* of prominent Arab families (Alatas, al-Junied, al-Tikriti) provided the same model, though one relatively little emulated by Southeast Asian Muslims. Westernized Javanese and Sundanese aristocrats appear to have begun the pattern of combining a Muslim personal name with a surname-like aristocratic name (for example, Hussein Djajadiningrat, Mochtar Kusumaatmaja) early in the twentieth century. In South Sulawesi and Maluku a similar pattern is observable among the elite (Hasan Walinono, Saleh Putuhena). More widespread, however, and almost universal among Malaysian Malays, has been the pattern of adopting ever more consistently an Arab practice of adding the father's name (*nasab*) with *ibn* or *bin*, while resisting any move toward inherited family names.

Where exogamous clans were particularly important a factor in marriage alliances, the retention of a signifying clan name as a modern surname was more likely to be the result. The diverse Batak groups of North Sumatra, who have in common the *Dalihan na Tolu* system of categorizing kin into wife-givers, wife-takers and agnates, are a particularly interesting study in this regard. Their entry into the modern world was largely a nineteenth and early twentieth-century phenomenon, through the medium of Islamization (primarily in the south) and Christianization. While the earlier phase of Islamization encouraged a Malay style of language and naming, the Christianization carried out by German Rhenische missionaries from the 1860s emphasized the retention of indigenous language and identity — partly as a bulwark against Malayization. Batak names continued after Christianization, though in a very diverse pattern.

In the 1920s the interaction of Dutch and Batak officials working in the field of Batak customary law produced a huge chart linking all Toba and most Angkola and Mandailing *marga* (clans) with each other by tracing each back to branches developed from parent *marga*. Published in Toba Batak in 1926 and in Dutch in 1932,[17] this schema canonized and eventually popularized the notion that every Batak had an identifiable *marga*, ultimately related in some way with every other *marga*. Toba Bataks studying in mission schools, and eventually in state schools, began using the *marga* name as a surname indicating their patrilineage. By the 1960s, in effect, every Toba Batak used *marga* names like Simatupang, Siahaan, Siregar, or Lumbantobing proudly as a family name inherited through the male line. This made the adjustment to western or Chinese-dominated societies particularly easy for them.

All the other Batak groups were affected by this process. Karo Bataks, who became Christian much more slowly and partially than the Toba, emulated this tendency to see the *marga* as an essential identifier of Karo-ness. For southern Batak groups influenced by Islam there was more uncertainty and conflict as to whether the *marga*, and with it Batak origins, should be emphasized in this way. Many of those educated in Tapanuli carried their Mandailing or Angkola identity proudly to the national Indonesian level as Abdul Haris Nasution or Mochtar Lubis. Those who migrated early to Malay-speaking areas were more likely to seek to hide their pagan "uncivilized" roots by using a simple Muslim name and passing as Malays. The Mandailings of Malaysia, following a pattern established long before the rise of "*marga* consciousness," have always been in the latter category.

In addition to these self-selected patterns of using a surname to reflect identity, the state explicitly uses surnames to brand and homogenize its people during peaks of state nationalism. The Turkish law of 1934 was the most explicit such instrument. Although the letter of the law exempted Christian, Jewish, and Armenian minorities from the rule that the new surnames had to be "Turkish," in practice officials used it as a tool of assimilation and homogenization, as did Prussians in imposing family names on the Jewish minority in the early nineteenth century.[18] A well-known Asian case was the "name order" of Governor-General Minami in 1939, "allowing" Koreans to adopt Japanese names as a means to assimilation into the imperial order. By 1944, 84 per cent of the Korean population had done so, not without a great deal of pressure from lower officials. Independent South Korea launched a campaign to eliminate these Japanese influences, and subsequent control of the system of names through the Family Registry Law was unusually strict in that country. Parents had to choose from a list of acceptable given names.[19]

Southeast Asian cases also show some of this state nationalist feature. The king's anti-Chinese sentiment was certainly a factor in the Siamese surname decree of 1913. The new surnames had to be distinctively Thai, and the king was ready personally to create such names for prominent Chinese wishing to be naturalized as Thai citizens.

Indonesia is too diverse to make such a strategy possible, and sur-names have never been proposed as a norm. Indonesian citizens of Chinese descent were, however, permitted to adopt "Indonesian" names (in practice extremely various) in a 1961 law. During the ferocious crack-down on communism between 1965 and 1967, the procedure for so doing was simplified in a manner that suggested to Chinese Indonesians that they might suffer if they did not make the name change. Since the Chinese name had included a family name, and many Chinese Indonesians sought temporal continuity of both a male lineage and a business, one consequence was to inaugurate Indonesian family names for many Sino-Indonesians at this time, in the way Reid describes for the Philippines and Thailand below. Corporate magnate Liem Sioe Liong, for example, became Sudono Salim, and his family and corporation retained the Salim as an inherited name.

Methodology: The Relationship between Name Types and Name Tags

The above sections show that changing patterns of naming in history have had repercussions on culture, economics, and politics and on the attendant institutions of administrations, corporations, schools, churches and even nations. This concern requires in our view a conceptual under-standing of what personal names are and do and how they differ in space and time. In other words the very phenomenon of anthroponymy has to be theoretically constructed in the social sciences. We need a methodology that will help us bring the many aspects of naming to a set of general principles. We also need these principles to help organize the multifarious local naming patterns in a cross-cultural and historical grid of sorts.

As there is no space here to undertake a comprehensive summary of name studies in history, anthropology, sociology, psychology, linguistics, and onomastics, we will move directly to the perhaps controversial conclu-sion that such a theory does not yet exist, despite recent attempts at proposing something like, for instance, an "anthropology of names and naming" (vom Bruck and Bodenhorn, 2006). Most authors concerned with names and naming in the social sciences have not been concerned to generate a real comparative framework and to pursue the matter with a view to classify naming systems as anthropologists since Morgan have done with kinship systems. Almost all authors look at individual systems and practices or even, at individual name types (like nicknames or patronyms) as exemplified by the discussions around the notion of teknonymy related by Sillander in this volume.

One of the most severe constraints on the development of an operational and comparative theory of personal names has involved becoming entangled in the semiotic intricacies discussed by linguistic philosophers who deal with the problem of proper names as opposed to common names. For instance, controversies regarding the question of sense versus reference locate the entire question of names within the logical triangle of the lexical item (the proper name), its meaning, and the thing or person to which it referred. The link, mostly semantic and psychological, between a label and a person or thing and an exaggerated attention to the semantic properties of personal names prove to be a methodological cul-de-sac when it comes to accounting for and bringing order into the richness and diversity of naming practices as observed by historians and ethnographers.

Lévi-Strauss' overemphasis on the classificatory function of personal names (which he discussed together with proper names) does not help clarify matters, in spite of some sharp and penetrating views on the subject. In his lengthy discussion of personal and proper names in *The Savage Mind*, the idea that proper names always and essentially classify is stated several times.[20] Moreover Lévi-Strauss sees personal names, in some instances at least, as a form of taxonomy. The Wik Munkan system of Australia is thus construed as a trinomial Linnaean taxonomy label.[21] This is particularly spurious.[22] Personal names can be classified as just words for things, but their classificatory function is never the main or even central contribution to the act of naming. Sometimes they do not classify at all. As Molino aptly wrote,

> The very existence of a plurality of names does not serve the purpose of a classificatory order, because it goes way beyond what is functionally necessary [for a purely classificatory purpose]. Naming may obey at times some principles of classification, but these principles do not form a system, they supplement each other endlessly. That is how the fundamental difference manifests itself between a classificatory and a naming practice: *the individual is not a species....* Classifications are used for classifying [species, groups, sets of elements], whereas in the case [of personal names], it is the individual which is the origin of the process and which is the object of several independent classifications that *serve only to enrich its social definition.*"[23]

Finally Lévi-Strauss' contribution to a theory of personal names as it was later on summarized by his followers was based on three functions: identification, classification and meaning (French "identification, classement, signification").[24] As those functions are too broad and overlap, and as the function of classification has been misconstrued as central, the entire framework became too imprecise or lopsided to be of real use.[25]

We advocate a different approach here. We believe that one must start with a clarification of the concept of name, and we propose to differentiate clearly the concept of name type (onomastic category) from the concept of name tag (onomastic label or personal-name-lexeme),[26] as explained more fully in Macdonald's contribution below. Most authors in this volume have used this most essential conceptual distinction. Using this analytical tool not only helps demonstrate that naming practices are organized into systems (that is, arrangements of name types with stable properties of their respective lexematic repertoires), but also how they are used pragmatically and how they differ from one culture to another, one speech community to another and one historical period to another. It is indeed the **relationships among name types and between name types and name tags** that provide the most convenient way to compare naming practices as well as offering a more encompassing view of this phenomenon. Instead of being a collection of name tags, naming systems are ordered arrangements of name types, which are categories such as "first name," "surname," or "nickname" in English. Those categories are emically defined and authors usually have no difficulty describing them. Confusion arises when this distinction is forgotten or discarded while developing interpretive rationales. Looking at naming as based on sets of name tags ordered by name types, and then looking at the entire set of name types current in a linguistic community, provides a sound and profitable pathway to discover how unique each system is, how it compares to others, and at the same time what social and cultural reality transpires through particular naming practices. The gain is tremendous in both directions: looking inside local naming practices and comparing different naming systems. An understanding of how naming systems relate to other aspects of human organization starts to emerge. A typology or classification becomes possible.

The Book

The volume is divided into four parts. The first takes the long view and investigates change in naming practices in the long term. Reid and Gealogo both address the modern trend toward surnames, an issue that has been most salient in recent works,[27] and that is representative of the globalized, hegemonic, binomial system imposed on people the world over. The two authors address this question from a slightly different angle.

Reid explores how surnames have helped create a new sense of corporatism leading to a form of family-based capitalistic entrepreneurship. Gealogo establishes the real intention of Governor-General Narciso Claveria's 1849 decree in the Philippines, which was not to "hispanize" the subjects of the crown, but to make them countable and accountable. Zheng Yangwen demonstrates the social and political values of naming styles throughout Chinese history. Her analysis brings forth a very strong sense of the expressive function of names in a highly complex civilization and how they reflect ideologies and cultural values.

Macdonald's contribution acts as a transitional essay. It is an attempt at classifying naming systems in insular Southeast Asia on the basis of formal properties of the latter and at the same time on what these systems reveal: a particular ethos, a kind of sociality that is specific to three different types of social organizations, egalitarian ("Class A"), competitive ("Class B"), weakly centralized ("Class C"). As such it provides a general framework for the following contributions.

The three articles in the second section by Sillander, Ananda Rajah, and Fiskesjö on the Bentian, Karen and Wa respectively provide insightful analysis and interpretations of what may be seen as variants of the "Class A" model. They all address the question of changes and the invasion into their midst of foreign hegemonic models, be it Chinese, Christian or lowland Malay-Indonesian. They all demonstrate how a traditional naming system works by a subtle but well articulated play on proximity and distance, familiarity and respect, incorporation and individuation. They take into consideration all name types, even if one of them (teknonyms for the Bentian) seems more salient. They all pay attention to how names are used in speech and communication. They all propose an anthropological model while paying attention to history.

In the third general section of this volume, naming practices belonging to what is tentatively dubbed "Class B" organizations are analyzed again in synchronic and diachronic terms. The Weyewa and Paiwan studied by Kuipers and Ku Kun-hui (as well perhaps as some of the Lamaholot groups mentioned by Barnes, though less clearly so) not only demonstrate the crucial position of names within their value systems (to the point of starting riots), but also how they relate precisely to a kind of acephalous, tribal social structure marked by status competition. Here name and prestige go together but the price sought is renown rather than power. Intrusion of another naming system results either in the development of new name tags, whether Christian or Chinese in origin, or in systemic change with binomial labels composed of a name and a surname, a *ming* and a *xing*.

The fourth and final part of the book is composed of contributions addressing aspects of naming practices belonging to the modern, complex, state-centered societies of Japan, Sri Lanka and Malaysia, which may be seen as belonging to "Class C" of Macdonald's typology, provided this is understood flexibly. In Macdonald's paper, small traditional polities are considered, such as the petty kingdoms and sultanates of the Malay world. The contributions in Part IV show some of the variations that arise in modern, populous and bureaucratic states. Naming systems reflect social complexity because individuals are identified by means of not one but several naming subsystems, each containing a set of name types. There is a huge contextual and structural variation with a multiplicity of name tags used by different subsystems at the same time.

In this section the authors also address specifically the question of change in naming, whereby actors change their personal names to the point of subverting the system. Nagata explains how this is done internally so to speak within an age-old established system of naming. Her historical and sociological approach demonstrates how merchants and peasants in early modern Japan (1600–1868) dealt with the complexity of changing their status by using new personal names and how corporations maintained continuity with head names. A number of manipulative strategies were employed in spite of a rigidly codified naming system enforced by law. De Silva's sociological analysis of the Sinhalese situation is exemplary. As elsewhere in South Asia, Sinhalese naming of persons is complex and seems to function at two levels: the local or village level and the wider caste/class/national level. Since recent history has allowed the second level to become a field where everybody can claim higher status regardless of caste, individuals have started manipulating their names to signal upward mobility. No less remarkable is the high level of hybridity exemplified by the Malaysian Chinese Muslims investigated by Hew Wai Weng. It is an apposite conclusion that this volume, which was initiated in Singapore, ends with a consideration of naming practices in the adjacent Peninsula. Here people may have three different name tags — one on their business cards, one on their Islamic cards, one on their identity card — reflecting the crisscrossing dimensions of ethnicity, religion, and nationality. Recognizing the power and centrality of names, people use them very consciously to cross borders constantly.

Westerners who inhabit very simple binomial systems can be dumbfounded at the pageantry of naming taking place in Asia: variegated, multiple, meaningful, versatile, with name tags aplenty. Those born in Europe with one or more name tags as first name, one name tag as family name, and perhaps one or two quickly dismissed nicknames, will live and die in name poverty. Those this volume celebrate, who may have nicknames and teknonyms, religious and corporation names, honor and death names, pseudonyms and retirement names, house names and clan names, local and foreign names, official and private names, know that a cornucopia of names can better express the abundance of identities we all enjoy.

Notes

1   The authors are grateful to colleagues in this volume for their insights, but also to Manjit Kaur, Jiang Na, Teo You Yenn, and Binod Khadria (all of ARI) for ideas and assistance.

2   Ayu Utami, *Saman. A Novel* [1998], trans. Pamela Allen, (Jakarta/Singapore: Equinox Publishing, 2005), p. 129.

3   Daniel 12:1; Hebrews 12:23; Revelations 21:27.

4   *Youth Daily*, quoted by the Associated Press in *Straits Times*, September 15, 2006.

5   http://en.wikipedia.org/wiki/Vietnamese_name.

6   Jonathan D. Spence, *The Question of Hu* (New York: Random House, 1989); George Dutton, "Crossing Oceans, Crossing Boundaries: The remarkable life of Philiphê Binh (1759–1832)," in *Viet Nam: Borderless Histories*, eds. Nhung Tuyet Tran and Anthony Reid (Madison: University of Wisconsin Press, 2006), pp. 219–55.

7   This information, for which I am much indebted to Didi Kwartanada, appears in the *Weekblad voor Indië*, March 31, 1907 and October 18, 1908.

8   Eddie Kuo and Bjorn Jernudd, "Balancing Macro- and Micro-sociolinguistic Perspectives in Language Management: The Case of Singapore," in *Babel or Behemoth: Language Trends in Asia*, eds. Jennifer Lindsay and Tan Ying Ying (Singapore: Asia Research Institute, 2003), p. 115.

9   I am grateful to Jiang Na for doing the research on NUS graduation lists.

10   Personal communication from Dr. Teo You Yenn, December 13, 2006

11   David G. Mandelbaum, *Society in India* (Berkeley: University of California Press, 1970), 1:14.

12   Ibid., 1:13–27; Louis Dumont, *Homo Hierarchicus: the Caste System and its Implications* (Chicago: University of Chicago Press 1970).

13   C.A. Bayly, *Rulers, Townsmen and Bazaars: North Indian Society in the Age of British Expansion, 1770–1870* (Cambridge: Cambridge University Press, 1983), pp. 174–83.

14   http://en.wikipedia.org/wiki/Indian_name; C.H. Philips, "India and Pakistan," in *Handbook of Oriental History*, ed. C.H. Philips (London: Royal Historical Society, 1951), pp. 51–5.

15   I owe this information to the research of Manjit Kaur in the records of the Sikh Education Foundation in Singapore, to both of whom I am most grateful.

16   Zadie Smith, *White Teeth* (London: Penguin Books, 2001), p. 326.

17   Waldemar Hoeta Galoeng, *Poestaha taringot toe tarombo ni halak Batak* (Laguboti: Zendingsdrukkerij, 1926). W.K.H. Ypes, *Bijdrage tot de kennis van*

de stamverwantschap, de inheemsche rechtsgemeenschappen en het grondenrecht der Toba- en Dairibataks (The Hague: Nijhoff for Adatrechtstichting, 1932).

18   Meltem Türköz, "Turkey's 1934 Surname Law." Macdonald, "Personal Names," p. 72.

19   http://en.wikipedia.org/wiki/Korean_name

20   Claude Lévi-Strauss, *The Savage Mind* (1962), pp. 261, 266, 283, 285.

21   Ibid., pp. 242–7.

22   Among the Wik Munkan the three name types that Lévi-Strauss compares to the three names given to a species within a genus, the "navel name," "big name," and "little name," do refer to clan totems but not in a classificatory manner (Thomson 1946). What they refer to are episodes in stories relating to these totems. Moreover, among the three name types derived from clan totems, one may not belong or relate to the person's own clan. As a result this trinomial sub-system would translate, in a supposedly taxonomic system, to a formula containing two elements referring differently to the same genus (clan), and a third to a second unrelated genus (clan). Both aspects of the Wik Munkan naming practice are therefore entirely alien to the intellectual and mental process that is characteristic of the Linnean taxonomy. It is definitely not a classificatory procedure. Moreover, the Wik Munkan naming system is not restricted to these mostly sacred and ceremonial names. They possess other name types that seem equally productive of social identity, in particular nicknames, and teknonyms: Thomson (pp. 159, 163). Titles — particularly necronyms — and kin terms, are essential to the general system of address and reference, but if we consider nicknames only, we can see that they form a very vital part of personal naming since they are used freely and without restraint. They are of a descriptive nature, indicating singular traits that identify individuals unambiguously.

23   Molino, Jean. "Le Nom Propre dans la Langue." *Languages* 66 (1982): 18 — our translation and emphasis.

24   Zonabend, F. "Nom." In *Dictionaire de l'ethnologie et de l'anthropologie*, eds. P. Bonte and M. Izard. Paris: PUF/Quadrige, 2002, p. 509.

25   Several authors have made the same remark concerning the conceptual value of the Lévi-Straussian model: Barnes, R.H. "Personal Names and Social Classification." In *Semantic Anthropology*, ed. David Parkin, A.S.A. Monograph 22. London: Academic Press, 1982, p. 222; Tonkin, Elizabeth. "Jealousy Names, Civilised Names: Anthroponymy of the Jlao Kru of Liberia." *Man*, n.s., 15 (1980) 4: 658–60.

26   "Tag" might not be the best choice of word as it refers here to a linguistic item, a lexeme like "Mary" or "Jack." "Tag" has been chosen for its convenient phonetic balance with "type." "Term" could be used if one accepts the phrase "name term" which would then contrast with "name type." This would parallel the use of the "kin term" and "kin type" in kinship studies.

27   Scott *et al.* "The Production of Legal Identities Proper to States: The Case of the Permanent Family Surname." *Comparative Studies of Society and History* 44, 1 (2002): 4–44.

PART I

The Long View

CHAPTER 1

Family Names in Southeast Asian History

Anthony Reid

Less than a century ago it was common to imagine that the adoption of inherited family names or surnames was a necessary stage in civilization. Did not the adoption of family names in Europe broadly coincide with the move out of the Dark Ages and into the Renaissance?[1] The westernizing King who imposed family names in Thailand in 1913 insisted, "Now we have surnames it can be said that we have caught up with people who are regarded as civilized."[2] The top countries had them, and those who wished to emulate those countries in progress should adopt them. A number of governments sought to impose them by legislative fiat on Asian populations — the Philippines first in 1850, Japan in 1875, Thailand in 1913, Tunisia in 1925, Turkey in 1926, and Iran in 1932.

Southeast Asia (minus Vietnam), apparently innocent of the idea of family names before the nineteenth century except as used by Chinese and Europeans in its midst, was early to adopt this approach to social engineering through family names. And yet Southeast Asia remains (with South Asia) one of the most resistant parts of the world to the idea of family names. The international media still had to labor the point when speaking of Presidents Sukarno or Suharto that most Javanese use only one name. And in the case of the Burmese even the relatively small stock of personal and relational names in frequent use appears not to have led, as it did elsewhere, to the addition of surnames as qualifiers.

Southeast Asia is therefore a useful historical laboratory to examine what the difference is between societies that use family names and those that do not, and what the assumption of such names at a particular point in history means. We may no longer believe that this is a necessary step on a path to civilization, but the family name remains central to the way families are constructed and imagined. The increasing (and overdue) contemporary reaction against patriarchy in Europe and Northeast Asia is currently challenging the belief in patrilocal societies that women at marriage became a dependent part of the male lineage and that the family name should pass down only in the male line. But historians have paid far too little attention to how and when that patriarchal pattern became established, and what if anything the connection is between family names and certain definitions of capitalism and modernity.

I want to explore four different explanations that have been given or can be given for the global shift toward inherited family names on the male side, and to test these particularly in light of what we know about the Southeast Asian cases. This may help us to understand how changes in name patterns are connected with broader social shifts in society, whether as cause or as consequence.

The Need to Distinguish Individuals

In England before the Norman Conquest, and most of the rest of Europe before Christian norms became strongly entrenched, names were as varied as in many parts of Southeast Asia today. Until the tenth century the church allowed great latitude in naming patterns, and a great variety of personal names appear in the few surviving registers of England or France at that time. But the cult of saints grew throughout Christendom in the ninth to the twelfth centuries, making saints' names increasingly the popular ones as baptismal names. Although it was not until the Council of Trent in 1563 that the Catholic Church decreed that only saints' names could be used for baptismal names, it had in fact become the usual practice over the several centuries before that.[3] The pattern spread from France to England at the Norman Conquest, resulting in a great impoverishment of the available stock of names.

Hence Reaney describes what he calls the accepted, albeit oversimplified, theory that surnames arose in England "due to the Norman Conquest when the Old English personal-names were rapidly superseded by the new Christian names introduced by the Normans. Of these, only a few were really popular and in the twelfth century, this scarcity of Christian names led to the increasing use of surnames to distinguish the numerous individuals of the same name."[4] So many Johns and Peters necessarily gave rise to John Black or White, Peter the Miller or Baker, Matthew the son of William or Williamson.

However, this is an oversimplification even for Europe because so many other factors determined the way first surnames (add-ons) and then inherited family names gradually gained ground over several centuries, in some places and among some classes more than others. Everywhere it was nobles who first insisted on a name that defined their landed property, then townsmen, and finally peasants. The gradual spread from Italy to France to England and Germany was very much determined by the way the literate classes of clerics, lawyers, and officials chose to record things, and specific decisions of authorities definitely moved the process along. Thus even in Europe this argument may explain why qualifiers were needed, but not why, when, or how this evolved in the direction of male-inherited family names.

When we move to Asia, this argument falls away altogether. For if the adoption of Christian saints' names reduced the stock of personal names and made a few names vastly popular, the adoption by Muslims of the names of the Prophet and his companions is an even more striking example of the same factor at work. As Islamization has proceeded in Malaysia and Indonesia, it appears, the overlap in names has become extraordinary.[5] The large number of people adopting a restricted number of names has not however led to a pattern of family names. Other devices are found to differentiate, pre-eminently in the form of the father's name, but it would be true to say that the Muslim populations of Southeast Asia have been unusually resistant to the globalizing push toward inherited family names.

The Need for a "Legible" Population

We are all familiar with the way in which modern states pressure everybody into having a family name. Forms that people complete for various purposes in Singapore require one, as do those in the US. If you want to get your salary paid, your visa issued, or your bills correctly addressed, you have to invent a family name for yourself. I advise people with only a personal name to put that name in the "Family name" box of the form, since that is really the sine qua non of the western or Singapore system. But then we find charming phenomena like my Javanese former colleague at ANU, Soebardi, who having properly put his name in that box of his student form in the US, then put 'nil' in the personal name box, only to find that all his scholarship checks came to Mr. Nil Soebardi, so he had to open a bank account in that name.

James Scott puts this correlation in center stage: "The invention of permanent, inherited patronyms was ... the last step in establishing the necessary preconditions of modern statecraft. In almost every case it was a state project, designed to allow officials to identify … its citizens."[6]

Since it is the state that creates documents, it is easy to exaggerate its role in shaping naming systems. As states become more competent, however, we do see them acting in ways that will hold their subjects accountable by name. It is probably not a coincidence that the two strongest states of the ancient world, the Roman and Chinese empires, both developed strong family name systems, with some state intervention. Both were highly patriarchal. For the Romans the essential name (*nomen gentium*, or simply *nomen*) was a family name passed down through the male line, while personal names (*praenomen*) were given only to males and often simply initialized. In China the Qin Dynasty appears to have imposed the clan or surname (*xing*) in the fourth century BC as means of holding male family heads responsible for others under their roof. As everywhere there was an older pattern of very varied names and naming systems, but we have to go far back to find it.

As the Roman state faded, so did the system of family names, from around the fourth century AD, leaving the Chinese as the only continuous strong system of state-supported family names. Their gradual return to Western Europe in about the eleventh to the sixteenth centuries was also promoted at many points by the legal agencies of the state. The king's officers needed to know what his fiefs owed him in duties and taxes, and the barons in turn needed to know people's obligations to them, over several generations. "It was the official who required exact identification of the individual."[7]

The Italian city-states, ahead of their time in imposing secular order, also led Europe in this regard. In 1427 the state of Florence required that every citizen should be registered with both personal and family names in a *catasto* for tax purposes. Because it was so much ahead of its time, imposing surnames on the majority of the population who still did not have them, it had mixed success.[8]

A more fundamental trend in Europe was for the growing state power to lean on the church to enforce registration of births, deaths, and marriages. Parish priests had this duty in northern Italy by the end of the fourteenth century, and the first example of its spread to France was in 1411. The church increasingly required that family names be included in order to prevent consanguinial marriages; the state required them for tax and property purposes. In 1539, through the Ordonnance of Villers-Cotteret, King Francis I made it obligatory throughout his domains that parish registers be kept with a family name accompanying the baptismal name in each register. Only after the French Revolution, in 1792, did this registration function become secularized as the responsibility of local officials.[9] In Europe, therefore, the pattern was for the state to enforce, systematize, and make uniform a trend toward inherited family names that was spreading gradually alongside literacy and the classifying reach of church, law and tax-collection. In modernizing Asia, the state's role was generally more forceful and interventionist.

In the Philippines it was the reforming colonial state that imposed surnames (*apelyido*) on all its subjects. On the surface an astonishingly successful revolution from the top was achieved through Governor-General Claveria's decree of 21 November 1849. The Governor-General's motivation for imposing this change appears to have been the Scott-like urge for a population legible to the state. The Governor-General was concerned at the confusion caused in "the administration of justice, government, finance, and public order" by the lack of family names. Because the second names "are not transmitted from the parents to the children" he saw "far-reaching moral, civil and religious consequences," particularly in making the parish registers less useful in tracing people than they should have been in a Catholic country.[10]

Social change in popular practice was of course a different thing. Sixteenth-century Filipinos, like most Southeast Asians, had only a single personal name given by the mother at birth, while Spanish missionaries of the time were already sufficiently habituated to family names to find the fact noteworthy. As parents, however, they became known as "father/ mother of X (their firstborn)," their own name becoming too heavy a taboo to be spoken.[11] This personal name continued to be used inside the family and the village, alongside the official baptismal names recorded by the church. Prior to 1849 parish registers had recorded the Christian name or names given to a child at baptism, which already frequently recorded a second or qualifying name which might be Christian (like Jose de la Cruz), secular Spanish (Pablo de Leon), indigenous (Maxima Calumpang) or Chinese (Maria Tongco). This helped distinguish people but appears very seldom to have been inherited in the family. A separate column of the register identified the person's parents.

The official step of 1849–50 to require the second name to be an inherited family one was therefore not difficult to impose on the registers. Official records of the state and church thenceforth recorded Filipinos under both a personal given name (*ngalan*) and a family name (*apelyido*).[12] Alone of Asian governing authorities, the Philippine state could rely on a supportive and pervasive church to carry out its plans. A *Catalogo de Apelyidos* was circulated through parish priests, providing

thousands of acceptable names for citizens to choose from. The majority
of them were in fact indigenous names, although the elite appears to have
chosen Spanish ones. As a top-down revolution in the formal naming
system, Claveria's reform remains unusually effective, changing the formal
naming system of Filipinos to look like the Castilian one. In tandem with
various economic and political factors, it may have been responsible for
the divergence of the lowland Philippines social pattern from those of its
(similarly bilateral kinship-oriented) Austronesian neighbors by the great
emphasis placed on loyalty to a family lineage (see below). At the same
time rural and uneducated Filipinos remain largely oblivious of the surname system, and most Filipinos continue to subvert it with frequent
name changes and a universal pattern of unregistered nicknames.[13] Even
after Claveria's change it continued to be used, as did other naming systems explained in Dr. Gealogo's paper.

Meiji Japan is another striking example of state-sponsored westernization in names as in other respects. Before the Meiji period, the Japanese
naming system had been complex and hierarchic. The Tokugawa had
forbidden commoners to use surnames (with certain exceptions), and the
enforced registration of names with Buddhist temples as part of the anti-
Christian campaign included only personal names. But after adopting
a system of universal military conscription in 1870, which abandoned
the old assumption that only samurai could fight, the Meiji government
concluded that the same logic should require universal family names. In
addition to pressure from the war ministry, the newly installed post office
similarly required a universal system of family names. A decree of 13
February 1875 required all Japanese to register surnames. A register was
established and the rule was swiftly and strictly enforced, even against the
fear of some rural people that this would overturn the village hierarchy.
Women, contrary to the practice of the surname-bearing samurai class,
were obliged to adopt their husband's name on marriage.[14]

Among the other modernizing Asian states whose governments
imposed surnames in a self-conscious act of high modernity, Turkey sits
alongside Japan. Its Surname Law of 1934 was the climax of a series of
reforms designed, like Japan's, to break sharply with the imperial, feudal,
and theocratic past. It made compulsory the registration, stabilization,
and use of hereditary surnames.[15] As in the Thai case which follows, however, these Turkish family names remained secondary and artificial, seldom
used in addressing or referring to a person even in formal speech.

Finally, the state's need for a legible population was also prominent in
the second major Southeast Asian attempt to impose family names — the

Siamese decree of 22 March 1913. After relatively little prior discussion, England-educated King Vajiravudh (1910–25) decreed that surnames must be selected by every male family head, to be passed down in the male line "to ensure that government records of births, deaths and marriages would be clear and reliable."[16] A number of columnists supporting the move also mentioned this factor of convenience in identifying people, seemingly also the main argument in the future king's mind when he had first written on the subject in an essay of 1906.[17] In the plethora of royal writings on this subject as the King became preoccupied with its implementation in the years 1913–5, however, other motives appeared more central. Some of these will be discussed below, notably in the last section. Probably the overriding motive to emerge from these writings was straightforward emulation of "modern" and "civilized" western nations. One of Vajiravudh's essays in support of the decree compared the surnames of his imagined Thai modernity with the Chinese system of family names. The Chinese *xing*, he insisted, was not a proper surname, but an "old-fashioned" clan name. With this reform Siam leapt past China in civilization, for "Nations that have become civilized in the modern sense, even if they used clan names from ancient times, have changed to the use of surnames."[18]

The Need for a Uniform Pattern of Surnames in Modern Democracies

The thousands of names on the Vietnam War Memorial in Washington are a dramatic demonstration of what is broadly taken for granted in modern democracies — that each citizen, represented by a uniform personal and family name, has equal worth. War Memorials of this type are not very old. They sprouted everywhere after 1918; every village in each country that sent its men to die in unprecedented numbers in the First World War produced its concrete monument and list of names. In earlier wars, with democracy still a fragile plant, such lists of the fallen are rare. Most of these names are listed in alphabetical order of family names (though the Vietnam War Memorial is an exception, listing by date of falling in battle), a necessary device once huge numbers of names are thrown together. Telephone directories, electoral roles and library catalogues made such listings imperative in the twentieth century, however ill suited to Chinese or Thai scripts.

Homo hierarchicus had no use for such formal equality. Those at the bottom needed to master a set of complex honorific modes of speech to address superiors, but they themselves had only a personal name. There was an undoubted tendency in those parts of Europe where feudalism was strongly established, that emancipation of serfs went along with their acquiring of surnames. This is not to say they grabbed at the chance to better their status in this way. Rather the two phenomena were parallel, with inherited family names spreading downward as legal rights did, from the nobility to the townsmen and finally the farmers at the bottom.[19] But states acted more positively in the revolutionary period when hierarchy was self-consciously replaced by equality before the law. This formal equality of citizens, in their rights but still more in their duties of military service and taxes, was the project of the American and French revolutions, and both moved swiftly to enforce a uniform naming system through their civil registries.

It was the government agencies charged with exacting those duties — the army, the courts, the taxation and land registrations authorities, and the schools — that became the active enforcers of such uniformities, and the compilers and systematizers of the naming system. If in Europe these operated in societies where family names had already become wide-spread, in the later surname frontier of Asia they became pioneers of an often-revolutionary idea. Once the Japanese Ministries of War and Education had become convinced of the merits of universal military service and schooling respectively, they became the champions of the new uniform system of family names. But following the 1875 edict enforcing this, "people gathered in village offices, and many were in great uproar, unable to figure out what surnames to register without offending anyone and without disturbing the traditional village leadership.... Some peasants of low status assumed the family names of those of higher status.... Some peasants assumed the surnames of the main family (*honke*), with whom they were distantly related or for whom they worked."[20] The Japanese two-name system nevertheless did have enough roots in past practice and enough reinforcement by a vigorous reforming state to become universal within a generation.

This factor is not pronounced as a motive in the Southeast Asian cases. The *Bangkok Times*, however, did advocate surnames in advance of King Vajiavudh's decree on the grounds that they would place more emphasis on the individual.[21] Southeast Asian states such as Siam had dealt with the lowly only through the hierarchy of officials and nobles around the court, and this arguably was a step toward dealing with them directly as individuals, and ultimately as individuals whose names would be entered on an electoral roll.

Patriarchy and Capitalism

The adoption of family names inherited in the male line has much deeper causes and consequences than those discussed above. It affects the way in which families have imagined themselves existing through time, and it places exclusive emphasis on the male role in imagining that continuity. Contemporary gender differences, which appear at first glance to be cultural, have been profoundly affected by changes in the naming pattern. Capitalism itself, in the form it developed first in northern Italy and then the Netherlands and England, was encouraged through a draconian male primogeniture that conserved property in the male line which carried the family name. Capitalism in its English variant appeared to benefit from such accumulation of capital by the gentry, and perhaps even by the way this cruel system forced younger sons and daughters to fend for themselves entrepreneurially. For historians, therefore, comparative analysis of both causes and effects of surname introduction is overdue.

The large industry examining the causes for the rise of capitalism has given some attention to the unusually absolute system of male primogeniture in England as one of the factors serving to conserve wealth and encourage its accumulation in certain families. The passing on of a name along with the title is a factor in that phenomenon, though not one the literature has paid much attention to. Only more recently has the importance of lineage in the Chinese case been emphasized as a key element in the form of capital accumulation in business which developed there. Since the Chinese social model is the earliest and by far the most important in the development of a system of family names inherited in the male line, this attention is overdue.

David Faure points out that Ming and Qing era merchants made a distinction between their day-to-day business (*hao*) and the trust (*tang*) which held his property. *Tang* is also the character for hall, and specifically the ancestral hall honoring the male ancestor of a particular surname group. He instances the ferries of Yuen Long in Hong Kong which in the nineteenth century were held in the name of a clan ancestor from the Song dynasty. The lineage descending from such ancestors was the group who formed the trust, since by definition they were able to trust one another in property matters. Specific Chinese partnerships and businesses were not intended to last over generations, but the ritually sanctioned holding trust had to do so.[22] This Chinese mercantile concern with lineage and the family name that went with it had echoes in Korea and Vietnam, and fainter ones in Japan. But in Southeast Asia it put Chinese business families somewhat apart from the local elites with whom they interacted. Family names spread in nineteenth- and twentieth-century Asia predominately on the European model, not the Chinese one. Can we nevertheless trace a correlation between family name introduction and the tendency to treat the vertical family over several patrilineal generations as a corporation whose name should be upheld?

The Meiji surname reform was the most striking here. Two years before the surname introduction law required married women to use their husband's family name, a decree of 22 July 1873 had already established that only male heads of households had the right to inherit property. This looks like a purposeful attempt to use surnames as part of an attempt to conserve property in the male line according to the English model. Subsequently, the Civil Law of 21 June 1896 also emphasized the continuity of the family in the male line, with only the eldest son inheriting.[23] Nagata's chapter in this book shows an elite tendency even in the Tokugawa era to regard the family as a corporation needing continuity over the generations. The surname law appears to have generalized this pattern and prepared Japan for its most robust century of male-dominated capitalism.

In Southeast Asia the emergence of powerful family corporations carrying Southeast Asian family names is closely connected to the merging of diasporic Chinese enterprise and indigenous elite status. To begin with the Philippines, it appears that Claveria's motivations had little to do with bolstering the family as a capitalist institution. Yet in its aftermath, nobody ignores the power of names such as Lopez, Romualdez, Osmeña, or Cojuangco. Most of these powerful landowning families had their origins in Chinese mestizo families who in the mid-nineteenth century used their trading capital and relatively privileged position within colonial society to become a commercially-oriented landed elite, culturally very distinct from the new Chinese migrants who took over many of their former trading and retailing roles.[24] While many adopted Spanish family names, others ran together the polite form of address of their Chinese name ending in the Hokkien title, *k'o*, to produce names like Cojuangco. Wickberg asserts that the mestizos using such hybridized *apelyidos* "seem to have been accorded equal welcome" into the Filipino elite as those adopting Spanish names.[25] In the three decades after Claveria's decree, a profound commercialization overtook Flipino society, as trade was freed and urban capital was redirected to commercial agriculture. Most of the sugar land of Cebu had been taken over by the formerly urban Chinese or Spanish mestizo trading communities, with a few families emerging as both economically powerful and socially prestigious. Cebu generated a new aristocracy, owning mansions in the city, drawing wealth from their estates, and having seats on the councils of the region. Already they were known by their *apelyidos* — the Osmeñas, Velosos and Climacos among them.[26]

The same trend was noted in the Negros sugar lands, developed into "the most productive agricultural area in the Philippines" by Chinese mestizo families from the town of Iloilo in the second half of the nineteenth century. Al McCoy was able to trace the same family names (Lopez, Lacson, Benedicto, and Yulo) from the leading mestizo merchants that dominated the Chinese quarter of Iloilo in the 1850s to the dominant sugar plantation owners of the 1890s.[27] McCoy has powerfully reminded us of the absolute centrality of the family in Filipino politics and society. "Much of the passion, power and loyalties diffused in First World societies are focused upon family in the Philippines. It commands an individual's highest loyalty, defines life chances, and can serve as an emotional touchstone." He quotes the pragmatic justification given by a Filipino sociology text for this phenomenon: "The Filipino family ... protects its members against all kinds of misfortunes since the good name of the family has to be protected."[28]

The Siamese surname law of 1913, like the earlier Japanese one, specified that married women should bear their husband's surname. In the flurry of speeches and writings that followed the decree, the King made clear that one of the results he hoped for from the reform was a much greater cohesiveness in the Thai family and a pride in its achievements. A surname would provide "an aid in the maintenance of family tradition. It will also serve as an incentive to everyone to uphold not only personal honour but the honour of the family as well."[29] A royal official claimed that the family name would be "like a flag of victory promoting the pride of people who are members of the family."[30] Although property was not mentioned, the belief appears to have been that European societies were more successful because of this element of pride in the family achievements over time.

Analyzing the effects of the decree takes us into territory the King scarcely envisaged — the ways in which prominent Sino-Thai (*lukjin*) families came to identify themselves as the Thai commercial elite. Walter Vella, whose data and sympathies were in the old Thai elite that dominated the country before the 1970s, claimed that the surname law had had little effect. Despite its eventual success by the 1930s in fixing Thai names in the form of personal name followed by family name, the latter never became the principal name in daily use. "The Thai traditionally have felt no strong familial ties in time; there has been little or no interest in genealogy. Nor is there now [1970s] ... No perceptible change in attitudes toward the past or the future has been noticed."[31] This view needs revision after the dramatic effects of Thai commercial expansion since the 1960s. Having been sluggish for the previous century, the Thai economy took off in the 1960s, averaging about 7 per cent per annum growth as it transformed per capita GDP from US$100 in 1961 to US$2,750 in 1995. Like the Chinese mestizos of the Philippines a century earlier, the *lukjin* led this transformation soon after having accepted an official national pattern of personal name followed by family name. As capitalists they became, in the eyes of one analyst, "the dominant social class in contemporary Thailand."[32]

The first Sino-Thai oligopolists were the "big five" families that came to dominate Thailand's rice trade after the economic crisis and revolution of the early 1930s had undermined their aristocratic and European rivals. In the process they adopted Thai-sounding surnames, Wanglee (the Teochew Tan family), Bulasuk (the Teochew Lo family), Bulakun (the Cantonese Ma family), Iamsuri (the Teochew Hia family), and Lamsam (the Hakka Ung family). The founders had generally migrated from South China in the late nineteenth century, and it was their sons or grandsons who brought the families to their dominant position in the 1930s. Their descendents continued to control large corporate empires through to the end of the century.[33] By the 1950s, however, they began to be replaced at the top of the Thai economy by "the new big four," more active in banking and insurance and developing alliances of corporate groups rather than the old family firm. By the 1990s these in turn had given way to five major conglomerates, together controlling 281 companies. While alliances with other Sino-Thai families and with the government were important to these groups, there is no mistaking the importance of a family in providing continuity of capital ownership and business leadership over several generations.

A good example is the Sophanpanich family. Tan Piak Chin was born in Thailand (1910) but educated until age 17 in China. He became Chin Sophonpanich in the aftermath of the surname reform, and operated easily between Thai and Chinese identities. His exceptional abilities in money management led to a succession of ever more prominent management roles in the 1940s, finally becoming President of the Bangkok Bank in 1952, and guiding force of the Asia Trust group of companies. The Sophanpanich family survived all Thailand's upheavals to make the Bangkok Bank Southeast Asia's largest, and the family share in its ownership in excess of 30 per cent by the 1970s. Leadership passed in the 1980s to the western-educated son, Chatri Sophonpanit.[34] The Sino-Thai Chia brothers established an agricultural export business from Bangkok to China in 1921, but by the time one of their sons took over in 1951 the surname was Thai-ized as Chiaravanont and its company, known as Charoen Pophand, began to expand into a huge agribusiness. By the 1980s leadership had passed to the third generation through Dhanin Chiaravanont, and the corporation had wrought a transformation in Thai agriculture from peasant to commercialized production for export.[35]

Thaksin Shinawatra, Prime Minister from 2001 to 2006, is a prime exemplar of the trend. His great grandfather, Khu Chun Seng, migrated from Guangzhou to Siam in the 1860s as a boy. He and his sons married Thai women and rendered their names in hybridized Sino-Thai form when in Thai public space, though presumably retaining a Chinese name for commercial purposes. Khu Chun Seng became Seng sae Khu or simply Seng. His eldest son and principal commercial heir, Thaksin's grandfather, was Chiang, while the Khu family business was known in Thai as Sae Khu. But in 1938 Chiang's eldest son, Sak, the first of the dynasty to be sent to the military academy as the most strategic connection a rising family would need, registered the family name Shinawatra.[36] The rest of the family, including Thaksin's father Loet, gradually adopted the same family name, which thereby became the family corporate logo. At the time of Thaksin's birth in 1949, the Shinawatras were one of the dominant families of Chiang Mai, including two members of Parliament, and ran the city's leading silk manufacturing enterprise. The twelve children of Chiang married strategically into other *lukjin* families on the way up. Thaksin himself returned from the US in 1978 with a doctorate in criminology, and expanded the family business into telecommunications. When the family's controlling stake in Shin Corp was sold to Singapore's Temasek Holdings in January 2006 to avoid conflict of interest issues, it was worth 73 billion baht (US$2 billion).

Comparative studies of comparable populations living with and without the pattern of inherited family names are rare. One interesting indicator, however, is Tanya Li's work on the household economy of Singapore Malays, which draws numerous parallels with that of Singapore Chinese of similar social class. In general the Malays in question are "Southeast Asian" in the sense of having no family names, or any marked sense of solidarity over generations; the Chinese do have such a sense of obligation toward the welfare of the patrilocal family as a unit. Li's Malay informants were concerned with their personal "name," but not that of their families per se. She found that children in Singapore Chinese families, and especially unmarried girls, were expected to give a high proportion of their income to the family unit to support parents, the education of younger siblings, or the family business. Malay children also contributed, but as a gift from time to time at their own discretion. By contrast with the Chinese (surname-bearing) families, they "do not feel linked by an idea of family name and honor."[37]

The harsh high tide of European patriarchal capitalism has passed, or taken new forms less focused on the exclusive role of male primogeniture in concentrating productive wealth. The family name fixation may even have become a liability in the age of joint-stock companies and global competition for talent. A recent study by the London School of Economics has shown that the primary reason British firms are less productive than US ones is the much higher proportion of family-owned firms (30 per cent), and especially family firms passed to the eldest son (15 per cent), in the UK.[38] In their day family firms were, however, the engine of British capitalism, as they remained up to a much later period (and on different assumptions) in Chinese, Japanese, and Korean capital accumulation. Further south Chinese and Arab Southeast Asians were the pioneers in building family-named businesses that survived several generations.

The relative slowness of the majority populations in Indonesia, Malaysia, Cambodia, Burma, and most of India to shift to family names may be causally linked to their less intense engagement with the capitalism of the family firm, though which is cause and which effect remains to be researched. Some studies have shown a strengthening in the economic role of the male patriarch at the expense of increasingly homebound wives in upwardly mobile families in Indonesia since 1970, where the older pattern was one of bilateral descent and strong economic roles for women as well as men.

Family names are one of the more salient variables needing investigation as a key to understanding cross-cultural variations in the reactions to capitalist pressures and opportunities, as well as to global cultural models.

Notes

1   Albert Dauzat, "Le Nom de Famille Correspond a une Etape de la Civilisation," in *Les Noms de Famille de France* (Paris: Payot, 1945), p. 39.

2   King Vajiravudh's royal birthday speech of 1914, cited in Walter Vella, *Chaiyo: King Vajiravudh and the Development of Thai Nationalism* (Honolulu: University of Hawaii Press, 1978), p. 131.

3   Dauzat, *Les Noms de Famille*, pp. 34–5.

4   P.H. Reaney, *The Origin of English Surnames* (London: Routledge and Kegan Paul, 1967).

5   While I have not been able to quantify this in Southeast Asia, in South Asia the online Karachi telephone book has 4,302 names listed under Ismail, 3,889 under Ibrahim and 30,290 under Mohammad. "Pakistan Telephone Directory: Karachi," http://www.karachiplus.com/teledir/Search.asp (accessed January 2006).

6   James C. Scott, *Seeing Like a State: How Certain Schemes to Improve the Human Condition Have Failed* (New Haven: Yale University Press, 1998), p. 65.

7   Reaney, *The Origin of English Surnames*, p. 314.

8   Scott, *Seeing Like a State*, 66, drawing on David Herlihy and Christiane Klapische-Zuber, *Tuscans and their Families: A Study of the Florentine Catasto of 1427* (New Haven: Yale University Press, 1985).

9   Dauzat, *Les Noms de Famille*, p. 40.

10   Decree of Governor-General Narciso Claveria, 21 Nov. 1849, cited by Michael Cullinane, "Accounting for Souls," in *Population and History: The Demographic Origins of the Modern Philippines* (Madison: University of Wisconsin CSEAS, 1998), p. 296.

11   Pedro Chirino, *The Philippines in 1600*, trans. Ramon Echevarria (Manila: Historical Conservation Society, 1969), pp. 477–8.

12   Cullinane, "Accounting for Souls," pp. 294–6, 336–7.

13   Charles J-H Macdonald, "Personal Names as an Index of National Integration: Local Naming Practices and State-produced Legal Identities," *Filipinas* 42 (March 2004): 61–75.

14   Herbert Plutschow, *Japanese Name Culture: The Significance of Names in a Religious, Political and Social Context* (Richmond, Surrey: Japan Library, 1995), pp. 189–97.

15   Meltem Turkoz, "The Social Life of the State's Fantasy: Memories and Documents on Turkey's 1934 Surname Law" (PhD diss., University of Pennsylvania, 2004).

16   Royal birthday speech of 1914, cited in Walter Vella, *Chaiyo: King Vajiravudh and the Development of Thai nationalism* (Honolulu: University of Hawaii Press, 1978), p. 130.

17   Essay, "Chaya ru chusae" of May 1906, as translated in Vella, *Chaiyo*, p. 129.

18   King Vajiravudh's essay, "Priap nam sakun kap chusae," as translated in Vella, *Chaiyo*, p. 131.

19   Dauzat, *Les Noms de Famille*, pp. 38–9.

20   Plutschow, *Japan's Name Culture*, pp. 193–4.

21   *Bangkok Times*, October 3, 1911, cited in Vella, *Chaiyo*, p. 129.

22   David Faure, *China and Capitalism: A History of Business Enterprise in Modern China* (Hong Kong: Hong Kong University Press, 2006), pp. 38–41.

23   Plutschow, *Japanese Name Culture*, p. 196.

24   Edgar Wickberg, *The Chinese in Philippine Life, 1850–1898* (Yale University Press, 1965, reprinted Manila: Ateneo de Manila Press, 2000), pp. 29–35.

25   Ibid., p. 32.

26   Michael Cullinane, "The Changing Nature of the Cebu Urban Elite in the 19th Century," in *Philippine Social History: Global Trade and Local Transformations*, eds. A.W. McCoy and Ed. C. de Jesus (Sydney: Allen & Unwin for ASAA, 1982), pp. 271–80.

27   Alfred W. McCoy, "A Queen Dies Slowly: The Rise and Decline of Iloilo City," in *Philippine Social History: Global Trade and Local Transformations*, eds. A.W. McCoy and Ed. C. de Jesus (Sydney: Allen & Unwin for ASAA, 1982), pp. 314–6.

28   Alfred W. McCoy, ed. *An Anarchy of Families: State and Family in the Philippines* (Madison: University of Wisconsin Center for Southeast Asian Studies, 1993), p. 8.

29   King Vajiravudh's speech of 1914, cited in Vella, *Chaiyo*, p. 130.

30   Chamun Amorn Darunrak, as translated in Vella, *Chaiyo*, p. 130.

31   Vella, *Chaiyo*, pp. 135–6.

32   Kevin Hewison, *Bankers and Bureaucrats: Capital and the Role of the State in Thailand* (New Haven: Yale University Southeast Asian Studies, 1989), p. 128.

33   Suehiro Akira, *Capital Accumulation in Thailand, 1855–1985* (Tokyo: Centre for East Asian Cultural Studies, 1989), pp. 110–22.

34   Suehiro, *Capital Accumulation*, pp. 158–60, 245–9; Hewison, *Bankers and Bureaucrats*, pp. 192–204.

35   Hewison, *Bankers and Bureaucrats*, pp. 143–6; Suehiro, *Capital Accumulation*, pp. 270–1.

36   Pasuk Pongpaichit and Chris Baker, *Thaksin: The Business of Politics in Thailand* (Chiang Mai: Silkworm Books, 2004), pp. 25–34.

37   Tanya Li, *Malays in Singapore: Culture, Economy, and Ideology* (Singapore: Oxford University Press, 1989), pp. 155–8. The quote is from page 157.

38   http://cep.lse.ac.uk/briefings/pa_inherited_family_firms.pdf.

CHAPTER 2

Looking for Claveria's Children: Church, State, Power, and the Individual in Philippine Naming Systems[1] during the Late Nineteenth Century

Francis Alvarez Gealogo

Introduction

On 21 November 1849, Spanish Governor-General to the Philippines Narciso Claveria issued a decree that a catalogue of family names should be compiled for Filipinos to adopt. The aim of the decree was to put administrative order in the Philippine naming system, utilizing Spanish surnames, as well as indigenous words related to things like plants, animals, minerals, geography, or arts to be adopted as Filipino surnames. The result was the organized systematization of the Philippine naming system that has been viewed by some historians as Hispanicizing Filipinos by giving them Spanish surnames.[2] This paper takes a contrary view, and regards the Claveria decree not as an attempt to design an administrative system to Hispanize Filipino surnames, but one to regularize record-keeping so colonial officials could trace their subjects for purposes like taxation and law enforcement. This second view is suggested by the fact that the Spanish authorities allowed their subjects to adopt Chinese, Spanish, or indigenous surnames that were then entered into the colonial record system.

This paper analyzes the impact of Claveria's decree on Philippine naming systems, evaluates the actual rationale behind its implementation, and assesses the different orientations, characteristics, and types of Philippine naming systems put in place by the Claveria decree. This paper is limited to the description of the naming systems of lowland Christian Filipinos and does not include the naming practices of Filipino Muslims in the southern Philippine islands of Sulu, Basilan, Tawi Tawi, and the southwestern portion of the islands of Mindanao and Palawan. Also excluded are the naming systems of non-Christian and non-Muslim indigenous peoples, including those from the northern Luzon communities in the Cordillera mountains, the Mangyan communities on the island of Mindoro; the Negrito communities in Luzon, Negros, and eastern Mindanao; and the Lumad (indigenous peoples of Mindanao). Some of these communities remained "pagan," while others were later converted to Christianity or Islam during the twentieth century. But most of them retained their indigenous naming systems and never adopted Spanish or Islamic surnames.

Name Types and Naming Practices in Contemporary and Historical Lowland Tagalog Societies

One way of describing Philippine naming types and practices is to understand the differences of meaning between *binyag, bansag, pangalan,* and *apelyido*. The Christianization of Filipino communities meant ministering the sacraments of the Catholic Church to save the souls of the converted peoples. One important element in the sacrament of baptism is giving names to new Christians to reflect their new religious orientation. Called *binyag* in Tagalog, the term not only connotes the equivalent of a baptismal name but more importantly the notion of name giving.[3] In fact, Rafael mentions the caution made by the Spanish missionaries about using the terms *binyag* and *bautizar* interchangeably, lest it create confusion between the notions of Christian conversion and baptism, and naming practices.

The other concepts associated with the means of adopting formal names are *pangalan* and *apelyido*. *Pangalan* is the generic term used to refer to all naming types. It may refer to the full name of an individual, which usually includes a given first name, the mother's maiden surname as the middle name, and the surname. A more specific *pangalan* refers only to the given name without the surname. An informal *pangalan* may also refer to *palayaw*, or nickname, and all its many attendant variants. In fact the term *pangalan* itself is the closest term to the Anglo-American or European concept of name because the other terms indicate more specific name types of concepts related to naming practices. Another thing that must be highlighted is the total absence of an indigenous term that refers to the concept of surname or *apelyido* (from the Spanish *apellido*, "surname"). All of the dictionaries and vocabulary books consulted for this paper indicate the term as derived from Spanish and the absence of an indigenous equivalent to this. This indicates that the practice was never adopted until after Spanish colonization.

The other important concepts in Philippine naming systems are the terms associated with the less formal names that Christian Filipinos usually acquire, the *palayaw, taguri, bansag, tukso,* and *tawag.*[4] *Palayaw* is the more generic term used to refer to all forms of informal names and is the closest term to nickname. Giving a *palayaw* was a more informal mode of naming. It is interesting to note that the word *palayaw* comes from the root *layaw,* which may mean either freedom or a state of spoiled existence (usually to connote a lack of discipline in childhood).[5] The *palayaw* is often used only when people are at ease and familiar with each other and not used for identifying a person for official purposes. *Taguri, tawag, bansag,* and *tukso* are forms of *palayaw.* The *bansag* and *tukso* may also mean a nickname, but are usually given by other individuals and are used as a means of teasing an individual with a name normally formed in jest. *Taguri* and *tawag* are more neutral nicknames that are not the results of jesting, but are used in informal settings where relationships are familiar and personal between individuals. More often than not, *taguri* and *tawag* as forms of *palayaw* may be either self-referral or given by other people (both self-ascribed or used by others). This means that an individual may choose *tawag* or *taguri,* but may be referred to by others in forms of *tukso* or *bansag,* leading to the possibility of individuals having multiple, plural name tags. Moreover, the *tukso* and *bansag* may also refer not only to individuals but also to clans and family groups, while the *taguri* or *tawag* almost exclusively refer to individuals. The classic example of the Cavite bandit Leonardo Manecio is a case in point. All his records indicate his formal *pangalan* as Leonardo Manecio. But he was more popularly known as Nardong Putik, where Nardo[ng] was his *palayaw,* and *putik* (mud) was a *bansag.* His family was also referred to as pamilya Putik.

An interesting characteristic in the *bansag* and *palayaw* system is the fact that most of these names are adopted during an individual's childhood and carried into adulthood. Hence, during the period of American colonization, English *palayaw* like Baby, Boy, Junior or indigenous *palayaw* like Nene (small baby girl), Totoy or Boboy (small baby boys), and other such names were given to individuals during babyhood and carried until adulthood. Even now, one may therefore find odd references such as Lola (Grandma) Baby, Tatay (Father) Boy, Tiyo (Uncle) Junior or Jun, Nanay (Mother) Nene, and other strange combinations. Equally interesting are the *palayaw* that some Filipinos have grown accustomed to, which indicate the baby sounds that infants and toddlers may have uttered and were adopted by their parents as their *palayaw*, or sometimes, an alteration of the formal names, a repetition of some of the syllables of the formal given names or adaptation of new sound patterns, hence the *palayaw* Jingjing, Lingling, Dingdong, Bingbong, Bongbong, Jojo, Chin Chin, Lotlot, and Tonton.

The use of these informal names varies, depending on the levels of intimacy and familiarity of individuals, the context and audience of the giver and receiver of *palayaw*, the existence of relational hierarchies, and the formal and informal referral types existing between individuals. One may have many *palayaw, bansag, tukso, tawag,* and *taguri* at the same time. There is also a possibility that some of the *palayaw* (or its other forms) may be utilized and familiar only to some social groups but not others to whom a person belongs. Thus, an individual may have multiple *palayaw*, which are associated with different social circles. These informal systems of naming do not often find their way into official record systems, but are more used to refer to people in a more informal, familiar, and personal sense. The real methodological issue for the social scientist and historian is that *palayaw* and all its other variants are all informal and unofficial, and therefore do not enter into the formal historical record systems. And precisely because of that, the tensions between the formal, official, and institutional on the one hand, and the informal, familiar, and relational on the other hand are manifested in the differences between the *pangalan* and *apelyido*.

One may also note that the freedom of choice in naming practices is best exercised by the individual in the *palayaw* and *bansag* mode. Formal names are given to individuals usually in a non-consensual manner. But individuals can choose to have their own *palayaw*, usually upon reaching the age of maturity. In this manner, the formal first names and the informal *palayaw* given by the parents are discarded and in their place individuals use a *palayaw* of their choice.

Indigenous Naming Systems

The pre-Claveria, pre-Spanish Filipino naming system among those who were eventually converted to Christianity exhibited an entirely different mode and orientation. Most of the non-Islamic inhabitants of the islands did not use surnames; instead they used a single indigenous name to refer to an individual's identity. Clan and family identities were reckoned, not through surnames or other identifying systems, but rather through the location of one's residence in the indigenous communities called *barangays*, composed mainly of related individuals.

The pre-Spanish naming system also involved changing parents' names after the birth of their first-born child. Parents discarded their original given names and were renamed Inani (Mother of) or Amani (Father of) plus the name of their first-born.[6] For example, a man named Bituin (Star) as a child would have a father named Amani Bituin and a mother named Inani Bituin. Amani Bituin and Inani Bituin may have had different names before Bituin was born, but these were discarded after Bituin's birth. Once Bituin had his own first child, he would no longer be called Bituin. If his child were called Ilog (river), he would be called Amani Ilog and no longer Bituin.

This system is significant in highlighting the pre-Claveria, pre-Hispanic naming system in the Philippines in many ways that are completely similar to the teknonymic tradition of other Austronesian societies.[7] First, this indicates the great value given to children during this period. Second, it may be surmised that this system denotes that one's identity was strengthened with the birth of a child and that the child's identity was usually regarded as more determinant than that of the parents. This is the complete reverse of patronymic naming systems of some societies where adopting the father's name is the defining characteristic of one's name, as is illustrated by the prefix Mc- or Mac- (as in McArthur) and the suffix -son (as in Jackson) that indicates that one is somebody's son.

Amani and Inani were oftentimes recorded as one word in the historical records, and not two words (Ama ni or Ina ni). The reasons for this is because the foreign colonial record keepers of the period mistook these names as single first names and did not understand that they were teknonyms. Hence, Ama ni Calao was recorded as having Amani as his *nombre* (first name) and Calao as his *apellido* (surname) because teknonyms had no place in Spanish naming practices, which made the local naming systems unreadable to the colonial mind.[8] As a result, record keepers reinterpreted teknonyms to conform to the conventions of Spanish naming practices with the confusing consequences unobserved and not considered.

Baptisms and Spanish Names

The advent of Spanish colonization changed this orientation altogether. Not only were Christianized Filipinos given Spanish first names, they

were usually given surnames carried across generations following a patrilineal system. Early eighteenth-century baptismal registers usually list
the names of early converts with a Spanish baptismal first name derived
from the name of a Catholic saint and an indigenous second name.[9]
Some historians are unclear whether these indigenous second names were
passed on to the next generation as second names, but some research has
shown that in some parish records the indigenous second names were
not used as surnames to be passed on to succeeding generations of individuals. What appears to be the case in some parish registers after the mid-
eighteenth century is that these indigenous second names were replaced by
Spanish names. However, neither indigenous nor Spanish surnames seem
to have served as surnames at this time. Further there is no indication
that the names of parents were linked with those of their children or that
children shared a surname with their siblings.[10] In some registers the
parents and children could have entirely different names. For example, if
a couple, Juan Esteban and Maria Josefa, had four children, they could
have names as different as Pedro de la Cruz, Jose Santos, Nicolasa Mariana,
and Felipe Julian.

Equally important is the lack of standardization and permanency in
the naming system. A more extreme case is cited by a researcher who found
that the same woman appeared in the parish record systems (baptismal,
confirmation, marriage, burial, and the annual parish census) under ten
different names.[11]

Looking at the Claveria Decree

A second look at the Claveria decree indicates that regularizing the administrative record-keeping and systematization was the foremost aim of the
decree, contrary to suggestions by some researchers like Kautz and Zaide
that the Hispanization of Filipino naming systems was the main objective.
Claveria indicated as much in the decree:

> The natives in general lack individual surnames which distinguished
> them by families. They arbitrarily adopt the names of saints, and this
> results in the existence of thousands of individuals having the same
> surname. Likewise, I saw the resultant confusion with regard to the
> administration of justice, government, finance, and public order, and
> far-reaching moral, civil and religious consequences to which this
> might lead, because the family names are not transmitted from the
> parents to their children, so that it is sometimes impossible to prove
> the degree of consanguinity for purposes of marriage, rendering use-
> less the parochial books which in Catholic countries are used for all
> kinds of transactions.[12]

Claveria's issuance of the catalogue of surnames, therefore, addresses the issue of civil and religious administration rather than cultural Hispanization. The colonial church and state found it necessary to overhaul their confusing system of recording names, which involved transforming the naming system in order to keep track of individuals and record their various transactions with the church and state in order to manage their colonial subjects.

It is thus essential to correlate the decree with the institutionalization of a system of civil and religious registers designed to increase the power and efficiency of the state and church through a standardized recording, classifying, and categorizing of individuals.

> In view of the extreme usefulness and practicality of this measure, the time has come to issue a directive for the formation of a civil register, which may not only fulfil and ensure the said objectives, but may also serve as the basis for the statistics of the country, guarantee the collection of taxes, the regular performance of personal service, and the receipt of payment for exemptions. It likewise provides exact information of the movement of the population, thus avoiding unauthorized migrations, hiding taxpayers, and other abuses.[13]

More specifically, the colonial state aimed to systematize its capacity to create usable statistical data to better serve the bureaucratic needs of the state.

The partnership of the church and the state is mirrored in the last paragraph of the Claveria decree. The decree enjoined the religious authorities to lend their full cooperation and support to the decree, ranging from the compilation of the catalogue of acceptable surnames that were either pre-existing or culled from missionaries' interactions with the local population, to the implementation of the decree at the village level.

It should be noted that the decree never prohibited the local population from adopting indigenous names. As a matter of fact, the fourth article of the decree states that "natives of Spanish, indigenous or Chinese origin who already have a surname may retain it and pass it on to their descendants."[14] What was important, therefore, was not for the Filipinos to adopt Hispanized names, but for the colonial subjects to have a recordable, consistent, constant, and regular surname expressed in a regularized format using a binomial formula with *pangalan* as first name and *apelyido* as surname to create a singular recordable identity for individuals.[15] The Claveria decree clearly indicates that the bureaucratic imperative took precedence over the demands of institutionalizing the cultural legacy of naming practices.

Enter the Chinese

The decree recognized the existence of Chinese communities in the Philippines and permitted those with Chinese surnames to keep them. A perusal of the entries of the catalogue highlights this tendency. Included in the catalogue were common Filipino-Chinese names that are still currently used like Chioco, Chia, Chinco, Chua, Co, Dizon, Limpin, Linjoco, Tan, Tuanco, Tuazon, Tingco, and Yi. Some Chinese families adopted their surnames from their original Chinese names, but others are more descriptive of their birth order, status, or relationship with other Chinese relatives who migrated with them. Thus, for example, Tuason/Tuazon, Dizon, Samson, Sison, Gozon, and Lacson were derived from the southern Fujianese terms for the first, second, third, fourth, fifth, and sixth grandson respectively.[16]

This system of retaining Chinese surnames varied accordingly, as Antonio Tan points out:

> Sometimes, a mestizo (child of mixed Chinese and indigenous blood) retained the name of his Chinese father, making such transliterated names from the Chinese ideograph as Co, Tan, Lim, Yap, Ong, Uy, as Filipino surnames. Another way was to create a Filipino name by combining parts of the full name of the Chinese father. Thus when the full name of the Chinese father was Tee Han Kee, the mestizo children might decide to create a new name, Teehankee. The same also explains the proliferation of names once Chinese and later Romanized into forms like Yuzon, Limkao, Limcuaco, Leongson; if a Chinese name like Yap Tinchay had been popularly known as Yap Tingco, using the Hokkien polite suffix Ko (meaning elder brother) with the personal name, the new name might be Yaptinco. This explains why there are today numerous Filipino names that end in co, names like Sychanco, Angangco, Tantoco, Tanchoco, Tantuico, Tanlayco, Cojuanco, Syjuco, Ongsiako, Soliongco, Yupangco, Tanco, Yangco, etc.[17]

One important development in this regard, with particular reference to Chinese surnames is the development of polysyllabic Romanized Chinese surnames. While monosyllabic surnames are still prevalent among the Chinese Filipinos, equally noticeable is the survival of polysyllabic Chinese surnames that go with Spanish Catholic first given names. Moreover, while the decree never prevented the Chinese from retaining their names, some Chinese families opted to adopt Spanish surnames. There were many means of acquiring a Spanish surname. A common mode was the adoption of the Spanish name of the Spaniard who was the godparent in the Catholic baptism of converted Chinese or their children. Another method was the adoption of the surname of a Filipino Christian mother. Sometimes, the combination of the Spanish name and the Chinese name was initially recorded, but the Chinese names were eventually dropped in the records. In other instances, the indigenous surname of the Filipino wife of a godfather was adopted by the Chinese family. Thus, some Filipino Chinese or Chinese mestizo families may have Spanish surnames like Velasco, Poblete, Sanguilayan, Aguinaldo, Encarnacion, Lazaro, Cuenca, Bustamante, Nazareno, or other common surnames in the Philippines that no longer reflected their Chinese heritage.

Resilience of Indigenous Names

Indigenous surnames form another large category in the entries in the catalogue that were drawn from the suggestions of missionaries in the field, whom Claveria tasked to propose possible surnames from indigenous terms referring to minerals, plants, animals, and other appropriate terms. Moreover, indigenous surnames that were already in use by Filipinos as surnames were permitted to be retained. Thus, surnames like Macapagal (tiresome), Magsaysay (to make sense of), Kalaw (hornbill), Dimagiba (indestructible), and others found their way in the catalogue and are still contemporary Filipino surnames.

It is interesting to note that some of these surnames date back to the sixteenth-century indigenous names of the local ruling elites who were recruited by the Spaniards to assist in transforming indigenous communities into colonial communities. These families made sure that their local communities met quotas for goods and services set by the Spanish authorities. As a reward for their services to the church and crown, these families were exempted from paying tribute taxes and rendering forced-labor services, and allowed to retain their indigenous names. This demonstrated to the local people the elites' continuing leadership role while also indicating that ultimate power rested in Spanish hands. Thus, some of these names were retained not because of the elites' refusal to submit to the Spanish crown, but as a result of their role in increasing the power of colonial rule.

While the abovementioned names were socially acceptable surnames, other entries from the catalogue were either obscene or absurd but were nonetheless adopted. Some Filipino surnames that can be traced back to the Claveria decree are the following: Daga (rat), Unggoy (monkey), Buwaya (alligator), Utut (fart), Bayag (testicles), Utim (small penis), Bagungajasa (just been raped), Mabayag (with big testicles), and Bacla (homosexual). One possible reason for this is the multilingual nature of

Philippine communities. Terms that may sound neutral and acceptable to some linguistic communities are absurd or offensive to some. Hence, after Claveria asked the missionaries assigned to different regions for possible suggested surnames to include indigenous terms, they submitted local terms that may have meant something positive from their linguistic area of proselytization.

Spatial Patterns of Philippine Naming Systems

The implementation of the Claveria decree developed logistical problems and resulted in a unique geographical distribution of surnames in some locales. The catalogue was an alphabetical listing of possible surnames that the local population could adopt. Unfortunately, some copies of the catalogue were sent with missing pages, or only one copy was sent to cover a large area, prompting the local governors, in some cases, to divide the catalogue and assign different sections to municipal mayors from different communities. From these truncated lists of alphabetically arranged names, the local population chose surnames,[18] which, for example, resulted in the inhabitants receiving a choice of surnames beginning mostly with Q, while other towns chose from surnames beginning mostly with F. These patterns were provincial- and even regional-wide. For example:

> In the Bikol region in southern Luzon, the entire alphabet is laid out like a garland over the provinces of Albay, Sorsogon, and Catanduanes which in 1849 belonged to the single jurisdiction of Albay. Beginning with A at the provincial capital, the letters B and C mark the towns along the coast beyond Tabaco to Tiwi. We return and trace along the coast of Sorsogon the letters E to L; then starting down the Iraya Valley at Daraga with M, we stop with S to Polangui and Libon, and finish the alphabet with a quick tour around the island of Catanduanes. Today's lists of municipal officials, memorials to local heroes, even business and telephone directories, also show that towns where family names begin with a single letter are not uncommon. In Oas, for example, the letter R is so prevalent that besides the Roas, Reburrianos, Rebajantes, etc, some claim with tongue in cheek that the town also produced Rizal and even Roosevelt![19]

Temporality and Naming Patterns

If the surnames in the catalogue were spatially distributed in some towns in the Philippines, the Catholic calendar of saints' feast days gave lowland Christian Filipinos' traditional first names a temporal spread. It became a tradition to name children after the patron saint whose feast day coincides with the child's birthday or the day of the child's baptism. The Catholic calendar became an unofficial catalogue of sorts for the first names of most Filipinos born during the Spanish colonial period. If the *Catalogo de Apellidos* provided the list of possibilities for Filipino surnames, the calendar provided the possibilities for their first names. Combined with the geographical pattern of some surnames, the full name of the individual could mirror the geographical space and the calendrical time in which the individual was located. Time, space, and the individual became intrinsically united through the naming patterns.

After the Claveria Era

The end of Spanish colonization of the Philippines at the turn of the twentieth century not only marked the end of political and economic Hispanization of the archipelago, it also marked the beginning of new naming patterns in the Philippines. While the legacy of the Claveria decree continued because the United States maintained the surnames of the Filipinos in their record systems, several noticeable changes were reflected in the naming patterns. Foremost of this was the adoption of the system of the Anglo-American naming order in the Philippines. While in most Spanish and former Spanish colonies, the sequence is the given first name, surname, and mother's maiden name, the Anglo-American system sequences the names with the surnames coming last. Thus, while most Mexicans, Puerto Ricans, Spanish, and Argentineans would have their surnames as their middle names and their mother's maiden names as their last names, Filipinos adopted a different sequence, with surnames last and the middle name actually reflecting the mother's maiden surname.

The other transformation was in the way first names were given. While Filipinos still gave children first names following the Catholic calendar, in some localities during the twentieth century, the influence of American cultural hegemony was also felt in the formation of Filipino first names. Juan gave way to John; Arturo to Arthur, Jose to Joseph, Maria to Mary.

The other tendency was religio-political in orientation. The Philippine revolution against Spain not only created the possibility of an independent political system free of colonial domination, but also gave rise to a form of an indigenous Filipino Christian tradition with the establishment of the Iglesia Filipina Independiente. One interesting cultural legacy of this church was the formulation of what was popularly called the *Calendariong Maanghang* (literally, "spicy calendar"), which not only did away with the celebration of Spanish feast days, but also provided alternative, indigenous names for each day of the calendar year, for members of the church to choose from. This resulted in the re-emergence of Filipino indigenous names such as Bayani (hero), Liwayway (dawn), Kalayaan (freedom), Ligaya (bliss) as common first names for Filipinos, while retaining the surnames found in the Claveria catalogue.

The advent of the American regime broke the monopoly of the Catholic Church over first names, and many other modes of uniquely Filipino first names arose. Names like Thucydides, Herodotus, and Aristotle were given to children of history teachers. A couple who taught physics named their twin sons Vector Atom and Hector Ion, while combination of names and terms like Filamer (Philippines and America), Ameurfina (America, Europe, Filipinas), Luzviminda (Luzon, Visayas, and Mindanao) were not uncommon. Moreover, American words like Joker, Cherry Pie, Strawberry, Lollipops, and others became popular names.

Conclusion

The Philippine naming system in the nineteenth century as realized in the Claveria catalogue exhibited varied responses from the population. It was relatively successful in regions where bureaucratic control and religious documentation of individuals were more established. One should note that the Claveria decree was a product of its time, an indication of the growing realization that an effective state needed a system of documentation for the recording and surveillance of its people. The recording of individual names, tracing their existence vis-à-vis the religio-bureaucratic demands of the state, and the assigning of surnames to groups of people became essential functions of church and state control. Name-giving acquired a non-neutral sense in this particular regard. Surnames, in particular, became essential tools for cataloguing the individual as they negotiated for themselves and dealt with the institutions of the state and the church. However, the survival of the Chinese and local names indicates that identity formation and cultural influence were not given as much priority in the Claveria decree as the demands of bureaucratic efficiency. The level of tolerance granted to the evolution of Chinese names in the records that were not in the original catalogue were observable in most of the *padrones generales* (inhabitants lists) up to the end of the nineteenth century. This indicates that the colonial state was able to accept the existence of new surnames provided that they were classifiable in the record system and useful for tracing individuals. Although the catalogue seems to have been intended to establish a naming system amenable to record-keeping, it had other unintended consequences with long-term effects, of which "alphabetized" Filipino naming patterns in some localities is one aspect.

One must also note that while the Christianized Filipinos may have subscribed to the surname rule in the Claveria decree, they also had localized naming systems that departed from the official, state-regulated project. The system of giving informal names in the form of *palayaw*, *bansag*, *tawag*, *tukso*, *taguri*, and others may be viewed as the local populations' attempts at circumventing the Spanish naming system. During the periods of anti-colonial resistance, these indigenous naming practices took anti-establishment forms as they sought to ignore, if not totally replace, the officially recorded names of individuals. This is particularly true for those whom the authorities considered as bandits and brigands living on the outskirts of the pueblo. Thus, anti-establishment personalities were more popularly known by their *palayaw* and *bansag* rather than their *pangalan* and *apelyido*. From the above, one can argue that the naming system created by the Claveria decree as well other Philippine naming systems highlight the potential of naming as a space for individuals to contest, negotiate with, accommodate, and resist the colonial state. However, the propensity of the Filipino to adopt names not reflected by the Spaniards' formal legal naming systems is not necessarily an indication that the local population resisted the new mode of name-giving and the reasons behind its creation.[20]

Nevertheless, one must be cautious about seeing the persistence of indigenous Filipino names among the contemporary population as an indication of the failure of the Claveria decree or an indication of local resistance to the state-initiated naming system. While some communities resisted colonial occupation through various means, Filipinos' retention of indigenous surnames does not automatically indicate a refusal to submit to the colonial regime. The numerous entries of indigenous terms in the catalogue refute the idea that the catalogue was made in order to give the Filipinos a sense of Spanish identity.

What is less obvious about the Claveria project is its major goal: to record, classify, catalogue, and categorize people into a systematic record group in order to trace people more efficiently and thoroughly. Colonial identity formation and the attendant contestations surrounding the act of adopting a name were but secondary effects of this state-directed project.

Notes

[1]   The author is grateful to the comments made by Reynaldo Ileto, Charles Macdonald, James Scott, Anthony Reid, Trina Tinio, and Mercedes Planta on the earlier drafts of this paper.

2   See, for example, Gregorio Zaide, *Philippine Political and Cultural History*,
     vol. 2 (Manila: Philippine Education Company, 1956), p. 80; Charles Kautz,
     "Bansag and Apelyido: Problems of Comparison in Changing Tagalog Social
     Organizations," in *Studies in Philippine Anthropology*, ed. Mario Zamora
     (Quezon City: Alemar Phoenix Publishers, 1967), p. 397 as well as Domingo
     Abella, "Introduction," in *Catalogo Alfabetico de Apellidos* (Manila: Philippine
     National Archives, 1973), p. vii.

3   Vicente Rafael rightly gave the differentiation in the translation from Tagalog
     to Spanish of *bautizar* to *binyag* and referred to the process not only as an act
     of Christian conversion but also the adoption of names. See Vicente Rafael,
     *Contracting Colonialism: Translation and Christian Conversion in Tagalog
     Society under Early Spanish Rule* (Quezon City: Ateneo de Manila University,
     1988), p. 117.

4   See Juan de Noceda and Pedro de Sanlucar, *Vocabulario de la Lengua Tagala*
     (Manila: Imp. De Ramirez y Giraudier, 1860), pp. 39, 229, 237, 344, 370; Jose
     Villa Panganiban, *English-Tagalog Vocabulary* (Manila: University Publishing,
     1946), pp. 68–9, 120; Jose Villa Panganiban, *Fundamental Tagalog* (Manila:
     Philippine Educational Company, 1939), pp. 277–8; and Leo James English,
     Tagalog-English Dictionary (Quezon City: Congregation of the Most Holy
     Redeemer, 1986), pp. 65, 151, 937, 973, 1463.

5   See Reynaldo Ileto, *Pasyon and Revolution: Popular Movements in the Philippines,
     1840–1910* (Manila: Ateneo de Manila University Press, 1979), pp. 107–8.

6   Giovanni Francesco Gemelli Careri, *A Voyage to the Philippines* (Manila:
     Filipiniana Book Guild, 1963).

7   Hildred and Clifford Geertz, "Teknonymy in Bali: Parenthood, Age Grading
     and Genealogical Amnesia," *Journal of the Royal Anthropological Institute of
     Great Britain and Ireland* 94, 2 (1964): 94–108. See also Kenneth Sillander's
     article in this volume. For a description of this naming system in the unhispanized
     Philippines, see Francisco Colin, "Native Races and Their Customs" (from
     Labor Evangelica), in *The Philippine Islands*, vol. 40, eds. Emma Blair and
     James Robertson (Cleveland: AH Clark, 1903–9), pp. 58–62. One must note
     that even though scholars have identified the practice as teknonymy, there is
     no local Tagalog term for teknonymy either.

8   For Calao and Amanicalao, the son and father listed as two of the co-
     conspirators with Magat Salamat against the Spaniards during the late six-
     teenth century, see Santiago de Veyra, "Conspiracy Against the Spaniards,"
     in *The Philippine Islands*, vol. 7, eds. Emma Blair and James Robertson
     (Cleveland: AH Clark, 1903–9), p. 100.

9   Michael Cullinane, "Accounting for Souls: Ecclesiastical Sources for the
     Study of Philippine Demographic History," in *Population and History:
     The Demographic Origins of the Modern Philippines*, eds. Daniel Doeppers
     and Peter Xenos (Quezon City: Ateneo de Manila University Press, 1998),
     pp. 294–5.

10 Ibid.

11 Norman Owen, "Life, Death and the Sacraments in a Nineteenth Century Bikol Parish," in *Population and History: The Demographic Origins of the Modern Philippines*, eds. Daniel Doeppers and Peter Xenos (Quezon City: Ateneo de Manila University Press, 1998), pp. 225–52.

12 *Catalogo Alfabetico de Apellidos* (Manila: Philippine National Archives, 1973), p. x.

13 Ibid.

14 Ibid.

15 Charles Macdonald suggested this line of analysis to me.

16 I am grateful to Clark Alejandrino and Karl Cheng Chua, both of the Ateneo de Manila University Department of History for the above information.

17 Antonio Tan, *The Chinese Mestizos and the Formation of the Filipino Nationality* (Manila: Kaisa Para sa Kaunlaran, 1994), p. 5.

18 Diosdado Asuncion, *Ang Kasaysayan ng mga Pangalan, Palayaw at Apelyido sa Pilipinas: Ilang Komentaryo* (Quezon City: University of the Philippines Diliman College of Social Sciences and Philosophy Professorial Chair Papers Series, 1997).

19 Domingo Abella, *Introduction to Catalogo Alfabetico de Apellidos* (Manila: Philippine National Archives, 1973), p. vii.

20 This was earlier pointed out by Charles Macdonald. See his "Personal Names as an Index of National Integration: Local Naming Practices and State-Produced Legal Identities," *Pilipinas* 42 (March 2004): 61–75, as well as James Scott's remarks in the naming conference that resulted in the production of this volume — giving officially recognized surnames became a matter of implementation of state projects.

CHAPTER 3

From 居正 *Live Righteously* and 小蘭 *Small Orchid* to 建華 *Construct China*: A Systematic Enquiry into Chinese Naming Practices

Zheng Yangwen 鄭揚文

Chinese people live and communicate with multiple names. They use different types of names to identify themselves depending on where they are and to whom they speak. In other words, each type of name functions in a different sphere of life or has a different audience as the following Table 1 shows:

Table 1 Name Types

Sphere	Name
Home	Pet or childhood name (小/乳名) and clan name (族名)
School	School name (學名)
Adulthood	Adult name (字), given to men when they reach adulthood and women at marriage
Profession	Examination title (學位名), occupation qualification (職業名)
	Business names for merchants and artisans (商號/名), literary and artistic studio names (室/斋名, 笔名), stage names (戲/藝名)
	Official titles for public officials (官衔名，爵名)
	Native or posthumous name for ranking officials[1] (宦地名)

Table 1 *continued*

Sphere	*Name*
Emperors	Reign name/title (年號)
	Temple and posthumous name (廟號)
	Given name (俗名)
	Literary name/title (笔名)
	Unofficial and tomb names (墓名)
Well-known persons	Pseudonyms (假名，无名)
(Martial artists, pirates, fugitives, etc.)	Nicknames (外/绰號，別名)
Religious believers	Religious name (教/法名)
Resident abroad	Foreign name (洋名)

Many ordinary Chinese have at least two names: a pet name and a school or adult name; while extraordinary figures, well-known artists/writers and emperors, for example, would have multiple names or titles. The Qing dynasty scholar-official 王士正 (Wang Shizheng), for example, had more than 100 names and titles. Most Chinese surnames are one-character although there are a few two-character surnames. Chinese given names, which occur after the surname, consist of one or two characters. A surname followed by a one-character given name is 單名 (*dan ming*), a single name or uninominal whereas a surname followed by a two-character given name is 雙名 (*shuang ming*), a double name or binominal. Charles Macdonald provides definition and analysis of uninominal and binominal names in Chapter 4. The first character of a double name or the only character in a single name can be a verb. In other words, a single name can be a short sentence consisting of a subject (the surname) and a verb (the given name), while a double name can be a sentence with a subject (the surname), a verb (the first character of the given name), and an object (the second character of the given name). This sentence-like nature and structure made it possible for parents and name-givers to create and differentiate; this explains why some Chinese names are vivid and literary, some action-oriented, and others informative of the era and its idiosyncrasies like the following:[2]

劉勝	Liu Sheng 'Liu Triumph' (Han)
彭沖	Peng Chong 'Peng Dashes' (CCP)
孔安国	Kong Anguo 'Kong Stabilises country' (Han)
李建華	Li Jianhua 'Li Constructs China' (CCP).

Chinese names offer a wealth of information about political change, cultural continuity and social origin that have shaped identity and lay bare a mechanism that merits systematic studies. Chinese naming is an art; it is also a science.[3] The dynamics between naming and the sociopolitical change and cultural practice of a particular era beckon academic investigation and synthesis. The first part of this chapter presents a brief history of Chinese naming practice in the past two millennia to highlight the development of name giving, especially the emergence of new types. The second part explains the cultural properties of Chinese given names. This will allow us to mine deep into the color and fiber of names which will shed light on the idiosyncrasies and making of Chinese identity. The last part discusses naming in the twentieth century, a very interesting case that reveals both change and continuity in the age of globalization. The majority of the names used as examples come from dictionaries and official histories (hence they are real people!) compiled by academic institutions and by the various regimes beginning with the Qin dynasty founded in 221 BC, ending with the Chinese Communist Party (CCP).[4]

From the Han to the Qing: A Précis of History

One cannot talk about Chinese naming practice without discussing surnames, which is intimately related to the emergence and development of Chinese civilization.[5] The few mainland scholars who have studied surnames and naming agree that it is difficult to pinpoint when exactly the practice of giving surnames began; but the sources they used in their works point to the Xia dynastic period (twenty-first to sixteenth century BC).[6] Surnames originally belonged to princes and aristocrats, some inherited and others granted. More surnames appeared during the Western Zhou dynasty (eleventh century to 771 BC) when the Zhou emperor, by way of holding his territory together as an empire of confederated states, created dukedoms and fiefdoms upon whom he also bestowed the privilege of surnames. As the population grew, more people inherited or were granted surnames. The hundred or so of the Zhou dukedoms and fiefdoms fought for survival and supremacy in wars of political consolidation during the Spring-Autumn period (771–475 BC). This led to changes in naming. As the Zhou Empire disintegrated, the practice of granting surnames to garner loyalty to the Zhou emperor came to an end. The small surviving polities were led by a new emergent class of leaders who ruled because of their competency, not just bloodline. This kind of political consolidation made it absolutely necessary for political regimes to register and control their male population, and naming served as the best mechanism of control by the fifth century BC. Surnames enabled the government to register every adult male and his household; identity cards were common as they helped regulate taxation, trade and travel.

Only seven larger kingdoms remained at the beginning of the Warring States period (475–221 BC). It took another 254 years for them to battle it out and for a dominant power, the Qin dynasty, to emerge. In this time of monumental change, radical reforms were undertaken. Centuries of war left many people not only homeless but also stateless. Some people used the names of their old dukedom or fiefdom as their surnames, some gave up their surnames for fear of discrimination or persecution, while others were given surnames by their conqueror and founder of the new dynasty. The increase in surnames made it necessary to further differentiate; hence given names emerged to help adequately identify the new Qin subjects. The first given names were numbers. 天干 (*tiangan* 'heavenly branch') with its 10 characters and 地支 (*dizhi* 'earthly branch') with its 12 characters were used in naming. These characters combine and form [into] the first 60 numbers in the Chinese mathematical system. Numbers were known to many and easy to remember, and the practice survived and thrived in later dynasties, interestingly among scholars and artists who used it with creative sophistication to escape the bureaucratic control which "numbered" given names were intended to achieve. Surnames and naming are intimately related to historical development in the past two millennia; the subject needs far more study than it has received.

Chinese given names began to increase rapidly after 221 BC when the first Qin emperor unified China and standardized the written language. However, the Qin dynasty was short-lived, a mere 15 years. It was left to the Han dynasty which followed to develop further the naming system. One striking innovation occurred during the Western Han (206 BC–24 AD) when the dynasty adopted Confucian ideals as its ruling ideology — names, then, took on a Confucian moral flavor. This can be seen from the following examples:

建德　Jiande 'Construct morality'
賢　　Xian 'Virtuous'
忠　　Zhong 'Loyal'
元　　Yuan 'First'
次　　Ci 'Next'
恭　　Gong 'Reverent'

君	Jun 'Gentleman'
師	Shi 'Teacher'
偉	Wei 'Great'
孝	Xiao 'Filial'

Likewise contemporary events and politics also appeared:

安国	Anguo 'Stabilizes country'
平胡	Pinghu 'Conquers barbarians'
長樂	Changle 'Long-lasting joy'
千秋	Qianqiu 'Thousand autumns'

王莽 (Wang Mang), the first emperor of the Eastern Han dynasty that followed the Western Han, promoted the use of single names which proliferated as a result. This can be seen from *Hou Han Shu* (*History of the Latter Han*) in which all the Eastern Han Emperors and nearly all the historical characters from 25 to 220 have single names.[7] This practice continued in the Three Kingdoms period (220–280) that followed as can be seen from the names in the *Sanguo Zhi* (*The Official History of the Three Kingdoms*) and *Sanguo Yanyi* (*The Unofficial History of the Three Kingdoms*). Single names remained predominant in the Jin dynasty (265–420); they surfaced again in the Sui (581–618), Song (960–1279), and Ming (1368–1644) dynasties as well as in the post-Mao era (1976 onwards).

Naming underwent important transformation in the Southern-Northern dynastic era (420–589). This was a time of division as China broke up into smaller kingdoms. People seemed to have also broken away from the confines of Confucian ideals and moral philosophy; this also coincided with the gradual adoption of Buddhism (introduced during the Han period) and the popularity of Daoism and *Xuanxue*.[8] The characters denoting the Buddhist notion of wisdom 志慧 (*zhihui*) began to appear in given names, sometimes in single words and other times [together] as a phrase. These two characters remained favorites in the twentieth century, with 志 (*zhi*) for male names and 慧 (*hui*) for female names. Non-Chinese words made their ways into Chinese names as China came under the rule or influence of its nomadic neighbors. New ways of assembling given names appeared as well; one of the most innovative is a neutral and sophisticated direct object word 之 (*zhi* 'this/it') as the second character of a given name. For example:

安之	Anzhi 'Stabilize it'
偉之	Weizhi 'Make it great'
悅之	Yuezhi 'Please it'

The Tang dynasty (618–907) ended more than 300 years of division and ushered in a golden age where Confucianism, Buddhism, and Daoism flourished. This dynasty also marked a new era in naming as it saw the standardization of double names; single names would never regain their eminence. The Tang dynasty saw the emergence of new types and produced new ways of assembling given names as examination titles and official ranks appeared. The famous scholar-official poet 韓愈 (Han Yu) was 韓十八郎 (Han Shiba Lang 'Han the Eighteenth Vice Minister'). This extended to women; 徐三娘 (Xu Sanniang) or 'Xu the Third Lady' was a prominent example. Color, nature, animals and mundane things appeared in names as can be seen from poet 李白 (Li Bai 'Li White'), 白居易 (Bai Juyi 'Bai Lives Easily'), and 杜牧 (Du Mu 'Du the Shepherd'). As did professions such as 李百藥 (Li Baiyao 'Li Hundred-medicine'). Profession designations from then would become the norm [since then] as China began to urbanize and commercialize. 'Li Hundred-medicine' not only denotes his profession but also his place in the social hierarchy.

One character alone can sometimes identify the naming trend of a particular dynasty or era; this was true with the Tang. As the Tang dynasty reached its zenith, so did its naming practice. The use of such scholarly words as 文 (*wen*) or 'letters and culture' and 士 (*shi*) or 'gentleman scholar' appeared in many given names. They reflected the Tang dynasty's inventiveness and sophistication. Although the Five Dynasty period (907–960) that followed was short, it saw the frequent use and popularity of the word 彥 (*yan* 'virtuous and talented gentleman') in names. Mainland specialist Wang Quangen states that *yan* appeared in the names of more than 140 prominent people.[9] Perhaps this mirrors the qualities that many sought after during this era of disorder and division.

The Song dynasty (960–1279) saw the return of words from Confucian ideals and moral philosophy in names. This had much to do with the revival of orthodoxy and the emergence of 理學 or *lixue*, a new school of thought that combined Confucianism and certain elements of Buddhism. The influence of *lixue* can be seen in given names such as:

安仁   Anren 'Stable-kind'
居正   Juzheng 'Live-righteously'
德儒   Deru 'Virtue-Confucius'

and characters like:

恕   *shu* 'forgive'
謙   *qian* 'modest'
老   *lao* 'old'

The Song dynasty also saw the return of 五行 (*wuxing*) or 'five elements' (some have translated it as 'five phases'): they are 金 (*jin*) or 'gold,' 木 (*mu*) or 'wood,' 水 (*shui*) or 'water,' 火 (*huo*) or 'fire,' and 土 (*tu*) or 'earth.' This had much to do with the popularity of Daoism, which believes that the universe is made of these five elements and that they complement as well as oppose each other, making it important to balance them in the human universe. The act of balancing can be achieved through naming, that is, through the careful selection of words. This is vital in a marriage. For example, if a man lacks the element of wood and even if his parents have tried to compensate this in his name, he should not choose a wife whose nature and whose name contain the element of fire since fire destroys wood; he would fare better with someone whose personality and whose name are endowed with the element of water.

The Song dynasty is a particularly important period in naming because it also saw a revival of family or clan histories. Large and established families or clans recorded their own births, marriages, migrations, undertakings and achievements of all sorts. This made it necessary to identify each generation within the family or clan, and naming was one major and, in many ways, the only mechanism of identification adopted. A modern and easy-to-follow example is the communist leader 毛澤東 (Mao Zedong), his younger brothers, 毛澤民 (Mao Zemin) and 毛澤覃 (Mao Zetan), and their cousin 毛澤建 (Mao Zejian). Ze obviously identifies Mao's generation. Family/clan names are a very important aspect of Chinese naming practice, which is further elaborated in the next section.

The Mongols (1271–1368) brought new words into Chinese names. A typical example is the character 哥 (*ge* 'elder brother'). It has replaced the more classic word 兄 (*xiong* 'elder brother') as in 大哥 (*dage* 'elder/ big brother') and 二哥 (*erge* 'second brother'). Many ethnic Mongols took Chinese names, especially those who settled in China; some were more hybrid than others, 冒襄 (Mao Xiang) is a good example of that. This pattern of indigenization would repeat with the Manchus in the Qing dynasty. The return of Chinese rule in the Ming (1368–1644) restored Han Chinese tradition and reinforced Han Chinese values. The Ming saw the return of the five elements; this can be seen from the imperial family that adopted the five elements [see earlier comment] as generation identifiers. The second generation used "wood" characters in their given names, the third generation "fire" characters, the fourth generation "earth" characters, and the fifth generation "water." But more importantly the Ming saw the return of Confucian ideals and moral philosophy in names. This can be seen from such characters as 德 (*de* 'morality') and 恭 (*gong* 'reverent') as the character 中 (*zhong* 'middle') surfaced in names.

This can be seen from 時中 (Shizhong 'Time-middle') and 柄中 (Binzhong 'Handle-middle'). Perhaps this reflects the conservative and middle of the road nature of the Ming.

The Ming dynasty also witnessed the return of single names. For a few decades, single names were suddenly popular among some scholar-officials and eunuchs; as a matter of fact, the majority of eunuchs seemed to have single names. 王振 (Wang Zhen), 汪直 (Wang Zhi) and 劉瑾 (Liu Jin) are perfect examples. Does this indicate solidarity of a kind or reveal the extent of the internal strife that would ultimately bring down the House of Zhu? Ming dynasty Chinese did come up with new characters and new ways of assembling names. Among the characters were 汝 (*ru* 'you'), 爾 (*er* 'me'), 吾 (*wu* 'I'), 以 (*yi* 'use/depending on'), 于 (*yu* 'at'), 在 (*zai* 'in') 與 (*yu* 'with'), 其 (*qi* 'that/then'), 此 (*ci* 'this/now'), 也 (*ye* 'too/as well'), 若 (*ruo* 'like') 亦 (*yi* 'just as'), and 又 (*you* 'again'). These words mean little but they made it possible to assemble new and different names; and they contributed to the increasing sophistication of name giving.

The Qing dynasty (1644–1911) ushered in another era of economic growth and cultural development. Manchu reign saw the emergence of new words and concepts in Chinese names when new ways of naming along with new characters appeared. One distinct feature is that the Qing produced pleasant-to-hear and easy-to-remember names. Some reflect the beauty of nature, architecture and objects, some the pursuit of refined personalities and tastes, and others inspirations and aspirations of all kinds. Examples include 紀曉嵐 (Ji Xiaolan 'Ji Sunny-cloud'), 陳鳳翔 (Chen Fengxiang 'Chen Phoenix-flying'), 李秋庭 (Li Qiuting 'Li Autumn-pavilion'), 王玉峰 (Wang Yufeng 'Wang Jade-peak'), and 葛雨田 (Ge Yutian 'Ge Rain-field'). These names demonstrate Qing creativity; they also reveal the state of Qing politics, an aspect of which was its literary inquisition or 文字獄 (*wenzi yu*) — the Manchus persecuted many Chinese whose literary works were considered by the official censors to contain anti-Manchu sentiments, irrespective of whether they did or did not in reality do so. Under such conditions, people looked for non-political words and neutral phrases to use in given names. Qing naming conventions broke away from the practice of using terms associated with Confucian ethics, moral virtues and the five elements; instead it prioritized natural, neutral and ordinary ideas and things. Perhaps this had something to do with the fact that the dynasty was non-Han in origin.

One of the most significant aspects of the Qing which no historian has studied is the "disappearance" of Manchu names after 1911. The

Manchus brought in and used their own naming practice until the eve of and even after the Nationalist Revolution. But the Manchu people virtually "disappeared" in the 1920s, and it is almost impossible to find old Manchu surnames or given names today.[10] Did they adopt Chinese names? If so, how was this effected? Was it a collective endeavor or individual decisions? Did they omit their long surnames which in many cases contained four characters when written down in Chinese and retain their given names which in many cases contained only two characters to make them look like Chinese names? Where are the descendants of the legendary Aixin Jieluo clan that founded the Qing dynasty? The disappearance of not just Mongol and Manchu but also other ethnic names, like the Wa people elaborated in Chapter 7, demands academic attention. They will undoubtedly shed light not merely on the issue of the assimilation of the Manchus at least through naming practice to the majority Han population, but also on the matter of the making of modern Chinese identity.

To recapitulate, Han Chinese rule in the Han, Song, and Ming dynasties seemed to have encouraged the use of words related to Confucian philosophy and ethics in names. Division during the Three Kingdoms and the Jin-Southern-Northern periods seemed to have encouraged innovation whereas ethnic rule saw the addition of alien words. The pool of names enlarged overtime as new words and new ways of naming were fashioned and refashioned throughout history. Names can help us identify a certain historical era and help us gauge the political thought, social psyche, and cultural norms that dictated the lives of ordinary people. From a structural point of view, while new name words and new ways of naming appeared throughout history, older naming practices also returned in new forms, enlarging the pool from which given names can be taken or re-assembled.

燿祖 'Glorify Ancestors' to 玉環 'Jade Earrings': the Cultural Properties

Chinese names are not just combinations of surnames followed by given names made up of one or two characters which might be pleasant to hear and easy to remember. More often they are endowed with moral, political, cosmological and cultural properties that tell much about the person and his/her name givers. Chinese poetry, literature, drama and history provide a vast and rich pool of words, phrases, characters and stories from which a name may be chosen or appropriated to suit a particular individual, his/her character or the occasion. Literary allusions in a given name reflect the class origins and/or the educational background on the part of the name givers, or at least their social aspirations. One needs time to acquaint oneself with the vast reservoir of literature, drama and history in order to develop the knowledge to construct names. This is what Pierre Bourdieu calls "close relationship linking cultural practices to educational capital and to social origin."[11]

Aristocrats, literati, and ranking officials often have hard-to-understand, eccentric, and enigmatic given names and literary titles, such as 西溪居士 (Xixi Jushi 'Gentleman of West Brook') and 桃園老人 (Taoyuan Laoren 'Old man of Peach Blossom Cave'). Those who are less exposed to history and literature tend to have names with straightforward meanings. 鄧小平 (Deng Xiaoping 'Deng Small-peace') is a great example as his parents wished 'small peace' for him in turbulent times. The poorly educated sometimes paid for the naming of their children, especially when it was a boy while others used the simplest terms, such as 張九四 (Zhang Jiusi 'Zhang Nine-four' [Ming]), 田万頃 (Tian Wanqin 'Tian or Land Ten-thousand Acres' [Qing]), and 麥有金 (Mai Youjin 'Mai Has Gold' [Qing]). However, we cannot assume that ordinary people did not come up with sophisticated names to reflect their expectation for their children. 孫來臣 (Sun Laichen 'Sun Arrives Minister'), a historian of Southeast Asia and a colleague, is an example of this. Laichen was the only one from his village to attend Beijing University but he did not enter officialdom and become a minister as many would have in the old days and as his parents had hoped. Chinese parents can express their aspiration or expectations for their children in given names; this ranged from moral standards to worldly accomplishments. They can use given names to commemorate historical figures/events, cultivate interest/enthusiasm, compensate for biological defects according to Chinese cosmology, rank seniority and mark gender among their children.

Ethical

Social contact and exchange in China are based on Confucian moral principles, and Chinese naming practices reflect this concern with being moral. Parents often embed desired moral standards and the names of those who personify these standards in their children's given names to express their reverence for these values, their admiration for those who have faithfully upheld them, as well as their hope that their children will emulate them. Among the most important moral principles are 仁 (*ren* 'benevolent, kind-hearted, merciful'), 和 (*he* 'harmonious, gentle, mild, affable, amicable'), and 德 (*de* 'virtuous'). Below are examples of names incorporating these principles:

仁   Ren
李懷仁   Li Huairen 'Li Remember/Cherish-kindness' (Song)
梁志仁   Liang Zhiren 'Liang Determines-to-be-kind' (Ming)
張体仁   Zhan Tiren 'Zhang Considerate-and-kind' (KMT)
和   He
蔡和   Cai He 'Cai Peace' (Song)
陳知和   Chen Zhihe 'Chen Know-harmony/peace' (Song)
德   De
陸樹德   Lu Shude 'Lu Plant-virtue' (Ming)
林立德   Lin Lide 'Lin Establish-virtue' (Qing)
楊學德   Yang Xuede 'Yang Learn-virtue' (Contemporary)

Most of the above names, except the single name Cai He, feature [action] verbs followed by moral values, standards and aspirations. These verbs include 敬 (*jing* 'respect'), 遵 (*zun* 'abide'), 從 (*cong* 'follow'), 希 (*xi* 'hope'), 幕 (*mu* 'admire'), 應 (*ying* 'echo'), and 思 (*si* 'think of'). They are often combined with characters denoting values such as 良 (*liang* 'good'), 忠 (*zhong* 'loyal'), 正 (*zheng* 'upright, honest, serious, solemn, earnest'), 容 (*rong* 'forgiving'), and 誠 (*cheng* 'honest'). Examples are:

袁遵尼   Yuan Zunni 'Yuan Abide-Confucius' (Ming)
張繼儒   Zhang Jiru 'Chen Continues-Confucianism' (Ming)
林則徐   Lin Zexu 'Lin Looks-up-to-Xu' (Qing: Xu was the surname of a governor)
張學良   Zhang Xueliang 'Zhang Learns-to-be-good' (KMT)

Of the important moral values is 孝 (*xiao* 'filial piety'); this can be achieved in many ways such as sacrificing the self for the family, ensuring the continuation of the family line, honoring ancestors, or taking care of the elderly. *Xiao* can be found in many Chinese names throughout history; so can [be] 祖 (*zu* 'ancestor'), which many families/clans systematically incorporate in the names of their children or a particular generation. Note the use of 祖 (*zu*) in the following names:

念祖   Nianzu 'Remember-ancestors'
紀祖   Jizu 'Commemorate-ancestors'
耀祖   Yaozu 'Glorify-ancestors'
孝祖   Xiaozu 'Filial-to-ancestors'

Political

The literary nature of Chinese naming practice makes it possible to express or suggest political thought, affairs, awareness, or bias in given names. On the one hand, this demonstrates innovation in naming practice throughout history as dynasties changed hands, and as politics and philosophies came and went. On the other hand, it shows democraticization at work as ordinary people participate in the voicing, if not the making, of politics, even though, admittedly, a limited exercise. This indeed is a most interesting aspect of Chinese naming practice. A name can help us pinpoint the socio-political change and popular spirit of a certain era; it can also help us see the undercurrent of a particular dynasty or regime. Given names can be highly explicit and political such as 陸平胡 (Lu Pinghu 'Lu Conquers/Wipes-out-barbarians'), which is a reference to the Chinese people's struggle with the ethnic Siongnu people to the North and West of Han dynasty China. They can be metaphorical and subtle like 鄭思肖 (Zheng Sixiao 'Zheng Thinks *Xiao*'), where 肖 (*xiao*) sits in the word of 趙 (*zhao*), the surname of the Southern Song imperial family.

The most political of all is the naming of emperors who, as I mentioned at the beginning, have many names. Their reign name/title is the most important because that is what they would be remembered by their subjects. Reign names are most ostentatious and auspicious. 永樂 (Yongle), the Ming emperor who commissioned the 鄭和 (Zheng He) voyages, translates as 'perpetual joy.' 'Zheng He' was the name that the Yongle emperor granted to his favored eunuch-turned-admiral, who voyaged to Southeast Asia, the Indian Ocean and East Africa from 1404 to 1433. '*Zheng*' means 'accurate, serious, and upright' while '*he*' means 'peace or harmony.' Perhaps this was indeed the Yongle emperor's intention for the epic voyages. The Manchus came to rule China in 1644; they adopted many Chinese practices, including naming. The reign names of the first five Qing emperors further illustrate how names reflect their wishes:

順治　Shunzhi 'Smooth-rule'
康熙　Kangxi 'Healthy-and-prosperous'
雍正　Yongzheng 'Poised-and-righteous'
乾隆　Qianlong 'Heaven-earth-thrive'
嘉庆　Jiaqing 'Excellent-celebrate'

Qianlong had many literary names, one of them was 十全老人 (Shiquan laoren 'Old man of Ten Enumerations'), a reminder of his ten victories that enlarged China's territory. Many political figures had very political names. Some would have changed names according to their changing fortunes or conviction throughout history, especially at times of dynastic/ regime change — the Song general who became 秦再雄 (Qin Zaixiong 'Qin Once again great') is a case in point. Other examples are:

王辟疆   Wang Bijiang 'Wang-opens-up-new-territory' (Song)
謝恩昭   Xie Enzhao 'Xie Thank-Majesty's-decree' (Qing)
劉華清   Liu Huaqing 'Liu China-clear/s' (CCP)

Cosmological

Cosmology runs deep Chinese culture, shaping naming practice from its beginning. The 八字 (*ba zi* 'eight characters') are the most important. These eight characters are grouped in four pairs that indicate the year, month, day, and hour of one's birth based on the lunar calendar. Years, for example, are represented by a cycle of 12 animals: rat, ox, tiger, rabbit, dragon, snake, horse, goat, monkey, rooster, dog, and pig. Each of them symbolizes different attributes, bearing different fortunes. The tiger for example symbolizes strength, bravery, independence and pride — all you could want for a boy and his name. But, if a girl is born in the year of the Tiger, parents need to be careful in naming her. The same principle applied to the 24 solar signs that mark the seasonal changes of a year and to the 12 months. The days in the month of January, for example, are marked by 29 pairs of different terms. In the past, many parents used the terms associated with the birthday of their children to name them. This also includes the lunar calendar which marks each day with 12 pairs of characters, the first part of each pair indicating the earthly branches and second indicating the sequence of the 24 hours. For example, the hour between 11:00 AM and 12 noon is 午初 (*wu chu*), and the hour between 12 noon and 1:00 PM is 午正 (*wu zheng*). In the past, many people were named after these lunar terms, some with one character, others with both terms. Following one's cosmology from birth was the best way for the ordinary people to give their children a head start in life.

If this is complicated, it is only the beginning. 五行 (*wu xing* 'five elements') is even more important when it comes to choosing names. Daoism holds that the five elements of 金 (*jin* 'gold'), 木 (*mu* 'wood'), 水 (*shui* 'water'), 火 (*huo* 'fire'), and 土 (*tu* 'earth') make up the cosmos, operating in two cycles. In the reproductive or generative cycle, wood causes or leads to fire, fire to earth, earth to metal, metal to water, and water to wood. In the destructive cycle, water clashes with fire, fire with metal, metal with wood, wood with earth, and earth with water. These elements underpin the constitution of the human psyche as well. We are each born with some but not with all of them. It is therefore vital to ensure they are balanced, which can be achieved through giving names that refer to them. Many people, especially the elderly, know them by heart and in the old days, fortune-tellers made a good living suggesting auspicious names to uninformed parents. Today many rely on Chinese dictionaries and lunar calendars, which come with this kind of information, to choose an appropriate name for their children. A worksheet fell out of a book which I borrowed for my research.[12] The family name Chen is obvious on the worksheet and Chen is a "metal" character. Since metal clashes with fire and wood, the choices of this hardworking parent were limited to water and earth. This parent needed water or earth characters that can also do the job of differentiating gender, a hard enough job that turned him or her to read academic publications. Here are some of the characters which this parent could have chosen:

Water
冰   *bing* 'ice'
帆   *fan* 'sail'
慧   *hui* 'intelligent'
媚   *mei* 'charming'
華   *hua* 'magnificent'

Earth
威   *wei* 'power'
溫   *wen* 'warm'
文   *wen* 'literary'
業   *ye* 'business'
友   *you* 'friend'

Names Indicating Occupation, Region, Nature, and Objects

The literary nature of the Chinese naming practice allows parents and name-givers to put occupation, region, nature, weather, the environment, objects, religion, ethnicity, and many other ideas/things in given names. Despite the great desire for upward social mobility, most people lead ordinary lives and ordinary names do the job of identifying oneself in an ocean of people. Here are some instances of names acquired in adult life through careers and occupations:

宋公明   Song Gongming 'Song Fair-and-transparent' (Song official who became a rebel)
彭和尚   Peng Heshang 'Peng Monk' (Rebel leader in the Yuan period)

包青天　Bao Qingtian 'Bao Blue sky' (Ming upright/incorrupt official)
陳布衣　Chen Buyi 'Chen Cotton cloth' (poor scholar's clothes versus official robes)
李石匠　Li Shijiang 'Li Mason'

Having a name that refers to one's occupation was and still is the norm because it served to uphold professionalism. Teachers and doctors are good examples. It is impolite and disrespectful to address one's teacher or doctor by his/her given name. Occupational names have been very popular in the performing arts world where many performers have stage names. In the Tang dynasty when the performing arts flourished, many popular performing artists had very literary stage names like 飛鳥 (Fei niao 'Flying Bird') and 輕風 (Qing feng 'Breeze'). Whereas those from the late Qing to the Republican era had stage names that contained the character 玉 (*yu* 'jade') like 常香玉 (Chang Xiangyu 'Chang/Often-fragrant-jade') and 白玉霜 (Bai Yushuang 'Bai/White-jade-frost'). Another idiosyncratic characteristic was that many actors had feminine stage names. 梅蘭芳 (Mei Lanfang 'Mei/Plum-blossom Orchid-fragrant'), the great Peking opera singer, is a great example.

Naming had much to do with place names in the past as I mentioned earlier. Many people took the names of their fallen kingdom or locality when they were rendered stateless, while others had names forced upon them during the period of political consolidation that led to the Qin dynasty in 221 BC. Many still used their own or their children's birth places or provinces to make a given name. They ranged from whole words or abbreviations for provinces, regions, rivers, mountains, and local specialties. Examples of places/regions used as given names can be seen from:

陳楚舟　Chen Chuzhou 'Chen Hunan Boat' (Yuan)
丘念台　Qiu Niantai 'Qiu Remembers Taiwan' (Qing)
張杭杭　Zhang Hanghang 'Zhang Hanghang [Hangzhou]' (CCP)

Nature, weather, the environment, architectures, plants, animal and objects can be found in the following given names:

陳禾　　Chen He 'Chen Grain' (Song)
顧亭林　Gu Tinglin 'Gu Pagoda-forest' (Ming)
李漁　　Li Yu 'Li Fish' (Qing)
王石谷　Wang Shigu 'Wang Stone-valley' (Qing)
王崑崙　Wang Kunlun 'Wang Kunlun (Mountain in China)' (CCP)
周谷城　Zhou Gucheng 'Zhou Grain-city' (CCP ranking official)

The list below illustrates some interesting ideas and phenomena:

辛棄疾　Xin Qiji 'Xin Rid-disease' (Writer from the Song dynasty)
李自成　Li Zicheng 'Li Self-made' (Ming rebel leader)
康有爲　Kang Youwei 'Kang Does-something-great' (Qing reformer)
楊虎城　Yang Hucheng 'Yang Tiger-city' (KMT general)
贾笑寒　Jia Xiaohan 'Jia Laughs-at-cold weather' (Contemporary)

Names Indicating Generation

The family/clan has always been the basic social unit of China. Historians have only just begun to mine deep into the thousands of family/clan histories that exist. Naming is after all a family/clan affair. Many families, both royal and ordinary households, followed their own naming practices. One of the challenges is to identify the different generations within because a large family/clan might have hundreds of people scattered over a large region, the whole country or even the globe with unprecedented migration since the late nineteenth century. Clan names are not intended for public use even though some may choose to use them in public. The first character of a clan name identifies the generation to which one belongs within the family/clan. For example, the given names of the sons of the Xuande emperor (Ming) were Zhu Jianshen, Jianlian, Jianchun, Jianshu, Jianze, Jianjun, Jianzhi and Jianshi, where *jian*, a water character, identified this generation and indicated that this generation was believed to lack the element of water. The Manchus also used a common character to identify princes of the same generation even though it might not have been a Manchu tradition, as illustrated by the use of 弘暉 (Honghui), 弘時 (Hongshi), 弘曆 (Hongli, the Qianlong emperor), and 弘昼 (Hongzhou), whose bearers were all sons of the Yongzheng Emperor.

How do families/clans come up with the all-important first character of a clan name to identify generations within? In the past, they came from verses composed precisely for naming purposes at the foundation or revision of the family/clan genealogy. Different families of a clan would follow the verse word by word and generation by generation to distinguish their offspring. This way, the satellite families kept track of their children and the different generations could easily identify themselves. This again demonstrates the family's education background and social origin. One can usually find these naming verses in the beginning pages of family/clan histories. My research has revealed a number of them, including Mao Zedong's family in Hunan. Here is the Mao family naming couplet:

立顯榮朝士
文方運際祥
祖恩貽澤遠
世代永承昌

澤 (*ze*), the fourth character in the third verse, identifies Mao's generation (see the examples mentioned earlier) whereas 遠 (*yuan*) the fifth or the last character in the third verse identifies the next generation and so on. Mao's family was of middling peasantry at best, yet even such a modest family kept their own naming practices. So we can imagine the set up of more established families/clans. A close-to-home example is Zheng Yongnian (鄭永年), Director of the East Asia Institute, National University of Singapore and former Professor of Chinese Politics and Founding Research Director of the China Policy Institute at Nottingham University. When I was first introduced to him, his name reminded me of my father's clan name Zheng Yongle (鄭永樂). I knew that the character Yong identifies my father's generation. In this case, 'Uncle' Yongnian might have used his clan name in public which I verified with him later. Professor, "Uncle" to be more precise, Zheng and my father were born thousands of miles apart, he in Zhejiang and my father in Hunan, and they have never met and led very different lives; but one character identifies kinship and the enduring naming practice of their clan.

However, using a common character to identify the same generation of a family is not limited to a verse from genealogy. Many families found ways to identify their children with a common character that is significant to the parents or to their generation. For example, tree-related words mark Deng Xiaoping's three daughters 鄧林 (Deng Lin 'Deng Forest'), 鄧楠 (Deng Nan 'Deng Phoebe-tree'), and 鄧榕 (Deng Rong 'Deng Small-fruited-fig-tree') as sisters. The girls obviously lacked wood; this was compensated for in their names. In the past, daughters did not usually have family/clan names since they were considered members of their husband families/clans. But things changed with reform and revolution in the late Qing and throughout the twentieth century as we can see from Deng Xiaoping's daughters. Some would use a common second character to identify their girls. The Song patriarch Charlie Soong (宋嘉澍) used a common last character to identify his daughters who married into wealth and power; they were 宋藹齡 (Song Ai*ling* 'Song Kind-*time/age*'), 宋慶齡 (Song Qing*ling* 'Song Celebrate-*time/age*'), and 宋美齡 (Song Mei*ling* 'Song Beautiful-*time/age*'). Other examples include sons of Nationalist-era warlord general Zhang Zuolin: 張學良 (Zhang Xueliang), 張學思

(Zhang Xuesi), and 張學民 (Zhang Xuemin), and the children of a famous literary-artistic family: 黃宗洛 (Huang Zongluo, son), 黃宗漢 (Huang Zonghan, another son), and 黃宗英 (Huang Zongying, a daughter). This Huang family did not discriminate against their daughter as she shared the first character of her name with her brothers.

Pet or childhood names are also a most important aspect of Chinese culture and society because daily life revolves around family. Indeed a number of scholars — Lu Gumeng from the Tang dynasty, Chen Min from the Song dynasty and Shen Hongzu from the Ming dynasty — have written about pet names. Children are often given pet names when they are born, and they are identified by their pet names until they go to school when they are given a school name. Pet names tend to reflect memorable events of one's childhood, things that only matters to the immediate family, or unique characteristics of a child. The rule of the game is that the more unusual and funnier, the better. They tend to be explicit like 老三 (Laosan 'Number three'), hilarious like 臭宝 (Chou bao 'Foul fool'), affectionate like 毛它 (Maotuo 'Hairy chunk'). Many pet names do not make sense except in local or indigenous dialects; this indeed is a most fascinating aspect as a dialect can be Greek to people from outside the area. The first day of school presents a most interesting spectacle when teachers call pupils by the school names with which their parents registered them, and the pupils do not respond until their parents push them forward because the new pupils are not used to their school names. Even today, many parents would prepare their children when they approach the age of seven with a question like "What is your name?" to familiarize them with their new name to be used in school and in public. Later in life, pet names identify kinship and family; no one in my family/clan calls me Yangwen (school name).

Names Indicating Gender

Chinese given names are endowed with masculine and feminine properties. This originated, if not earlier, then at least, from the time of Confucius (552–479 BC), who advanced the idea that men and women were different with males being superior to females. Men should participate in affairs of the world and be the breadwinners of their families while women should care for the home, have children, and serve their husbands. Therefore, boys were given names befitting their role; their names often had built-in lofty aspirations, noble qualities, strong personalities, wisdom, responsibility, and power with such characters like 宏 (*hong* 'grand'),

偉 (*wei* 'great'), 大 (*da* 'big'), 勇 (*yong* 'brave'), 軍 (*jun* 'military'), 鵬 (*peng* 'eagle'), 飛 (*fei* 'fly'), 俊 (*jun* 'handsome'), 聰 (*cong* 'smart'), 安国 (*anguo* 'stabilize country'), 光宗 (*guangzong* 'glorify ancestors'), 居正 (*juzheng* 'live righteously'), 禮仁 (*liren* 'courteous and kind'), and 志堅 (*zhijian* 'will strong'). Girls are given names befitting their presumed submissive nature and supportive, nurturing roles. They were named after plants and flowers, animals, birds, seasons, natural phenomenon, inner chamber accessories, colors, and objects such as earrings and powder, and with adjectives like filial, warm, virtuous, obedient, modest, forgiving, beautiful, elegant, fragrant, refined, graceful, quiet, and small. In a word, girls and women were reminded of the conventional set of moral and beauty standards indicated by their names. The *Huaxia Funu Mingren Cidian* (华夏妇女名人录 or Dictionary of Famous Chinese Women) lists more than 3,300 eminent women in the past two thousand years. Except for a small portion of those with gender-neutral names, the majority of these women had feminine given names:[13]

于蘭馥	Yu Lanfu 'Yu Orchid-fragrant'
馬金鳳	Ma Jinfeng 'Ma Gold-phoenix'
王淑珍	Wang Shuzhen 'Wang Tender-precious'
楊玉環	Yang Yuhuan 'Yang Jade-earrings'
張靜安	Zhang Jingan 'Zhang Quiet-peace'
顧媚	Gu Mei 'Gu Charming/Seductive'
梁守靜	Liang Shoujing 'Liang Remains-quiet'

What Distinguishes the Twentieth Century

The twentieth century saw monumental political changes; it also saw cultural continuity. This can be seen from naming practices. When political change transformed many aspects of society, it also enriched the pool of names. New characters emerged and new ways of naming came into fashion. The Nationalist and Communist eras were no exception. They might have destroyed many old elements of Chinese culture, but naming attained a high level of political correctness and cultural sophistication. The Nationalist regime started the engine of fundamental change whereas the Communist rule brought unprecedented upward social mobility. Increased industrialization and modernization demanded convenience and transparency on an individual level. What distinguishes twentieth-century naming practice is unprecedented politicization, de-feminization, and the return of single names in the post-Mao era.

Unprecedented Politicization

Twentieth-century China saw three very different kinds of political regimes — Imperial, Republican, and Communist. These political changes are reflected in Chinese names. The late nineteenth and early twentieth century saw the rise of Han Chinese nationalism; many Chinese had Han names or changed their names to make them anti-Manchu. The 1911 Nationalist Revolution ushered in the New Culture Movement where many intellectuals blamed tradition for China's backwardness and advocated modernization or even Westernization. Many European and American ideas flooded China and began to work their way through not just Chinese polity but also Chinese society. This can be seen from naming and this was the beginning of a cultural revolution, and it continues today. In theory, this is not different from dynastic change and the introduction of foreign religions and cultures that China had come to accept and indigenize over time. In practice, this was the beginning of an intensified egalitarianization and modernization of Chinese society, which would be carried to an extreme under Communist rule. New characters, new names, and new ways of naming that bear the special symbol of the twentieth century appeared. For example, many twentieth-century names contain the character 'three,' which is short for Dr. Sun Yatsen's three revolutionary principles.

包達三　Bao Dasan 'Bao Arrives-three'
馮鼎三　Feng Dingsan 'Feng Uphold-three'
李立三　Li Lisan 'Li Establish-three'
王遵三　Wang Zunsan 'Wang Respect-three'
張省三　Zhang Shensan 'Zhang Reflect-three'
鄭位三　Zheng Weisan 'Zheng Position-three'

Many twentieth-century names contain characters expressing Han nationalism.

康克清　Kang Keqing 'Kang Overcomes-Qing'
胡漢民　Hu Hanmin 'Hu Han-people'
廖漢生　Liao Hansheng 'Liao Han-born'
李漢俊　Li Hanjun 'Li Han-handsome'
李漢魂　Li Hanhun 'Li Han-soul'
林漢雄　Lin Hanxiong 'Lin Han-hero/great'
潘鎮亞　Pan Zhenya 'Pan Shakes-Asia'
張震球　Zhang Zhenqiu 'Zhang Shakes-globe'

And, many twentieth-century names contain characters expressing revolutionary zeal.

建華	Jianhua 'Construct-China'
援朝	Yuanchao 'Support-Korea'
衛東	Weidong 'Defend-Dong' (reference to Mao Zedong)
衛青	Weiqing 'Defend-Qing' (reference to Jiang Qing, Mao's wife)

De-feminization

The New Culture Movement and the Communist Revolution advocated women's rights and promoted feminism. Indeed, in no other part of the world did women experience so much change as they have in twentieth-century China. These changes can be seen from the gradual neutralization or de-feminization of female names during the height of Communist rule. There is no doubt that the post-Mao era saw the return of traditional female names, a backlash against the revolutionary Mao era. But I believe that female modernity and the single child policy will continue to shape socio-cultural norms related to female naming. When there is only one child in the family, the gender element is less important than it would have been otherwise. Below are some twentieth-century female names:

楊開慧	Yang Kaihui 'Yang Opens-up-wisdom' (reference to Mao Zedong's first wife)
馬仰班	Ma Yangban 'Ma Looks-up-to-Ban' (Ban is a woman historian in the Han dynasty)
李鉄軍	Li Tiejun 'Li Iron-army'
陳慕華	Chen Muhua 'Chen Admires-China'
熊鉄生	Xiong Tiesheng 'Xiong Iron-born'
陳自強	Chen Ziqiang 'Chen Self-strong'

According to Xu Jianshun's 1982 research, the ten most used words in female names were:

英	*ying* 'flower/outstanding'
秀	*xiu* 'elegant/excellent'
玉	*yu* 'jade'
華	*hua* 'magnificent, splendid'
珍	*zhen* 'precious'
蘭	*lan* 'orchid'
芳	*fang* 'charming'
麗	*li* 'beautiful'
淑	*shu* 'virtuous'
桂	*gui* 'osmanthus'

Despite so much change, it seems tradition dies hard. This is the same with male names as noted by Xu [who also listed the ten most used words for male names]:

明   *ming* 'clear/transparent'
国   *guo* 'country'
文   *wen* 'culture/letters'
華   *hua* 'China'
德   *de* 'virtue'
建   *jian* 'construct'
志   *zhi* 'will/want'
永   *yong* 'forever/lasting'
林   *lin* 'forest'
成   *cheng* 'succeed'[14]

Return of Single Names in the Post-Mao Era

Single names or uninominal, that is surname followed by only one character, was popular in early imperial times from the Eastern Han to the era of the Three Kingdoms as I described in the early part of this chapter. The following table provides a big picture of single names versus double names or binominal, surname followed by two characters, from the Han to the Qing dynasties.[15] The South-North Period seems to be the dividing line as uninominal names dwindled and binominal names became the norm even though there appears to be even in the Ming dynasty as the following table shows:

Table 2   Single Versus Double Names in History

Historical Source	Period	Percentages Single Names	Percentages Double Names
Han Shu	206–24 BC	77	23
Hou Han She	25–220	98	2
Sanguo Zhi	220–280	99	1
Jin Shu	265–420	95	5
South-North Period	420–581	50	50
Sui Shu	581–618	59	41
Tang Shu	618–907	43	57
Wudai Shi	907–960	40	60
Song Shi	960–1279	52	48
Ming Shi	1368–1644	50	50
Qing Shi Gao	1644–1911	25	75

Single names have made a major comeback in the post-Mao era. I came across the 1997 winner list of national undergraduate honors theses in the humanities and social sciences. The distribution [of their names] is as follows:

Table 3 Percentage of Single Names among National Honors Undergraduates in 1997

Subject	No. of Single Names	Total No. of Names	Percentage of Single Names
Philosophy	6	25	24
Arts	13	23	56
Psychology	9	16	56
Economics	7	20	35
History	7	20	35
Total	42	104	40

These honors students were born in the post-Mao era; forty per cent of them have single names. So are many of my students whom I taught at the University of Pennsylvania, the National University of Singapore and now at the University of Manchester. What do we know about this cycle of social change and cultural continuity? This return of single names can be credited to the one-child policy, which was first implemented in 1978 and has been reinforced ever since. One child means no siblings, rendering the tradition and function of identifying generation and sometimes gender unnecessary. The consequence of this is yet to be seen and will need to be analyzed as history unfolds. From a psychological perspective, it seems that people are tired of social upheavals, as many of these single names seem spontaneous and convenient like 江洋 (Jiang Yang 'River Ocean'), 夏爽 (Xia Shuang 'Summer Cool'), 楊多 (Yang Duo 'Yang Many'), and 錢博 (Qian Bo 'Money Many or Learned').

This return of single names has generated serious concern among the various central and local authorities because many people, sometimes hundreds, have exactly the same name. This has created problems for identification and conscription, especially with regard to the criminal justice system. Which 張軍 (Zhang Jun 'Zhang Army') should the police arrest when they are faced with 20 Zhang Jun's in the city? Mainland specialist Xu Jianshun believes that Chinese naming practice is in grave danger now. There are too many similar names, and there is a shortage of non-political but well-meaning names like those of the Qing. What would be the naming practice or trend in the twenty-first century? It might well reflect a desire for de-politicization after a century of political upheaval and a return to tradition as China rises again not just as an economic but also as a cultural power. And, it may well see globalization making its way into Chinese names.

Notes

1   Native-place or hometown names sometimes replaced given names in the case of many ranking officials. This would distinguish them from others who shared the same surname or even the same ranking. It also shows the intimacy because hometown names are like nicknames. A good example is Zhang Nanpi. Nanpi is the name of the county in which the famous Qing minister, Zhang Zhidong, was born.

2   All examples of names in this paper begin with the names in Chinese characters, followed by an English transliteration and gloss of the Chinese characters. In cases, the historical period when a name appears is listed between parentheses. Note that KMT denotes Kuomintang (Chinese Nationalist Party) rule and CCP denotes Chinese Communist Party rule.

3   Chinese naming practice has interested some scholars and popular writers. See Xiao Yaotian, *Zhongguo Renming de Yanjiu* (Penang: Penang jiaoyu chubanshe, 1970); Ji Xiuqing, *Zhongguo Renming Tanxi* (Beijing: Zhongguo guangbodianshi chubanshe, 1993); Liu Xiaoyan, *Best Chinese Names: Your Guide to Auspicious Names*, 3rd ed., trans. Wu Jingyu (Singapore: Asiapac books, 1999); Xu Jianshun and Xin Xian, *Mingming: Zhongguo Xingming Wenhua de Aomiao* (Beijing: Zhongguo shuju, 1999); Wang Quangen, *Zhongguo Renming Wenhua*, trans. Wu Jingyu (Beijing: Tuanjie chubanshe, 2000); and Hou Tijun, *Shuoxin Jieming* (Beijing: Dandai shijie shubanshe, 2004). It also interested Jesuit Joseph Anne Marie de Moyria de Maillac, who devoted a long section on Chinese naming titled "Des Nien-hao ou Des noms que les Empereurs de la China ont donne aux annees de leurs regnes." See *Histoire Générale de la Chine ou Annales de cet Empire* (13 tomes. Paris: l'Abbé Grosier, 1777–85), tome 12, pp. 1–4.

4   All official histories 二十四史 since the Qin dynasty contain sections on the ranking officials, which is a reservoir of names. I have used many of them here and surveyed all the 人名字典 name dictionaries deposited at the Library of 近史所 Institute of Modern History, 中央研究院 Academia Sinica where I did most of my research.

5   The Chinese character 姓 (*xing* 'surname') consists of two characters; the one on the left denoting female and the one on the right denoting birth; surnames thus identified a matriarch in ancient times.

6   Hou Xudong, "Zhongguo Gudai Renmin de Shiyong Jiqi Yiyi: Zunbei, Tongshu Yu Zeren," *Lishi Yanjiu* 297, 5 (2005): 3–21 and Ma Yong, "Zhongguo Xingshi Zhidu de Yange," in *Zhongguo Wenhua Yanjiu Jikan* (Shanghai: Fudan daxue chubanshe, 1985).

[7] *Hou Han* or "the latter Han" refers to the Eastern Han dynasty.

[8] This was a philosophical sect that thrived in the Wei and Jin dynasties, pp. 220–420.

[9] Wang, *Zhongguo Renming Wenhua*, p. 96.

[10] It seems that some members from the clan of the Empress Dowager Cixi took a very common Chinese surname Li.

[11] Pierre Bourdieu, *Distinction: A Social Critique of the Judgement of Taste* (Cambridge, MA: Harvard University Press, 1984), p. 13.

[12] Liu, *Best Chinese Names*.

[13] Huaxia Funu Mingren Cidian Bianweihui, compiler, *Huaxia Funu Mingren Cidian* (Beijing: Huaxia chubanshe, 1988).

[14] Xu and Xin, *Mingming*, p. 8.

[15] Wang, *Zhongguo Renming Wenhua*, pp. 94–5.

CHAPTER 4

Toward a Classification of Naming Systems in Insular Southeast Asia

Charles J-H Macdonald

Introduction

My general aim in this paper is twofold. I would like first to show how formal properties of naming systems are determined, or at least constrained, by cultural and social factors. Second, I would like to propose the beginning of a typology of naming systems for Southeast Asia. But, before doing so it is necessary to raise a number of theoretical points and define some key concepts.[1]

I am not pursuing a final definition of personal or proper names in the way linguistic philosophers do[2] and I feel satisfied with a general definition of personal names based on the consideration that they fulfill two opposite functions: to identify a single individual person as different from other people and incorporate or qualify this person to make him similar to other persons. I am critical of the classificatory/taxonomic role of personal names, a point I will not discuss here, except for saying that the Lévi-Straussian emphasis on the classificatory, and even taxonomic, dimension of names is seriously ill-inspired.[3] A more pragmatic view of personal names — which I see primarily as linguistic objects together with other proper names and with other linguistic items like deictics, articles, affixes, titles, pronouns, and kin terms — focuses on their behavior in speech acts rather than their semantic content or ultimate status as "rigid designators."

Formal properties of naming systems can be analyzed by using the following conceptual framework.

1. Probably the single most important concept is that of "name type" which has to be distinguished from the notion of "name tag" — technically a lexeme. In English, "given name," "surname," and "nickname" are name types. John, Peter, Elizabeth, Mary, Smith, Mayer, Reid, Macdonald, Pete, Tony, Lizzy, Chuck, etc. are name tags. This obvious distinction usually gets lost in the course of analysis. I submit that an anthropological study of personal names is one that focuses on name types, rather than name tags. I would thus contrast onomastics as primarily a study of name tags, as against an anthropological or ethno-pragmatic study focusing on name types.

2. An important observation has to be made at this point. It seems that *all* existing naming practices (the way different cultures name individuals) contain not one but several name types — to my knowledge so far.[4]

3. Another crucial observation is that apparently *all* naming systems seem to put an emphasis on one of the name types, which I call the "autonym" (variously dubbed the "real," "true," "primary," "big," "beautiful," "good," "main," and so on, name). The morphological sociological and pragmatic characteristics of the autonym are of paramount significance, as is its relationship to other name types.[5]

4. It is the relationship, organization, and combination of name types that make up the study of naming systems since this is how I see naming, not as a collection of name tags but as an organized set of name types with rules of combination and use.

5. As stated previously name types combine in various ways, and their use in speech acts and utterances characterize a naming system. Among the different ways this happens two seem more salient: whether name types are used together (causing name tags to be strung together) or when one is used instead of the other (causing different name tags to be used exclusively of others according to circumstance, identity of speakers, etc.). Most naming systems do both, but I submit that systems show a tendency to predominantly or characteristically use one rather than the other. This would result in extreme situations which we may see as ideal types, for instance:
    a. Systems that use few name tags for each individual, usually strung together in a certain order (Syntagmatic Systems); and
    b. Systems that use a great number of names tags for the same individual, but one at a time (Paradigmatic Systems).

6. The morphology of name types and particularly the autonym can be studied from grammatical, lexematic, and morpho-syntactic points of view in order to decide whether it is simple or complex, and if complex, how and to what degree.

7. Moreover to each name type is attached a specific set, stock, or repertoire of name tags. Such sets or repertoires can easily be characterized as:

    a. Either closed or open, that is, narrowly restricted or restricted but large;

    b. Motivated or not motivated, that is, the name tags belong or do not belong to an already existing lexical set; and

    c. As being productive or unproductive of name tags for the same individual.

These formal properties of naming systems can in turn be correlated with socio-structural dimensions and non-onomastic factors such as the size of the speech community and the presence or absence of a ranking system with competitive status achievement. But between the purely morphological aspects of naming systems as defined above and the more general aspects of the culture and the society wherein they operate, a number of rules and properties are directly attached to names and naming practices. Among those one may pay special attention to:

1. The social rules of bestowal of name tags (with or without a ceremony or formal ritual marking it, chosen by divination, dream or free choice, created anew or inherited);

2. The restrictions on the use of the autonym (always prohibited according to the relationship between speaker and hearer versus generally prohibited on an occasional basis);

3. The social value of name tags (treated as social capital in the literal sense of being private and/or precious property, or of no special value whatsoever);

4. The change and accumulation of name tags for individuals which is both a formal property of name types (productive or unproductive repertoire) and a social aspect of naming practices; and

5. The spheres wherein names are used, especially the public and the private.

Two Opposite Systems

Palawan Names

The Palawan people, an ethnic group inhabiting the southern part of Palawan island in the southern Philippines, and particularly a section of this ethnic group in the Kulbi river basin (Barangay Taburi, Rizal

Municipality), use a traditional system of naming that is characterized by several traits (Macdonald 1999, 2004). First, each person has an individual name, *ngaran*, which is the first name given to him after birth and which serves as his main and permanent referent (autonym). It is his "true" (*tigbung*) or "real" (*banar*) name. This name is made of two or more syllables and has no meaning. It does not, except very occasionally, belong to a lexical set (like animal names or plant names). Second, again with a few exceptions, each individual has a name that is like no other person's name. We will say that the autonym in Palawan is a name type belonging to (1) an open list (as many names as individuals with endless possibilities of creating new names) and (2) a "non-motivated" list (i.e., a list of terms that have no other meaning).[6] Thus the name, Djuari, means nothing except as the name of a person called Djuari. And nobody else in the community is called Djuari. This resembles the English system in one way. Djuari like John is just a name that means nothing else. But where there are millions of "Johns," there is only one "Djuari."

On top of having one autonym, like "Djuari," Palawan people use two other name types. One is a nickname, *palajew* or *gegbekan*;[7] the other is a "friendship name," *lalew*.[8] The nickname and the friendship name are used instead of, not together with, the autonym. The nickname is either a shortening of the autonym (like Dida for Rusida or Rus for Rusita) or is descriptive in nature, *gegbekan* being derived from *gebek*, meaning "to quarrel, to tease." Ersin is thus nicknamed Lindepan meaning "setting sun," and Magdalena is Penaj meaning "she who shines from afar" (actually a reference to her naked bottom when she was a child!). The main difference between the nickname and the friendship name, which is a kind of nickname, is that the latter is used only between two persons who use the *lalew* reciprocally — whereas a *gegbekan* can be used by everyone. This friendship name type is an interesting institution that has been described for other groups in this area, namely the Batak (Eder 1975), the Ilongot (Rosaldo 1984), and the Penan (Needham 1971). People in Palawan have many such reciprocal friendship names. I listed about 16 such *lalew* for one of my informants. The use of the *lalew* denotes intimacy and familiarity like the use of the singular French pronoun *tu* instead of the plural pronoun *vous*. It is not possible to have such a reciprocal naming with a person of superior status like a father-in-law. The *lalew* frequently commemorates an event or incident. So Taya called Turing "Lawaq" and Turing also called Taya "Lawaq" (that is, they call each other Lawaq), because they used to court girls together when they were teenagers. Lawaq comes from *luminawaq*, meaning "she who has been abandoned," because Turing loved one girl but eventually left her.

Parallel to this traditional naming system, people nowadays have acquired a surname, *apeledo*, introduced by the national administration (Macdonald 2004). Among the traditional name types (autonym, reciprocal name, descriptive nickname, and short form of the autonym) the rule is to use one at a time, never two or more strung together.

Names in Hursu (Selaru, Tanimbar)

Let us look now at the situation described by Pauwels for the people of Hursu in Tanimbar island (Pauwels 1999), in the far eastern part of Indonesia. The people from Hursu have a multi-type autonym, with a "small" and a "big" name. The small name is morphologically complex (it can be broken down into several parts). One part of the small name means something, like "Lady" or "territory." The small name is used in daily interaction. The "big name" is attached to the small name and is also complex and motivated, but it is never or rarely used in normal social intercourse, since it is loaded with ancestral and prestige connotation. Both the big and the small names belong to closed repertoires, there is a limited supply of available names and no new ones are created. Autonyms are those of linear ancestors.

Other name types are Christian names, masked or disguised names (used for infants), nicknames (shortening of "small names"), and teknonyms. A person's name is composed of several name types strung together like: Amasama Telyavar (binomial autonym) + Abner (Christian name) + Tété Tinggi (nickname) + Maso (short form of Amasama), which gives Amasama Telyavar Abner Tété Tinggi Maso, quite a long string of name tags. If we now compare the two naming systems, Palawan and Hursu (Selaru), a number of traits and dimensions stand out as saliently contrastive (Table 1).

These two systems offer the maximum number of salient contrasts. The point I want to make is that these traits taken together vary according to deep underlying rules binding all of them together. Name morphology, social rules, and the behavior of name types in speech acts are all interdependent.

First of all the morphology of the Palawan autonym stands in complete opposition to the Hursu autonym: simple versus complex, uninominal versus binomial, not motivated versus motivated. Second, the social rules commanding the bestowal and use of the autonym are completely different. The Palawan name is invented but the Hursu name is inherited, passed from one generation to the other, usually the second descending generation. The Hursu autonym, like that of various other

Table 1   A Comparison of the Palawan and Hursu Naming Systems

	Palawan	*Hursu (Selaru)*
Autonym: Morphology	Uninominal Simple Open repertoire Not motivated	Binomial, Multiple Complex Closed repertoires Motivated
Autonym: Social rules	Invented, bestowed through individual choice, used but not preferred in general address or co-reference; restricted use contingent on relationship between speakers	Inherited, bestowed through choice or by dream, • small name: used in general address or co-reference • big name: never used in general address or co-reference except on special ritual occasions
	Prohibition is individual and permanent	Prohibition is general and occasional
Number of other name types	2	3
General rule for combining name types	Paradigmatic	Syntagmatic

Eastern Indonesian naming systems (Geirnaert-Martin 1992, Forth 1983) is basically an ancestral name, bearing a heavy semantic load. The person bearing such names is either the ancestor reborn or is like the ancestor, programmed as it were to be like the ancestor (Forth 1981, 1983). The name carries the destiny of the person who bears it. In the Palawan case the autonym refers to nothing, especially not a dead relative. The name bears no reference to events or persons and has no historical dimension. In the Palawan case again, people prefer to use nicknames and reciprocal names of a more anecdotal significance. Rules of restriction are telling. Palawan autonyms are not prohibited except between certain relatives, especially with the parents and spouse-giving in-laws. In the Hursu case whether name types are permitted or prohibited is conditional upon circumstances (they are *sometimes* prohibited during ceremonies and ritual events) and not contingent upon relationships between individuals (as in the Palawan case).

It is finally clear that name types associate with one another differently; in one case a simple lexeme is enough, in the other, names extend horizontally and form long and complex syntagms (strings of name tags), as instanced above.

What can account for this systematic variation in all traits? I shall venture the following explanation. The entire set of name types and its behavior in speech acts (its ability to produce syntagmatic or paradigmatic arrangements) are related to what the name must say not only about the person in a given social environment but, in a more complex and essential way, about the ethos or norms of social conduct prevailing in a given social context. Among all the features that may define a social environment with its ethos and norms of conduct, three seem particularly relevant in this case:

1.   Whether the "speech community" is demographically small or large;
2.   Whether the society is stratified or not, with or without competitive behavior in status achievement; and
3.   Whether the theory of personhood rests or does not rest on the idiom of ancestry (whether the person is considered as made of ancestral "stuff") and more largely whether ancestry plays a structural role or not.

It is easy to show that each of the previous dimensions relate to formal properties of the respective naming systems. Palawan dialectal communities tend to be small demographic isolates (from 1,000 to 3,000 members) with communities of a few hundred people interacting frequently on a daily and long-term basis. They are members of a purely egalitarian social system with no status competition whatsoever. Furthermore, ancestors worship and corporate descent groups are absent, genealogies are shallow, and apical ancestors are not recognized. The Palawan ideology of personhood is not constructed with an idiom of ancestral qualities or traits inherited from forebears and passed down to the living, but rather with a vocabulary of individualistic psychological traits and personal history of private events, encounters, and interpersonal associations. We may call this a "spontaneous/contextual" or "idiosyncratic" definition of personhood.

Since they live in sufficiently small, tight groups, they can be privy to the name history of each other; a rich repertoire of personal name tags can be remembered and used by everyone.[9] Besides, with no high status to assert, the name is not much, apart from being an individual tag. It does not include any status marker or prestige meaning. With no ancestors to worship or to reincarnate, names are not inherited; instead name tags are produced from an endless supply of invented forms. A name tag can easily be discarded or dismissed in favor of better, more congenial name tags with individual connotations of shared events or private jokes. Palawan people remind one of schoolchildren or inmates constantly inventing new labels in jest and jocularity. Thus they tend to replace their autonym by a number of other name types particularly the "reciprocal names" or "friendship names" that tell the story of an acquaintance and refer to recollected incidents that bind the members of the community together. This is in complete contrast with names that look back into the past, reflecting an unchanging order of things.

Let us turn now to the Tanimbar situation. The people of Hursu certainly live or lived in rather small island communities with enough daily interaction to know each other's personal naming history. This would make them similar to the Palawan case and explain why they could accumulate and use a great number of name tags. However, in their case, prestige and ancestry are of paramount importance, and this is clearly reflected in names both at the semantic and speech levels. The autonym (the "big" name) indicates social status and ancestral predestination. The name bearer carries a name like a flag that must be either seen by all, or enshrined away from the public gaze. The name is so important that it must be either publicly displayed or protected in secrecy. Even informality is restricted in its expression since nicknames are not descriptive, being short forms of the "small name." Like other Eastern Indonesian people, the Hursu tend to be self-important status-bearers harboring the marks of their own high status, precedence and ancestral pedigree. Whereas among the egalitarian Palawan the paradigmatic dimension was preferred on the ground of how unimportant each name tag was, and on how desirable it was to acquire new name tags marking new relationships, among the status-conscious people of Hursu, one never wants to abandon one's ancestral name, and when new names are added, the old one has to be recalled. Hence, the people of Hursu string together a longer syntagm of the more salient and the less salient segments of a name, creating a more complex structure of autonyms. Since ancestral names contain so much meaning for the bearer, their form is more complex, whereas with the disposable Palawan names, complex forms are not required.

A core of traits thus provides the entire gravitational system of names with a high degree of cohesiveness. The traits and dimensions called forth to explain the structure of the naming system analyzed so far are linguistic and morphological on the one hand, and socio-structural on the other. Together they form contrasted and cohesive patterns. But now, is this situation exemplified by two isolated cases only, or is it applicable to a larger number of cases? Is it exceptional or regular? The following examples will provide us with an answer. Let us call the Palawan situation "Class A" system, and the Hursu case "Class B" system. Which other societies may be considered as belonging to either "Class A" or "Class B"? Or, phrased differently may be similar enough in their formal and structural properties to either the Palawan or Hursu cases?

"Class A" Systems ("Paradigmatic"): Peninsular Malaysia-Borneo-Philippines

Naming systems that resemble the Palawan type are located in the Peninsular Malaysia-Borneo-Philippines zone. One is a well-documented and celebrated case in the anthropological literature, that of the Penan described by Needham in a series of articles (1954a, 1954b, 1965, 1971). This ethnic group uses a naming system containing five name types (autonym, necronym, teknonym, friendship name, and death name). In common with the Palawan, the Penan use the highly specialized friendship name which I have defined as a reciprocal dyadic appellative. The Penan are hunters and foragers in the interior of Borneo and live in small bands/groups with a mean membership of 32 individuals per group (Needham 1971: 204). Their naming system is such that each individual has a rich and varied naming history with a number of name tags shifting according to the births (teknonyms) and deaths (necronyms) occurring in his/her family environment, a situation characteristic of small speech communities with intense interaction over a long period of time. There is no ranking, and the Penan naming system contains no status markers or prestige titles.[10] Although necronyms and teknonyms can occasionally be added to or precede the autonym, the overall system is clearly paradigmatic, and names types are used in place of each other rather than strung together into long syntagmatic phrases.

Demographically small groups with an egalitarian ethos, a rich naming history, and paradigmatic axis of use of this kind are represented by the Temiar as described by Benjamin (1968). The Temiar of Peninsular Malysia display one of the richest naming systems described so far with no less than eight name types (autonym, necronym, teknonym, death name, birth-order name, nickname, foreign name, and spirit/dream name), plus a number of specific terms of addresses. They also live in small groups with an egalitarian ethos. Prestige names and markers of ranking order are absent, but there is an obvious wealth of name tags and appellatives to choose from when referring to or addressing any adult member of the group. The Temiar, the Penan, and the Palawan autonym is characterized by an open repertoire of lexematically and syntactically simple tags, which are not motivated.

The Ilonggot of Northern Luzon (Rosaldo 1984) and the Batak of Palawan island (Eder 1975) offer an almost identical naming structure: the autonym is simple, with an open list (but sometimes motivated) tag, together with the same main paradigmatic axis of use. Both societies have four name types including the autonym. In common with the Penan and the Palawan, they use the friendship name (reciprocal dyadic name type). To this they add another name type, a special name used between affines, and finally nicknames.

We thus have with some slight variations (especially the number and definition of name types) in a class or group of naming systems with an identical or very similar formal structure, correlating very closely with the kind of society that we have described: demographically small, egalitarian, with little or no emphasis on ancestry and a "contextual" definition of personhood.

This however is not always the case, and a number of other naming systems, while resembling the above, borrow and combine certain aspects or dimensions so as to create an admixture of traits diverging from the initial model. The Punan Bah of Sarawak are a good example of this kind of "mixed" system.

According to the clear and complete description provided by Nicolaisen (1998) the Punan Bah from Central Borneo have six different (traditional) name types: an ancestral name (autonym), dream name or spirit name, trivial name, nickname, teknonym, and necronym to which they add a more recent "government" or "passport" name. All of these name types are labeled in the vernacular.

The autonym belongs to a closed but very large (several thousands of items) list of names belonging to ancestors. It is also a gender-specific list and one that connotes rank in a stratified social system (traditionally including aristocrats, commoners and slaves). One very important aspect of the autonym is that it is very seldom or never used except in the case of aristocrats. Another meaningful aspect is that children receive two or more ancestral names and that the name is bestowed through a divination ritual. Part of the explanation lies in the belief that the soul of the ancestor is reincarnated in the newborn child. Finally these autonyms are morphologically simple and mean nothing (are not motivated in our parlance).

Teknonymy is used very frequently and is of the "extended" kind, meaning that the name not only of children (the firstborn is preferred) but that of grandchildren is also used. Teknonymy, together with other name types that are also abundantly used, is used *instead of the autonym, and never with the autonym.*

The government name, as the label clearly indicates, derives from an external administrative practice whereby each individual is provided with a string of name tags consisting of a first (ancestral) name and a patronym (surname), a sub-system similar to what can be observed elsewhere as a result of an administrative imposition of a European-like binomial form of identity (Macdonald 2004).

The main difference with the preceding systems of the Palawan type is the formal structure of the autonym, which is complex (binomial with two name tags strung together) and a closed albeit large repertoire. Moreover, it contains a semantic dimension connoting rank and indeed the naming system reflects an important aspect of this stratified society. Characteristically, the autonym is inherited and not invented. But it remains an essentially paradigmatic naming system as far as the rules of combination for the various name types apply. It also shares the typical "Bornean" necronym with the Temiar and the Penan.

Table 2   Punan as an Example of a "Mixed" Naming System

Autonym: Morphology	*Uninominal*
	Simple
	Multiple
	Closed but large list
	Not motivated
Autonym: Social rules	Inherited
	Bestowed through divination
	Not used in general address or reference
Number of other name types	6
General rule for combining name types	*Paradigmatic*

"Class B" Systems ("Syntagmatic"): Eastern Indonesia

Let us now turn our attention to a different naming system, that of the Weyewa (or Wewewa) of Western Sumba, described by Kuipers and Renard-Clamagirand (Kuipers 1998: 102–24, and this volume, Renard-Clamagirand 1999), which is typical of the Eastern Indonesia part of insular Southeast Asia. A close examination of this particular naming system will show its structural similarity with the Tanimbar naming system described previously. There is a minimum of five traditional name types, including the autonym (birth name, "foundation of the name"); and two name types which can be subdivided into a number of sub-categories (or considered as different name types altogether). Two other name types, a Christian forename and a patronymic, have been more recently added.

According to Renard-Clamagirand, the autonym is always binomial, being composed of a "soft" and a "hard" name. The "soft" name is used throughout one's life and commonly used, while the "hard" name is never used before adulthood and then only under certain conditions. The "soft" name belongs to a limited repertoire of non-motivated terms. The "hard" name is motivated and seems to belong to a larger if not open repertoire. To the first "hard" name, another one (second "hard" name) is appended. To the birth name or rather to its first "soft" part is also added a variety of other name types. One is the "companion name" which has a descriptive content, then a choice of "added names." Those include most notably teknonymy, surnames, prestige names (mentioning valuable possessions), "calling names," endearment names, and "house names." Lastly Christian names are used together with Indonesian titles (such as Pak "sir, father"). An individual will thus be called, for instance: Pak Mike Mali Lalo Ama Male. This name is composed of an Indonesian title (Pak), a Christian name (Mike), followed by the first part of the autonym or "soft" name, Mali, followed by the companion name, Lalo, followed by the teknomym, Ama Male (father of Male). "Hard" names form a much more formal and parallel syntgagm that is not used in daily life. The second "hard" name seems particularly secret. Names used in address are composed of a basic sequence of three name types: "soft" birth name + companion name + added name.

Kuipers also identifies five name types, not including the Christian and new patronymic names. The autonym is composed of a "soft" and a "hard" name, the first one being used in daily interaction and the second rarely uttered. In addition there are teknonyms, sobriquets (nicknames and descriptive names), and prestige names. Prestige names have a trinomial structure and refer to an object or prized possession, such as a horse. They are composed of two attributes and a head noun, for example, "Swift Conqueror, the Water Buffalo" or "Upright Tail, the Horse." Obviously such names belong to an open motivated list.

Finally let us note that the Weyewa people spend considerable time "seeking a name," that is, acquiring prestige names through feasting and an elaborate ritual process. The table below outlines the main features of this system, particularly the paradigmatic play among sub-name types.

Table 3   Weyewa as an Example of a "Class B" Naming System

Autonym: Morphology	Binomial, Simple, Multiple • "Soft" name: *Close but restricted list*; not motivated • "Hard" name: *open or unrestricted list*; *motivated*
Autonym: Social rules	• "Soft" name: inherited, bestowed through divination; *used in general address or co-reference* • "Hard" name: inherited, not used in general address of reference
Number of other name types	4
General rule for combining name types	Very saliently *syntagmatic* with paradigmatic dimension in name types

The paradigmatic dimension within the structure of the autonym itself displays a complexity of a much higher order than the Punan's autonym for instance. It is not only made of several name tags but *several name types*, each having its rules of use and composition. Compared to the Temiar naming system with its eight name types, the Weyewa seem to add a third dimension by creating a system within a system. It produces long syntagms stringing together a number of name tags and uses specific name types to denote rank and status, some of which are acquired (prestige names) while others are inherited ("hard" names). Naming practices saliently display the values of ancestry, inheritance and what J. Fox so aptly called the "social competition for precedence" (1996: 131). What has been said before for the Tanimbar naming system applies even more to the Weyewa, namely concerning the twin dimensions of social status and ancestral predestination. The name is either publicly displayed or protected in secrecy. Even informality is restricted in its expression since nicknames and teknonyms have a limited definition and do not seem to be extensively used. Like other Eastern Indonesian people, the Weyewa tend to be assertive in their claim to self-importance.

Due to incomplete information I am not absolutely sure to what extent various other systems from the same area (Timor, Sumba) fit this model. Data found in the works of Renard-Clamagirand on the Ema (1982: 133), Geirnaert-Martin on the Laboya (1992: 65–7, 204), and Forth on the Rindi (1981: 144–6, 219, 226, 266, 323, 419, 462, 464, 477 and 1983: 655–8) definitely point toward similarity in the structure of the autonym, which is always complex at the lexematic level and refers to both status and ancestry. Autonyms are inherited, highly motivated, and belong to closed repertoires. Lacking a complete list of other name types for these systems I cannot venture further, but the impression is that it is limited in number (the Ema have a teknonym and a "house name," the Laboya have temporary infant names, and the Rindi have "slave names," "sheltered names," and nicknames. The syntagmatic dimension in the formation of name tags (syntagms) seems to always result in complex formulas stringing together several name types and/or titles, according to circumstances. The entire apparatus aims at promoting the social standing of the bearer to the point of having even inherited nicknames — in Rindi — denoting qualities of the forebear (Forth 1981: 226). The Woisika from Alor described by Stokhof (1983), center their entire system on a (grammatically, lexematically, and semantically) complex autonym that is highly productive. But the rest of the naming system does not seem to match what could be called the "Eastern Indonesian" class of naming systems, as seen above.[11]

"Class C" Systems ("Titles/title system"): Central Indonesia

A great number of naming systems in the region have yet to be accounted for. So far we have established that at least two kinds of formal structural types of naming systems match rather closely corresponding specific social organizations and ideologies of personhood. "Class A" systems located in Peninsular Malaysia, Borneo, and the Philippines match a simple egalitarian social structure with a "spontaneous/contextual" definition of personhood; "Class B" systems from Eastern Indonesia match stratified societies with a focus on competitive status and an "essentialist/inherited" definition of personhood with the name sometimes indicating a kind of reincarnation of the ancestor-namesake.[12] However, all of these are rather small-scale demographic sets and lack the kind of state apparatus present in other large-scale societies with a developed class system, kingship, central bureaucracy, and so on. This is the kind of systems that we are now going to examine.

The Javanese naming system, according to Uhlenbeck (1969) rests on three name types: the autonym, with a name tag that changes once at least during one's lifetime, a birth order name, and teknonym. The masculine autonym is double. A child keeps his "little name" until marriage and then changes it for a "second name" or "old name" (Jones and Phillips 1995: 903) which he himself chooses. The little name has an open repertoire of simple, motivated and/or unmotivated name tags. The second name belongs to a closed list, with a complex (binomial) name tag that is motivated and has one element often indicating one's occupation. Married women take the name of their husband or a teknonym and discard their small name. Honorifics and titles are attached to autonyms in the form of a prefix like *su-*, articles like *si* and *pun*, or distinct words like *Pak* and *Bu*. Javanese persons bear essentially one name tag, which is expanded by means of honorifics and sometimes teknonyms as well.

In spite of some differences, the Balinese system described and interpreted by H. and C. Geertz (1964); also Geertz (1973: 368–89), is structurally identical to the Javanese. As in Javanese, it contains three name types: the autonym, the teknonym (extended) and the birth-order name.[13] These name types behave in a fashion similar to Javanese. In the latter case the little name is discarded for an adult name. In Balinese the autonym given at birth is discarded in favor of a teknonym. The Balinese teknonym and the Javanese second autonym are functionally identical. A common feature of both systems is how compatible name types are with titles. In Javanese the honorific/title is added to the autonym, while in Balinese it seems to associate with the birth-order name (Geertz 1973: 383). Let us point out an important detail mentioned by Geertz: Balinese titles denote "spiritual composition" and not "status discrimination" (1973: 381–3).

Table 4 A Comparison of the Javanese and Balinese Naming Systems

	Javanese	*Balinese*
Autonym: Morphology	Binomial, multiple • Little name: open list, simple, not motivated • Adult name: closed list, complex	Uninominal Simple, open list, not motivated
Autonym: Social rules	• Little name: discarded when adult • Adult name: chosen by individual, used in general address or reference, includes status/occupation marker	Autonym discarded when adult, use of teknonym in general address or reference
Number of other name types	2	2
General rule for combining name types	Paradigmatic with name types, syntagmatic with titles	Paradigmatic with name types, syntagmatic with titles

In sum, Balinese and Javanese people are denominated with a binomial syntagm (onomastic tag) that indicates a stable honorific position (*varna*, "occupation") and a kinship status (teknonym). The autonym is not really concealed like a "military secret" as Geertz and Geertz have stated (1964: 375), since it is displayed in the teknonym of the parent, and the system does not essentially rest on the teknonym but on the ability of various name types to combine with honorifics and titles. Balinese society, it is true, is not interested in a fixed ancestral essence that would be transmitted to the living, but teknonymy is not meant to forget ancestors. It is meant to provide honorific and alternate name tags. Geertz's interpretation of teknonyms as creating sociologically functional age classes is also debatable. But the general principle here is that a naming system can never be interpreted on the basis of only one name type — in this case teknonymy.[14] It is the interplay of all name types that matters, and in this particular instance the most meaningful aspect of the system is its ability to open up and expand into the realm of honorifics and titles which become ultimately embedded into the onomastic syntagm.

Looking now at the Malay system described by Massard-Vincent (1999), one is faced again with an essentially similar structure comprising an autonym, a birth order name, a nickname, and a teknonym. The major difference lies in the presence of another name type, the patronym, with a connector (*bin*, *binti*). As in the Javanese little name and the Balinese autonym, the repertoire is made of simple tags from an open or large list and generally not motivated. The main difference here is that the Malay system thus described is a "mix" of an indigenous naming system and the Arabic naming system with its dual or binomial autonym composed of a first name and a surname (patronym) connected with *bin/binti*. Titles in Malay are intimately interwoven with name types in the onomastic syntagms. One of these titles, *haji*, becomes part of the name and loses its "title" value.[15] A number of other honorifics and titles, like Datuk, Pak, or Doktor, gravitate around name types. The existence and survival of an indigenous naming practice under the Arabic veneer is clearly demonstrated in this case by the wealth of descriptives, nicknames and sobriquets used in daily life (Massard-Vincent 1999: 205–7). Here again names (particularly the autonym) are not meant to commemorate forebears.

Let us recap this section briefly. Balinese, Javanese, and Malays use a three- or four-tired naming system, with rather unproductive name types, stable uninominal or binomial tags, and an ability to combine name types with honorifics and titles, which are an effect of etiquette rather than status competition, that is, a desire to conform to decorum rather than advertise inherited qualities. The structure of the autonym (simple binomial, open list, and partly or not motivated) and its syntagmatic axis of combination with other name types but primarily honorifics reflect an ethos and a way of life. As with the Malays, or Javanese, perhaps less so with the Balinese, naming systems adapt to large speech communities that cannot tolerate too rich a store of names tags for each individual. Standardization and reduction in the productivity of name types is called for. On the other hand, these societies discourage the formation of strong corporate kin groups but encourage a sense of hierarchy based on an unchanging order of things desired by a central state with its own hopefully unchanging ranking system. Here again the *formal* properties of the naming systems match the *structural* properties of social organization.

This general naming pattern — we could call it "Central Indonesian" — has probably influenced or inspired various local naming systems that were originally of a different style. What possibly happened was a steady pressure exerted by a central state on small communities with paradigmatic systems containing a number of name types, some yielding a wealth of changing and varied name tags — an intolerable situation for any census-taking bureaucracy (see Scott *et al.* 2002). This kind of transformation is readily observable in the Kadayan system. A similar trend can probably be exemplified by local states like the Bugis.

The Kadayan system from Brunei (Western Borneo), described by Maxwell (1984), displays the typical Malay-Arabic binomial syntagm (first/personal name and patronym linked by a connector *bin/binti*) plus other name types, nicknames and "special" names like infants' names, pen names, and other pseudonyms and descriptives (epithets). The latter are used instead of the patronym and with the autonym. Interestingly the Kadayan have a friendship reciprocal title, *nama samarang*, reminiscent of the old Bornean-Philippine friendship name. The autonym in itself has a complex structure in the sense that it contains several name tags used in alternation (paradigmatically). Autonyms are either Arabic or Malay, that is, belong to either an open list of simple unmotivated name tags, or to an open list of simple motivated name tags. Name types (autonyms, nicknames) are productive and "close friends regularly create new names for each other in play" (id. 34). The naming system is clearly paradigmatic and productive of a rich store of appellatives for each individual, quite like the Palawan-Penan-Temiar type with basically a simple name tag mostly replaced by — or less frequently, added to — all sorts of other name tags. This we could call the "Class A" aspect of this system which, at the same time, displays unmistakable features of a "Class C" naming system. Naming patterns (onomastic syntagms) include a number of honorifics and titles to which they are attached as in the name Yang Mulia Haji Putih bin Haji Hitam, with an honorific (Yang Mulia) and courtesy title (Haji) that are thus embedded in the onomastic syntagm. This is a result of direct imitation or conformity with the dominant stratum of Brunei society, the Barunay aristocrats whose names are even longer.[16] This kind of syntagmatic development within a Bornean paradigmatic type is a clear instance of a "Class A"-"Class C" hybrid, a marriage so to speak between the forest and the city.

The Bimanese system described by Brewer (1981) is no less intriguing. The whole naming system comprises three name types, the autonym, the teknonym (extended form, including "grandparent of") and the patronym. Actually the autonym can be analyzed in two ways: either as formed by three different autonyms (multi-type, as it is among the Woisika for instance) or as one productive autonym with three forms — the proper, the common and the respectful. Its repertoire is formed of Arabic name tags, simple and by definition not motivated.[17] In one form or the other, the autonym combines with the patronym or the teknonym. A man whose proper name tag (for the autonym) is Ishaq will be called Ishaq Abidin (autonym + patronym without connector) and after the birth of a first child Ishaq ama Mariam (Ishaq father of Mariam). In other circumstances he will be known as Haka (common form/tag of the autonym) or Heko (respect form of the same) (id. 205–7). The Bimanese naming system has furthermore devised a neat and original trick to introduce gender, status, formality, and even group membership in the naming practices. It consists of specific connectors for the teknonym, each specific connector indicating gender, membership in a male descent line or the status of Haji. Thus Ishaq ama Mariam is signaled as being an aboriginal Bimanese. If he were a descendant of Makasarese immigrant he would be called Ishaq dae Mariam, and if he had accomplished the pilgrimage to Mecca he would be called Ishaq umi Mariam. On top of all these, a great many titles are added to the name tags. These titles indicate sex, age, religious position, official and nobility ranking, academic achievement, and more. They are all integral parts of onomastic syntagms (id. 209).

The hybridity of this system is of a different order from the previous Kadayan one. It closely resembles the Javanese or Balinese in its overall three-tiered structure, the structure of the autonym itself, and its affinity with titles and honorifics. But it has devised a way to incorporate status indicators in teknonymy and a substitutive dimension in the autonym itself. This makes it a genuine "Central Indonesian" type with a stylish dash of its own.

Finally I like to briefly examine the Bugis system, which might be considered as belonging to the class of systems examined in this section. Pelras stresses its extreme syntagmatic development by giving the longest onomastic syntagm recorded so far for a historical character whose complete name (full syntagm) includes about 25 components (various name tags belonging to several name types) (Pelras 1999: 167).[18] He also stresses the need to distinguish between naming practices of aristocrats and of commoners. We would have thus a double naming system or two sub-naming systems, a situation which is not at all unusual for complex class-based societies.[19] For commoners the naming system contains three name types (autonym, teknonym, and nickname). The autonym is grammatically complex, belongs to an open repertoire of motivated name tags, and is followed or preceded by an honorific. Aristocrats have an autonym, which is more complex lexematically (binomial) than that of commoners and consists of a teknonym, death or posthumous names, and decorous nicknames. All these name types can be and usually are strung together. The autonym is always complex since it includes what Pelras calls a "forename," actually a morpheme (an article indicating gender, a teknonym connector, a status title or honorific) which does not preclude, for aristocrats, additional titles indicating rank and nobility (like Datu or Sultan). Here again several important traits mark this system (1) its rather limited number of basic name types (three or four); (2) its affinity with a title apparatus embedded in the onomastic syntagm; and (3) its extreme syntagmatic development. In spite of some differences, it is structurally very close to the Javanese and Balinese systems which are equally characteristic of small states with a rigid ranking or class system.

Concluding Remarks ("Schoolchildren," "Stuffed Shirts," "Kings and Bureaucrats")

The variety and complexity of naming practices render any typological exercise futile if one wants to pigeonhole one and every system into a neatly laid category. Conversely, the focus on one dimension only (like the formal structure of the autonym, the arithmetical number of name types, or the presence of one salient name type only) would also lead one into some kind of empty academic exercise. That is why the formal properties of naming systems must be matched with the social, cultural, and even psychological dimensions of naming practices and with their historical environment.

In order to make this point a bit more vivid, allow me to force the analysis into a Weberian caricature of the typical agent for each class of naming systems thus far distinguished. Because they do not put any stock in status and self-importance and because they relish nicknaming, reciprocal naming, and all manners of contextual and relational appellatives, given in jest and jocularity, members of the "Class A" systems are like schoolchildren or inmates, tribal people "free in the forest" to the point of companionable anarchy.[20] The principle underlying the whole system is what I might call "contextual distance" and kin terms are the most appropriate lexical items with which personal names combine.

"Class B" people are different. In a way they are reminiscent of Protestant capitalists trying to prove by their worldly achievements what they are supposed to be in the first place. Overly concerned with status and prestige they accumulate name tags and hoard them like precious crests which they like to display in a show of self-importance. Let's call them the "stuffed shirts." In a way names *are* titles in a game aptly described as "social competition for precedence."

Entering the realm of "Class C" societies, one enters an atmosphere of hushed formality where individuals conform to a strict etiquette, where stern bureaucrats list names in ledgers and flamboyant aristocrats adorn themselves with endless strings of titles. We could call these the "kings and bureaucrats" and the kind of social structure to which they belong is hierarchical and holistic. Personal names are tightly associated with titles which eventually become embedded in the naming system.

Table 5   Classification of Naming Systems in Insular Southeast Asia

"Class A" (Borneo Type)	*"Class B"* (East Indonesia Type)	*"Class C"* (Central Indonesia Type)
Contextual distance	Social competition for precedence	Holistic hierarchy
• Palawan	• Hursu (Tanimbar)	• Javanese
• Penan	• Weyyewa	• Balinese
• Temiar	• Ema	• Malay
• Batak (Palawan)	• Laboay	• Bugis
• Ilonggot	• Rindi	
	• Woisika	

The above classification is obviously very far from being a complete typology of naming systems in insular Southeast Asia. Aside from hybrid systems such as the Punan and Nuaulu (A and B), Bimanese (B and C) and Kadayan, (A and C) there are many other naming systems not examined so far and probably a few more general classes of systems. The study of naming must continue and is certain to yield other interesting conclusions.

Notes

1   I have suggested this approach and proposed similar methodological principles in several previous publications. See Charles Macdonald, "De l'anonymat au renom: Systèmes du nom personnel dans quelques sociétés d'Asie du Sud-Est (notes comparatives)," in *D'un nom à l'autre en Asie du Sud-Est: Approches ethnologiques*, eds. Josiane Massard-Vincent and Simonne Pauwels (Paris: Karthala, 1999); Charles Macdonald, "Personal Names as an Index of National Integration. "Local Naming Practices and State-produced Legal Identities," *Pilipinas* 42 (March 2004); Charles Macdonald, "Can Personal Names be Translated?" *IIAS Newsletter* 36, 2005.

2   Russell, Wittgenstein, Frege, Searle, Kripke to name a few. See *The Encyclopedia of Language and Linguistics*, eds. R.E. Asher and J.M.Y. Simpson, volume 5 (Oxford and New York: Pergamon Press, 1994), art. "*Names and Description*," pp. 2667–72.

3   Lévi-Strauss, C., *La Pensée Sauvage* (Paris: Plon, 1962), pp. 261, 266, 283, 285. Also see "Introduction," this volume.

4   One possible exception could be the Inuit system or some variants of this system. See Charles Macdonald, "Inuit Personal Names. A Unique System? Or the Needle in the Haystack." Paper presented at the 15th International Inuit Studies Conference, Paris, 26–8 Oct. 2006. *Proceedings of the 15th International Inuit Studies Conference*, eds. B. Collignon, and M. Therrien (in press).

5   The morpho-syntactic structure of the autonym is the result of the presence and arrangement of lexematic and grammatical elements. The autonym is made of one lexematic element or more. If the autonym is made of two lexical elements (name tags) strung together, it will be called "binomial," but if these elements behave independently and obey different rules of use for the same name-bearer, it will be called "multi-type." It includes or does not include affixes and other morphophonemic elements. As the case may be, the autonym can be morpho-synctactically productive, for example, where John becomes Johnny. The autonym can thus have a complex structure, being composed of several lexematic and grammatical/syntactic items. It can be simple with one lexeme only and no affixation. It can be complex from a purely morpho-syntactic point of view, a purely lexematic point of view, or from both.

6   In one sample 797 names were used for 848 individuals. Homonymous instances exist but are few.

7   The first, *palajew*, is rather a diminutive, whereas the second, *gegbekan*, is a descriptive. The first is most probably a borrowing from Filipino (Tagalog) but the Kulbi people today use both terms as more or less synonymous.

8   So called in R. Needham, "Penan Friendship-Names," in *The Translation of Culture*, ed. T.O. Beidelman. London: Tavistock, 1971, pp. 203–30.

9   In a recording of a discussion between several Palawan speakers that I translated, I found the name "Timbagu" used by one of them to refer to someone who had been dead 20 years previously at least. This particular name tag belonged to the name type *lalew* (reciprocal dyadic type used mainly in address and only between two persons). It did not seem to cause anyone to wonder who "Timbagu" was!

10   Necronyms are borderline cases and can be considered as being titles rather than names, but even so they do not position individual bearers in a hierarchical scale.

11   The Nuaulu naming system of Seram, described by Ellen, contains traits that are unmistakably "Eastern Indonesian" (like a complex autonym, highly motivated, inherited, and belonging to a closed list), while allowing the creation of simple autonyms belonging to an open list, as in the "Class A" systems. See Roy Ellen, "Semantic Anarchy and Ordered Social Practice in Nuaulu Personal Naming," *Bijdragen tot de Taal-, Land- en Volkenkunde* 139, 1 (1983). Also see Macdonald, "De l'anonymat au renom", pp. 116, 119.

12   Ida Nicolaisen, "Ancestral Names and Government Names," p. 363. This feature is present in the naming ideology of the Punan Bah which is why they are considered a "mixed" system.

13   By extended we mean in the form of "parent of X" and "grandparent of X."

14   However, see Sillander in this volume.

15   Witness the case of the writer Muhammad Haji Salleh, whom I questioned about his name. "Haji" in his case is a pure name tag and not a title (since the name bearer has never been to Mecca) and an inherited part of the name at that (his father's name tag included Haji" since he had been a pilgrim to Mecca).

16   For instance, "Yang Mulia Awang Haji Bungsu bin Awang Haji Chuchu" including likewise an honorific (Yang Mulia), a title (Haji), a class label (Awang), and the father's title (Haji).

17   In my definition Arabic name tags although having a meaning in Arabic — a meaning that might or might not be known to Bimanese speakers — is not a Bimanese word and therefore is considered as "not motivated."

18   The name is *La Tenritatta' Daeng Serang ToA' patunru' Arung Palakka Arung Palette Arung Pattiro Datu Mario Arung Mpone Sultan Sa'aduddin Torisompa-e Malampe'-e Gemme'na Matinro-e ri Bonto Ala.*

19   In modern France, up to the beginning of the twentieth century, names of aristocrats and names of commoners obeyed different rules of formation and included different name types. See T. Barthélémy, "Noms patronymiques et noms de terre dans la noblesse française (XVIIIe–XXe siècles)," in *Le patronyme: Histoire, anthropologie, société*, eds. Guy Brunet *et al.* (Paris: CNRS 2001), pp. 61–79.

20   The naming practices of the deaf offer numerous and striking similarities to "Class A" systems. See Y. Delaporte, "Des noms silencieux. Le système anthroponymique des sourds français," *L'Homme* 146 (1998).

PART II

"Class A": Simple Egalitarian Societies

CHAPTER 5

Teknonymy, Name-Avoidance, Solidarity, and Individuation among the Bentian of Indonesian Borneo

Kenneth Sillander

Introduction

This chapter analyzes the sociological importance of teknonymy and what I call pseudo-teknonymy among the Bentian, a small Dayak group of Indonesian Borneo.[1] In conjunction with this analysis, I also discuss other forms of address and reference in this society, paying particular attention to the literature on teknonymy and descriptions of name-avoidance practices based on anthropological fieldwork.[2] Teknonymy is analyzed both in the total context of Bentian naming practices, and a cross-cultural context.

The Bentian case is unusual in that teknonyms are used inter-changeably with a special type of teknonym-like nicknames that derive, not from descendants' names but from various habits, attributes, or events associated with the namebearer.[3] My principal purpose is to examine the combined effects of these designations and the true teknonyms, with a particular view to how they affect social relations and subjectivity. Thanks to the work of authors such as Marcel Mauss, Claude Lévi-Strauss, Hildred and Clifford Geertz, and Rodney Needham,[4] it is now widely recognized that names are not incidental cultural artifacts but matters of elementary social significance, influencing — among other things — social organiza-tion, notions of personhood, and solidary relations in society. Names obviously "do things"; they have in Maybury-Lewis' formulation, an "instrumental function," permitting, at a minimum, reference to and address of the persons that they designate,[5] and thus, in Weber's terms, "social action" involving these persons.[6] In addition to facilitating social action, names inevitably communicate something about the name-bearers and their social relationships, and thereby influence such action. The principal conclusion of this chapter is that Bentian teknonyms and pseudo-teknonyms promote socio-centrism, egalitarianism, and a local culture of sociality. Another, related conclusion is that they represent both status terms and names and that individuation and integration do not form opposing forces in Bentian society.

The Bentian number about 3,500 people living in a thinly populated and relatively remote upriver area. They are swidden cultivators who for much of the time reside in dispersed farmhouses, and periodically stay in small villages. Cash-income is principally obtained from rattan grown in the rice fields as an integral part of the system of swidden cultivation. The household is the principal economic unit. Local leadership is weak and social relations are mostly egalitarian. There is extensive individual autonomy and people generally have significant latitude in affiliating with other individuals and groups. Authority, solidarity, and other social connections are largely the result of achievement: products of social practices such as rituals and speeches; the sharing of game, food, and services; and frequent formal and informal visits, which establish egocentric networks and dyadic bonds among a multitude of complexly cross-cutting bilateral kinship relations. However, despite this ostensibly weak structural foundation of Bentian society, an ethos of social solidarity prevails, and people often respond affirmatively to claims made in the name of kinship and engage in substantial reciprocal exchange of gifts and services.

Bentian Teknonymy

Teknonymy, understood in a narrow sense, is the practice of naming parents after their children. In a broader sense, the concept encompasses the practice of naming grandparents after their grandchildren and occasionally other categories of people after other relatives. In most societies practising teknonymy, the name-bearers are designated as "father of so-and-so," "mother of so-and-so," etc.[7] The institution is common in Southeast Asia, especially in Indonesia, and found all over the world.[8] In many societies, it is a dominant form of reference and address, although kinship terms are often a preferred alternative, especially for address. Teknonymy occurs in all kinds of societies — matrilineal, patrilineal, bilateral — although more commonly in small-scale and "traditional" as opposed to large-scale and modern societies.[9] Where it occurs, it is mostly used restrictively for parents (sometimes for only one parent). However, extended usage including grandparental teknonyms is also common, for example, in Borneo.[10]

The Bentian have both personal or "true names" (*aran bene*) received some time after birth and parental and grandparental teknonyms received after they obtain children and grandchildren respectively or when they acquire adult and old-age status. The standard Bentian teknonyms read as follows: Ma X (Father of X), Nen X (Mother of X), Kakah X (Grandfather of X), and Tak X (Grandmother of X).[11] The first elements of these designations are similar to or derived from the kinship terms for father (*uma*), mother (*ine*), grandfather (*kakah*), and grandmother (*itak*). Teknonymy is the dominant form of reference for Bentian adults, and, together with kinship terms, the dominant form of address.

When Bentians become known by parental teknonyms, their personal names will, according to a typical pattern in teknonymous societies, gradually fall into disuse, and when they acquire grandparental teknonyms later, their parental teknonyms will become progressively obsolete. Although these processes are gradual (some people adopt new designations much later than others), a general pattern emerges: young people are referred to by personal names, middle-aged people by parental teknonyms, and old people by grandparental teknonyms. Thus, Bentian teknonymy divides Bentians into three broad age categories or strata. This property of teknonymy has been identified in many societies,[12] with the most famous examples drawn from Bali. As in the Balinese case, the age categories of Bentian teknonymy divide communities into roughly corresponding sets of "social organizational layers of minors, active citizens, [and] elders," a division into which the above-noted gradual acquisition of teknonyms, in fact, represents an adjustment, delaying the conferment of adult status for immature adults (who may continue being called by personal names after marrying and receiving children), and old age status for politically or economically active elders (who may continue being called "fathers" and "mothers" long after receiving grandchildren).[13] This is an important structural function of Bentian teknonyms, shared by the pseudo-teknonyms.

True Bentian teknonyms are typical teknonyms. Normally, they derive from the name-bearers' first-born children or grandchildren (irrespective of sex) and they are usually not replaced upon birth of additional descendants, as in some societies. Nevertheless, people are occasionally named after later born descendants, particularly if they obtain these after remarrying or moving to new villages, in which case different people often know them by different teknonyms. They are also commonly named after their spouses' children or other adopted children.[14]

Nearly half of the adult Bentian population is not known by true teknonyms, but by a form of structurally similar designations made up of the same kinship term-like first elements as true teknonyms and a second element designating different qualities, habits, or life experiences of the name-bearer. Thus Bentians are called, for example, Ma Minyak (Father Oil), Nen Ue (Mother Rattan), Kakah Bekok (Grandfather Frog), and Tak Rosik (Grandmother Sharp). Such designations represent a kind of nicknames and are not teknonyms in an analytical sense. Antoun, who encountered similar designations in Jordania, referred to them as "descriptive teknonyms."[15] As they are not really teknonyms, I have used the term pseudo-teknonym in this chapter.[16] However, although analytically different from true teknonyms, they are similarly constructed and used in the same way and contexts with the same consequences. Bentians do not regard them as a special name type. Unlike the pseudo-teknonyms investigated by Antoun, they do not generally have a derogatory connotation or impose social control by designating immoral behavior. They are as common and normal as true teknonyms, and are adopted along with the latter when name-bearers become adults or reach old age. An understanding of Bentian teknonymy thus requires it to be analyzed in tandem with these designations, which occupy the same niche in the naming system, and when I speak of Bentian teknonyms or teknonymy, the expression covers both true and pseudo-teknonyms.

That some people become known by pseudo-teknonyms rather than true teknonyms appears to be incidental and not, for example, an expression of moral or other qualities. People without children are somewhat more likely to acquire pseudo-teknonyms; however, many of them go by teknonyms derived from relatives' children. But nearly half of those Bentians who have children also go by pseudo-teknonyms. This does not mean that their children mean less to them, nor that the personalities, habits, or life-histories of these Bentians necessarily are distinctive although they sometimes are, and this occasionally explains why they acquire pseudo-teknonyms. Whether or not one acquires a pseudo-teknonym is most importantly due to the creative wit of one's consociates: if someone comes up with an apt or poetically appealing pseudo-teknonym (it is not customary to invent one's own) there is a good chance that it will become established.

Bentian teknonyms are established through usage, not through ceremony or formal decisions. They are invented and circulated by relatives or neighbors who, for some reason such as entertainment, aesthetics, interpersonal politics, or others' opinion, find it appropriate to define a particular person with reference to a particular condition (for example, parenthood or idiosyncratic habits). Pseudo-teknonyms often compete with ordinary teknonyms, and only time will tell which eventually will stick. Indeed, people are commonly known by both types of designations. My fieldwork indicated that many individuals are known by alternative teknonyms because when people know a person but not his or her spouse, they often use a similarly constructed teknonym for the spouse as for the person they know. People who knew Nen Simur but not her husband called him Ma Simur even if he already had a distinct teknonym, Ma Bure. Women are a little more likely to become known by teknonyms resembling their husband's than vice versa, and men are slightly more likely to acquire pseudo- as opposed to ordinary teknonyms. Grandparental as opposed to parental teknonyms, in turn, more often consist of true teknonyms than pseudo-teknonyms, especially in the case of grandmothers.[17]

Ultimately, the meaning or derivation of one's teknonym usually means little. Like names in many places, Bentian teknonyms and pseudo-teknonyms are "just names," in that people normally do not read a secondary significance into them. As they become established, they evoke only the name-bearers, not any of the characteristics, events, or descendants from which they are derived. Often, the attributes from which pseudo-teknonyms are derived are not very important in the first place. Although some pseudo-teknonyms refer to something continually salient about the persons they designate, as in the case of Nen Wase (Mother Axe), who was so-called because of her split upper lip, most do not. More often they derive from some no longer pertinent past event or condition associated with the name-bearer's youth or childhood. This was the case, for instance, with Nen Pore, who received this designation from her penchant for a certain forest fruit (*pore*) as a child, and with Ma Lutar, who, when newly married, was frequently seen leading his father's water buffalo in a field of open grazing ground (*lutar*). Often, pseudo-teknonyms are not really descriptive. The most important way in which they are devised is probably through wordplay — an all-important activity in Bentian society — connecting them through a phonological or semantic likeness to the personal name. Two examples are Ma Tuak (Father Liquor), who received this designation from its auditory resemblance with his personal name (Atok) not because of his drinking habits, and Ma Kalak, who received his pseudo-teknonym because of its semantic similarity with his personal name Buu (*kalak* signifies one kind of fish trap, *buu* another).[18] Frequently, these designations are acoustically or semantically connected to the personal name even when they are descriptive, as in Ma Lombang's case, who obtained his pseudo-teknonym partly from its sound likeness with his personal name (Mangong), and partly because he in his youth carried around a distinctive rattan box (*lombang*) containing flintstones.

The Bentian Autonym

There are thus several different principles by which Bentian teknonyms and pseudo-teknonyms are established, but they nevertheless form an integrated system in usage. Several principles are also utilized in the construction of Bentian personal names (that is, autonyms), which are characteristically short two-syllable or, less frequently, one-syllable words. It is necessary to consider these names, from which true teknonyms derive, in an analysis of Bentian teknonymy. Wordplay plays a part in the construction of the autonym, too, as indicated by the fact that sibling names are often phonologically similar (for example, Yan, Yati, Ida, Kiwot, Nawot, Wawot; or Sina, Selia, and Kamsia). As these examples also demonstrate, foreign names (Yan, Yati, Ida) including Malay, Javanese, and Western are often used, and have been used for a long time. The same is true of names associated with Christianity like Thomas, Johannis, and Josep, particularly among Christians. Muslim names like Kadir, Karim, Saleh, and Kuan are also common although they are usually taken without an intention to signal affinity with Islam or Malay culture. Some names derive from foreign words that are not names in their original context, for example, Hong Kong, Damai (Indonesian, 'peace'), and Dinas (Indonesian, 'agency, official'). However, most Bentian autonyms are purely local. Often, they lack other meaning (for example, Wawot, Nawot, Mangong, Dut), and when they have a distinct meaning, they frequently say nothing about the name-bearer as in the case of Buu, above, or Padeng, '*alang-alang* grass.' However, they may also be descriptive, as in Mokak's case, whose name derives from a verb meaning "to split rattan," and which he, like Nen Wase, received because of his split lip. Autonyms sometimes commemorate events, and they may be constructed through modification of another word as in Ma Lutar's case, whose autonym (Tawir) derives from the location (Mengkatip) where his father was away doing road construction work when he was born.

Even more than teknonyms, autonyms are "just names" that rather exclusively denote only their human referents. Autonyms are not given at birth, or during the *ngulas bidan* ritual held to bless the child and thank the midwives a few days later, but usually only after a year or more.[19] Infants are often referred to as just *tia* "children" or *tia mea* "red children," or with nicknames such as *basung ure* (young bamboo shoot), or *semeritek* ("willy" referring to male genitalia), and often treated with a degree of reservation at first. This practice reflects fears of attracting malevolent spirits' attention to the child and of becoming too closely attached to it until its survival seems likely. (Infant mortality is very high.) Autonyms are usually given by the parents or the often co-resident (maternal or paternal) grandparents, but other relatives, neighbors, influential elders, and shamans (*belian*) also frequently suggest them.

A principal consideration in selecting an autonym is to provide a name not shared by anyone else. Autonyms are unique within the speech community. The names of recently dead ancestors are not used — and people are reluctant to mention them.[20] Those of people long dead are sometimes reused, but not systematically, in contrast to the Punan Bah, among whom everyone takes the name of a particular, long-dead ancestor, in a sense representing an incarnation of that person.[21] Autonyms, which can be "hot" (*layeng*) or "cool" (*rengin*), are frequently changed, especially during childhood (but also later), and in connection with prolonged illness or misfortune. New names are typically given during curing rituals, often by a *belian*.[22] Nevertheless, a certain intimate (metonymic) connection is perceived to exist between individuals and their autonyms (and generally between names and referents), which contributes to a general reluctance to openly use them, for example, from fear that they become used in black or love magic. By contrast, teknonyms are not changed during rituals since a similar connection does not exist between them and their referents.[23] In a sense, autonyms represent the personal or intimate aspect of a person, for which reason their use is inappropriate. As in many societies, people are somewhat uneasy in supplying their own autonyms.

In many respects, however, the autonym is rather insignificant. Once people reach adulthood, it will largely fall out of use, and they will be addressed by teknonyms and kinship terms instead. Autonyms are used for adults in some relationships, however. For example, older people in the grandparental generation often continue addressing their children and other close middle-aged people by autonyms, and one can, in principle, address cognatic relatives on one's own generational level with them. However, the use of adults' autonyms in public discourse is restricted even in these relationships. In other relationships, using adults' autonyms is strictly prohibited, and sanctioned both by customary law regulations making violators liable to pay fines and by fear of supernatural retribution (*bunsung*). One cannot mention the autonyms of generational elders or same or higher generation affines; in these cases teknonyms or, preferably, kinship terms must be used. Consequently, autonyms are poorly known outside the family, especially those of older people.

In everyday life, adults' autonyms have limited social significance. Like Balinese personal names, their role "in ordering ... social relations is essentially residual."[24] Their greatest social significance is, in fact, "negative": it consists of the prohibitions to use them. However, these prohibitions have important consequences. The use of teknonyms and kinship terms, which Bentians reportedly practise more actively than their neighbors, is motivated precisely by them and by a converse concern to address consociates (and some more than others) in more respectful ways. Bentian teknonymy — and the institution more generally — cannot be understood without reference to these motives. However, before developing the implications of this point, I will review previous theories of teknonymy.

Parenthood and Descendants: Early Explanations of Teknonymy

The widespread occurrence of teknonymy prompted several early commentators to explain the origins and general function of the custom. The term was coined by Tylor, who argued that teknonymy survives from an earlier period and provides a means whereby the father is given parental status and integrated in the wife's family. Tylor based this hypothesis on a statistical correlation in a sample of societies between teknonymy, matrilocal residence, and ceremonial avoidance by the husband of the wife's relatives (which was ceased when he acquired a child and teknonym).[25] Wilken suggested that teknonymy served to recognize paternity, especially in connection with an assumed transition from matriarchy to patriarchy.[26] Steinmetz saw it as a means whereby both parents demonstrated parenthood at an early promiscuous stage of human history.[27] Miller argued that teknonymy mirrors a significant transformation in the parents' social personalities.[28] Crawley claimed that the practice served, through the parents' mutual reference to the child, the functions of protecting the child and supporting a union between them.[29]

In contrast to most early commentators, Lowie regarded teknonymy as an example of "convergent evolution" and dismissed the value of "generic theory" for understanding it.[30] Steinmetz and Crawley renounced Tylor's hypothesis on the grounds that many patrilineal and patrilocal societies practise teknonymy and that the mother is named after the child nearly as frequently as the father.[31] Steinmetz and Parsons dismissed Wilken's hypothesis on similar grounds,[32] while Steinmetz's theory was discounted as speculative by Parsons.[33] Parsons also dismissed Crawley's protection theory, pointing out that parents are usually named only after the first-born child and often only when the child reaches puberty or becomes distinguished in society.

Clearly, the heterogeneity of teknonymy and the variety of societies practising it make speculation about its ultimate origins and function difficult and insufficient, at any rate, for understanding it in many present-day societies. There is limited explanatory value for evolutionary hypotheses in this field, at least of a unilineal kind. As with kinship, the near-universal status of teknonymy is more plausibly explained by its "natural availability." The recognition of parenthood (and grandparenthood) makes it an obvious logical possibility, and from occasionally calling someone, for example, "Father of John" — something which presumably occurs virtually everywhere — there would not seem to be such a great step to institutionalizing this usage.

Quite naturally, parenthood has also provided the key to understanding teknonymy. Most analyses have assigned central importance to the institution's assumed role of expressing the importance, or promoting the well-being, of children. Sumner and Keller, for example, suggested that the custom is "strongly indicative of the place offspring hold in the eyes of primitive people,"[34] while Crawley noted that adoption of the child's name amounts to an adoption of "a religious surname for the parents," which "renders them in a real sense the spiritual parents" or "godparents" of the child, in addition to being its biological parents.[35] Later interpreters of teknonymy have also emphasized this aspect. Charles contended that the custom "constitutes an ultimate form of respect for the newcomers' importance" and that "teknonymy suggests that, having helped create a remarkable new thing, the parent has already begun to die as a person."[36] Lévi-Strauss, in his analysis of Needham's material on Penan teknonymy, made a somewhat similar statement: "the reasons why parents may no longer be called by their [personal] name when a child is born is that they are 'dead' and that procreation is conceived not as the addition of a new being to those who already exist but as the substitution of the one for the others."[37] To mention a Borneo example, Hudson and Hudson argued that "since people [Ma'anyans] are not really considered to have reached adult status until he or she has a child, the teknonym signals the attainment of this status."[38] Even the Geertzes, who saw teknonymy as a "vital social mechanism with important structural impact both on village organization and the process of corporate kin-group formation"[39] and thus moved the focus of analysis outside the domestic sphere, contributed to this tendency by claiming that Balinese teknonymy expresses "the enormous value which is placed upon procreation," and has the effect that "one is not defined [...] in terms of who produced one [...] but in terms of whom one has produced."[40]

Respect: An Alternative Approach to Understanding Teknonymy

For an outside observer, it is understandably easy to get the impression that teknonymy focuses attention on children. Children are undeniably important in most societies practising teknonymy (although probably not significantly more than in others), and in some of them, local inter-pretations support such theories. But there is reason to believe that theories of teknonymy which regard it as expressing the importance of children suffer from a misplaced emphasis. Teknonymy is obviously not only about children. Indeed, it may not even be primarily about children.

Most frequently it is not, as Alford noted, the importance of children which members of teknonymous societies provide as a motive for the practice, but instead, respect for those addressed by teknonyms.[41] This is also the rationale for using teknonymy (and pseudo-teknonymy) that Bentians suggest. Teknonymy represents a respectful way of addressing and referring to those whose autonyms cannot be mentioned (and, to a lesser extent, others). A similar interpretation was proposed earlier by Parsons,[42] who claimed that "teknonymy is merely one case of the wide-spread practice of avoiding the personal name by substituting a status name, a title, or a nickname."[43]

The kin categories for whom Bentian prescribe use of teknonymy or kinship terms are affines and elders, categories with which joking and avoidance relationships have often been recorded. Relations with these categories are illuminated by reference to Radcliffe-Brown. His division "within the wife's family" between "those who have to be treated with extreme respect [elders], and those with whom it is a duty to be disrespectful [same-generation affines]"[44] is descriptive of differences in emphasis in the general style of Bentian interaction with same-generation affines, on the one hand, and elders (cognatic and affinal), on the other. Extreme respect is perhaps not always expected; joking occurs between the generations (especially among cognates), and one should certainly not be too disrespectful all the time with one's same-generation affines. But an atmosphere of joking and teasing, often associated with vulgarity or indecency, characterizes same-generation relations in particular (and there is a special, reciprocal joking relationship between the wife's brother and sister's husband) while one is expected to show considerable respect (for example, in choosing terms of address) for elders, particularly affinal elders.

More specifically, Radcliffe-Brown's discussion about joking, avoidance, and respect is useful in demonstrating that these behaviors represent alternative ways to manage relationships which simultaneously involve "conjunction" and "disjunction," that is, which are close but involve a potential for conflict.[45] The Bentian relationships characterized by name-avoidance are also such relationships, and they are generally associated with joking, avoidance, and respect.[46] Indeed, the Bentian are simultaneously more inclined to show respect, practise various taboos, and engage in disrespectful teasing than their neighbors, and there exists an important relation between this condition, and their greater inclination to engage in solidary social relations.[47]

Of further value in Radcliffe-Brown's discussion is his emphasis on respect as a generally important issue in social life: "the whole maintenance of a social order depends upon the appropriate kind and degree of respect being shown toward certain persons, things, ideas or symbols."[48] A central issue in Bentian name-avoidance and teknonymy is precisely exhibiting "the appropriate kind and degree of respect," an exercise which benefits from being tempered — in some relations more than in others — by a playful style of interaction characterized by joking, banter, and verbal artistry. In such interaction, pseudo-teknonyms, which are often born in this context, have special value in promoting a sense of familiarity, intimacy and in-group identification like nicknames elsewhere. In addition to other things that they do, forms of reference and address serve an important function in setting the tone of interaction and marking the general atmosphere of social context.[49]

One consequence of using teknonyms as opposed to autonyms is especially significant for the question of respect: that which results from substituting a designation entailing direct, non-contextualized, personal reference (the autonym) by what is, in effect, a "status term" (the teknonym). The teknonym, as Parsons observed,[50] calls attention to the status of the person who it denominates, or more exactly, to his or her status as parent or grandparent, or as adult or elder in the Bentian case.[51] As Parsons expressed it: "teknonymy is a means of concentrating attention upon kinship or status, diverting it [...] from the individual to his or her position.[52] Thus, not only is it "part of the system of avoiding personal names [...] of itself it emphasizes the status relationship."[53]

Alford observed that teknonyms perform a similar operation to kinship terms, which as noted are a preferred, more effective alternative to teknonyms in address although they are sometimes unnecessarily or inappropriately powerful as such and not always applicable or sufficient for purposes of reference. Both types of terms "place individuals in the social network, and call forth role-appropriate behavior."[54] Certainly teknonyms, and particularly pseudo-teknonyms, have the effect of connecting people, not the least because of the naming process. As is the case with kinship ideology in Bentian society,[55] the most important general social consequence of teknonymy may well be its contribution to the reproduction of solidary local relations. A similar connection presumably pertains between Bentian teknonymy and the "particular form of social solidarity" that Needham observed to correlate with the presence of "mourning terms" or "death-names" in different Penan communities and other similar societies.[56] At least the Bentian are, in comparison with their more modernized neighbors, to a higher degree characterized by such solidarity — described by themselves and the latter in terms of greater *adat* (customary law, tradition) orientation and greater respect for kin — at the same time as they practise name-avoidance and teknonymy more extensively.

Teknonymy seems to have similar, structural functions also in other Borneo societies. Among the Land Dayaks, who commonly take their teknonyms from other relatives' children rather than their own (and occasionally from non-relatives' children), teknonymy reflects "the ruling requirement of [...] society [which] is to produce a broad sentimental basis for the community through many interlocking personal attachments, while at the same time avoiding divisions within it."[57] A somewhat more specialized structural function is attributed by Nicolaisen to the remarkable system of Punan Bah teknonymy.[58] Punan Bah teknonyms derive partly from people's own children, but partly also from others', in particular, their oldest sibling's first-born child, a practice which results in a special category of people (the firstborns of firstborns) becoming "anchors of symbolic relations," and later, the custodians of heirlooms and family authority in society.

A specific way in which teknonymy helps reproduce the Bentian social order is by emphasizing the asymmetrical character of intergenerational relations: the fact that elders may, and often continue to, refer to middle-aged adults by autonyms while the latter usually refer to the former in the more respectful form of teknonymy, serves as a constant reminder of the nature of these structurally fundamental relations in Bentian society. On the other hand, the symmetrical character of teknonymy use and prescribed name-avoidance in the ideally respectful *and* close relationship between same-generation affines represents an ideal model for these relations. By emphasizing these complementary ideals, teknonymy promotes an ideal social order similar to that promoted by Bentian kinship, which I have characterized elsewhere, inspired by Robert McKinley,[59] in terms of "the twin principles of intergenerational respect and collateral reciprocity."[60] Indeed, teknonymy promotes the same socio-centric ideology which the use of kinship terms for address is taken to symbolize by Bentians.[61] Also like kinship, teknonymy divides people into age-sets resembling (but not exactly corresponding to) the generational categories into which the kinship system, in a less age-sensitive manner, divides people, thereby further enhancing the importance of age as a principle of social organization.

Besides helping us understand teknonymy, the status-stressing effect of teknonymy also suggests what is wrong with the autonym: "personal names are disrespectful of or indifferent to status relationships."[62] Being "non-relational," it refers just to the referent without connoting a connection to a social context.[63] Hence, it symbolically deprives, for example, an elder of the seniority that a teknonym or kinship term would attribute, or suggests lack of respect for the norms regulating interaction between affines when it involves not identifying an affine with a status position. The fact that the autonym, in Benjamin's Lévi-Strauss-inspired expression, "sets apart whoever bears it openly as not yet having entered the system,"[64] that is, associates personal names with children and immature youths (*tia*), indicates a related reason for name-avoidance.[65] Certain properties of the autonym, such as its non-incorporated, non-relational character, thus have social implications, which can make it disrespectful, at least in societies characterized by an incorporated notion of personhood.[66]

Individuation, Egalitarianism, and an Upriver Culture of Sociality

Bentian teknonyms, then, may be regarded as a kind of status terms. However, it would be inappropriate to regard them, like the Geertzes described their Balinese counterparts, as "essentially impersonal status terms."[67] Even though Bentian teknonyms, in contrast to autonyms, externalize a certain (quite generalized) social status in a name, they invoke this status only relatively weakly. Moreover, they are not impersonal. Notwithstanding that they represent a preferred alternative to autonyms, and enable their avoidance, they do not establish an "anonymization of persons."[68] Like autonyms, and unlike kinship terms, they are unique (at least within the speech community). Indeed, they are not only, or really, status terms: they are names.[69] While indicating adult or elder status, they also discriminate between individuals who are referred to and remembered by these names, at least for restricted periods of time in particular social settings, but sometimes long after death. This suggests another, previously overlooked, property of teknonymy. Teknonymy individuates, and this is not merely a residual function, especially not among the Bentian for whom pseudo-teknonymy lends special importance to this function.[70]

Even though they are perceived as less direct and more respectful than autonyms, Bentian teknonyms do not just designate social roles or the "social personality."[71] They also function as personal names, and signify individuals whose personalities and manners do not to me seem significantly less variable than those of people in an average European town. The Bentian, of course, do not all conform to a single ideal type, and are not mere reflections of their statuses as men, women, shamans, elders, etc. Furthermore, attaining such a condition is not a general Bentian aspiration, nor a goal of the Bentian naming system. Even though the naming system, in Benjamin's terms, serves to "suppress the autonym,"[72] it does not suppress individuality. Unlike the Balinese, it cannot be said of the Bentian that they make "a persistent and systematic attempt to stylize all aspects of personal expression to the point where anything idiosyncratic, anything characteristic of the individual [...] is muted."[73] Rather, they are more poignantly described through Weinstock's characterization of the Luangan (the larger, "tribal" group of whom the Bentian form part) as "individualistic by nature."[74]

As the extensive Bentian use of pseudo-teknonyms suggests, idiosyncrasies are not systematically suppressed but rather given a fair amount of expression in public life. Similarly, autonomy, although publicly recognized as an ideal, is an important covert ideal and goal toward which people often strive in practice (for example, by evading their relatives by keeping to their swidden fields).[75] This is not to say that Bentian social relations are not generally solidary; it is rather the opposite. But it is to say that autonomy and individuality cannot be eliminated and that these conditions have to be dealt with in attempts to establish solidarity between people.

In Bentian society, as in the small-scale "segmentary" societies using mourning-terms and sharing "a particular form of social solidarity" analyzed by Needham, "individuals are in direct social dependence upon each other, and [...] related as persons rather than as members or representatives of groups."[76] In such a society, solidarity is rarely established through coercion. Indeed, there are weak structural foundations for such an exercise. Neither is it simply the result of conformity, of an archetypal Durkheimian "mechanical solidarity" built on likeness. Rather, solidarity results from an *incorporation of individuals* who have internalized a sense of responsibility which is part of their conceptions of whom they consider themselves to be, and successfully acted out in large part because of how moral virtue is articulated with their personal interests as local leaders, elders, and adult persons. In such a society, a name type designating not only status but also individuality caters to notions of subjectivity which it is less advantageous (and perhaps impossible) to categorically suppress than to incorporate. Teknonyms, which Murdock characterized as "intermediate between personal names and kinship terms,"[77] are well-adjusted to the structural requirements of such a society. Replacing autonyms but retaining an individuating quality, they socialize individuality, and at least in the Bentian case, incorporate it in a system of intergenerational and afffinal relationships structured by the principles of respect and reciprocity.

Another way which Bentian teknonyms contrast with Balinese teknonyms is by not setting apart an upper stratum in society. In the first place, they do not, at least not to a similar extent, result in "genealogical amnesia, foreclosing the reckoning of descent."[78] Secondly, they are used for everyone, also leaders, that is, house-group leaders, and community leaders, including village heads (*kepala desa*) and the descendants of the former title-holding leaders, who often act as "heads of customary law" (*kepala adat*). All leaders of this sort may be addressed by the generic leadership term *manti*, but are typically addressed (and referred to) by teknonyms.[79] Even the title-holding leaders of the colonial period, who owned slaves and held elevated positions of authority held by no one today, are often referred to by teknonyms. (In the past, titles to a variable degree, depending on the position achieved by the leader, substituted for, although probably never entirely replaced, teknonyms.)

This preference for using teknonyms for everybody, including outsiders like myself if they stay long enough among them, reflects a prevailing egalitarian ethos which strongly influences Bentian attitudes toward social life.[80] Teknonyms — even though they individuate — in a sense treat all people the same; they make everybody "like-named." Using teknonyms (and especially, pseudo-teknonyms) for leaders or outsiders, therefore entails, as Antoun has observed for Jordanian nicknames and pseudo-teknonyms, "a way of saying [...] that you are no better than me, whatever power, knowledge or money you may have." Indeed, it seems appropriate here to talk in Antoun's terms about "abusive equality."[81] Bentian teknonymy involves symbolic incorporation within a symbolically undifferentiated group, and is expressive of an often obtrusive inclusiveness, motivated by an ideology of sharing and affirming relations.

As such a means of incorporation, Bentian teknonyms function primarily in very small-scale social contexts. Indeed, they incorporate people particularly within small networks of intimate consociates outside of which their teknonyms are often unknown. Interestingly, if one moves, one likely becomes known by a new teknonym in the new locality.[82] As this indicates, Bentian teknonyms represent vehicles of incorporation particularly in *new* settings, such as new villages or families, or adulthood in villages where they previously were "children." An example of this is Ma Adir, a man who was named after his child from his first marriage in his home village but who became known as Ma Putup (a name derived from the word *putup* which signifies the kicking movements of infants) in the village of his wife by his second marriage. She, in turn, was called Nen Adir in his home village, and also, by some of her closest cognatic relatives in her village, who thereby wanted to acknowledge her new union. However, most people there who lacked this concern persisted in using her old teknonym, Nen Bujok. In other words, giving someone a new name often functions somewhat like an acknowledgment, if not quite a welcome (although it may do that as well), of a person's new status as part of a group, community, or relationship. An example of how this can purposively serve to welcome the newcomer is Ma Denia ("Father of the World"), a young inmarried man and successful hunter, who was given this somewhat flattering pseudo-teknonym by an old *belian* in recognition of his experience of having traveled widely and of always being on the move, visiting various relatives in his new village who had quickly come to depend on him.

However, teknonyms exclude as well as incorporate, and by the same means. They represent a restrictively local idiom. Like the Gaelic "by-names" investigated by Dorian, their understanding demands "an intimate knowledge of the community's social structure available only to its members," and they represent "unofficial designations used [in the local context] almost to the exclusion of official names."[83] Because of not occurring in official records such as village statistics or land titles (or on identity cards) in which the autonyms, in accordance with national practice, are used, teknonyms are often unknown to outsiders such as government officials for whom this contributes to make local discourse inaccessible (all the more so as one person may be known by several different designations even in one locality).

Another respect in which Bentian teknonymy represents a local idiom is by way of perceived contrast to the larger, national society. It represents local culture as opposed to "downriver custom" (*adat sawa*), something which the Bentian are frequently reminded of through increasing contacts with government officials and other downriver people with whom they usually use their autonyms. Consequently, Bentian teknonymy has become an example of persisting local tradition, or primitiveness, depending on how one wants to define it.

Another way in which Bentian teknonymy contrasts the local society with the national relates to consequences of its use. Bentian teknonymy, especially pseudo-teknonymy, sets the tone for a distinctively Bentian, as opposed to downriver, style of public discourse. It is expressive of a delight taken in creative, intimate, and context-sensitive wordplay, and a preference for descriptive as opposed to "inscriptive" designations (in Foucault's sense). It expresses and exemplifies a style of interaction often characterized by horseplay and joking, or by what Antoun calls an "idiom of abusive familiarity."[84] Indeed, Bentian teknonymy represents a particularly vernacular name type, and is as such rather discordant with the anonymous, universalistic, and affective-neutral ideals associated with state administration and modern citizenship.

Interestingly, however, the fact that Bentian teknonyms do not qualify as official designations (already the fact that they do not consistently designate people from birth to death makes them unacceptable as such) is not much regretted. In the first place, although Bentians still strongly disapprove of autonyms in some contexts, they regard them as their "true names," and understand the administrative need for objective and standardized identification. Furthermore, a sentiment prevails that they, too, should, become "ordered" and modern, and therefore necessarily more like downstream people in some respects. Of course, this does not need to stop them — and so far has not — from using teknonyms, or avoiding autonyms, in the local setting. Interestingly, the fact that autonyms become circulated and sometimes uttered because of this use appears also does not bother them much.

Teknonymy is notably also not first on the list of valuable traditions constituting the Bentian cultural heritage and it is little objectified. Unlike kinship, little significance is attributed to it in discourse, and a sense of embarrassment is even associated with the fact that pseudo-teknonymy is absent among downstream Dayaks. The Bentian would probably also practise teknonymy less extensively if it was not for the fact that dealings with outsiders and the presence of the government in their area are rather restricted. Not all Bentians are, in fact, equally keen to use them. There is a tendency among modernization-minded individuals to use autonyms in the local context whenever possible, and among city-dwelling Bentians teknonymy is probably rare. Already in the larger downriver Christian Bentian communities where I did not usually stay, the use of autonyms seemed much less restricted. Here, modernization-mindedness and government and outsider influence were also more evident, and here, I was told, respect for seniority, kinship, and tradition is less important. The use of teknonymy indeed seems likely to decrease with increasing integration in a wider social universe. Comparative Indonesian findings testifying to this were reported by Brewer who in a relatively accessible lowland Bimanese village observed autonymy to be more common (and preferred), and teknonymy less dominant, than in a relatively isolated mountain village in the same region; further, he found this tendency to be still more pronounced in the town and government seat of Kota Bima where teknonymy was already inadequately known.[85] As this suggests, teknonymy is important and motivated mainly under certain social conditions, an understanding of which this article has attempted to articulate.[86]

Conclusion

Like its more well-known Balinese counterpart, Bentian teknonymy is a dominant form of address and reference, and as such a complex multifunctional institution and "cultural paradigm." As in Bali, it results in people become like-named and divided into broad age categories. However, involving use of asymmetric as often as symmetric teknonyms for married couples, Bentian teknonymy inconsistently promotes "identification of man and wife as joint procreators."[87] Indeed, it is incorrect to talk about "procreational strata" here. Rather than parent or grandparent status, Bentian teknonymy designates adulthood and elder status. Contrary to the Balinese case, as interpreted by the Geertzes, we have here an "upward looking" rather than "downward looking" system.[88] Bentians are defined more through their ascendants than their descendants, and it is respect toward elders, and affines, not children, that Bentian teknonymy serves to establish, as indeed generally is the case with teknonymy.[89]

Teknonymy functions much like kinship among the Bentian. It is an integrative medium which promotes connections between people. It also expresses the persistence of the kinship orientations: its continuing use reflects the continuing relevance of socio-centric values associated with kinship. Conversely, where its use is in decline, this expresses the deterioration of these values, and integration into a larger demographic setting in which other ideologies and principles of organization are equal or more important than kinship. Like kinship terms, teknonyms invoke status or position, as indicated by the fact that the principal motivation for using them is replacing the autonym, which is deemed disrespectful because of representing non-contextualized, personal reference. Another crucial function of Bentian teknonymy, shared by kinship terminology, which results specifically from contrastive use with autonymy, is that it emphasizes the asymmetrical character of intergenerational relations and the reciprocal and respectful relations of intragenerational affinal relations, and thus helps reproduce a fundamental aspect of Bentian social structure.

However, teknonymy also complements kinship in some ways. Bentian teknonyms individuate and assign people unique positions in small social networks. They define them in respect to the continually moving stream of social life, and often to aspects of it only perceived from within, like the "shared events" or "private jokes" that Macdonald (this volume) mentions as examples of sources of names among the Palawan of the Philippines. Indeed, the Bentian naming system seems to be characterized by similar contextual orientations that characterizes the "paradigmatic naming systems" discussed by Macdonald, and it forms a typical example of such systems.[90]

In this context it is illuminating to note that Bentian parental teknonyms resemble, in terms of structural functions, the "affinal names" of some other peoples.[91] They are assigned to mature social actors who assume a role in public life and kinship affairs, and they are established in social interaction between relatively equal and intimate peers, in relations typically characterized by continuous negotiation, carried out, for example, through forms of address. It is also against this background that the distinctive institution of pseudo-teknonymy should be understood. Although it is impossible to reconstruct its emergence, it undoubtedly functions to define personal identity in a more expressive and charismatic way than true teknonymy is capable of doing, and on the basis of positions in networks of adult consociates rather than positions within families. It represents a name type particularly well-adapted to such interaction because it has a capacity to simultaneously individuate and reduce social distance while maintaining a degree of respect and enabling avoidance of the autonym. Thus, it serves to complement teknonymy and adjust the institution in closer alignment with an upriver culture of sociality predicated upon such values as egalitarianism, socio-centrism, individualism, and familiarity.

Notes

[1]   "Dayak" is a generic term for the indigenous non-Muslim peoples of Borneo who mostly are or used to be swidden cultivators in the island's interior. The term is frequently contrasted with "Malay," a generic term for the indigenous Malay-speaking Muslims of Borneo who generally live in closer proximity to the coast.

2   Eighteen months of fieldwork were conducted in 1993 and 1996–7 mainly among upriver, non-Christian (Kaharingan) communities in West Kutai district of East Kalimantan and North Barito district of Central Kalimantan. The fieldwork was conducted under the auspices of Universitas Indonesia and Lembaga Ilmu Pengetahuan Indonesia in cooperation with Isabell Herrmans (University of Helsinki). It was funded by the Academy of Finland, the Finnish Ministry of Education, the Swedish School of Social Science at the University of Helsinki, the Nordic Institute of Asian Studies, the Nordenskiöld Society, the Ella & Georg Ehrnrooth Foundation, and the Oskar Öflund Foundation. Participation in the conference on "Naming in Asia" in Singapore in February 2006 was enabled by grants from Waldemar Frenckell's Foundation and the Ella & Georg Ehrnrooth Foundation.

3   I only know of pseudo-teknonymy occurring among the Bentian and their Luangan and Meratus neighbors (Anna Lowenhaupt Tsing, *In the Realm of the Diamond Queen: Marginality in an Out-of-the-Way Place* (Princeton: Princeton University Press, 1993), and, to a more limited extent, some other Dayaks (W. R. Geddes, *The Land Dayaks of Sarawak: A Report on a Social Economic Survey of the Land Dayaks of Sarawak Presented to the Colonial Social Science Research Council* (London: Her Majesty's Stationery Office, 1954); Pascal Couderc, personal communication, 2006) and Jordanian men (Richard T. Antoun, "On the Significance of Names in an Arab Village," *Ethnology* 7 (1968): 158–70).

4   Marcel Mauss, "A Category of the Human Mind: The Notion of Person; the Notion of Self," in *The Category of the Person*, eds. Michael Carrithers, Steven Collins, and Steven Lukes (Cambridge: Cambridge University Press, 1985); Claude Lévi-Strauss, *The Savage Mind* (Chicago: University of Chicago Press, 1966); Hildred Geertz and Clifford Geertz, "Teknonymy in Bali: Parenthood, Age-grading and Genealogical Amnesia," *Journal of the Royal Anthropological Institute of Great Britain and Ireland* 94, 2 (1964): 94–108; and Rodney Needham, "The System of Teknonyms and Death-Names of the Penan," *Southwestern Journal of Anthropology* 10 (1954a): 416–31.

5   David Maybury-Lewis, "Name, Person, and Ideology in Central Brazil," in *1980 Proceedings of the American Ethnological Society*, ed. Elizabeth H. Tooker (Washington: American Ethnological Society, 1984), p. 1.

6   Max Weber, *Economy and Society*, vol. 1, eds. G. Roth and C. Wittich (Berkeley: University of California Press, 1978), pp. 22–3.

7   In some societies, teknonyms are constructed differently, for example, through modification of the child's name. See Geoffrey Benjamin, "Temiar Personal Names," *Bijdragen tot de Taal-, Land- en Volkenkunde* 124 (1968): 99–134.

8   Ernest Crawley with Thedore Besterman, *The Mystic Rose: A Study of Primitive Marriage and of Primitive Thought in its Bearing on Marriage*, vol. 2 (London: Methuen, 1927), pp. 189–91; Robert H. Lowie, *Primitive Society* (London: George Routledge and Sons Ltd, 1921), p. 102; and W.G. Sumner, and A.G. Keller, *The Science of Society*, vol. 3 (New Haven: Yale University Press, 1929), p. 1899.

9   Richard D. Alford, *Naming and Identity: A Cross-Cultural Study of Personal Naming Practices* (New Haven: HRAF Press, 1988), pp. 90–1, 180–3.

10   In Borneo, grandparental teknonyms are used at least by the Land Dayaks, Punan Bah, Ot Danum, Meratus, Ma'anyan, and Bentian, and other Luangans. See Geddes, *The Land Dayaks of Sarawak*; Ida Nicolaisen, "Ancestral Names and Government Names: Assessing Self and Social Identity among the Punan Bah of Central Borneo," *KVHAA Konferenser* 42 (1998): 361–82; Pascal Couderc, personal communication, 2006; Tsing, *In the Realm of the Diamond Queen*; Alfred Hudson and Judith Hudson, "The Ma'anyan of Paju Epat," in *Essays on Borneo Societies*, ed. Victor T. King (Oxford: Hull Monographs on South-East Asia, Oxford University Press, 1978); and my fieldwork data). Outside Borneo, they are found, for example, in Seram, Bali, Sumbawa, and northern Thailand (Roy Ellen, "Semantic Anarchy and Ordered Social Practice in Nuaulu Personal Naming," *Bijdragen tot de Taal-, Land- en Volkenkunde* 139, 1 (1983): 18–45; Geertz and Geertz, "Teknonymy in Bali;" Jeffrey D. Brewer, "Bimanese Personal Names: Meaning and Use," *Ethnology* 20, 3 (1981): 203–15; and Rajah, this volume).

11   The Benuaq Dayak equivalents of *Ma* and *Nen*, *Tamen* and *Tinen*, are also occasionally employed, especially by Bentians living near the Benuaq area.

12   Tsing, *In the Realm of the Diamond Queen*, p. xiii.

13   In Bali, teknonymy additionally results in a fourth social organizational layer (corresponding to the great-grandparents) designated by the Geertzes as "senile dependants." See Geertz and Geertz, "Teknonymy in Bali," p. 97; cf. Geddes, *The Land Dayaks of Sarawak*, p. 15; Brewer, "Bimanese Personal Names," p. 212.

14   Adopted and biological children have a similar status in Bentian society, and unlike in Penan society, the same type of teknonyms is used for both. See Needham, "The System of Teknonyms," p. 416.

15   Antoun, "On the Significance of Names."

16   I am indebted to Joel Kuipers (personal communication, 2006) for suggesting this term.

17   This may reflect the fact that very old people, and especially grandmothers, have relatively unimportant public roles. See Antoun, "On the Significance of Names," p. 166, where he explained the fact that rural Jordanian women do not generally have nicknames (or teknonyms) with the same argument.

18   The Bentian process of coining pseudo-teknonyms resembles Ilongot practices of devising personal names. And like these Ilongot practices, the Bentian process "uses techniques of semantic association and phonological alteration" found in various linguistic contexts among both people and elsewhere in the region. See Renato Rosaldo, "Ilongot Naming: The Play of Associations," in *1980 Proceedings of the American Ethnological Society*, ed. Elizabeth H. Tooker (Washington: American Ethnological Society, 1984b), pp. 16–9.

19   Here my information may not be representative for all Bentians. It may reflect the fact that I did fieldwork predominantly in upriver, non-Christian (Kaharingan) communities.

20 As among the Ilongot, name uniqueness is "a regularity more empirical than normative," and partly reflects the same consideration that Rosaldo suggests ("Ilongot Naming," pp. 14–5): fear of invoking the spirits of the dead through reference to living namesakes or, more to the point in the Bentian case, fear of becoming tainted by death. An example of this is the event when a young Bentian man (Dula) climbing a honey tree fell to his death, and his namesakes in other villages quickly took new names.

21 Nicolaisen, "Ancestral Names," pp. 367–71.

22 Name change is not always consistent, however. People often continue using the old names. This was the case, for example, with a seriously ill woman who during a curing ritual was given the name Darma — a "politically" motivated name expressing affiliation with the Hindu Kaharingan religion, which was an important issue discussed during the ritual. For an analysis of this ritual, see Isabell Herrmans, "Representing Unpredictability: An Analysis of a Curing Ritual among the East Kalimantan Luangan," *Journal of Ritual Studies* 18, 1 (2004): 50–61. This name did not become widely accepted; most people continued using her old name, Resa.

23 However, if a child's autonym is changed during a ritual, then its parents' teknonyms will also change as part of the effort to avoid the old, inauspicious name.

24 Clifford Geertz, *The Interpretation of Cultures* (New York: Basic Books, 1973), p. 370.

25 Edward Tylor, "On a Method of Investigating the Development of Institutions; Applied to Laws of Marriage and Descent," *Journal of the Royal Anthropological Institute of Great Britain and Ireland* 18 (1889): pp. 248–50.

26 G. A. Wilken, *Handleiding voor de Vergelijkende Volkenkunde van Nederlandsch-Indie* (Leiden: Brill, 1893), pp. 212–9.

27 S. R. Steinmetz, *Ethnologische Studien zur Ersten Entwicklung der Strafe*, vol. 2 (Leiden and Leipzig: Van Doesburgh, 1894), pp. 239–42.

28 Nathan Miller, "Some Aspects of the Name in Culture-History," *American Journal of Sociology* 32, 4 (1927): pp. 598–9.

29 In these respects, Crawley notably saw teknonymy as analogous to the *couvade* (*The Mystic Rose*, pp. 188–202), while Wilken saw it as analogous to this practice in that both served to assert paternity (*Handleiding*, p. 212).

30 Lowie, *Primitive Society*, pp. 102–4.

31 Steinmetz, *Ethnologische Studien*, p. 240; Crawley, *The Mystic Rose*, pp. 190–1.

32 Steinmetz, *Ethnologische Studien*, p. 240; Elsie Clews Parsons, "Teknonymy," *American Journal of Sociology* 19, 5 (1914): 649.

33 Ibid.

34 Sumner and Keller, *The Science of Society*, p. 1899.

35 Crawley, *The Mystic Rose*, p. 192.

36 Charles, "Drama in First-Naming Ceremonies," p. 28.

37 Lévi-Strauss, *The Savage Mind*, pp. 194–5.

38   Hudson and Hudson, "The Ma'anyan of Paju Epat," p. 218.

39   Geertz and Geertz, "Teknonymy in Bali," p. 94.

40   Geertz, *The Interpretation of Cultures*, pp. 377, 379.

41   Alford, *Naming and Identity*, pp. 93–5.

42   Parsons, "Teknonymy;" Elsie Clews Parsons, "Avoidance in Melanesia," *Journal of American Folklore* 29 (1916).

43   Parsons, "Teknonymy," p. 650. Rivers also noted an "evident connection between this practice and the avoidance of names of relatives," See W.H.R. Rivers, *The History of Melanesian Society*, vol. 2 (Cambridge: Cambridge University Press, 1914), p. 336, and Tylor, too, can be credited for emphasizing a connection between avoidance and teknonymy, even though he tried to explain the institution too restrictively with reference to the son-in-law. See his "On a Method of Investigating," p. 189.

44   A.R. Radcliffe-Brown, "On Joking Relationships," *Africa* 13, 3 (1940): 198.

45   Ibid., pp. 196–7.

46   Relations between the generations are perhaps less likely to result in conflict (or were, at least, until recently), but this reflects the highly asymmetrical character of authority exercised in these relations, and the fact that special support of this kind helps maintain this authority, which is vital for the reproduction of the social order.

47   An instructive example of how the Bentian differ from their closely related neighbors in this respect is that they address their same-generation affines with the kinship terms *ayu* and *ongan*, and are prohibited from using their autonyms, while their neighbors typically address these relatives by the second personal pronoun (*ko*), and are less strictly prohibited from using their autonyms. This was suggested to me as an instance of the Bentian's greater propensity to use roundabout (*mengkelotes*) or refined (*halus*) as opposed to direct (*kentes*) or coarse (*kasar*) language.

48   Radcliffe-Brown, "On Joking Relationships," p. 196.

49   Rosaldo, *Ilongot Headhunting 1883–1974*, p. 12. Anyone familiar with Swedish society understands what significant bearing on the general climate of interaction that the far-reaching substitution of the formal and honorific second person pronoun *ni* by its informal counterpart *du* has had. This change in address has contributed significantly to the dehierarchization of Scandinavian society, as well as to what Orvar Löfgren called the "informalization of Sweden." See Orvar Löfgren, ed. *Hej, det är från Försäkringskassan: Informaliseringen av Sverige* (Stockholm: Natur och kultur, 1988).

50   Parsons, "Teknonymy," p. 650; Parsons, "Avoidance in Melanesia," p. 290.

51   Pseudo-teknonyms are status terms too although not derived from descendants or denoting parent- or grandparenthood. They still invoke these statuses, and, more primarily, adult and elder status.

52   Parsons, "Teknonymy," p. 650.

53   Parsons, "Avoidance in Melanesia," p. 290.

[54] Alford, *Naming and Identity*, pp. 92–3. This is true mainly in address. In reference, however, teknonyms identify people more neutrally without invoking social obligations. This shows that kinship terms and teknonyms are not identical, and indicates that they may perform different functions in address and reference.

[55] See Kenneth Sillander, *Acting Authoritatively: How Authority is Expressed among the Bentian of Indonesian Borneo.* (PhD diss., Helsinki: Swedish School of Social Science Publications No. 17, University of Helsinki Press, 2004), pp. 109–64.

[56] Needham defined this solidarity in terms of "reciprocal dependence, the common recognition of a moral duty to help each other, and the consciousness of being at one in interests, sympathies, and values." See Rodney Needham, "Mourning-Terms," *Bijdragen tot de Taal, Land- en Volkenkunde* 115, 1 (1959): 80. He also argued that the abandonment of death-names "marks the disintegration of the solidary character of the traditional Penan group," and that "the social significance of the statuses defined by the relationship terms and the congruent death-names is ... diminished" as a result of integration of the Penan in a "wider range of social life," developments which are paralleled by analogous ones affecting solidarity and teknonymy among the Bentian. See Rodney Needham, "Death-names and Solidarity in Penan Society," *Bijdragen tot de Taal, Land- en Volkenkunde* 121, 1 (1965): 72.

[57] Geddes, *The Land Dayaks of Sarawak*, p. 16.

[58] Nicolaisen, *Ancestral Names*, p. 376.

[59] Robert McKinley, "Cain and Abel on the Malay Peninsula," in *Siblingship in Oceania: Studies in the Meaning of Kin Relations*, ed. Mac Marshall (Lanham: University Press of America, 1983), pp. 355–6.

[60] Sillander, *Acting Authoritatively*, pp. 148–51, 270–1.

[61] In this respect, the Bentian resemble the Punan Bah among whom the use of kinship terms is seen "not simply as an expression of a harmonious world, but as the very means by which such a world is maintained" (Nicolaisen, *Ancestral Names*, pp. 376–7). To continue comparing teknonymy with kinship, it may be noted that what is above all expected of Bentians with parental and grandparental teknonyms, and kinship terms on the same levels, is mature, socially responsible behavior (and from younger people addressing them, respect). Indeed, teknonymy is a means by which an ideal notion of adulthood is prescribed. Like kinship, in McKinley's characterization, it may be likened to a "philosophy ... about what completes a person socially, psychologically, and morally, and how that completeness comes about through a responsible sense of attachment and obligation to others." See Robert McKinley, "The Philosophy of Kinship: A Reply to Schneider's Critique of the Study of Kinship," in *The Cultural Analysis of Kinship: The Legacy of David M. Schneider*, eds. Richard Feinberg and Martin Ottenheimer (Urbana: University of Illinois Press, 2001), p. 143.

[62] Parsons, "Avoidance in Melanesia," p. 285.

63   Benjamin, "Temiar Personal Names," p. 127.

64   Ibid., p. 126.

65   The Ilongots motivate autonym avoidance similarly. They "avoid the names of their in-laws in order to show respect by not shaming or commanding them" (Rosaldo, "Ilongot Naming," p. 19).

66   Autonyms are of course not disrespectful in all societies. They seem to be thus perceived particularly in societies having what Macdonald (this volume) calls "paradigmatic naming systems."

67   Geertz and Geertz, "Teknonymy in Bali," p. 94.

68   Geertz, *The Interpretation of Cultures*, p. 377.

69   Cf. Benjamin, "Temiar Personal Names," p. 111.

70   Intrigued by teknonymy's quality of defining people through relationships, observers have paid little attention to its individuating function. Making people like-named and defining them all through their descendants is "rarely a distinctive way of labeling an otherwise notable individual" (Kuipers, this volume). However, unlike in Sumba, where there is a limited stock of autonyms, Bentian teknonyms adequately function to discriminate individuals, and they are used to label prominent and charismatic individuals. Although they are not particularly charismatic labels, unlike pseudo-teknonyms which have a special capacity to designate personal identity in a distinctive way (Kuipers, personal communication, 2006), they are no less charismatic than the autonyms which they replace and whose individuating capacity they retain. Teknonymy also only superficially, or nominally, "subordinates the identity of the owner of the name to that of the child" (Kuipers, this volume). The fact that it ascribes a certain generalized status to people does not deprive them of individuality.

71   A.R. Radcliffe-Brown, *The Andaman Islanders* (New York: The Free Press, 1964), pp. 284–5.

72   Benjamin, "Temiar Personal Names," p. 125.

73   Geertz, "'From the Native's Point of View'", p. 63.

74   Joseph Weinstock, "Kaharingan and the Luangan Dayaks: Religion and Identity in Central East Borneo" (Ph.D. diss., Cornell University, 1983), p. 117.

75   The same is true for the related ideal of economic self-sufficiency which is also not an acknowledged value, but nevertheless a universal desire and an incentive for some to look down on others.

76   Needham, "Mourning-Terms," pp. 86–7.

77   George Peter Murdock, *Social Structure* (New York: The MacMillan Company, 1949), p. 97.

78   Geertz and Geertz, "Teknonymy in Bali." Although older people's autonyms are rarely expressed in interaction, many opportunities to obtain knowledge about them exist. Genealogies are also often memorized (possibly more than in the past, because of increasingly pressing land right issues), and it is possible to state ascendants' names in private in the absence of the affected persons. Writing also provides a way around the problem: it is not prohibited to write

down names. Autonyms are also widely used in government records without meeting from local resistance. As this shows, supernatural sanctions are not the principal motivation for name-avoidance; prohibitions are not absolute but contextual. Furthermore, although teknonyms rather than autonyms are typically used of ancestors, it is not too problematical to find about who was related to whom and how. Thus, the Geertzes' notion of genealogical amnesia is not really applicable to the Bentian. One reason for this may be that there is no absolute need for it; maintenance of the social structure does not require it as it supposedly does in Bali.

[79] However, kinship terms are less often used for high-ranking leaders than other people (at least by people not closely related to them), suggesting that the importance of rank correlates negatively with that of kinship in Borneo. See Victor T. King, "Introduction," in *Essays on Borneo Societies*, ed. Victor T. King (Oxford: Hull Monographs on South-East Asia, Oxford University Press, 1978), pp. 11–2; Jérôme Rousseau, "The Kayan," in *Essays on Borneo Societies*, ed. Victor T. King (Oxford: Hull Monographs on South-East Asia, Oxford University Press, 1978), p. 88.

[80] Sillander, "Acting Authoritatively," pp. 155, 264, 326. For example, the one pseudo-teknonym, of several tried out, that stuck in my case was Kakah Komkom (that is, "Grandfather Komkom"), a designation derived from a puppy that I befriended, and often called on with the Swedish words *kom, kom* "come, come," as a result of which first the dog, and then I, became known by it. The interesting, and for me slightly disturbing, fact that I was then in my early thirties, but through this usage became addressed as "grandfather," which testifies to the flexibility of Bentian naming, and to the tendency to devise contextually relevant and amusing labels. I believe this designation was considered appropriate because it was superficially respectful by attributing age-associated status to me while simultaneously connoting my marginal and somewhat puzzling role in society — lacking children, social responsibilities, and not engaging in productive work — a role which my special relationship with this dog symbolically expressed.

[81] Antoun, "On the Significance of Names," p. 166.

[82] For a similar example, see Tsing, *In the Realm of the Diamond Queen*, p. xiii.

[83] Nancy C. Dorian, "A Substitute Name System in the Scottish Highlands," *American Anthropologist* 72 (1970): pp. 303, 305.

[84] Antoun, "On the Significance of Names," p. 169.

[85] Brewer, "Bimanese Personal Names," pp. 213–4.

[86] However, as long as conditions like an egalitarian ethos, socio-centrism, respect for elders and affines, and smallness of speech community continue to prevail in the local setting, teknonymy might well continue to be practised, even if autonyms become more extensively employed in contacts with outsiders. Just like people are capable of keeping apart different registers of speech, they are capable of consistently using different types of names in different settings as Macdonald has shown for the Palawan among whom a

government-enforced binominal naming system has been comprehensively adopted for legal identification, without replacing the indigenous naming system in internal identification. See Charles Macdonald, "Personal Names as an Index of National Integration: Local Naming Practices and State-produced Legal Identities," *Pilipinas* 42 (March 2004).

[87]   Geertz and Geertz, "Teknonymy in Bali," p. 104.

[88]   Ibid., p. 105.

[89]   Alford, *Naming and Identity*, pp. 93–5.

[90]   Among other things, the Bentian naming system shares with Macdonald's paradigmatic naming system: similar restrictions on autonym use, a number of alternative name tags used only one at a time, an "open and productive repertoire" of name tags, a "contextual definition of personhood," and an egalitarian ethos.

[91]   J. Eder, "Naming Practices and the Definition of Affines among the Batak of the Philippines," *Ethnology* 14, 1 (1975); Rosaldo, *Ilongot Headhunting 1883–1974*; and Uhlenbeck, E.M., "Systematic Features of Javanese Personal Names," *Word* 25, 3 (1969).

CHAPTER 6

The Karen Naming System: Identity and Sociocultural Orientations[1]

Ananda Rajah

Introduction

The Karen is an ethno-linguistic group found in Thailand and Burma. They have been estimated to number 240,000 in Thailand and perhaps up to 2.4 million in Burma.[2] Karen studies, in their most general sense — ethnological, anthropological, historical, and plainly descriptive — have a long history, but to the best of my knowledge, there has been no systematic effort to describe Karen naming systems and explain the cultural logic(s) of their naming systems. This essay is an attempt at filling this gap in Karen studies.

This essay examines the naming system of the Palokhi Karen, a small Sgaw Karen community located approximately 90 kilometers northwest of Chiang Mai city in northern Thailand. The cultural significance of their naming system, in which teknonymy is an important feature, cannot be fully understood without consideration of other aspects of Palokhi Karen culture, that is, sex and gender differentiation, kinship terminology, religion, and the subsistence system. The essay sets out some of these complex relations with a focus on sex and gender differentiation, relevant kin terms, and only briefly, with regard to Palokhi Karen religious and subsistence systems. The analysis is sociological in intent: an understanding of the naming and related systems of the Palokhi Karen in terms of socio-cultural orientations and, by implication and extension, societal types.

A Brief Comparison: Burma and Thailand

In mainland Southeast Asia, the Karen in Burma represent perhaps the greatest success story in terms of Protestant Christian conversion and demographic numbers, although Karen acceptance of Buddhism (which has greater historical depth) has probably involved far more Karen people as well as a change in ethnicity from Karen to Mon and Burman. The spread of the idea of the nation-state, on the other hand, resulted in a highly intransigent Karen separatist movement whose leaders are mostly Christian. Historically, Christianity played no small part in the emergence of Karen nationalism.[3]

Christian conversion has had some consequence for the Karen naming system in Burma (and also in Thailand), but this has been very gradual, considering that Christianity in its Baptist form first took root in Burma in the 1830s. The situation varies depending on where Christian Karen are found in Burma. Field research in Burma has not been possible, but visits to Karen (and Karenni) refugee camps in Thailand suggest that many more Christian Karen have Karen (language)-based names than English (that is, Christian) names.[4] Teknonymy is practised, but it is my impression that this is generally confined to Christian Karen from hill-tract villages and small townships. There can be little doubt that Christian Karen in these camps, however they are named, are committed Christians, and their Christianity is not some syncretized version of Christianity and animism. This suggests a degree of tenacity in the Karen naming system.

It should be noted, however, that among more "Western"-oriented Karen (by whom I mean those fluent or near fluent in English), Karen-language autonyms are not necessarily based on events but on euphony and what parents consider to be exemplary qualities. It does not take a great stretch of the sociological imagination to understand that the conferment of names in this way represents what is wished for as attributes in infants and in their subsequent adult lives. It is also, of course, a considerable departure from the system of event-based names of the kind found in Palokhi, which I shall later examine in detail. Among nationalist Karen, there is an important example that helps to illustrate the complex relationships between the Karen naming system, religious and political change, changes in socio-cultural orientations, and the kinds of analytical challenge they pose.

Until he retired or was "eased out" of the KNU and KNLA in 2002, General Saw Bo Mya was President of the separatist Karen National Union and Commander-in-Chief of the Karen National Liberation Army.

Bo Mya, a Sgaw Karen who speaks Burmese but very little English, came from an animist community in lower Burma, served in the British colonial constabulary, and later in Force 136 under the overall command of Orde Wingate (of "Chindit" fame) during the Second World War. He was a late convert to Seventh-Day Adventist Christianity, by which time he had established himself as the foremost Karen resistance leader. He did not assume an English or Christian baptismal name. Also in this time, he had several children and many grandchildren, but to this day Bo Mya goes by this name and has never been known teknonymously, except possibly within his immediate family.

Saw is the honorific in Sgaw Karen derived from the notion of elder brother and is used among urbanized Karen, both Christian and Buddhist.[5] Bo Mya, on the other hand, was a self-applied name replacing his birth name when he came to see himself playing a Karen nationalist role after the Second World War. *Bo* comes from Burmese and the same term served to designate, for example, General Aung San and the *thakin* "masters," the anti-British Burman nationalist leaders described as the "Thirty Comrades." In its pre-modern sense, *bo* meant something like "military leader." Mya (*mya*) on the other hand is a Sgaw Karen term meaning "fierce."

Bo Mya (and he is not the only one) "embodies" — obviously in a metaphorical sense — the coming together of the historical spread of a monotheistic religion and the idea of the nation-state among Burma Karen. The retention of his self-given name may well be explained by the fact that many adult Karen converts from hill-tract areas and townships follow the practice as a matter of general preference despite conversion. This is also the case with Karen adult converts in Thailand. The preference has to do with the retention of embedded individual and social identities within the local community.

In Bo Mya's case, however, a further name change upon conversion would have had far greater consequences. At the time of his conversion, he had already acquired iconic status as a military commander and Karen nationalist leader. His name, Saw Bo Mya, in other words was co-identified with the Karen struggle for independence and the Karen quasi-nation-state, Kawthoolei, as it is officially called. Many Karen villagers who had never seen Bo Mya in person were nevertheless familiar with his name and image through the distribution of calendars, propaganda posters, and photographs in village schools (see Plate 1, General Saw Bo Mya, 1981).

The assumption of an English or Christian baptismal name would have destroyed that iconic co-identification. And what would KNLA

Plate 1

sub-unit commanders in their dispersed bases of operations in the forests of eastern Burma have made of directives and orders from General Headquarters previously signed off by "General Saw Bo Mya" and then replaced by "General Saw Peter" or "General Saw Paul"? I do not know whether the avoidance of a publicly declared baptismal name was arrived at intuitively or through reflexive deliberation. The avoidance, however, is not difficult to understand in the larger socio-political context of the Karen quasi-nation-state which once had a palpable autonomy.[6] Given his role in the Karen insurgent movement, Bo Mya's name and identity had a far greater significance than that of the individual and personal. The significance is intimately linked to the idea of a Karen nation-state and attempts by the KNU and KNLA to establish such a state. In these circumstances, a change in name would have required consideration of its impact on that "imagined community," the Karen nation.

This contrasts sharply with conditions in Palokhi. In supra-local political and administrative terms, the Palokhi Karen are undoubtedly part of the modern Thai state, at least in formal institutional terms as the modern Thai state would "see" it, although contacts with Thai district officials are irregular. They are also part of an economic network that stretches from the Chiang Mai plains into the highlands. This network includes exchanges with other ethnic hill minority peoples such as the Lisu, as well as northern Thai peasants who have migrated upland. The Thai state does not loom large in their consciousness. Their orientation is primarily focused on their subsistence system, which includes swidden cultivation and wet-rice cultivation in micro-terraces, the latter system being adopted from the northern Thai. Their religious system is an animist one. Despite their contacts with Thai officials, participation in an extensive network of economic exchanges (the intensity of which varies seasonally), and adoption of wet-rice cultivation, they are fundamentally "subsistence oriented."[7] By this, I mean a clear attachment to place or locale upon which their subsistence depends. Yet, the Palokhi Karen naming system indicates an"openness" toward the outside world.

The Naming System in Palokhi

The essential feature of the naming system in Palokhi is a fortuitous event which occurs in the village and which usually (though not always) concerns the conjugal family or stem family if one or both of the parents of the wife are still alive at, or close to, the time a newborn infant is given its name. This generally takes place around the time when the stub of the baby's umbilical cord drops off after it has been ligatured at birth.[8] The events are drawn upon in a variety of ways to form the names of children.

Autonyms: Event Names

Autonyms, in Palokhi, may well be regarded as "event" names. The names parents give to their children on the basis of such events may be nouns, adjectives or verbs, or compounds of these. For example, the name Mi' Zo is a compound of the Thai word *miit*, "knife," (not a loan word) and *zo*, the Karen word for Northern Thai and Shan or, as David Marlowe suggests, for all Tai speakers.[9] This name was given to a boy when some Northern Thai came to Palokhi and asked the boy's father, the blacksmith-cum-gunsmith in the village, to repair some bush knives. Another name, Khae' By, is a compound of two terms. *Khae'* is a loan word from the Thai *khaek* ("stranger," "guest," "foreigner"), which the Karen use ethnonymic-ally to designate non-Karen and non-Thai, as in *Khae' Lisau* (the Lisu) and *Khae' Hau* (Haw or Yunnanese Chinese). *By*, on the other hand, is the generic term in Karen for rice. This name was given to a girl because some Lisu from a distant village had come to buy rice in Palokhi.[10] A further example is Ty We, where *ty* means "to arrive" and *we* means "town" (derived from the Northern Thai *wiang*, whose original pre-modern meaning was "fortified city" or "walled city"). This name was given to a girl when her father was accidentally shot by his eldest son and had to be sent to Chiang Mai for medical treatment. I hasten to add that not all Palokhi Karen names are based on events that relate to the outside world or people outside the community. The point about these examples is that the naming system acknowledges the existence of the outside world and interactions with that world, the significance of which I shall discuss later.

While these examples serve to describe the essential aspects of the naming of individuals, there is more to the way in which the naming system operates in Palokhi. Most Palokhi Karen retain the names given to them in childhood until they become parents, after which they are known teknonymously. Nevertheless, it sometimes happens that individuals have more than one name bestowed upon them by grandparents, siblings, or age-mates on the basis of some personal idiosyncrasy or other. These names are more in the nature of nicknames and they generally do not replace the names given to them at birth. Names may, however, be changed for specific reasons such as prolonged illness. For instance, a girl by the name of Ti Ka was sick for several months and when her parents consulted a ritual specialist, he said that apart from his ritual ministrations, her successful recovery would also depend on changing her name to a new one. Her parents renamed her Mi Sau meaning, literally, "new name."[11]

What is important in the Palokhi naming system is that the names — and the social identities they represent — are formed on the basis of events that are *unique* or non-replicable; thus, the proper names created from such events are themselves also unique. In a discussion of the social significance of naming systems in *The Savage Mind*, Claude Lévi-Strauss pointed out that proper names, or autonyms, possess an individuating function and also imply a distinction between "self" and "other."[12] The discussion is instructive and the distinction is wholly appropriate in approaching the significance of the relationship between the naming system and certain kin terms in Palokhi.

In the Palokhi naming system, this individuating function of autonyms and the "self-other" distinction is carried to the extreme. The autonyms are not drawn from a common pool of names available to all members of the society but, on the contrary, are formed from unique events. The "self-other" distinction and the distinctiveness of individual social identities in Palokhi are, therefore, highlighted by the very uniqueness of all autonyms, which, incidentally, accords with a high degree of personal or individual autonomy in Palokhi, extending even to children (see Plate 2,

Plate 2

Pha Dek Chaj and Pha Saw Di Enjoying a Cheroot). It also suggests a
reason for the practice of naming children when the stub of the umbilical
cord drops off: children are given names only when the last vestige of
their connection with their mothers is lost, and hence acquire a persona
separate from that of their mothers.

Name-giving

In Palokhi, name-giving is not accompanied by ritual or ceremony, nor
does it involve designated name-givers of any special status. The occasion
(if such it may be called) for name-giving happens, as noted above, after
the stub of the infant's umbilical cord falls off. As may be expected, when
this occurs it is known to members of the immediate family, especially to
the mother who has more frequent and intimate contact with the infant.
Fathers are not ignorant of this either, for they too are much involved in
carrying babies and washing their bottoms, while elder siblings also carry
the infant. When the stub of the umbilical cord has dropped off, the
event is noted and remarked upon in everyday conversation.

Name-giving occurs through what we might call everyday communicative function with the infant. Someone (it could be the mother,
father, or an elder sibling) in the family, cuddling or rocking the infant,
"speaking" to the infant, may refer to an event, in repetitive or sing-song
manner, to attract the infant's attention or to entertain the infant. This
is recognizable as play behavior. If others are around, they may then join
in the refrain. In this way, the name "takes" or "adheres" to the infant.
There is no conscious intentionality or deliberation in the name-giving
process. This system of naming and name-giving is deeply embedded in
socio-cultural praxis, such that no reflexive thought is given to the process
of name-giving.

Relinquishing Autonyms: The Conjunctiveness of Spouse Relations

There are two instances when autonyms are relinquished in Palokhi. The
first is when a man and woman marry, and commence using the term
ma (spouse). The term is not sex or gender differentiated, and is used in
address and reference by both husband and wife. The second is the advent
of parenthood, when teknonymy is used. There is an important difference
between the two. In the first case, although a married couple does not
use autonyms, they are nevertheless known by their autonyms as far as
others are concerned. In the second case, teknonyms replace the autonyms
by which they are known to others. These two cases should, therefore, be
examined separately.

If autonyms and their use stress the distinctiveness of individual
identities — the "self-other" distinction — then the abrogation of the
use of autonyms upon marriage by husband and wife must be seen to
stress the opposite relation, namely, a downplaying of such a distinction
between spouses, as opposed to others who, nevertheless, continue to use
their autonyms. In other words, the relinquishment of personal names in
favor of spouse terms marks the conjunctiveness of spouse relations and
the conjugal bond as against all other relations.

Teknonymy

We can now turn to the question of teknonymy in Palokhi. Lévi-Strauss
has observed that whereas autonyms stress the individuality of persons,
teknonyms and necronyms, on the other hand, are "relational" terms
where the definition of self is derived from another whose autonym forms
the teknonym whereas necronyms effect this definition negatively since
the names of the dead are never mentioned.[13] Teknonymy in Palokhi is

no different. The relations expressed in teknonyms are links of affiliation that are evident in teknonyms such as De' Chaj Pa (Father of De' Chaj) and De' Chaj Mo (Mother of De' Chaj). In Palokhi, however, teknonymy is extended into the second ascending generation as well (on a matrilateral basis because of uxorilocal residence at marriage), so that the parents of De' Chaj's mother would be known, after the birth of De' Chaj, as De' Chaj Phy (Grandfather of De' Chaj) and De' Chaj Phi (Grandmother of De' Chaj).[14] The point of reference in the system of teknonymy in Palokhi is, therefore, the eldest surviving child in the last descending generation.

Although the Palokhi Karen kinship system is a cognatic one, in pragmatic relational terms, the use of *phy* and *phi* is matrilaterally oriented because of the custom of uxorilocal marriage.

In Palokhi, necronymy does not exist, so that unlike the Penan system that Lévi-Strauss discusses, and which he describes as possessing three types of "periodicity" (necronym → necronym, autonym → necronym, teknonym → necronym), the Palokhi system possesses only a single "periodicity": autonym → teknonym. Lévi-Strauss has proposed that in systems characterized by these three types of periodicity, "teknonymy and necronymy are a single problem and amenable to one and the same solution." More contentiously, Lévi-Strauss has also proposed that as far as teknonymy is concerned, "the reason why parents may no longer be called by their name when a child is born is that they are "dead" and that procreation is conceived not as the *addition* of a new being to those who already exist but as the substitution of the one for the others" (emphasis added).[15] This was strongly criticized by Rodney Needham (see also the discussion by Barnes in this volume).[16] In a system such as that in Palokhi where teknonymy but not necronymy exists, the significance of teknonymy is in fact otherwise (see also Sillander, this volume). Parents revert to the system of reference and address employed prior to the birth of their first child if the child dies, and hence "avoid" the "negative" definition of "self" through necronymy.

Moreover, if there is more than one child, the death of the eldest child does not mean the end of teknonymy; teknonymy then becomes based on the autonym of the next child. Furthermore, when there are three generations, the autonyms appropriated from the second generation to define the first generation teknonymously become replaced by autonyms appropriated from the third generation.

Teknonymy in Palokhi, therefore, stresses the positive definition of self in which procreation is conceived as the addition of a new being to those who already exist. The relational nature of teknonymy in Palokhi thus emphasizes *continuity* of filiative links as part of an ideology that treats the conjugal bond as a reproductive union within the "continuous flux of generations."[17] It is possible to analyze Palokhi teknonyms more generally, in the sense of "name type" and the "Class A" naming systems discussed by Macdonald (this volume). As with the Palawan referred to by Macdonald, and the Bentian (Sillander, this volume), social relations in Palokhi are markedly egalitarian with a high degree of individual autonomy that extends even to children, as noted before. There is no rigid pecking order, so to speak. Palokhi teknonyms constitute friendly and respectful forms of address and reference. Insofar as role situations are concerned, the use of teknonyms reflects egalitarian, congenial forms of consociation within the community. Within such role situations, teknonyms, however, also reflect differentiated status, that is, those who have attained adult reproductive status as against those who have not and who, therefore, are addressed and referred to by their autonyms.

Sex and Gender Differentiation

There is another feature of the naming system that is worth noting, that is, sex and gender differentiation apart from an egalitarian ethos in social relations, the recognition of generational distinctions, and the attainment of adult, reproductive statuses, noted above. Within the category "human beings," the Palokhi Karen make a general distinction between males and females in the following way: *phau'khwa* (male) versus *phau'my* (female). Unmarried males are referred to as *phau'khwa* and unmarried females as *mykoe'nau*. Married males are known as *phaukhwapgha* and married females as *phau'mypgha*.

As we have seen, autonyms or "event names" in Palokhi do not, in themselves, contain any distinction between sex or gender because they are made up of simple verbs, adjectives, or nouns. However, when they are used with respect to individuals, they are usually preceded by articles that specify sex and gender in address or reference according to context. These articles are *pha*, for males, and *nau* for females. *Pha* and *nau* do not function as honorifics; their function is to indicate the gender of the person bearing a particular autonym.

Very generally, these terms are used together with autonyms when ego is addressing or when referring to another person who is older than, or is an age-mate of, ego. Age-mates of the same gender who are on intimate terms may, however, drop the gender term in direct speech if they are speaking to the person concerned, or if they are referring to the person when speaking with other age-mates. The gender term is, however, usually retained if ego is referring to an age-mate, notwithstanding the closeness of the relationship, if ego is speaking to an older person.

On the other hand, these gender terms are retained if ego is referring to a person who is either older than ego or an age-mate, when ego is speaking to someone younger. If, however, the person referred to is younger than ego but is of the same age as the person spoken to, or younger, then the gender term may be dropped. The reason why relative age is a factor in these usages is that wide disparities in the ages of individuals within any particular generation are not uncommon.

Gender differentiation also exists in the case of teknonyms where the kin terms *pa* (father), *mo* (mother), *phy* (father's father, mother's father) and *phi* (father's mother, mother's mother) are prefixed to the autonyms of eldest children. These kin terms are, in themselves, gender differentiated. Teknonyms are not merely relational terms; they also identify the gender of the person bearing a particular teknonym. At the same time, they distinguish between generations by virtue of the fact that the kin terms express generational relationships.

It may be noted here that tracing generational relationships depends on the availability of relevant genealogical information and the social field of the individuals concerned. In Palokhi, the necessary information is wholly available because the community is small. This is not necessarily the case when the Palokhi Karen deal with Karen from other villages in the area because local knowledge then tends to be less than complete. In such circumstances, general kin terms such as *phati* (father's brother, mother's brother), *mygha* (father's sister, mother's sister), *phy* and *phi* would be used in address and reference. This is not an unusual feature of Southeast Asian cognatic systems. As terms of reference, they are of course extremely vague and other information would then be necessary if there is a need for precision in referring to the person concerned.

The core features of the naming system in relation to gender differentiation and generational distinctions are set out in Table 1.

Table 1 Gender Differentiation, Generational Distinctions and the Naming System

	Human Male *(phau'khwa)*		Human Female *(phau'my)*	
Unmarried	*phau'khwa*	*Pha* + autonym	*mykoe'nau*	*nau* + autonym
Married	*phau'khwa* + *pgha*	autonym of eldest child + *pa*	*phau'my* + *pgha*	autonym of eldest child + *mo*
		autonym of eldest grandchild + *phy*		autonym of eldest grandchild + *phi*

None of the pertinent oppositions *pha/nau, pa/mo, phy/phi, pau'kwha/ phau'my* displays markedness. The fact that gender differentiation is characterized by unmarked oppositions indicates that the male/female oppositions are non-hierarchical, since marked oppositions are hierarchical by nature. The various oppositions constitute an embedded system of social classification which recognizes the *complementarity* of males and females and a life-course progression of males and females from non-reproductive → reproductive → non-reproductive states of being.

Quite evidently, the naming system of the Palokhi Karen functions with other category systems: kin terms, gender differentiation, and generational differentiation. To understand the interdigitation of the naming system, specifically teknonymy, with these category systems, we need to consider a broader Palokhi Karen conceptual schema in their animist religion that links marriage with another aspect of male-female differentiation, and rice cultivation. In this sense, the naming system is embedded in other aspects of Palokhi Karen cultural ideology and praxis. On the other hand, the creation of autonyms (for example, based on events involving people and places outside Palokhi) also reflects an "openness" to economic relations existing in the highlands of northern Thailand, not to mention the adoption of methods of wet-rice cultivation from the northern Thai.

This requires an examination of other aspects of the Palokhi Karen ethnography which I shall summarize below in terms of "embedded-ness" and "openness." My use of these terms is intended as a typology of an analytically complex ethnographic situation. The presentation of this summary ethnography is also intended to provide additional, comparative ethnographic data to the ethnographic material on the Palawan and Bentian cases (see Macdonald and Sillander, this volume). My overall purpose in doing so, however, is to show *how* the naming system in Palokhi may be situated, analytically, in relation to Macdonald's ideal-type classifications of naming systems as set out in this volume, despite this ethnographic complexity, within a broadened ethnographic context and conceptual-theoretical framework. For this, it is necessary to mount an argument that takes into consideration how historically-constituted societal types may be conceptualized in a way that bridges ethnographic complexity and ideal-type classifications. This argument is presented in terms of socio-cultural orientations and indigeny and tribality after the following consideration of embedded-ness and openness.

Embedded-ness

As we have seen, the Palokhi Karen naming system and the use of associated kin terms place an emphasis on the union of males and females, their procreative roles, and links of filiation within the continuous flux of generations. This emphasis is also extended into the domain of rice cultivation. In the Palokhi Karen conceptual schema, intimately associated with religious ideas, rice is conceived of as female. This may be seen from the term for a ritual crop of rice, the *By Mo Phga*, "Old Mother Rice" (see note 2). Rice is grown from seed kept specifically for this purpose when a crop is harvested. The crop of rice symbolizes the entire rice crop that is planted in swiddens and is the focus of rituals that nurture the rice to ensure a successful harvest. When the ritual crop of rice is harvested, it becomes the focus of a "first fruits" ceremony conducted in the village.[18] Here we see, in rice cultivation, a concern with continuity of the rice crop that parallels the concern with generational continuity exemplified in the Palokhi Karen naming system, specifically the interdigitation of teknonymy, sex and gender differentiation, and as I have argued, the attainment of adult, reproductive statuses. The relationship between the *By Mo Pgha*, rice cultivation, and these aspects of the naming system hold together within what may be termed the cultural ideology of the Palokhi Karen.

A simple interpretation might see this conceptual association in Palokhi Karen thought as recognition of fertility embodied in femaleness or the necessity of females in biological reproduction. While this explanation should not be discounted, the explanatory weakness is that it does not explain *why* the (interpretive) notion of fertility or the necessity of females in human and animal reproduction (which the Palokhi Karen recognize no more and no less than that of males) should be extended to the domain of crop cultivation.

In "gender" terms, it is worth noting that *localities* in which the Karen live have tutelary spirits (generically known as *Thi Koe'ca, Kau Koe'ca*, the Lord of the Water, Lord of the Land) that are conceived of as male. The tutelary spirit is the focus of a great many agricultural rituals that are propitiatory in nature and are intended to ensure bountiful harvests and harmony in the village community. These agricultural rituals show a clear association between male and female in rice cultivation. It is worth noting that in the rituals, these conditions are referred to in ritual texts that are aoristic in form, which, again, demonstrate a concern with continuity.

When we also consider two other aspects of Palokhi Karen cultural practice, marriage and agricultural rituals, the matter acquires an even greater degree of complexity. The Palokhi Karen have marriage rules but these are by no means inflexible. In general, however, these rules prohibit (1) marriage between first cousins and second cousins and (2) intergenerational marriages between traceable consanguineal and affinal kin.

Plate 3

The rules are of interest in terms of the comparative analysis of Southeast Asian cognatic kinship systems, but these comparative issues need not detain us here. Where the present analysis is concerned, what is significant are the *consequences* of transgressing the rules that relate marriage (the union of males and females) to rice cultivation. The transgressions are said to result in *kau takho* (the land heating up) and *by haghau* (the rice will be destroyed). These religious beliefs are, in short, part of a cultural ideology.

In crop cultivation, a ritual accompanies the first planting of rice seed after swiddens have been cleared. It is simply called *lyta thi toe* ("rite of the water container"; see Plate 3).

There is no Palokhi Karen exegesis for this rite other than the claim that "this should be done" and that "we have always done it this way." The symbolism, in other words, may well be so deeply embedded in a socio-cultural orientation that it eludes any form of reflexive explanation or exegesis on the part of the Palokhi Karen. Nevertheless, I shall attempt an explanation: the *lyta thi toe* is symbolic of sexual intercourse, a natural human (and animal) act that ensures the perpetuation of life applied to the domain of subsistence-in-nature which is no less essential to the sustenance and continuity of human life. (The fully assembled ethnographic details that would support this view are impossible to present here because of length constraints).[19]

The fertility interpretation fails to address a world view reflected in an animist religion that dialectically articulates the human and the natural, and involves marriage and place. It is also related to the fact that the Palokhi Karen, at least as far as swidden fields are concerned, observe usufructuary rights rather than possessory rights. If anything, it is the Lord of the Water, Lord of the Land that has these latter rights.

Openness

The Palokhi naming system, however, also requires us to consider a certain degree of openness in their social, cultural, and economic life. Palokhi is not a closed system. The autonyms and their derivative teknonyms are based as much on events that occur within the community as they are on contacts with the outside world or civilization. These events and contacts (as and when they occur) are fortuitous and contingent, but they nevertheless occur within a larger structural economic and political context. The contacts can also occur through deliberate engagement on the part of the Palokhi Karen. We have seen that individuals can be named on the basis of, for example, northern Thai villagers coming to seek the services of the Palokhi blacksmith, Lisu tribespeople coming to buy rice in Palokhi, and a father seeking medical treatment in Chiang Mai. This "openness" is encoded in these names.

Despite an openness that admits the existence of the outside world and is reflected in their names and identities, there is a strong identification with place that is intimately linked with the religious system, as I have noted. The local economy is not entirely based on swidden agriculture and dry rice cultivation. The community has adopted wet-rice agriculture on a small scale in the form of micro-terraces and, with that, irrigation techniques such as the building of weirs borrowed from the northern Thai. The ritual that accompanies the completion of a weir is, however, situated within a schema of religious ideas based on swiddening rituals in which the weir ritual is subordinate. The agricultural system of the Palokhi Karen by no means ensures self-sufficiency. Sufficiency and insufficiency are related to the life cycle of domestic groups and has a bearing on the availability of household-based labor throughout this cycle. In periods of insufficiency, Palokhi Karen engage in wage labor for northern Thai to earn money which they use to buy rice from northern Thai shops. The rice, it may be noted, originates from the Chiang Mai plains. This cyclical dependency has not resulted in any sense or sentiment that it would be preferable to engage in full-time wage work on a permanent basis and thus assure oneself of a continuous or permanent source of rice. If anything, that way of life is viewed as precarious. In structural terms, cyclical engagement with the outside economy in the form of wage labor helps to support a way of life in Palokhi that is subjectively experienced as being essentially Karen and preferable.

Socio-cultural Orientations: Palokhi Karen Indigeny and Tribality

It may seem that I have ventured farther away from the naming system in Palokhi than may be warranted. I have been guided, however, by Geoffrey Benjamin's approach in his "Temiar Personal Names."[20] In that study, he says: "names are more than just ethnographic details or minor nomenclatural usages; on the contrary they are inextricably bound up with those features that anthropologists regard as lying at the very base of society."[21]

The Karen naming system is not a thing in itself. Karen names are inseparable from gender differentiation, the use of specific kin terms that include a stress on the conjugal bond (spouse terms), and generational distinctions. I have sought to show that an examination of Karen names leads us to yet other considerations in Palokhi Karen society and culture: embeddedness and openness. The naming system is clearly embedded in social relations and religious ideas that extend to rice cultivation; yet the naming system accommodates interactions with the outside world, including economic interactions and the adoption of wet-rice cultivation methods from the northern Thai. Embeddedness and openness have to do with socio-cultural orientations: the first inward-looking and the second outward-looking. Nevertheless, it is the first orientation that is dominant. What does this tell us about the basal features of Palokhi Karen society?

The expression, socio-cultural orientation, is derived from Benjamin, who refers to "attitudes and orientations encoded in the habitus of daily life" in his delineation of "indigeny."[22] On a general level, this may be applied to "exogeny," the ideal-type corollary of indigeny and a condition that Benjamin also discusses. Indigenous and exogenous socio-cultural orientations have different characteristics. The ideal-type features of indigeny may be summarized as follows: attachment to *place*, not territory, implying *use* rights; long inhabitation of place; land as the foundation of existence/being; a conservative approach to land and nature (environment); a monophysite orientation; a tacit and non-articulated knowledge and understanding of the world; inheritance; small populations; and low organizational separation of activities/functions. Central to the notion of indigeny is a grounding in "*family*-level connections to concrete *places*" rather than "the connection of whole ethnic groups (whatever they may be) to broad territories."[23] It is important to note that these are ideal-typical features and that, empirically, gradations may exist between indigeny and exogeny.

The notion of socio-cultural orientations, then, refers to ways of cognizing and perceiving the natural and socio-cultural worlds and, among other things, is associated with the *flexible regulation* of social relations (internal and external to the community) — in the sense of a "culturally mediated social *strategy*."[24] Socio-cultural orientations are produced through a process of adaption in long- and short-term human history. The notion of socio-cultural orientations also implies ontology or a "state of being" that is constituted through historical, dialectical adaptive processes.

Benjamin also deals with the concept of "tribal," a concept that is as much misunderstood as the notion of "indigenous."[25] He provides a typology of what in anthropology were regarded as different types of society (tribal, peasant, and state): "Tribespeople," "Peasants," and "Rulers." The terminological difference is not as trivial as it may appear. First, Benjamin emphasizes that this typology is not an evolutionary series. Tribespeople, Peasants, and Rulers may be regarded as socio-political formations, but they are all part of a single complex. These types emerge out of the "classical civilizing process." Rulers refer to those actively engaged with formation and maintenance of the state. Peasants provision the Rulers but have no counter control. Tribespeople strive to stay outside the state. Together, they constitute:

> a single complex, formed of alternative, mutually dissimilatory responses to the same sociopolitical circumstance — the imposition of a hierarchically organized, supralocal state appearance. On this view, all historically and ethnographically reported tribal societies are *secondary* formations, characterized by the positive steps they have taken to hold themselves apart from incorporation into the state apparatus (or its more remote tentacles), while often attempting to suppress the knowledge that their way of life has nevertheless been profoundly shaped by the presence of the state, or whatever locally represents its complexifying effects. The structure and formation of tribal societies, especially in Southeast Asia, is best understood as an adaptation to the broader state situations in which they are found.[26]

This, then, is the condition of *tribality* which, as Benjamin emphasizes, is not the same thing as indigeny. Indigenes can be tribal or non-tribal. In terms of Benjamin's theoretical distinctions, the basal features of Palokhi Karen society, as revealed through an examination of their naming system and related empirical (ethnographic) evidence, are indigeny and tribality. Their socio-cultural orientations are primarily indigenous and secondarily tribal. The indigenous orientation lies in the cognitive associations that link names with sex and gender differentiation, generational differentiation, place, and the cultivation of rice in swiddens — associations that constitute a "cultural paradigm" in Benjamin's sense of "internally coherent systems."[27] The tribal orientation, on the other hand, lies in how external interactions can and do provide names and identities, and indeed augment their subsistence system. The dissimilatory aspect of this orientation lies in how such names and augmentations of their subsistence system are subsumed under a dominant cultural paradigm which is fundamentally indigenous.

"Class A, B and C" Naming Systems; the Notions of "Tribal," "Peasant," "Rulers," "Indigeny-Exogeny;" and the Palokhi Karen Ethnography

Macdonald's "Class A, B and C" naming systems are "ideal types." They are, as such, valuable in directing anthropological and comparative sociological attention to how naming systems may be understood and explained in relation to what might be termed historically-constituted "societal types." There are parallels between Macdonald's ideal-type classifications and Benjamin's ideal-type delineations of "Tribal," "Peasant," and "Rulers," as well as indigeny versus exogeny, which are no less valuable. For those familiar with one or the other set of delineations but not both, the parallels may not be entirely obvious. Part of the purpose of my argument here has been to establish these parallels, with a view to a more comprehensive explanation for the kind of naming system that we find among the Palokhi Karen and, for that matter, the symbolic content of General Saw Bo Mya's name. Benjamin's ideal types offer a way of bridging ethnographic complexity — of the kind exemplified in the ethnography of the Palokhi Karen — and Macdonald's formal classifications of naming systems.[28]

I see, in other words, a complementarity in these classifications and formulations, which taken together offer a way of understanding and explaining how the naming system of the Palokhi Karen functions in relation to their "lifeworld" beyond ethnographic particularities. If the

Palokhi Karen naming system in all its ethnographic complexity is to be situated, analytically, in terms of a classification of naming systems, this would require equal consideration of what societal type they are.

Conclusion

This paper has been concerned with demonstrating that the Palokhi Karen naming system can tell us a great deal about their individual and collective local identities, but only if we view these systems in relation to other aspects of their culture, for example, their religion and how religion, in turn, is intimately linked with their system of subsistence-in-nature, and their primary indigenous and secondary tribal orientations. The Palokhi Karen, however, are not representative of *all* Karen-speaking peoples. Given their demographic distribution, Karen-speaking peoples are found in a wide range of ecological situations in Burma and Thailand. While many in Thailand and Burma live in situations similar to those of the Palokhi Karen, there are perhaps just as many who are peasant-proletariat or urban dwellers. Then there are a much smaller number, in Burma, who have experienced Christian conversion and colonial rule and think in terms of a pan-Karen identity and a Karen nation-state.

The case of General Saw Bo Mya, with which I began this essay, was intended to provide a basis for showing this cline of adaptation, in contrastive terms, in relation to Karen naming systems. The considerations involved in how Bo Mya came to his name and identity and retained it could not be more different compared with how names are given and gradually sloughed off through teknonymy in Palokhi. The contrast might well be expressed in the following way. Whereas the socio-cultural orientations of the Palokhi Karen are indigenous and tribal, the orientations of Karen like Bo Mya are exogenized and nation-state focused.

Notes

[1] I would like to thank Geoffrey Benjamin, James J. Fox and the late Gehan Wijeyewardene for invaluable comments on various parts of this paper in its earlier forms. I am also most grateful to Charles Macdonald for his comments on this paper when it was presented at the International Conference on Naming in Asia: Local Identities and Global Change, 23–4 February 2006, organized by the Asia Research Institute, National University of Singapore. Beyond that, I am especially grateful to Professor Macdonald for his subsequent editorial comments and observations. I would also like to thank Professor Anthony Reid and Dr. Zheng Yangwen of the Asia Research Institute who, together with Professor Macdonald, were the joint conveners of this conference, for inviting me to the conference, and for their editorial patience.

2   Opinion about the linguistic status of Karennic is divided, that is, whether
     Karennic (of which there are many dialects or varieties) should be placed
     within the larger class of Sino-Tibetan or the sub-class of Tibeto-Burman.
     This difference of opinion does not have a direct bearing on the analysis pre-
     sented here.

3   Martin Smith, *Burma: The Insurgency and the Politics of Ethnicity* (London and
     New Jersey: Zed Books, 1991); Ananda Rajah, "Ethnicity, Nationalism and
     the Nation-state: The Karen in Burma and Thailand," in *Ethnic Groups across
     National Boundaries in Mainland Southeast Asia*, ed. Gehan Wijeyewardene
     (Singapore: Institute of Southeast Asian Studies, 1990), pp. 102–33; Ananda
     Rajah, "Transformations of Karen Myths of Origin and Relations of Power,"
     in *Patterns and Illusions: Thai History and Thought*, eds. Gehan Wijeyewardene
     and E.C. Chapman (Canberra: The Richard Davis Fund and the Department
     of Anthropology, Research School of Pacific Studies, The Australian National
     University, 1993), pp. 237–76; and Ananda Rajah, "A 'Nation of Intent' in
     Burma: Karen Ethno-nationalism, Nationalism and Narrations of Nation,"
     The Pacific Review 15, 4 (2002): 517–37.

4   See Jonathan Falla, *True Love and Bartholomew: Rebels on the Burmese Border*
     (Cambridge: Cambridge University Press, 1991) for some of these names,
     and my review of this book in *Man*, n.s., 29 (1994): 198–9. "True Love"
     and "Bartholomew" in the title of Falla's book are the personal names of two
     of the many Karen Falla came to know in the Karen separatist movement.
     The Karen and Karenni speak a mutually-intelligible form of Karennic. The
     Karenni (literally "red Karen") are also known in the anthropological and
     ethnological literature as Kayah. The Karenni are to be found in Kayah state in
     Burma, north of Karen state. The present-day term, Karenni, is a pre-eminently
     political one intended to distinguish their separatist movement from the Karen
     separatist movement. The distinction is related to a long historical process of
     ethno-political differentiation and Buddhist-based millenarianism beginning
     in the nineteenth century. See F.K. Lehman, "Kayah Society as a Function
     of the Shan-Burman-Karen Context," in *Contemporary Change in Traditional
     Societies*, eds. J. Steward (Urbana: University of Illinois Press, 1967); and F.K.
     Lehman, "Who are the Karen, and If So, Why? Karen Ethnohistory and a
     Formal Theory of Ethnicity," in *Ethnic Adaptation and Identity: The Karen on
     the Thai Frontier with Burma*, ed. C.F. Keyes (Philadelphia: Institute for the
     Study of Human Issues, 1979).

5   See Robert Jones, *Karen Linguistic Studies* (Berkeley and Los Angeles: Univer-
     sity of California Press, 1961), p. 179. Jones notes that whereas in most Sgaw
     dialects in Burma, *sau* (cognate to *cau'* in Palokhi Karen) means "Mr." never-
     theless, in Moulmein Sgaw, it has the additional meaning of "elder brother."
     Jones offers no further comment, but it is by no means unlikely that the
     original meaning of the term was "elder brother" and that it was at some later
     stage employed as an honorific beginning, perhaps, in an urban setting.

6 In 1992, the headquarters at Manerplaw along the Thailand-Burma border-lands was overrun by the Burmese armed forces. KNU and KNLA control over territory in eastern Burma has since then been greatly reduced, a change accompanied by a reduction in the administrative capacity of the KNU. Kawthoolei is now far less of a quasi-nation-state than it once was.

7 David H. Penny, "Growth of 'Economic Mindedness' Among Small Farmers in North Sumatra, Indonesia," in *Subsistence Agriculture and Economic Development*, ed. C.R. Wharton (Chicago: Aldine Publishing Co., 1969); Ananda Rajah, "Implications of Traditional Karen Land Use Systems for the Introduction of New Cropping Systems: Some Observations from Ban Hua Lao, Huai Thung Choa, Northern Thailand," in *Natural Resource Development and Environmental Stability in the Highlands of Northern Thailand: Proceedings of a Workshop Organized by Chiang Mai University and the United Nations University*, eds. E.C. Chapman and Sanga Sabhasri; *Mountain Research and Development* 3, 4 (1983): 352–6; and Ananda Rajah, *Remaining Karen: A Study of Cultural Reproduction and the Maintenance of Identity* (PhD diss., Canberra: Department of Anthropology, Research School of Pacific Studies, The Australian National University, 1986).

8 See also Donald Smeaton, *The Loyal Karens of Burma* (London: Kegan Paul, Trench and Co., 1887), pp. 81–2; and Harry I. Marshall, *The Karen People of Burma: A Study in Anthropology and Ethnology* (Columbus: Ohio State University, 1922), p. 170.

9 David Marlowe, "In the Mosaic: The Cognitive and Structural Aspects of Karen-Other Relationships," in *Ethnic Adaptation and Identity: The Karen on the Thai Frontier with Burma*, ed. C.F. Keyes (Philadelphia: Institute for the Study of Human Issues, 1979), p. 196.

10 The word for rice is reserved exclusively for female names suggesting an association between femaleness and rice. This association is also to be found specifically in the cultivation of rice, where a small crop of rice, which is grown solely for ritual purposes, is called *By Mo Pgha*, "Old Mother Rice."

11 My own arrival in Palokhi resulted in the creation of a compound autonym. I was introduced to the village by Mr. Chaiwoot Hongthong, a village primary school teacher who worked for the Thai Royal Forestry Department within which area of operations Palokhi was included. Mr. Chaiwoot, who is of Shan descent and known as Khruu Wuud (Teacher Wuud), introduced me as an *ajaan* (Thai for university professor, although I was only a PhD. student). Not long after I arrived in Palokhi, a baby was born. He was named Aja Wu.

12 Claude Lévi-Strauss, *The Savage Mind* (London: Weidenfeld and Nicholson, 1966), p. 192.

13 Ibid.

14 The name De' Chaj is derived from the Northern Thai/Thai term, *dek chaaj*, "male child"!

15 Lévi-Strauss, *The Savage Mind*, pp. 194–5.

16   Rodney Needham, "The System of Teknonyms and Death-Names of the Penan," *Southwestern Journal of Anthropology* 10 (1954): 416–31.

17   Lévi-Strauss, *The Savage Mind*, p. 191.

18   Ananda Rajah, "Commensalism as Practical Symbol and Symbolic Practice among the Sgaw Karen of Northern Thailand," *Southeast Asian Journal of Social Science* 17, 1 (1989): 70–87.

19   See also Rajah, "Remaining Karen."

20   Geoffrey Benjamin, "Temiar Personal Names," *Bijdragen tot de Taal-, Land- en Volkenkunde*, 124 (1968): 99–134.

21   Ibid., p. 124. One important aspect of Benjamin's analysis of the Temiar naming system was a consideration of the Temiar kinship system. I have, here, considered the Karen kinship system only very briefly because of space constraints.

22   Geoffrey Benjamin, "Indigeny-Exogeny: The Fundamental Social Dimension?" (Unpublished manuscript, 2003), p. 8.

23   Geoffrey Benjamin, "On Being Tribal in the Malay World," in *Tribal Communities in the Malay World: Historical, Cultural and Social Perspectives*, eds. G. Benjamin and C. Chou (Singapore: Institute of Southeast Asian Studies, 2002), p. 15.

24   Ibid., p. 8.

25   Benjamin, "On Being Tribal in the Malay World."

26   Ibid., p. 9.

27   Benjamin, "Temiar Personal Names," p. 124.

28   This kind of complexity is hardly confined to the Palokhi Karen. A close reading of, for example, the chapters in this volume by Sillander and Kuipers, bears this out. While Macdonald is, in this volume, concerned with naming systems, we should not forget that one of Benjamin's major contributions to Aslian studies was also a contribution to the study of naming systems and religion, which progressed to his current theoretical formulations of societal types.

CHAPTER 7

The Autonomy of Naming: Kinship, Power, and Ethnonymy in the Wa Lands of the Southeast Asia-China Frontier

Magnus Fiskesjö

Introduction

This paper concerns the naming system of the Wa, a Mon-Khmer speaking people about a million strong who live between Burma and China. It also discusses recent Chinese transformations of Wa naming practices, considered in the context of the unequal historical relations between the Chinese center and indigenous peoples on China's periphery. Thus, the paper contributes to the broader field of research on the history of Chinese imperial expansions. Despite my attention to historical precedents, however, I am more concerned with the recent period, especially after the 1950s, when the land of the Wa first came under outside rule and the ways in which that recent history illuminates how naming of both persons and peoples is embedded in cultural, historical, and linguistic contexts and how it is inseparable from the question of autonomy.

Re-naming of the Chinese Other: Historical Precedents

The Wa lands were once far beyond the pale of Chinese civilization, but today Chinese names are assigned even here.[1] In contrast to former imperial times, China's version of modern territorial nation-state ideology dictates that names be given to every person in its charge, and even the Wa must now be classified, named, enumerated, and processed into the sort of statistics upon which the state machinery relies for taxation, population control, and so on.[2]

In imperial times, Chinese officials in distant southern frontiers issued Chinese names mostly to native elites and local lieutenants such as the *tusi* "native chiefs." They received *xing* (Chinese surnames, drawn from a limited range) as well as *ming* (personal names chosen more freely to reflect each individual's service to the empire), which linked them directly with Chinese imperial power and civilization. Because of the potential benefits of rising above fellow non-Chinese and attaching oneself directly to superior sources of political, military, and commercial power, there were many spurious claims to Chinese ancestry — as when *tusi* would claim to be descendants of Chinese soldiers deserving recognition for conquering their "barbarian" lands.

Most imperial-era Chinese re-naming seems to have been limited to such local elites. True, indigenous populations in areas where there was heavy immigration of Chinese settlers might have switched to Chinese naming practices and some even lost their language entirely so that they became minorities in their own lands. From the early 1700s onwards, the native chief system began to be abolished.[3] More indigenous peoples came to be governed directly, subject to taxation by regular officials who further promoted Chinese names.[4] Still, many people, even commoners nominally governed by *tusi*, were not affected by any such naming impositions but continued to name themselves according to local practice, in non-Chinese languages. In the case of the Wa, who were mostly beyond Chinese control until the 1950s, Chinese names were apparently not used at all before the modern period.

Wa Society and Its Autonomy: Historical Background

The Wa number about one million people today, divided between Burma (about two-thirds of the total, centered on the Wa State), and China (one-third, mainly in two nominally Autonomous Counties with ethnic Wa county chiefs). Historically, they practised swidden farming in the mountainous lands midway between the Salween and Mekong Rivers. Independent, self-sufficient groups moved at will, opening up virgin forests for shifting agriculture. As an indirect consequence of external circumscription over the last few centuries, especially since the late nineteenth century, such itinerant swiddening was replaced with more intensively farmed forest tracts claimed by settlements that had now become fixed, and there was competition for land among them. Food grains were farmed on intricate field rotation schedules, and the crops were supplemented with export-oriented cash crops like opium, as well as mining, all organized under a reinvigorated framework of traditional lineages.[5]

Wa culture thus persisted (and still does) through an idealized reconfiguration of older traditions and social and moral norms derived from a heroic past of forest farming and hunting. At the same time, the increasing internecine warfare over land and other resources, plus the hostile posture of alien powers intent on encroaching on Wa lands, combined to promote both fragmentation and entrenchment. Settlements were heavily fortified, and strongly localized dialect distinctions developed in each area, even as the language of one important trading center, Yong Soi (now in China), achieved *lingua franca* status. This volatile situation of proud independence and fragmented politics was firmly established by the late nineteenth century and basically continued until the mid-twentieth century. It is worth noting (as British observers did in the late nineteenth century) that the Wa historically were not poor. Wa populations were large and notably denser than those in surrounding areas. There was considerable wealth and trade in opium and other items.

The central Wa lands, without any centralized state structure of their own but still capable of uniting against outside invaders, persisted as loosely associated autonomous polities until the 1950s. This was the Wa heartland.[6] Its own peripheries fell under the influence or control of various neighboring Shan Buddhist principalities, Chinese or Burmese powers, British colonial Burma, or Christian missionaries, and the like.[7] The supposedly "primitive" but powerful heartland itself at times extracted tributes, "turning the tables" on the exterior, and certain no-nonsense outsiders, like opium buyers, had no trouble distinguishing such key distinctions, often calling central Wa the "Big Wa" and the peripheries the "Small Wa."

Other, self-identified "civilized" neighbors of the Wa instead chose to see the autonomous Wa as fearsome "barbarians," the most violent and dangerous edge of civilization — thus "Raw" or "Wild Wa" — and the subjugated peripheries correspondingly as the "Cooked" or "Tame Wa." "Civilized" outsiders have been particularly infatuated with the historical form of Wa warfare, the headhunting war raids, typically de-historicized as "primitive custom" and thus deterring acknowledgment that such wars, whether directed at intruders or internecine adversaries, can really only be understood historically, and not as static "custom."

The peculiar geopolitical position of the Wa center, quite unlike the usual dependent and exploited "peripheral situation,"[8] has an instructive parallel in the equally powerful Yi ("Lolo") of the border area of the Chinese provinces of Sichuan and Yunnan, which are closer to central China.[9] The Yi similarly reversed the conventional situation of peoples occupying peripheral positions by exploiting rather than being exploited by the center, setting themselves up as a "predatory polity"[10] known for raiding the Chinese for slaves (as the Wa also did on occasion). While fiercely autonomous, the Yi were also simultaneously deeply implicated in the world beyond, especially the Chinese economy, and in the attendant fantasies of the "primitive" and the "civilized," which again recall the Wa.

Another salient Yi-Wa similarity is the importance of patrilineal descent groups in the organizing framework of autonomous social repro-duction, maintained not least by genealogical mnemonics. The autonomy of these societies, which were facing immense outside pressure, rested on this framework, and it is an indispensable context for understanding indigenous naming practices. As we shall see, this remains true in the Wa center on the Chinese periphery, and its legacy continues to be highly relevant even though Wa autonomy came to an end in the 1950s.

The Wa Naming System in Its Social Context

In the Wa setting, memorized genealogies of the personal names of suc-cessive lineage ancestors remain highly important. These genealogies once served as a historical memory of heroic moves across the landscape, linking the names of newly claimed places with each associated ancestor. It also gives form to the memory of historical wars and refugee waves, when Wa lands were lost to others. Such connections between forefathers and the places they lived faded as the Wa became more sedentary. Today genealogies mainly serve to affirm the possession of already-settled land by highlighting the depth of the Wa presence, which is traced back to the very origins of humanity. Even today, adults in central Wa country are expected, and most are able, to recite their own lineage (*ntoung*) genealogy (*ndax* "track") listing the personal names of male ancestors all the way back to the *Sigang lih*, the primordial event of humanity's emergence out of a hole in the ground (located at Blag Dieh in the central Wa country, just inside the Burma side of the new border).

Historically, hundreds of such named *ntoung* are known from the central Wa country,[11] which was divided into *jaig' qee* or Wa "realms." Each *jaig' qee* was made up of an ancestral village, its original seat, and groupings of kindred villages established by lineage members in a process that combined fissioning with entrenchment.[12] The Wa *ntoung*, lineages, themselves most likely formed and multiplied in that very process of territorialization. Stories that refer to an ancient time without lineages, when the Wa used only birth-order terms as names, may refer to an era with unlimited supply of land for swidden farming. Because such expansion is a thing of the past, lineages are no longer newly created.

The data that I cite derives from the *jaig' qee* of Yong Ou, known in Chinese and Lahu as Masan. It is in the "Big Wa" lands, which were incorporated into new China in the 1950s and are situated right on the new international border.[13] The founder, Ou, set up the ancestor-village 17 generations ago. His name, which literally means "mute," also denotes "dull," and "not easily thrown off balance." These multiple layers of meaning suggest the traditional ambivalence surrounding *ai* "the elder brother" as being less entrepreneurial than subsequent younger siblings (who venture into the unknown), staying behind instead to serve important ritual functions on behalf of his kin. (Thus, when the origin myths personify the Wa as *ai*, the elder brother of humankind, this is to suggest the role of the Wa people as the supreme sacrificer/guardian for all humanity).

Having arrived at what was to become Yong Ou, a place with a wealth of promising virgin forest lands, Ou stayed on. He was then reportedly joined by another man, A Meang (literally "Chief"). They became ancestors of two of the most important local intermarrying lineages. As Yong Ou grew into a "circle," the founder's village was elevated into a ritual ancestor center called Yong Ou Dax or Yong Ou Ting ("Ancestral" or "Great" Yong Ou), with over ten lineages represented, namely: Siu'ei, Yam, Muid Nku, Npoung Ki, Yong Glaih, Gon Qeim, Krim, Si Ku, plus A Meang and the still revered Yong Ou.[14]

When recited, the *ndax ntoung* of one of these lineages might sound like the following example from the late Jen (Blae Ge Jen), a village elder in Yong Ou and member of the Yong Glaih lineage, who died only recently:[15]

> Jen; Jen Van; Van Leid; Leid Sian; Sian Kri; Kri Soux; Soux Ki'eid; Ki'eid Lan; Lan Hou; Hou Boi; Boi Gan; Gan S'reng'; S'reng' Hong; Hong Peh; Peh Nge; Nge Ki'eim; Ki'eim Gang … daom eix dao Sigang! ["we come from the Sigang"].[16]

The repetition of each name is a mnemonic device which builds on the Wa genitive, for example, "Jen Van" means "Jen, son of Van."[17] This reinforcing device is also the short answer to the everyday question "Jen who?" — to which the full answer is the full *ndax ntoung*. The short form "Jen Van" is an abbreviation, which is also used frequently in daily life.

Because the patrilineal exogamy framework continues to govern kin relations, these genealogies persist even in Wa lands annexed to China. They obviously also serve as stores of personal names that might be recycled in later generations, but I should note that Wa lineages (which in the past maintained specific drum shrines, aqueduct systems, and so on, and which might also be referred to as "clans") do not seem to have ever "owned" personal names documented in other ethnographic contexts. Wa kinship is but a framework for social relations in which power under an ideology of fierce egalitarianism is placed in the hands of autonomous adults, as manifested in the fact that naming remains the prerogative of parents.

We must note that the fabled Sigang aperture — expounded in origin myths and ubiquitous in everyday parlance — signifies the legitimating claim that the Wa rightfully possess the lands where they live today. The Wa first appeared on earth and remained at this "ground zero"; non-Wa latecomers on earth were forced to move farther away, for example, to China or America; modern-era outsiders moving back into Wa lands are intruders. In the past, such definitions helped to overcome internecine conflicts and unite the Wa. These claims combine the mythic and the "anti-mythic,"[18] forming the bedrock of Wa self-identification and ethnonymy, the system of names for ethnic identities, both of the self and others ("autonym" versus "exonyms"). Ethnonymy is never just a neutral catalogue of names for Others, in themselves fascinating instances of referential practice and packed with sediments of etymology and history. More importantly, the salient kinds of non-Wa foreigners are noted in their order of appearance on history's stage: the Siam (Tai-speaking Shan); the Gui (Tibeto-Burman speaking Lahu or Muhso, nineteenth-century immigrants); the Houx (Chinese of different kinds, such as Muslim Chinese caravan traders whose long history in the region explains why Houx is occasionally mentioned ahead of the Gui); the Man (Burmese); as well as (in some versions, but only in the northern Wa country) the Kang (Kachin/Jingpo); and Grax (Indo-European traders arriving through Burma from distant India, and any other Westerners).

Ethnonymy is meaningful classification in a social context, and the Wa case underlines how both autonyms used to define communities themselves as well as exonyms, which are used for others, form part of an autonomous ordering of the world.[19] Founded on a powerful historical narrative reinforced by memorized name-genealogies, Wa ethnonymy is directly linked with the lineage framework within which Wa name themselves and their persons, both on the level of "a people" constituted in practice by the lineages and of their members, that is, individual Wa persons.

Nowadays, lacunae frequently appear in the famous genealogies, usually somewhere in the less salient middle. This is due to the post-1958 disruption of Wa autonomy and social order, which is discussed at length below. But the most recent string of forebears is remembered, along with the crucial early sequence which connects with the primordial beginning of humankind and qualifies each Wa person as sharing through their lineage, in the potency of that narrative.[20] Furthermore, the macro-level of ethnonymy and the micro-level of personal naming are strikingly linked through the identification of the Wa in their role as *ai*, the oldest sibling of humanity's family, which seizes on the importance of birth order in the main form of personal naming.

Children in each nuclear family are enumerated by nine birth-order terms that combine with the name of the weekday of the birth to form the name of a person. This core two-part "name type" (in Macdonald's terminology)[21] — birth-order designation and weekday name (or a substitute given name) — seems to apply across Wa country, with only some geographical variation.[22]

Wa "name types" also include the already mentioned posthumous names for the recently dead, nicknames (discussed briefly below), and kinship terms that either replace or accompany given names. Lineage names figure mostly in the background and serve as an actively used "name type" only on serious and formal occasions internal to local Wa society and not historically in foreign relations. (This is part of the convoluted story of how Chinese surnames were imposed on the Wa and how lineage names were also explicitly deployed as part of the personal name, which is explained further below.) Let us first focus on the standard personal name, which is binomial, that is, combining two parts.

By virtue of birth order, sons are known by one of the following nine terms: *ai, nyi, soi, sai, sam, laog, niu, meig'*, and *uig'*. Daughters are referred to in the following terms: *yiex, ei, og, ui, am, eib, iad, ou*, and *uig'*. (The term *uig'* also means "the last." However, if one has more than nine children of either sex, as actually happened in the past, number ten is again *ai* or *yiex*). In Yong Ou, the Wa week has nine days: *brag, hrax, naom, raong, goum, s'rom, riex, miong*, and *o*. These day names double as basic building blocks of personal names.[23] Thus, we have two-part classical-sounding and ubiquitous Wa names like Ai Naom and Nyi Raong, and Yiex Goum, and Og Miong,[24] names that surely denote with connotation of Wa identity.

Certain flexibility allows for not always using the two parts together. For example, for a person like me who was born on a day believed to have been Riex, being the middle child but the eldest son of my parents, my Wa name would be Ai Riex. However, in everyday situations, I might be called either the full Ai Riex, which is slightly formal; simply Riex (especially by familiar people of my age); or just Ai. The latter is often politely used by people who do not necessarily know my given name or birth-order position. If more conversation were to ensue, one may follow up with questions like: "That's it? You're *ai* or *nyi*?" Local people are treated in the same way. Since Wa villages may comprise several hundred people (in many places, settlements are but shadows of their once formidable size), few know the formal names of every person, especially the children.

In Wa villages, kinship relations and lineage membership are well known by all. They serve as the main framework for social relations, tabooing certain sexual relations, etc. Kinship terms may often be appropriate in place of personal names, as when young people address a person of the previous generation. If an older man is an agnate, a member of one's own lineage, he is called *geeing* ("uncle," also "birth father"). An older woman who is an agnate is called *mex* ("aunt," also "birth mother"). An older man from another lineage, that is, a potential affine, is called *boux* ("maternal uncle"), while a woman is called *ting* ("maternal aunt"). In all these cases personal names are left out. Female elders can be addressed as *dax* or *ya*, and *dax* also can be used for any unfamiliar older man.

Note that it is precisely for lack of lineage affiliation that a foreigner cannot participate fully in Wa society. This means that there is no answer to a question like "Riex who?" The foreigner is nobody's kin. (My own Wa name thus remains little more than a matter of convenience.) All this highlights the enduring importance of the lineage system for the "anchoring" of persons, male and female.

Among people of the same generation, personal names are frequently used in everyday address, and they are mandatory when referring to a couple, in which case addressing always starts with the woman's name, as in Brag ha Kam.[25] In the case of people older than oneself, the personal names can also be combined with kin terms, again dropping the birth-order part of the binomial autonyms, as in Geeing Van "Uncle Van" or Box Jen "Maternal Uncle Jen." When the audience is multi-generational or when speaking across a generational boundary, teknonymy is also widely used (though not mandatory). It can involve grandparents, such as *dax* Naom Gin "Gin, grandfather of Naom," but it is mainly used for fathers or mothers with the given name of their first, or oldest, living child. For example, *mex* Hrax "the mother of Hrax" leaves out the mother's personal name. In this case, one can be sure that she herself is not Hrax because children are rarely, if ever, given the same weekday name as either parent, even if they are born on the same weekday.

Such a circumstance is but one of several that can prompt the giving of a name other than weekday names. Names (*ngai*) are given right after birth by the parents themselves or by an older lineage member present on the occasion. Names are usually not changed over a lifetime, except when the child encounters accidents or disease (the result of evil spirit attacks). In this case village oracles will often suggest that the name is taboo (*tueh*) and that it should be changed (*vai*, conveying the sense of "repair"), along with the required sacrifices for warding off spirit attacks. In such situations, it is again usually the parents who decide on a new name. They may, following traditional practice, pick names that advertise to the evil spirits that the child is someone they would not want. Common words like *diag* "throw away" and *nbri* "dirt" are used for boys' names while *brah* "leave aside" and *gam* "[rice] chaff" are used for girls. Some are used for both sexes, like *s'reng'* "disdain," as in the disgust one may feel for something unclean, or as in the common expression, *Po s'reng' nah kod* "do not avoid old people because you think they are unbecoming." Even the verb *vai* "change" can be used, thus, Vai "Changed ." This kind of name is quite common. Strange as it may seem, such names carry no stigma: every member of society is aware of the intended audience. An interesting variation is when birth-order names are shuffled to fool the spirits. (One can even rename boys using girls' birth-order names and vice versa!)

Instead of weekday name tags, other given names may be plugged into the "name type" by parents. Some are recycled names and some invented anew, whether at birth or in response to misfortune. Like weekday names, they are used in combination with a birth-order term. They often lack explicit lexical meanings but are chosen for ease of pronunciation and because they sound nice, on a whim or according to the wishes of the parents. Examples of names other than weekday names used in Yong Ou in recent memory include, for men — Kiad, Vui, Ven, Man, Hah, Hian, Jang, Dang, Diam, Song, De, Nte, Nge, Teh, Leang, Li, Tu, Bai, and Gou. Women's names include Huan, Heim, Heng, Hang, Ham, Peh, Pen', Puad, Mah, Ah, Briad, Kruad, La, Loid', S'rie, Suan, Jang, and Guoi. (Unlike weekday names, a few of these names can be used for either males or females.)

As mentioned, some of these conferred names follow historical ancestors (= *plug ngai* "fill in the name"). Others are chosen explicitly to resonate phonetically either with birth-order name tags, or alongside the father's names in the inevitable recitation of genealogies. Thus Ban ("grove" or "stand" of a plant) was once chosen for the son of a certain Riex, which is itself not just the name of a weekday but also the word for banyan tree, thus the name Ban Riex ("Ban, son of Riex," which sounds like "Banyan tree stand," — a positive image). Sometimes there is humor or irony involved. A father named Sen recently had one daughter beyond the limit set by the Chinese authorities and faced penalties for what the Chinese call *chao sheng* "excessive births." She was named Qao; thus, every time she is mentioned as his daughter (Qao Sen), this "excess" (*chao sheng*) comes to mind. Occasionally, such seemingly whimsical names revert to traditional names when the child meets with disease and a name change is required. Thus, a boy named Lu (Chinese for "road," after his mother gave birth to him on the road), was later renamed using the ancestral Qi. This also exemplifies the present widespread wavering between the Wa repertoire and the fashionable adaption of Chinese words as Wa names (fuelled by the resigned — but practical — insight that "we now live in *nqu* Houx" (a "Chinese-[dominated] era").[26]

Names that refer to an event or circumstance at the time of birth include Pi "Forgotten" (the name of a man whose father died before he was born); Kuad "Cold" (evoking the weather that day); and Kan, suggesting a difficult birth. However, many such seemingly meaningful names, even names that explicitly suggest wariness toward evil spirits (as in Kui "Careful" and "Slow") are not always acknowledged as such. When asked, people will typically emphasize the freedom the parents have in naming, their only consideration being that the name must sound good. This surely involves not only phonetic but also social values, and that unspoken standard also covers other names with obvious lexical meanings but unclear implications. For example, the name Soux "Dog" (which is rarely used today but figures in several Yong Ou genealogies), and in some areas, Lig "Pig" have served as names. One scholar suggests an express intention to have children grow up quickly like these animals, but this point is difficult to confirm.[27]

The nickname is another "name type" that is invariably descriptive and attached to given names, such as Nbrah Hled, "Nbrah the Deaf," but never replacing them. (The famous Ou is sometimes thought to have been a descriptive nickname which persisted; others say it was given to harmonize nicely with the name of his own father, O, to produce the melodious "Ou O").

Historically, yet another kind of name-change occurred. The names of children purchased for adoption, a trade occurring mainly within Wa country, seem to have been left unchanged except in the case of disease or other troubles.[28] However, in headhunting warfare, children might be spared as war captives and renamed. In the 1940s, one such boy was captured, adopted into a lineage, and given the name Pun "Captured," memorializing the defining event and marking him as a perpetual newcomer. (Eventually, this new name was undone under Chinese rule when he returned to his ravaged home village and reverted to his previous name!)

The Chinese Re-definition and Re-naming of the Wa After the 1950s

Before the 1950s, Chinese presence in the vicinity of the Wa was sporadic, as exemplified by opium and salt traders and mining adventurers. Only a few Wa knew the Chinese language and Chinese officials dealt with the Wa mainly through intermediaries like the Shan and Lahu, as revealed in the older Chinese ethnonym "Ka-wa" or "Ka-la" for the Wa, using the Shan (Tai) terms "Wa" or "La/Lua" plus the prefix *khaa* which refers to non-Buddhist, "primitive" people and "natural slaves." "Ka" was not dropped from the Chinese language ethnonym for the Wa until the 1950s, when government anthropologists charged with classifying and renaming the non-Chinese peoples of China realized its separate meaning.[29]

After their 1949 victory in China's civil war, the Communists imposed direct control over imperial China's former peripheries to an extent only hoped for, but never realized, by Republican-era governments (1911–49). Troops were sent to the Wa country as early as 1952 but at first they mostly avoided confrontation and were even withdrawn from Wa areas ceded by China to Burma when the international boundary was finally installed, thus dividing the Wa lands. In 1958, the policy of conciliation collapsed and a minor Wa-Chinese war in the central Wa country sent waves of Wa refugees into Burma. There has been no challenge to Chinese rule since that time. Within China (as in the Burmese parts of the Wa lands, later taken over by the Chinese-supported Burmese Communist Party),[30] much of the Wa social order was disrupted. The crucial drum-shrines and the associated lineage-based forest, land, and water management systems were destroyed or abandoned. Chinese institutions were imposed by army-backed "work teams" featuring government ethnographers preparing for subordination and integration into the Chinese state and economy. As a prerequisite for inclusion into the new state structure, non-Han peoples were re-classified as "minority nationalities" and their native institutions of power and wealth were analyzed and targeted for "reform." Only since the 1980s has the transformation of

Chinese state management of rural areas permitted a limited restoration of self-governance and religious practices, among other things.[31]

Collecting and recording the names of each person was critical for this project of a "modern-scientific," "multi-national" nation-state under Chinese command. However, questions arose as to how the Wa people would be named, and how their names would be written. At the outset, "minority" policies expressly included respect for local customs, including naming, and real linguists and anthropologists participated in the research. Scientific Chinese reports initially list ethnic Wa names in phonetic transcriptions using Chinese characters, a practice that was awkward but at least attempted to account for both lineage and personal names.[32]

This practice was observed by knowledgeable ethnographers who were sympathetic to the locals in their charge and thus mindful of choosing neutral or positive characters from the sets of Chinese characters ordinarily used to transcribe foreign names. It was subsequently abandoned in favor of assigning Chinese-style *xing* "surnames" and *ming* "given names."[33] One reason was the limited education and ethnocentric outlook of state, party and military officials, who would not learn Wa and envisioned a totally Chinese-speaking future. They saw their task as ensuring a peaceful but steady expansion of Chinese control — with the major exception of the Cultural Revolution, when many Chinese in authority were instead primarily driven by zealous hopes for instant reform of "backward" non-Han "primitives." Either way, imposition of the Chinese language, in the form of spoken Yunnanese dialect and written standard Chinese was and still is perceived by government officials as modernization through sinicization.

After the initial period of diligent transcription, these officials shifted toward assigning names. In the Yong Ou area, they took pragmatic cues from local Lahu, living in close association with the Wa, whose men they called "Ai," and the women, "Na."[34] This was copied in official Chinese transliterations and used as surnames for Wa people instead of lineage names, as if the Wa were all "surnamed" Ai and Na. However, this caused an unmanageable proliferation of duplicates, which is one major reason why Chinese names began to be assigned instead. Today the Wa names are organized in line with the time-tested Chinese administrative model of a one-syllable ordinary Chinese surname plus a Chinese personal name *ming*, in either one or two syllables, which is sometimes still the attempted transcription into Chinese of the basic Wa birth-order position plus weekday name.

Because of the stark differences in Chinese and Wa phonology and phonotactics (e.g., both as regards salient phonetic distinctions, and the peculiar Chinese system of writing syllables, which further severely constrains the representation of Wa phonemes), representations of Wa in written Chinese cannot be accurate. They cannot, for example, account for either the initial consonant cluster or the final consonant of the ubiquitous weekday name Brag. Instead, three Chinese words awkwardly make "Bu-la-ge" (alternatively reduced to "Bu-la" to conform with the normative two-character limit and dispensing with the final one). Hrax is written with the character for *la* (obscuring the initial sound and omitting the glottal stop expressed by the Wa "x"), Naom is written as "Na" or "Nao," Raong as "Long," "Goum" as "Gao," and so on. This is the sad mess of ambiguous transliterations found nowadays in tax and population registers, on ID cards, and other documents indicating Wa names.[35]

The wholesale assignment of Chinese surnames started in earnest after 1958, when Chinese policy shifted decisively from conciliatory to activist. The surnames generally derive from the limited sets acceptable for Han Chinese. These have been successively imposed for every Wa person on Chinese territory who will now be identified as yet another Zhang, Wei, Li, Chen, Yang, Xiao, Tian, or Zhao (these are among the most commonly used). The surname precedes transliterations of Wa personal names (for adults and others who never attended Chinese school), or a *ming* with typical, explicit Chinese meanings, like those often assigned to Chinese-schooled Wa by their teachers, for example, Chen Xueming (Chen "Study Bright") or Li Jianhua (Li "Build China").[36] Such Wa persons now have fully "Chinese" identities, and if they belong to the ranks of cadres or businessmen living in county seats who may emulate Chinese ways in every respect and speak Yunnanese Chinese instead of Wa at work, and at home, the complete disuse of Wa naming is already a distinct possibility.

This situation, with successively sinicising officials and predominantly ethnically Wa subordinate general populations, has direct parallels across the border in the Wa State of Burma. Its currency is Chinese; official publications are often only issued in Chinese; place-names appear in Chinese rather than in Wa; and the Wa State leaders, under Chinese influence compounded by the failure to promote Wa writing as well as the legacies of historical fragmentation, are often known publicly mainly by their Chinese names, complete with *xing* and *ming*.

Chinese *xing* have not been assigned altogether randomly. The Chinese recognition of the existence of Wa lineage affiliations, the mistaken equivalence of lineage-names with surnames, and the cohesion of Wa lineages all have contributed to certain consistencies. For example, when descendants of the Yam lineage were registered, the Chinese surname "Yang" seemed a convenient choice because of phonetic proximity. After several decades, the association of Yam with Yang has begun to be taken for granted by lineage members themselves. Even when phonetic similarity is non-existent between some Wa and Chinese names, some lineages now also have come to associate themselves with particular Chinese surnames. This is so even when the *xing* chosen for the same Wa *ntoung* lacks consistency and varies by locality; conversely, in many places distinct Wa *ntoung* have ended up represented by the same Chinese surname (for example, at least 23 different central Wa lineage names have been subsumed under the ubiquitous "Zhang.")

Wa naming is, of course, still the default in rural areas, where only a minority of the population is bilingual. But decades of Chinese schooling have now created a situation where many rural persons see themselves as having two sets of names. As time goes by, propositions like "We in the Siu'ei lineage *xing* Li" come to seem self-evident, signaling the beginning of the end for the Wa lineages as cornerstones of an autonomous generative framework. After a few generations, the process has created the illusion that a fixed Chinese *xing* is a natural correspondence, when in reality it indexes an already effective social transformation. The next steps might be the abandonment of Wa kinship, the genealogies, the land claims they once embodied, or the emulation of the cadre-class practice of complete sinification.

The change from autonomous Wa kin-based societies to governance as Chinese commoners (named, counted, taxed, and controlled) often occurs as a default transformation accompanying the demise of autonomous generative structures in the face of overwhelming Chinese colonization. This can be traced mostly in the Shunning, Zhenkang, and Yongde districts north of the central Wa lands, where the immigration of Han Chinese into areas formerly dominated by Mon-Khmer speakers has a history of several centuries. In some remote areas settlers assimilated with local cultures, but many remained Chinese and claimed land for themselves. They were in a position to demand Chinese law and order, and they would not entertain the sort of respect and fear of the old ghosts of the land once displayed by the Shan when immigrating into the region and building the fleeting Shan galaxy of Buddhist principalities.

However, local Chinese (descendants of such earlier Chinese colonists) still acknowledge the local Wa people as the *benren*, "autochthonous people." Some of these *benren* are still bilingual and retain elements of their Wa culture; in terms of power relations, however, they have completely lost the native structures that previously governed their social life. They once lived like landless peasants of Chinese landlords, but in the 1950s unexpectedly encountered Communist Government land reforms, in which they obtained some land, plus recognition as Wa, an officially ack-nowledged ethnic minority. In the new atmosphere of ethnic revival since the 1980s, some are even seeking to "re-translate" themselves by finding and reviving Wa equivalents to their current Chinese names, revealing further the central relationship between naming and power.

Conclusion: The End of Wa Naming?

I once journeyed to these Northerly Wa areas and returned to the central Wa country relating what I had learned to my long-standing interlocutors there. Some of what I had to say was no surprise: these "Wa" must be the people in the stories about terrible wars of the past when many Wa were forced to flee south from those northern lands; some forged ahead, reaching what is now the central Wa country, leaving their brethren behind, but "cutting forest plantains along their path for the benefit of such stragglers. However, the plantains had already shot up again by so much, that the stragglers figured they would never catch up, and decided to stay behind." These are, then, the *benren*, and no wonder they were compelled to "sinicize."[37]

One point offended several knowledgeable community members who had never traveled to Zhenkang — my claim that Zhenkang "Wa" had no *ntoung* (lineages). They felt I must be altogether mistaken, and suggested that the people I met may have said something which I heard as Wa, or may even have said they were Wa, but without *ntoung* it was impossible that they could be Wa. I countered that those Wa had simply experienced the same historical development which they themselves were now witnessing in central Wa country. Although the Wa *ntoung* with attendant marriage rules still exist there (and even if the role of the lineages is now being reinforced and revived in some respects), I suggested that the Chinese names that people are adopting and increasingly regard as part of their identity would ultimately lead to giving up the *ntoung* altogether, just as what happened in the Wa lands to the north? But they replied: "Never!"

Perhaps indeed the Wa, in their "peripheral situation," can continue a dual system, naming and to some extent governing themselves, even while they are named to be governed from the outside. This, however, remains to be seen.[38] The social arena in which Wa persons are realized — where one becomes Wa, and Wa ways are continuously reproduced and creatively re-fashioned by the very persons formed within those same sets of socio-logics — depends on some measure of autonomy, cultural if not political, as its foundation. The naming system's viability and the right to name oneself are obviously among the most salient expressions of this autonomy, reaffirmed every time the name for one's own people is reiterated — even when it merely figures as a silent foundation, as with the named lineages being missing from most explicit forms of address and barely figuring as a "name type", but which define the Wa person, in the eyes of the people of the central Wa lands. The link to land claims is still seen as crucial there, as the Wa make up the overwhelming majority, and their stake in the territory continues to be meaningful.[39] From their perspective, if minority Wa in the north are named only in Chinese, it is a sure sign that they have been reduced to being guests in their own land, in other words, as a subset of the Chinese.

Perhaps such reductions are the ultimate goal of the modern state policies. Because of the high stakes involved in the naming of persons, kin groups, ethnicities, or other social entities and their associated claims, they will quickly become a focus for external forces challenging the autonomous structures where the power to name is lodged. Even when externally imposed names merely appear to duplicate and coexist with the indigenous naming practice, seizing the power to define what are "official" names has crucial importance since it is key to the control of food production and trade, armaments, freedom of movement, as well as, more importantly, the harnessing and exploitation of (re-)named land and its natural resources. At Yong Ou, older people can point out vast lands recognized in the past as controlled or "owned" by their *jaig' qee*. Under the Chinese-configured economy of representations, much of the land and its resources are exploited by state agro-forestry and other industries. No license fees are paid: the *jaig' qee* Yong Ou is not only obsolete, but actively obscured. The name has been suppressed to block property claims, and the Wa of these areas have been reduced to the classic peripheral situation. It remains to be seen whether the Wa as a whole (including those in majority Wa areas in Burma, now under heavy Chinese influence) will indeed become a subset of the Chinese, or if a different kind of accommodation will be found.

One curious hint is found in the fact that domestic animals in the central Wa country nowadays often have Chinese names, given partly in jest and partly in mockery. The Wa have a limited range of *kreng ei* (*kreng* "belongings," *ei* "to raise"): dogs, pigs, chickens, buffalo, and cattle, which are presently given names in Chinese, such as Xiao Hua, "Little Flower."

Map 1 "Map of the Kawa area," showing the 1950s' Chinese understanding of the division of central Wa country and its peripheries, and indicating the Salween as the future western border of Chinese territory. From Fei Xiaotong, "Outline of Kawa society," in *Zhongguo minzu wenti yanjiu jikan* 2 (1955), 103–40, p. 105. Note Yong Ou in the center of the map. For more maps of the Wa lands see "Maps of the Greater Wa-speaking Area," at the Wa Dictionary Project, SOAS, http://mercury.soas.ac.uk/wadict/wa_maps.html

(Perhaps because of their short life span, chickens are usually not so named.) This Wa "sinification" of their own animals may seem oddly out of line, but it mirrors the Wa anti-myths poking fun at powerful outsiders while also recognizing their overwhelming powers,[40] granted that in the world we live in, the main characteristic of human-animal relations is, after all, one of domination. Animals are dominated by humans — they work for us and they are even killed and eaten by us. But as the origin myths recognized, things may very well have been the other way around.

Acknowledgements

Field research in Wa country was conducted in 1995, 1996–8, and 2006. I am deeply grateful to all my interlocutors there, and also for financial and other support for research and writing from the Wenner-Gren Foundation for Anthropological Research; the Pacific Cultural Foundation; the China Times Cultural Foundation; the Woodrow Wilson Foundation; the Department of Anthropology at Yunnan University; the Yunnan Institute of the Nationalities; the Institute for Advanced Study, Princeton; and Cornell University's Department of Anthropology and Southeast Asia Program, which funded my travel to Singapore and my most recent field research. I am grateful for the valuable comments and suggestions from the conference organizers and volume editors at the National University of Singapore. I also wish to thank Hjorleifur Jonsson, Nicholas Tapp, and Brook Hefright for valuable comments.

Notes

1   The old Wa lands were cut in two by the installation of the new Burma-China border in the early 1960s (after many failed attempts, starting in 1898). See my PhD dissertation, "The Fate of Sacrifice and the Making of Wa History" (Chicago: University of Chicago, 2000).

2   On the reconfiguration of non-Chinese peoples as "minority nationalities" in the new Chinese nation-state, replacing earlier designations as "barbarians," see my article "Rescuing the Empire: Chinese Nation-Building in the Twentieth Century," *European Journal of East Asian Studies* 5, 2 (2006): 15–44. On imperial-era precedents see my "On the 'Raw' and the 'Cooked' Barbarians of Imperial China," *Inner Asia* 1, 2 (1999): 139–68.

3   On the native-chief system and its abolishment, see John E. Herman, "Empire in the Southwest: Early Qing Reforms to the Native Chieftain System," *Journal of Asian Studies* 56, 1 (1997): 47–74; and Nicholas Tapp, *Sovereignty and Rebellion: The White Hmong of Northern Thailand*, rev. ed. (Bangkok: White Lotus, 2005), 167 ff.

4   On surnames as a device of state control, see James C. Scott *et al.*, "The Production of Legal Identities Proper to States: The Case of the Permanent Family Surname," *Comparative Studies in Society and History* 44, 1 (2002): 4–44; and James C. Scott, *Seeing Like a State: How Certain Schemes to Improve the Human Condition Have Failed* (New Haven: Yale University Press, 1998).

5   For an in-depth discussion, see my dissertation, "The Fate of Sacrifice and the Making of Wa History;" on the history of Wa farming also Yin Shaoting, *People and Forests: Yunnan Swidden Agriculture in Human-Ecological Perspective* (Kunming: Yunnan Education, 2001).

6   See Map 1 and my article "The Barbarian Borderland and the Chinese Imagination — Travellers in Wa Country," *Inner Asia* 4, 1 (2002): 81–99.

7   Some such Wa communities themselves became Shan-style principalities, with subservient-tributary ties to states further beyond like the Shan "galaxies" shifting ties to Chinese and Burmese states or to other Shan states.

8   Terence Turner, "Production, Exploitation and Social Consciousness in the 'Peripheral Situation,'" *Social Analysis* 19 (1986): 91–119.

9   Major differences include the distinct social stratification among the Yi, where core lineages came to form a sort of aristocracy; see Stevan Harrell, ed., *Perspectives on the Yi of Southwest China* (California: University of California Press, 2001), which contrasts with the fiercely egalitarian Wa.

10   A term borrowed from Jonathan Friedman's famous discussion of the China-Burma borderlands, *System, Structure, and Contradiction in the Evolution of "Asiatic" Social Formations*, 2nd ed. (Walnut Creek: Altamira, 1998).

11   Luo Zhiji, probably the foremost Chinese scholar of Wa culture, suggests that there are 125 different named lineages just in Ximeng, now a Chinese county. See her *Wazu Shehui Lishi yu Wenhua* [The society, history and culture of the Wa nationality] (Beijing: Zhongyang minzu daxue, 1995), p. 223; also Luo *et al.*, "Ximeng Wazu Xingshi diaocha baogao" [Report on investigations of Wa nationality lineage names at Ximeng]," in *Wazu Shehui Lishi Diaocha* [Investigations of the society and history of the Wa nationality] (Kunming: Yunnan renmin, 1986), 4: 20–50; and Xiao Zegong and Gao Dengzhi, "Wazu xingshi de xingcheng" [The formation of Wa surnames], in *Wazu Minjian Gushi Jicheng* [Collected Wa Nationality Folktales], eds. Shang Zhonghao *et al.* (Kunming: Yunnan minzu, 1990).

12   British colonial-era writers called them "circles;" the Chinese more recently use "tribes" (*buluo*).

13   I use the Chinese-devised Wa orthography (without prejudice against the missionary-created alphabet and its modifications), with minor modifications to reflect the "Ava" dialect. See my dissertation, "The Fate of Sacrifice and the Making of Wa History," pp. 401–6; also "Writing of the Wa Language" in the Wa Dictionary Project (http://mercury.soas.ac.uk/wadict/wa_orthography.html).

14   Yong means "village," here suggesting one of several ways in which lineage names were first created. See Luo Zhiji, *Wazu Shehui Lishi yu Wenhua*, pp. 225 ff.; 232 ff.

15   Blae and Ge are honorific terms attached to the names for recently deceased elders, as posthumous names pending their ultimate vanishing into unnamed, threatening ancestor spirits (*ge meang*).

16   Fiskesjö, Wa Fieldnotes, 1997, XV, p. 81.

17   The patronym we encounter here may look like "a kind of surname" (cf. "The Wa System of Personal Names," Wa Dictionary Project), even if it is not (it is not permanent, and shifts with each generation).

18   Anti-myths explain the history, power, and influence of this-worldly fellow humans, in contrast to myths that credit other-worldly forces with setting the basic conditions of existence (saying, for example, that people eat cattle, not vice versa). Anti-myths explain injustices regarding the possession of writing systems, modern machinery and weaponry, and the loss of ancestral lands, among others. See Terence Turner, "Ethno-ethnohistory: Myth and History in Native South American Representations of Contact with Western Society," in J.D. Hill, ed., *Rethinking History and Myth: Indigenous South American Perspectives on the Past* (Urbana: University of Illinois Press, 1988), pp. 235–81.

19   Gabriele vom Bruck and Barbara Bodenhorn, "'Entangled in Histories': An Introduction to the Anthropology of Names and Naming," in *The Anthropology of Names and Naming*, eds. vom Bruck and Bodenhorn (Cambridge: Cambridge University Press, 2006) suggest that Claude Lévi-Strauss, in his discussion of names in *The Savage Mind*, left behind the nuanced insights of Marcel Mauss on how names may simultaneously identify and classify (p. 8).

20   This applies to both men and women, who are often as eloquent as men in remembering their lineage. For all the emphasis on patriliny, women's personal names have a strong presence (for example, listed first in references to couples) and they have strong voices in Wa society. For a comparative view of Chinese women's namelessness and incomplete personhood, see Rubie Watson, "The Named and the Nameless: Gender and Person in Chinese Society," *American Ethnologist* 13, 4 (1986): 619–31.

21   Charles Macdonald, this volume.

22   The terms I quote here are those used in Yong Ou. See the comparative chart, "The Wa System for Personal Names," compiled by the Wa Dictionary Project at SOAS.

23   The names of the days of the Wa week differ with the locality, as well as its length (from seven to ten days). Local events are divined based on the local calendar, but just as elsewhere in the region one also keeps track of the ten-day Shan week in order to catch the larger marketplaces running on a five-day cycle (as is still done today, even as the "Chinese" Gregorian calendar is also gaining currency).

24   When birth-order terms become "name tags" in personal names, along with weekday names, they are appropriately capitalized.

25   Women who have become mothers are spoken of in the third person by the given name or weekday name only, plus the suffix "ha," for example, Huan ha. When addressed in person, one uses the peculiar pronoun *ba* "you (two)" used for mother and child whether or not a child is present.

26   Zhao Furong, *Zhongguo Wazu Wenhua* [China's Wa Culture] (Beijing: Minzu, 2005), p. 83, says only that the use of Chinese-sounding names is a widespread fashion. As elsewhere in his book, he seems to be taking the peripheral situation as the yardstick, not the central Wa lands.

27   Li Daoyong, "Wazu" [The Wa nationality], in *Zhongguoren de Xingming* [Surnames and Names of China's People], ed. Zhang Lianfang (Beijing: Shehui kexue, 1992), p. 337.

28   I discuss Wa "slavery" and adoptions in my manuscript "Both Kin and Antikin: On the Ambiguous Status of the 'Slave' in Wa Society."

29   See my articles, "Rescuing the Empire," and "Renaming the Barbarians: Ethnonymy, Civilization and Modernity in China and Southeast Asia" (ms.); also Frank Proschan, "Who are the 'Khaa'?", *Proceedings of the 6th International Conference on Thai Studies* (Chiang Mai, Thailand, 1996), 4.1, pp. 391–414.

30   Bertil Lintner, *The Rise and Fall of the Communist Party of Burma* (Ithaca: Cornell University Southeast Asia Program, 1990).

31   For an authoritative Chinese scholarly summary of the impact on the Wa in these periods, see Luo Zhiji, *Wazu Shehui Lishi yu Wenhua*, pp. 416–47.

32   Wa lineage names were often placed first, in Chinese fashion. Wa people, including both illiterate villagers and Wa writers educated in missionary traditions, tend to place them last.

33   On Chinese naming conventions and the importance of the surname (*xing*) as an organizing device, see Scott *et al.*, "The Production of Legal Identities" p. 11 n. 12, 31; Patricia Ebrey, "Surnames and Han Chinese identity," in Melissa J. Brown, ed., *Negotiating Ethnicities in China and Taiwan* (Berkeley: Institute of East Asian Studies, University of California, 1996), pp. 19–36; Viviane Alleton, *Les Chinois et la Passion des Noms* (Paris: Aubier, 1993); also Yuan Yuliu, *Zhongguo Xingmingxue* [The study of Chinese surnames and given names] (Beijing: Guangming ribao, 1994), Zhang Lianfang, ed. *Zhongguoren de Xingming* [Surnames and names of China's people] (Beijing: Shehui kexue, 1992), and Nari Bilige (Naran Bilik), *Xingming* [On naming] (Beijing: Central University of Nationalities, 2000); as well as Zheng Yangwen, this volume. One of the most penetrating recent monographs on naming among ethnic minorities in China and their interdigitation with Chinese practices is Chen Meiwen, *Cong Mingming Tan Guangxi Tianlin Pangu Yao Ren de Goucheng yu Shengming de Laiyuan* (The formation of the Pangu Yao people of Tianlin, Guangxi, and the origin of life as seen from the perspective of naming practices) (Taipei: Tangshan, 2003).

34   On Lahu naming, see He Jiren, "Lahuzu" [The Lahu nationality], in *Zhongguoren de Xingming*, ed. Zhang Lianfang, pp. 343–53, and on Lahu-Wa naming interaction (but *cum grano salis*!) Zhao Furong, *Zhongguo Wazu Wenhua*, pp. 82–91. Zhao explains that the Lahu "Na" originates with a female deity. It is also customarily used in women's names and often coupled with a birth-hour(!) name. The corresponding male term is Ja; it is unclear why the Lahu

would not apply it to the Wa. A full comparison of Lahu, Wa, Shan, and Burmese naming is beyond the scope of this paper, but note that certain terms, including "Ai," are shared with the region's Shan, whose naming system also deploys birth-order terms in personal names but is otherwise different, due to the marked hierarchies in Shan society. See Ai San, "Daizu" [The Dai nationality], in *Zhongguoren de Xingming*, ed. Zhang Lianfang, pp. 317–24. Wa and Shan are very old neighbors. Mutual borrowings and influences have certainly occurred. Shan influences are comparatively less evident in the central Wa country, but more so on the Wa peripheries (generally overrepresented in Chinese publications on Wa customs). On Wa-Shan interaction, we eagerly await the forthcoming important work by Liu Tzu-k'ai at the University of Illinois. As for Burmese, note that there too, part of weekday names are regularly used to form given names (I thank San San Hnin Tun, Cornell University, for pointing this out).

35   There are *two* writing systems, both adequate (cf. Wa Dictionary Project). Neither has been effectively promoted. Most schools in both China and parts of the Wa State in Burma today teach *Chinese only*, often with Chinese-trained Wa teachers. Most Wa are illiterate, only a minority attend school, and on the China side literacy has been fostered almost exclusively in Chinese. (As a result, even educated people hoping to record songs, stories, etc. have been reduced to miserable Chinese transliterations, or even to paraphrasing in Chinese, resulting in the loss of vast opportunities to record folklore traditions. The early state ethnographers used the International Phonetic Alphabet for some transcriptions, yielding results that are accurate but inaccessible for a wider Wa public). Another result of these developments is the new use of Chinese characters for writing the Wa language — fragmented and fledgling, to be sure, but unfolding in an old and widespread "Sinoxenic" tradition found in Japan, Vietnam, etc., as well as among some other people on China's peripheries. (For an insightful discussion, see Brook Hefright, "Language ideologies and linguistic practice among the Bai," paper presented at the Society for East Asian Anthropology conference, Taipei, Taiwan, July 5, 2009).

36   There are cases of special assigned surnames carrying particular meanings, for example, the Bao of the singular Wa chiefs of Banlong said to have "protected" (in Chinese, *bao*) China against British aggression in the 1930s. In areas closer to the imperial center, it is more common to find "irregular" Chinese-style surnames marking even assimilated people as different, as in the case of the Tujia who have largely lost their language (Philip R. and Cecilia Brassett, "Diachronic and Synchronic Overview of the Tujia Language of Central South China," *International Journal of the Sociology of Language* 173 (2005): 75–97).

37   These stories probably do reflect in part the historical explanation for the presence of scattered remaining populations of Mon-Khmer speakers in otherwise Chinese-dominated Zhenkang, and elsewhere.

38   Alternatively, a distinction of more Chinese and more "Wa-like" Wa may emerge in the short term, as in the case of Hmong distinguishing "Chinese Hmong" among themselves, based on the transformation of burial customs (cf. Tapp, *Sovereignty and Rebellion*, 161 ff.) much like in Chinese-ruled Wa areas today.

39   Note the insightful comparative discussion of land and resource claims in ethnic minority context by Janet Sturgeon, *Border Landscapes: The Politics of Akha Land Use in China and Thailand* (Seattle: University of Washington Press, 2005). On the relationship between naming and land claims, see also David Parkin, "Politics of Naming among the Giriama," in *Social Anthropology and the Politics of Language*, ed. Ralph Grillo (London: Routledge, 1989), pp. 61–89.

40   Compare the Malagasy peasants who talk to their cows in French, inverting the power relations of colonial rule. See Maurice E.F. Bloch, *How We Think They Think: Anthropological Approaches to Cognition, Memory and Literacy* (Boulder: Westview Press, 1998), pp. 193–5.

PART III

"Class B":
Competitive Societies

Personal Names and Changing Modes of Inscribing Identity in Sumba, Eastern Indonesia: "Bloody Thursday" in Linguistic and Social Contexts

Joel Kuipers

Introduction

On the morning of 29 October 1998, five months after the fall of President Suharto from power in Indonesia, more than 200 demonstrators gathered in front of the Regency Office in Waikabubak, West Sumba, in Nusa Tenggara Timur, eastern Indonesia. Carrying a banner inscribed with phrases like "Long live Reformasi!" [reform] and "Regent Malo must step down," the demonstrators prayed, sang songs, and vowed not to retreat until their demands were met (see Figure 1). By noon, they were met by security officers, who ushered 15 representatives to meet with the Regent, Rudolf Malo, to explain their grievances and deliver their demands. By 1:00 pm they met with Regent Malo. They asked why his nephew, Nedi Kaka, was listed as having passed the civil service exam when records showed that he never even took it. Demonstrators said the widespread practice of using surrogates (*joki*) to take tests under the names of other people was unfair and the whole test should be nullified. The competition for government jobs that year was particularly intense because the currency devaluation and political instability in Jakarta had

Figure 1 Protesters in West Sumba demand reform (Pos Kupang, 30 October 1998)

left the economy reeling and unemployment was high. Furthermore, with the fall of Suharto and his GOLKAR party cronies, people began to openly complain about corruption and nepotism. When Regent Malo, himself strongly in the GOLKAR camp, denied wrongdoing and called the Nedi Kaka case an "administrative error" at the provincial level, the protesters were not satisfied.

Protests grew in size and intensity for the next seven days. The increasingly vocal throng, mostly from the Loli ethnolinguistic group, created colorful banners and caricatures of the Regent and his second in command. They sang vivid and provocative songs in the Loli language, a language closely related and mutually intelligible with the native language of the Regent, Weyewa. The protesters' critique soon expanded to include the lavish renovations in the Regent's residence. They demanded that the Regent resign and his second in command be jailed.

Figure 2 The protesters' discourse became more personal (Pos Kupang, 31 October 1998)

At midday on 31 October 1998, in the courtyard of the Regent's Office, another dialogue took place between the Regent (Bupati) and the protesters, which was reported as follows:

> Regent: What are you doing here?
>
> Demonstrators: We told you yesterday about the things you had covered up.
>
> Regent: What have I covered up? Hey you in the red shirt! Come forward! (points to a protestor in a red shirt)
>
> Demonstrators: No! [They prevent him from going to the podium.]
>
> Regent: Oh, unfortunately you have no manners!
>
> Demonstrators: Is it we who have no manners or is it the Regent? [Demonstrators: "The Regent!"]

At some point during this exchange, the chanting demonstrators began using a specially stigmatized nickname for the Regent, his *ngara katto* or "hard" name, Mette. He withdrew from the scene and asked the local security to step in.

Two days later, at 8:00 am on 2 November 1998, the newspapers reported that at least 500 "family" (= relatives from the Weyewa ethno-linguistic group) members arrived at the Regency Office after an all night march from their highland homeland 18 kilometers away. The protesters asked that the security personnel form a cordon to protect the Regent so that his "hard" name would not be uttered again publicly in his presence. Aware of the mood of the demonstrators, the Regent rightly sensed that the presence of his "family" supporters would seriously escalate the conflict. He told them he appreciated their assistance, but that they were an "additional burden" at this time. As a way of defusing tensions about the use of the "hard" name, he made a curious statement: he told them he should not be considered a possession of his family, but of all of the Regency of West Sumba (*Saya bukan milik keluarga, tapi seluruh Sumba Barat*). For emphasis, he then used a phrase to refer to the Regency of West Sumba that was not its Indonesian name, but a couplet from the local register of ritual speech: *Pada Eweta, Manda Elu*. He asked that they return home peacefully.

As was reported the next few days on CNN, the *New York Times*, and many other international newspapers, things did not end peacefully. Tensions escalated, and eventually resulted in a bloody confrontation between the Regent's ethnic group, the Weyewa, and that of the people in the Regency capital, the Loli — leaving 26 people dead, many missing, 84 houses completely destroyed, and 891 people rendered homeless. Thousands of recent immigrants to this once thriving and highly plural region fled, many permanently. What came to be known as "Bloody Thursday" has reorganized politics and social life in West Sumba in ways that are likely to have long-term consequences.

While we must of course be careful not to oversimplify the matter by using a name-calling incident to explain the worst case of violence in the history of the Weyewa highlands, nonetheless, it would be equally fool-hardy to ignore the cultural significance of naming in the constitution of identity in this rapidly changing area of Indonesia. To understand the Regent's curious statement about the ownership and custody of his well-being, it is important to understand the relationship between identity, well-being, and naming among the Weyewa. Furthermore, to make sense of why this verbal incident could have sparked a conflict that led to so many deaths, it is crucial to understand how the protesters, by using his "hard" name in a public setting, were not simply being rude. They were challenging the boundaries of civil society as it was then defined in Indonesia. In what follows, I will describe how Weyewa ideas about the relation between "hard" and "soft" names are not simply part of a broader ideology of what it means to be a person; how they are *used* in social contexts are crucial ways of constituting what it means to participate in society. To understand how these two ideas are related, traditional approaches to proper names need to be re-examined in ways that take account of pragmatic usage as well as the denotative and designative properties of semantic reference.

Therefore, before I analyze the changing structure of the Weyewa naming system in its social and cultural context, I want to briefly outline some theoretical approaches to the study of proper names and how these approaches shed light on the case at hand.

The Ethnographic Study of Proper Names

Although the study of the nature of proper names has a long and distinguished history in philosophy, theoretically informed study of these universal linguistic phenomena has not been as widespread in anthropology.[1] D.J. Allerton has speculated that this may be because it is difficult to know what to do with proper names analytically. Are they individual possessions? Or are they social, collective, and conventional?[2] In a paper published in 1983, E. Mertz developed an argument that recasts these issues in a new way.[3] She argues for the need to appreciate the relation between the pragmatic and semantic functions of names, rather than focusing on their individual versus social attributes. On the one hand, names are semantic in that they serve to classify people into categories. For example, Clifford Geertz in a famous study argues that the Balinese system of teknonymy naming oneself after one's offspring, such as "mother of so-and-so" is such a powerful social classification system that it gradually erases individuality, even a certain perspective on time. According to Geertz, it results in the individualizing, personal name of the parent being forgotten altogether, thus producing a shallowness of genealogical knowledge that is flexible and strategically manipulable in times of successional crises.[4]

On the other hand, since at least the time of John Stuart Mill in 1870,[5] it has long been customary in linguistics and philosophy to stress the pragmatic functions of a name as a relation between the sign and the interpreter. Lévi-Strauss criticizes C.S. Peirce and Bertrand Russell for such views: Peirce for "defining proper names as "indices" and Russell for "believing that he had discovered the logical model of proper names in demonstrative pronouns." For Lévi-Strauss, "this amounts in effect to allowing that the act of naming belongs to a continuum in which there is an imperceptible passage from the act of signifying to the act of pointing."[6] In this view, carried to its extreme, names are a device for pointing and reference. While this perspective has its appeal, it erases all consideration of the role names play in what Geertz calls "symbolic orders of person definition."

What is needed is a way of understanding the relationship between these two functions. Mertz observes that "personal names play somewhat different roles in address and reference." Based on her fieldwork in a formerly Gaelic-speaking community in Cape Breton, Nova Scotia, she notes that in accordance with a community ideal of solidarity, the Cape Breton only allows familiar names in address. Thus, a speech situation is always defined as an exchange between intimate equals. However, the use of names in reference is changing significantly: Gaelic names are disappearing. The kinds and direction of the disappearances can be attributed to "changes in community boundaries and notions of "insider" and "outsider" definition." The more classificatory names, those that require community cooperation and "insider" knowledge for formation and use are falling out of use.[7] Thus while in address, familiar names were always used, the complex and evocative system of descriptive, classificatory, community, and kin names are dwindling, largely because they *presuppose* too much knowledge from the speakers, who are increasingly unfamiliar with the personal particulars of the individuals in the community. For people in Cape Breton, the changes in personal name use cannot be explained as reflections of modernization, or economic development, or aesthetic "taste." The patterns of change are neither a matter of phonological preference on the one hand nor economic interest on the other. Instead, the changing name use must be understood in the context of the overall system of changing semantic and pragmatic functions for the actors who use them.

In Cape Breton, first name use constitutes a space of familiarity; on the other hand, the last name, kin name, Gaelic names, and other classificatory names, employed in reference, create a sense of shared tradition. What Mertz describes is a changing system in which different names for individuals are invoked in different contexts, requiring different kinds of knowledge of the users. The use of first names creates a sense of situated familiarity based on face-to-face interaction; by contrast, the use of traditional kin and Gaelic names requires considerable background knowledge, and is beginning to fade as fewer and fewer people remember the shared lore, or even consider names as a way of keeping that lore alive. What is organizing the shift is an ideology about what language, and specifically, naming, is for and how it is supposed to function.

In the Sumbanese case of "Bloody Thursday," part of what was at stake was different ideas about the proper role of language. For the Weyewa defenders of Regent Malo, language played an essential constitutive role in the construction of his identity. The use of a "soft" name is a way of treating someone verbally with the gentleness they require, while using the "hard" name threatens his well-being. For the protesters who attacked Regent Malo for corruption, language was a device for representing their feelings and making their demands. While the demonstrators were aware of the implications of "hard" and "soft" names, they were also testing the limits of free speech in a newly emancipated political atmosphere.

Weyewa Native Naming Practices

Until the mid-1980s, relatively few Sumbanese had Western-sounding names like "Rudolf." The majority of Sumbanese were ancestor worshippers and not affiliated with any world religion. They lived on a dry and relatively barren island that was for centuries more or less isolated from the waves of Hindu, Muslim, and European influence that swept across the archipelago. Speaking one of about eight closely related but mutually unintelligible Austronesian languages, the various Sumbanese ethno-linguistic groups have had many shared cultural features — including hilltop villages consisting of large high peaked houses arranged in rows around megalithic ancestral sarcophagi; a system of subsistence agriculture based on swidden and irrigated cultivation of rice, corn, and root crops; a system of religious practice featuring animal sacrifice; and displays of parallelistic ritual speech used to communicate with the spirits of agnatic forebears. Their native system of personal naming was a dynamic one, and affected by the history of economic and political changes on the island, but only slightly by outside forces such as Javanese Hinduism, Bimanese Muslims, or European Christians.[8]

One of the crucial semantic, classifying functions of the traditional naming system was to define, and indeed constitute, a person. One of the ways in which this was accomplished was through the system of "hard" and "soft" names.

Personal Names: The "Soft" and the "Hard"

Ngara "name" in Weyewa refers primarily to a verbal label that is conventionally established (given or taken) as legitimately denoting an object through a culturally recognized act of bestowal. Grammatically, these are the only words in the Weyewa lexicon that accept the vocalic phonemic infix — i — as a way of indicating that the name is being used in "definite" reference, not address.[9] If the Balinese naming system emphasizes the classifying and ceremonial functions of naming as a system of person definition, the Weyewa system suggests an openness to the potentially problematic relationship between name and individual. The Weyewa system emphasizes importance of "fit" between a person and his or her name, and recognizes that some names may need to be changed. If the name does not fit, harm can come to the individual. Although the Sumbanese system is more volatile than the Balinese system, in the sense that it allows for more changes over the lifetime of an individual, it also permits individual embellishment and particularizing, especially later on in life, in conjunction with the feasting system.

Unlike Balinese personal names, which are highly individualized and unique from birth, Weyewa babies are traditionally given personal names from a rather limited stock. In a computer count of the names used in the 1992 census records for a subdistrict, I found that the vast majority of men (72 per cent) possessed one of just six forenames, and nearly the same was true for women (79 per cent possessed one of eight names). Second names were only slightly more differentiated. Such names are drawn usually from the same pool of names during a short ceremony held eight days after a child is born.

When the baby is born, it is regarded as "soft" or "tender" (*ndakke*) and somewhat amorphous, even alien. Acquiring distinctiveness and individuality as a person as one grows older is thus a process of "fixing" and "hardening" one's identity. To help provide a structure and form to this nondescript entity, agnatic relatives and the mother's brother (*loka*) assemble at the house of the child a few days after the birth, and a pig is slaughtered. A green coconut is opened up, and a finger is placed in the milk and then put to the mouth of the baby. Names of appropriately gendered ancestors are listed first, and if the baby sucks the finger (or in some cases, the mother's breast) while a name is uttered, then that name is chosen; it "fits" (*na moda*). To "revive an ancestral name" (*pa-kedde-we ngara umbu-waika*) is regarded as particularly desirable. To arrive at the second name, the process is repeated. The child is said to have a "namesake" (*tamo*) relationship to whomever shares its name, but particularly to an ancestral person. However, if the child later becomes sick, a divination may be conducted, and one possible cause may be that the child's ancestral *tamo* does not agree to having his or her name used. Because of their respective individual characteristics, and particular personality features, it may happen that they "do not fit" (*nda na modda-ki*). The assumption is that name and referent should be virtually inseparable.[10]

Table 1   Men's and Women's Personal Names

Men's names		Women's names	
"soft" names	*"hard" names*	*"soft" names*	*"hard" names*
N. ndakke	N. katto		
Malo	Mette	Peda	Roki
Zairo	Zokke	Ninda	Rede
Lende	Rua/Ngedo	Leda	Ponne
Mbulu	Mbennaka	Dada	Tiala
Ngongo	Ngilla	Koni	Mbiri
Mbili	Kurri	Zoli	Lawe
Dairo	Lade	Wada	Lew
Mbora	Tyalo	Lali	Pindula
Mete	Rangga	Winni	Tannge
Lelu	Atu	Louru	Ladde
Dowa	Kelo	Mbuta	Ngapu
Mali	Keba		

Table 1 shows how traditional personal names are typically two-syllable, and generally different for men and women. Names are typically binomial, with the last names selected at the naming ceremony also. In many common names, the same vowels are used in both first and second syllables as in the following: Ngongo, Mbulu, Mbili, Lende, Wini. Women's names seem somewhat more likely to end in "i", as in Wini, Lali, Soli, Koni, but there are men's names that end in the same way, for example, Dadi and Bili. The first name is more closely associated with the individual's identity, and may be used when addressing people of one's own age and status and younger. First names are more commonly used by peers, age-mates, and elders. When addressing an older person, it is more appropriate to use a teknonym, or title, or to avoid direct address altogether.

Most personal names are considered *ngara ndakke* "soft" names and each has a "hard" or "crude" name (*ngara katto*) associated with it. Much as Henry has Hank as a nickname, or Richard is linked with the more casual Rick, so Malo is conventionally associated with Mette as a "hard" name. It was the use of such a name in public by outsiders that resulted in the sense of grave injury to the Regent of West Sumba, and provoked a strong movement to protect his honor. These "hard" names are only used in address by those with whom one has the most intimate relations, such as one's wife of many years, and perhaps reciprocally among elderly siblings. Furthermore, the very use of a "hard" name presupposes a situation of familial, in-group intimacy among the hearers; otherwise using such a name is awkward. Because in most settings, people get angry when they hear their "hard" names, I was told to be especially mindful of this when I was learning to speak Weyewa so as not to inadvertently offend anyone. Regardless of one's intentions or who the audience is, all speakers are responsible for not uttering a person's "hard" name within earshot of the owner in public settings; such an act is cause for offense. It is said to be a provocation used in battle or in wild boar hunts. On the occasions when I have heard such names used, bearers respond with embarrassed laughter; but I have seen them occasionally get quite irritated, as when a child uses such a name in the presence of his or her parent to be disrespectful or deliberately insulting. On the other hand, older adults who know each other well sometimes address one another reciprocally with such names, and older married couples speak to each other in this way in domestic contexts. Children sometimes devise ways of using these names indirectly as taunts, deliberately violating the boundaries of inside and outside. I once heard a boy tease his friend named Ngongo by playing on the homonymy between the "crude name" for Ngongo Ngila and the word for "to whinny." He mocked his friend by calling out to him repeatedly "Hey, Ngongo, don't listen to that horse whinnying! Hey, Ngongo, don't listen to that horse whinny!" [*E Ngongo, ndu rengekana na ndara a ngil!. E Ngongo, ndu rengekana na ndara a ngila!*]

As a child grows into adulthood and becomes more defined and fixed as a person, its "softness" diminishes and its "hardness" increases. Only after a person is married and has a child, does one begin to use that person's "hard" name on a more regular basis. Even then, the *ngara katto* "hard" name is only used as a sign of great intimacy, by people who do not threaten (or are likely to be threatened by) the bearer of the name. "Hardness" is not only a feature of a person's name. A person with a "hard liver" (*ata pakattongge ate*) is a person who has shown evidence of the capacity to withstand adversity, such as hunger, stress, and conflict. In the past, Weyewa say, when things were more difficult than they are now, the elders preferred "hard" names as a sign of their toughness.[11]

Namesake System

Weyewa beliefs in the constitutive power of names are reflected in their namesake system. Because a name was traditionally viewed as integral to one's personhood, people who share a common name were thought to share a special bond that transcended kinship. Such individuals address one another not by their names but as *tamo* "namesake." Although neither women nor men change their names at marriage, both are expected to identify with the spouses' name in important ways. For example, two women whose husbands have the same name are said to be *tamo* "namesakes." The same is true for men with wives of the same name. For example, if Robert and Paul both have wives named Barbara, they call each other *tamo*. A male child who is named after a living grandparent is called *tamo ama* "namesake of father" and a girl is called *tamo inna* "namesake of mother" until the grandparent passes away, after which time the name may be used. It is interesting that the construction of a namesake label is from the perspective of the namer, not the named. For example, a small child labeled *tamo ama* "namesake of father" is *not* the namesake of its own father, but the father of the child's parent. To be accurate from the child's perspective, the label would have had to be *tamo ama kaweda* "namesake of grandfather." The namesake system thus assumes a sociocentric (rather than egocentric) perspective to meaning as a form of classification that decenters the individual.

Teknonyms

Another option available to the protesters for reducing social distance with the Regent would have been Rudolf Malo's teknonym. They did not apparently make use of this, or if they did, it went unnoticed by observers of the scene. Teknonyms are used by both men and women upon the birth of their first child. Thus, a woman becomes *inna Lende* "mother of Lende" and her husband is *ama Lende* "father of Lende." The eldest child is usually selected as the source name of the teknonym, regardless of whether it is a boy or girl, or whether it survives to adulthood. This unites the married couple in address; they are thus identified publicly in terms of the child they share. Since there are literally thousands of Lendes in the Weyewa-speaking region, however, teknonyms are not particularly helpful in differentiating identity. It does occasionally happen that a parent will take on the name of a younger child to show disapproval of the eldest, or to show particular favor toward a younger child. Teknonyms are also used in conjunction with Christian names; thus, one can be called *ama* Esther "father of Esther." They are most commonly used as names of address for adults of childbearing age; occasionally, if the child becomes famous, an older adult may retain the teknonym into old age.

Prominent individuals — such as Regent Malo — are seldom referred to by their teknonyms. This is because it is rarely a distinctive way of labeling an otherwise notable individual, and because it minimizes the individuality of the identity of the bearer. Teknonyms in some ways subordinate the identity of the owner of the name to that of the child (see the chapter by Kenneth Sillander in the present volume).

Prestige Names: *Ngara Ndara,* "Horse Names"

When the protesters challenged the authority of the Regent Malo, they sought to discredit him by pointing to lavish household objects as evidence of "corruption" (*korupsi*). They specifically singled out the elegant bar in his house and an expensive racehorse. This was particularly poignant, because such riches would once have been integral to his "name" in the traditional prestige system. In the post-Suharto era, the traditional image of a powerful man as one surrounded by objects of wealth and by followers is no longer freighted with such positive meanings.

Traditionally, wealthy Sumbanese sought to acquire special poetic names referring to possessions, particularly horses, dogs, ear pendants, water buffalo, pigs, spears, or swords as honorifics. Sometimes generically described as "horse names" (*ngara ndara*), they are used for addressing individuals on formal occasions, and for praising them indirectly in songs and in eulogies. In poetic genres of expression, such names typically have a trinomial structure to them, such as Attribute1 (Adjective) + Attribute2 (Nominal) + Head Noun. Examples are as follows:

> Dappa Doda, Karambo "Swift Conqueror, the Water Buffalo"
> Pera Dangga, Bongga "Trading Escort, the Dog"
> Mette Ngora, Bongga "Black Snout, the Dog"
> Ropa Lara, Numbu "Spans the Road, the Spear"
> Kaweda Ngara, Keto "Ancient Name, the Knife"
> Ndende Kiku, Ndara "Upright Tail, the Horse"

Attribute2 (nominal) may sometimes be derived from a verb, as is common in some Native American naming traditions (Mithun 1980). In "Swift Conqueror, the Water buffalo," *doda* is a verb meaning "to flatten, crush, vanquish." In this context, however, it functions like a noun. Such names may be inherited from an ancestor, or they may be acquired as a result of some special meaningful occasion accompanied by feasting.

Onvlee in his essay on the "Significance of Livestock in Sumba" sheds some light on the meaning of personal possessions:

> ... personal possessions are singularly linked with the life of their owner. They are not impersonal; rather they are part of the person who owns them and are related to his life in a particular way. A person's betel-nut case is a good example. In west Sumba when someone leaves behind his betel-nut case, his parang [knife], or cloth, his ndewa ("vitality") is affected: nakoba dengangge ndewara [sic] ("His ndewa becomes powerless").

He notes further that there is a "certain opposition to the sale of anything associated with the land or with the personal identity of the owner."[12]

I would also add that personal objects such as betel pouches, knives, cloths, horses, and buffalo are used as resources for the personal autonomy for boys in particular and a source of differentiating oneself from one's mother and father. Boys first acquire a cloth and a knife at around age 13 or 14; at about the same time, they begin to chew betel and areca nut and so, need a pouch. In an insecure world, differentiating one's identity and declaring one's autonomy from the nurturing environment of one's "house" (*umma*) was seen to require some "anger" and "boldness" (*mbani*) and even "hardness" (*katto*) on the part of the boy. One of the ways in which this is done is through the acquisition of objects through trade and negotiation, contexts that presume a potential for conflict.

Powerful and rich men, such as the Regent Rudolf Malo, were traditionally expected to be set apart from their peers by their names, their goods, their words, and their capacity to influence others and control their world. Their charisma comes partly from their "anger, boldness" and its capacity to motivate, attract, and repel people. Having a horse and dog name is part and parcel of this influence. To be truly *mbani* ("bold, angry"), it is not enough to simply possess animals. One must be named after certain selected ones. When one acquires sufficient wealth that one can devote valuable livestock and goods to the sole purpose of furthering one's prestige (since such animals cannot be traded), then these animals are given evocative names, such as "razorgrass, the spear." Once bestowed, the names are the preferred form of address on ceremonial occasions. As for the interlocutors of the name-bearer, on ritual occasions, it forces them to position themselves by how much respect they show.

Having oneself named and addressed with the label of certain personal objects was one of the highest forms of prestige; in the past, some men were named after their slaves, although this is no longer done.[13] Sometimes these names are handed down from a male grandparent on the father's side. One can also give oneself a horse or dog name, often as a way of commemorating a feast, or a particularly good harvest, or some successful event.

Horse or possession names are more than a way of denoting a person. They are a means of conjuring the memory of the individual. Listening to Weyewa talk about a powerful man or woman, one does not often hear connected, temporally organized biographical narratives about events during a lifetime; instead one hears about clusters of belongings, radiating out, as it were, from a charismatic center. These powerful nuclei both attract and cast a shadow on social inferiors. The life histories are organized as tales about personal objects, flowing in and out.[14] Powerful men *ata attu* "core person" as such men are sometimes called are idealized as never alone, but as always accompanied by an entourage of possessions of slaves, prancing horses, barking dogs, and elegant clothing. Like gigantic banyan trees, big men take care of those who are beneath their protective canopy.

From the standpoint of an addresser, by invoking the name of a prized possession, one avoids directly mentioning the name of the individual, which is regarded as too impolite. Plainly and openly speaking the name of revered individuals or spirits is forbidden. Indeed, a common way of referring to the Creator Spirit is "whose name cannot be uttered, whose title may not be mentioned" [*nda pa-zuma ngara, nda pa-tekki tamo*]. By naming a person in terms of a possession, one *mediates* the relation between the speaker and the addressee.

Personal relationships to belongings are *constituted* by the naming relationship. The act of bestowal results in a personal relationship that requires the owner to take the object out of circulation. As a person grows and becomes more of a unique individual, with more and more control over one's environment, part of one's identity includes the objects that one controls. It is as though a person's identity radiates outward and gradually comes to encompass valued objects metonymically associated with that individual, such as spears, knives, horses, and dogs. The image of a potent center, surrounded by a constellation of valuable and indeed magical objects, is one that resonates with descriptions of the classical Indic kingships, in which power is associated with an *exemplary center*.

As Onvlee suggests, such personal relationships with possessions is seen as incompatible with sale or exchange. When Weyewa name their horses, dogs, and cloths, for instance, they take them out of circulation. Selling (*batta*) or exchanging them is regarded as taboo (*erri*). That is not to say that it cannot be done, but it is not approved of, and there may be supernatural sanctions for doing so. Ideally, named goods are no longer available for exchange or slaughter at any feast other than the funeral of the bearer of the name. In Sumba, in which material exchange is a central idiom of sociability, this act of removal from circulation in itself is regarded as a bold and daring act.

Named animals may be sacrificed upon the death of their owner. When, for example, Mbaiyo Pote died, his burial was depicted as a return of his body to the ancestral mother and father. The named animals still alive (in this case, the horse and dog) were slaughtered at the funeral in order to accompany him as his body and possessions were reclaimed by the ancestors in partial repayment for the gift of life. Other named objects — pendants, cloths, and knives — were also offered to the spirits along with his body as gifts to the spirits of the unseen world.

Why are these names in ritual speech? The act of bestowing a name any name is an act of taking control over reference and distinguishing an object from a broader semantic category. The use of metaphoric elaborations provides semantic identity by adding a gloss on what is otherwise an opaque label. The use of ritual couplets for names takes a further measure of control by implying a spiritual audience for the speech act in which the names are uttered. If one addresses someone as "Mbulu of the white feather, Renda of the red scarf," the expression not only refers to a specific person, but it implies a spiritual, ancestral audience. It establishes the names as part of a discourse that occurs in exchange with the ancestral spirits. An important part of the audience for such names is thus not only one's peers, but the ultimate authorities in Weyewa social life: the "Mother and Father" spirits. Having a special couplet name thus at once differentiates one's identity and expands the audience for the use of the name to include at least implicitly the ancestral spirits.

Ngara Tana Dawa, "Names of the Modern World"

The process of "seeking a name" (*wewa ngara*) and the elaborate feasting system often associated with it, is now explicitly discouraged by officials from the district and regency level governments. The opposition to name-seeking is framed in economic and developmental terms: it is regarded as wasteful and backwards and impedes the progress of the Sumbanese people. In an interview in 1994 with the Regent Umbu Djima, he pointed proudly to the success of his program, which he calls *eka pata* "the new way." He noted that "[Fewer people are] feasting, wasting their resources; they are using their cattle, pigs and other animals [instead] for education and making a better life for themselves."

Name-seeking feasts do indeed seem to have declined. No one I asked in 1994 could think of any younger men or women under 40 years of age who use or even seek such names, and most of the traditional feasts performed in the past few years have tended to be rather modest by historic standards between one and four water buffalo slaughtered and only slightly larger numbers of pigs. What is not clear is whether the Regent can take any credit for this shift in priorities or even what role a shift in economic values may have played in this.

Naming Patterns in the 1980s and 1990s

In the late 1980s and 1990s, the use of Christian first names, patronymics, as well as the survival of certain kinds of prestige naming, were notable trends.

Ngara Keristen "Christian First Names"

Adopting a Christian name after baptism has a long history in West Sumba,[15] but initially anyway, these names were not often used in everyday address or reference. Indeed, there was some anxiety in the late nineteenth and early twentieth centuries about the meaning of these baptisms, since the names did not seem to be used by any of their recipients. Missionaries began to worry that Christianity was very superficial among the Sumbanese. Especially among the Calvinist missionaries such as Wielenga, there was a concern that any name change had to be accompanied by a transformation of consciousness. To reflect this change, "we seek a renewal of the language" as well, the Calvinist minister Lambooy declared in 1932.[16]

By the mid-1990s, anyone bearing a Western sounding Christian name could be expected to have a cultural orientation toward Indonesian-style modernity rather than traditional indigenous ancestor worship. With a name like "Rudolf," the Regent would be viewed as having a non-Muslim, but also modern and non-traditional identity. As the number of Christians has risen (see Figure 9), the number of Weyewa bearing Biblically derived names has risen as well. Based on a comprehensive computer listing of all the names in the 1990 census of Kalimbundaramane, I found that 67 per cent of all Weyewa in that subdistrict now possess Christian first names.

There is a greater variety of Christian names than native names. Among 1,481 people in the sample in the subdistrict of Kalimbundaramane, there were 481 names in total, but only 14 of those were *ngara tana mema* "native names," names which nonetheless were shared among 33 per cent of the population. Thus, 467 names were Ngara Keristen. Far fewer Christian names were shared than were native names and thus there were fewer people sharing a spiritual "namesake" (*tamo*) connection based on first names. The greater variety of Christian names makes it easier to identify unique individuals.

Another major incentive to adopting a Christian name is the desire to pursue schooling beyond elementary school. As of 1994, in order to register for continuing education in junior high (SMP) or SLTA Technical School, students have to present a birth certificate (*surat akte kelahiran*) notarized by a clergyman. Many Sumbanese believe that the clergymen will refuse to do so unless the student gets baptized and adopts a Christian name. In 1994, high level clergymen vigorously denied this; others called it a thing of the past, while others have smilingly acknowledged that it still occurs.

Uses of Christian and Modern Indonesian Names in Address and Reference

The difference between "hard" and "soft" names, and the palatalization function to distinguish between address and reference has not been carried over into Christian names. Nor does the Christian naming system have a way of addressing someone poetically with descriptive names that classify them in terms of their valuables and other possessions.

While the name-created boundaries between public and private, for instance, have been elided through the dwindling of "hard" and "soft" names, there are boundaries emerging between social distance and intimacy that are enacted through the use of the titles versus the more personal Ngara Keristen "Christian names." Table 2 displays the range of more "modern" forms of address and reference, the system which Sumbanese are likely to use when speaking to one another in Indonesian, and when employing Christian names.

Table 2 Contemporary Modes of Address and Reference in Sumbanese Indonesian

Nama Pangkat "Title"		
Address + function = e.g.	Pak Guru	Mr. Teacher
	Pak Camata	Mr. District Head
	Bapak Raja	Mr. Raja
	Ibu Menteri	Mrs. Minister
	Pak Dokter	Mr. Doctor
Title + Personal name e.g.	Pak Joel	Mr. Joel
	Dokter David	Dr. David
	Nona Janet	Miss Janet
	Pendeta Enos	Reverend Enos
	Guru Malo	Teacher Malo
Ngara Fam "Family Name"		
Title + Family Name	Ibu Dapawole	Mrs. Dapawole
	Pak Keremata	Mr. Keremata
Ngara Sefe [C.V.] "Enterprise name"		
Title + Company Name	Bapak Ujung Padang	Mr. Edge of the Field
	Bapak Dessa Ate	Mr. Good Hearted
	Bapak Emanuel	Mr. Emanuel

These names, however, may be used in both address and reference.

Patronymics

Another recent development has been the emergence of Western style patronymics. Although this is still a minority practice, it is an influential minority, since it tends to be done by Western-oriented and educated Weyewa elites. For instance, school teacher Sam Rewa, has named all his children with the patronymic Rewa as well, which in fact is a *ngara ndara* "horse name" from his male ancestors. Thus, his son is named Henk Rewa. Locally described as *ngara fam* "family name," patronymics generally follow a Western-type pattern in which children and wives adopt the last name of the father and husband. For wives, so far this is a matter of address forms only, but for children, the patronymic is their legal name.

The Survival of Prestige Naming

Partly because of the importance of the market, the meaning of personal possessions, particularly prestige items, has shifted. While prestige items were often named in the past, today highly prized prestige items, such as a "hardtop jeep," are not usually named to my knowledge. While in *tana mema* "the traditional world" named prestige items were viewed in some ways as objects that not only stood for but were referentially and materially *exchanged for* their owner (that is, by using the name of the object to address the owner and by sacrificing the object to compensate the ancestors for the deceased), valued commodities in the "contemporary world" *tana dawa* clothes, shoes, purses, wooden cabinets (*lemari*), television sets (*tifi*), and stone houses (*rumah batu*) are usually not named at all.

One important area in which the tradition of prestige names has persisted and indeed, developed, is in the domain of "horse names" applied to "racehorses" (*ndara malle*), covered pickup trucks used for transport called *bemo*s, and local businesses. An important theme linking these three categories is the association with risk, and this is particular clear in the case of racehorses. Most animals, if given names at all, are given descriptive names such as "white," or "black," or "patient." Since many pets such as monkeys, civet cats, birds, dogs, and cats are not routinely given names, it is all the more striking that racehorses should be singled out for naming, and usually names in the native language of the owner. Most of the racehorses in the annual 1994 horse races in the track outside of Waikabubak were given native language binomials that reflect sentimental themes, personal experiences, or unique features or attributes.

Table 3   Some Recent Racehorse Names

Racehorse Name	*Meaning*
Pangga Lewu	Prancer
Ole Ndewa	Soulmate
Reda Ole	Close Resemblance
Putera Kopi	Prince of Coffee
Pánde Pata	Knows How
Rita Bewa	Full Cottonwood
Peluru Kendali	Guided Missile
Manda Elu	Heaven Field
Engge Belli	Glad First
Eka Pata	New Ways

The two Indonesian-language names "Guided Missile" (*Peluru Kendali*) and "Prince of Coffee" (*Putera Kopi*) were either given by a non-Sumbanese speaking Chinese who owned the animal, or in cooperation with a Chinese financier for the horse. The majority of other names were in Sumbanese languages, and in some cases strongly evoked the traditions of prestige name-seeking and indeed legendary "angry" men, like Ole Ndewa "Soulmate." Even more striking, this is an activity in which the Regent, as well as a number of Sumbanese descent Indonesian officials participate and enter their own horses.

Another named valuable is the *bemo*, the small covered pickup trucks with benches in the back used as public conveyances within districts in Sumba, and the *bis* "bus" used to travel between districts on the island. In Sumba, these vehicles are always provided with names, which are spray painted on the side panels in often gaudy colors. Although the names are often in Indonesian, approximately half of them are in Weyewa or one of the other languages of the island. They also often use a line out of a couplet. Like racehorses, *bemo*s on Sumba are associated with the youthful autonomy and risk-taking of their drivers and ticket takers (*kornek*).

While both the horse and *bemo* names are used as a way of differentiating the identity of the conveyance from others, the names are also often corporate labels and refer to the business that owns it. Occasionally the name comes to attach to the owner as well, so that Weyewa will refer to the owner of a particular *bemo* by his *bemo* name. There is a diminished sense, however, of any special connection between the name and its referent; nor is there certainly any sense that the object somehow stands for or can be in some sense exchanged for the owner.

Why has the tradition of prestige naming been applied to racehorses, *bemo*s, and businesses? Like the traditional horse names, these names are

Figure 3   Colorfully decorated buses in West Sumba are sometimes given a "horse name"

bestowed upon objects that represent risk. The act of naming because of the link it establishes to the referent offers a way of attempting to control that risk. While the feasts in which the traditional horse names were bestowed were risky to one's prestige and indeed to one's whole social, religious, political, and economic well-being, a racehorse, a *bemo*, or a business entails risk more narrowly to one's financial well-being and personal reputation. Prestige names are thus at once expensive, but also potentially wealth-generating.

Bemo and racehorse names are different from the traditional prestige naming system, however. The use of prestige names for racehorses, *bemo*s, and businesses is indexicalized, in the sense that the name is viewed as *primarily* pointing to the actual referent vehicle, business, or animal and is not regarded as a metonym for the owner, a part of a verbal identity construed as a whole. No one has ever suggested as far as I know taking a named *bemo* out of service, closing down a business, or killing a racehorse — upon the death of its owner, as was customarily done for the objects named with traditional prestige names.

The prestige names in current use are more narrowly ostensive and indexical than their traditional counterparts. Whenever a local notable embarked on a traditional name-seeking quest, to a significant degree, the fortunes of his whole village lay in the balance. If he failed in an effort to drag a tombstone, to carry out a risky marriage negotiation, or to draw the necessary audience and participants to a feast, such a failure might have serious implications for the capacity of village members who were identified with his efforts to recruit labor for agricultural activities, to keep angry ancestral spirits from causing misfortune, and to create and maintain alliances of mutual protection. Currently, if the Regent's named racehorse fails in its bid for first place, it is the horse that loses, not him. He still has a job and his family can still eat.

Conclusion

With the rise of Christian naming, the salience of the distinction between "hard" and "soft" names is dwindling. Many Sumbanese children bear names that have no "hard" equivalents at all, for example, Christian names. Some residual aspects of the "soft"/"hard" name system have remained with the binomial practice of using a Christian first name in address and a traditional Sumbanese name as a second name. But since these traditional Sumbanese names are seldom used in address in such cases, in general, sensitivities about the use of "hard" name are on the wane, the case of "Bloody Thursday" notwithstanding. The reason for this has to do with a changing ideology about the role of language in the naming process.

For the protesters, their use of language — including the "hard" name of Rudolf Malo — was part of a legitimate process of *unjuk rasa* "expression of feeling." Language use is thus linked to its expressive function, rather than its denotative one. In the emerging, reform-era Indonesia, freedom of expression is regarded as crucial for democracy. From the perspective of the reformers, this use of language is a central tool in creating a modern democracy, and it should be tolerated, even embraced.

But as one commentator in the local newspaper put it, "[open protests] are something new for us in West Sumba." For those Sumbanese aware of the expression, *unjuk rasa* demonstration and expressive practices are associated with the fall of Suharto, a new sense of openness and transparency, and a crackdown on corruption, cronyism, and nepotism. The semiotic zone in which the "hard" name was uttered was not one governed by either family or the state, but by a fragile, fledgling but flourishing notion of civil society (*masyarakat sipil*).[17] From the language used on their banners, it was clear that the young protesters self-consciously saw themselves as part of a movement sweeping across Indonesia, criticizing nepotism, and its lack of boundaries between family and state control. To them, the rigged civil service exam was another example of these nepotistic practices. By calling Regent Malo by his "hard" name, they were challenging the supporters of the Regent to openly display their inappropriate family allegiances by protecting their family member from "hardness." Tragically, the Regent's supporters took the bait.

If the goal of Regent Malo's supporters was to protect his honor after his "hard" name (*ngara katto*) was used, they failed utterly. After assembling what "must surely have been the biggest war party ever assembled in the history of Sumba," on the morning of 5 November 1998, Weyewa attacked the houses and villages of the Loli people near the town center of Waikabubak. The Loli people retaliated by killing 26 of the attackers and threatening the members of Rudolf Malo's family living in the Regency capital.[18]

What had started as an expression of free speech in the context of civil society had been reinterpreted as a threat to the personal well-being of a member of a powerful extended family. Far from acting like an individual "hardened" to adversity, Rudolf Malo fled from the scene as the Loli people retaliated. Like a child who is "soft" (*ndakke*), Regent Malo sought protection from family members in the face of insults. Later confronted with the consequences of his neglect of his leadership role, Regent Malo wept publicly. As the discussion turned once again to the accusation of corruption and the boundaries of family and state, both Weyewa and Loli alike began to call for his resignation. The governor of the province eventually called for his removal and the Regent Malo left for Jakarta, where he now lives.

Prestige and renown were once described in terms of having a "name," and indeed this was seen as a central goal for Weyewa status and power seekers. By acquiring names in spectacular prestige feasts, they established themselves as individuals surrounded by key symbols of material value in Sumbanese life: horses, buffalo, pigs, spears, and cloths. As these name-seeking feasts began to run afoul of the Indonesian government's efforts at national development, and Christian names grew increasingly popular due to religious conversion. Prestige names did not die out altogether, but they have remained a way of referring to racehorses, *bemos*, and businesses. However, in the context of a post-Suharto Indonesia, the image of "renown" once so celebrated in name-seeking feasts began to look like another instance of KKN — *korupsi, kolusi, nepotisme* ("corruption, cronyism, and nepotism").

The Bloody Thursday incident sheds light on theories of personal names. Until the mid-1980s, few Sumbanese parents would agree with the view of Lieberson that selecting a name for one's child was a "matter of taste";[19] instead they would have argued that the name they choose "fit" (*moda*) the child and indeed helped constitute it as a person. The relatives of Regent Malo, in particular, would perhaps find themselves in agreement with Lévi-Strauss' assertions about the classificatory functions of personal names, especially in constituting people as "persons."[20] By contrast, the protesters argued that the function of such naming was part of their legitimate practice of protest, and ultimately the hearers were responsible for their own interpretation of the name use. Believing "like a state" that names were supposed to be for the identification and retrieval of actual individuals, the protesters were outraged when the name of someone listed as having passed the civil service test did not refer to anyone who actually took the test. For them — well-educated youths from many different ethnic groups (including Weyewa) — when one "sees like a state" in a bureaucratic testing context, using a name is an act of transparent reference, and should not be linked to further nepotistic ends.[21]

In this paper, I have a used a model of naming as a communicative practice in which semantic classification and pragmatic usage are both forms of participation used by ideologically interested actors in histori-cally dynamic social situations. Although the Indonesian state generally promotes the use of names as context free identifiers,[22] in this case a state functionary, Regent Malo, had a conflict of interest. On the one hand, in a rapidly changing and hostile political environment, he needed protec-tion against the illegitimate use of his "hard" name that this classifica-tion system implied; on the other hand, accepting the potency of this classification system amounted to a rejection of the government model for naming, and thus a key feature of his responsibility as Regent to "see like a state." The tragic unfolding of events in West Sumba reveals the importance of understanding names in the context of action and interests as well as formal semiotic relations.

Notes

1   But see Claude Lévi-Strauss, *La Pensée Sauvage* (Paris: Plon, 1962) and S.S. Bean, "Ethnology and the Study of Proper Names," *Anthropological Linguistics* 22 (1980): 305–16.

2   Allerton, D.J., "The Linguistic and Sociolinguistic Status of Proper Names — What Are They, and Who Do They Belong To," *Journal of Pragmatics* 11, 1 (1987): 61–92.

3   E. Mertz, "A Cape Breton System of Personal Names: Pragmatic and Semantic Change," *Semiotica* 44, 1–2 (1983): 55–74.

4   Clifford Geertz, "Person, Time, and Conduct in Bali: An Essay in Cultural Analysis," in *The Interpretation of Cultures* (New York: Basic Books, 1972 [1966]).

5   J.S. Mill, *A System of Logic, Ratiocinative and Inductive; Being a Connected View of the Principles of Evidence and the Methods of Scientific Investigation.* (New York: Harper & Brothers, 1870).

6   Lévi-Strauss, *La Pensée Sauvage*, p. 215, quoted in Mertz, "A Cape Breton System of Personal Names," p. 55.

7   Ibid., p. 70.

8   J.C. Kuipers, *Language, Identity, and Marginality in Indonesia: The Changing Nature of Ritual Speech on the Island of Sumba.* (Cambridge: Cambridge University Press, 1998).

9   L. Onvlee, *Palatalisatie in Eenige Soembaneesche Dialecten. Feestbundel Tegenover het 150 jarig Bestaan van het Bataviaasch Genootschaap*, Deel II. (Batavia: Bataviaasch Genootschaap 1930), pp. 234–45; C. Lyons, *Definiteness* (Cambridge and New York: Cambridge University Press, 1999).

10   Forth 1983.

11   Renard-Clamagirand, B., "Le Nom Wewewa: Jeu et Enjeu (Sumba, Indonésie de l'Est)," in *D'un Nom à L'autre en Asie du Sud-Est: Approches ethnologiques*, eds. J. Massard-Vincent and S. Pauwels (Paris: Karthala, 1999), pp. 27–44.

12   L. Onvlee, "On the Significance of Livestock in Sumba," in *The Flow of Life: Essays on Eastern Indonesia*, ed. J.J. Fox (Cambridge [MA]: Harvard University Press, 1980), pp. 196, 199.

13   (but, see Forth 1981).

14   J. Hoskins, *Biographical Objects: How Things Tell the Stories of People's Lives* (New York: Routledge, 1998).

15   H. Haripranata, *Ceritera sejarah gereja Katolik Sumba dan Sumbawa, dengan sejarah umum Sumba kuno sebagai latar belakang* (Ende, S.N: Arnoldus, 1984).

16   T.V.D. End, *Gereformeerde Zending op Sumba, 1859–1972: een Bronnenpublicatie.* (Alphen aan den Rijn: Aska, 1987).

17   W. Wolters, "The Making of Civil Society in Historical Perspective," in *Civil Society: In Search of Transition*, ed. H.A.I.A. Schulte-Nordholt (Yogyakarta: Pustaka Pelajar, 2002).

18   D. Mitchell, "Tragedy in Sumba: Why Neighbours Hacked Each Other to Death in a Remote Part of Indonesia," *Inside Indonesia* (1999): 58–9.

19   S. Lieberson, *A Matter of Taste: How Names, Fashions, and Culture Change* (New Haven, Yale University Press, 2000).

20   Lévi-Strauss, *La Pensée Sauvage.*

21   James C. Scott, *Seeing like a State: How Certain Schemes to Improve the Human Condition Have Failed* (New Haven: Yale University Press, 1998) (drawing on David Herlihy and Christiane Klapische-Zuber, *Tuscans and their Families: A Study of the Florentine Catasto of 1427.* [New Haven: Yale University Press, 1985]); James C. Scott, John Tehranian and Jeremy Mathias, "The Production of Legal Identities Proper to States: The Case of the Permanent Family Surname," *Comparative Studies in Society and History* 44, 1 (2002): 4–44.

22   Y. Yahya, *Ganti Nama* (Jakarta: Yayasan Tunas Bangsa, 1987).

CHAPTER 9

"Who is Your Name?" Naming Paiwan Identities in Contemporary Taiwan

Ku Kun-hui 顧坤惠

Anthropological studies of names (and terms of address) have been shaped by different theoretical frameworks over time, ranging from evolutionary, functionalist, structuralist, and psychological approaches to symbolic approaches.[1] Geertz's discussion on names and titles is more or less derived from the Maussian-Leenhardt position which assumes that people are incumbents of names, that is, they inhabit a position in a constellation of names. It is often used to make a point about the person being a localized refraction of a social whole, and it is meant to counter the notion of the person as an isolated individual. Renato Rosaldo urged a shift from a system-oriented Maussian-Leenhardt position to a practice-oriented study of names.[2] Names do not just reflect social categories but also what people often "do" with them. I have argued elsewhere that the strategic use of Paiwan names and naming is a social praxis in re-negotiating social relations in daily interaction.[3] This also has an impact on long-term historical trajectories for local social hierarchies and regional political dynamics. This article focuses on the interface between the Paiwan vernacular naming system and other dominant institutions to articulate the degree of changing identities and possible consequences of this interface on the global milieu.[4]

The Paiwan people are one of the Austronesian-speaking groups in Taiwan who reside in south and southeast Taiwan, which is divided by Mt. Tawu (Map 1).[5]

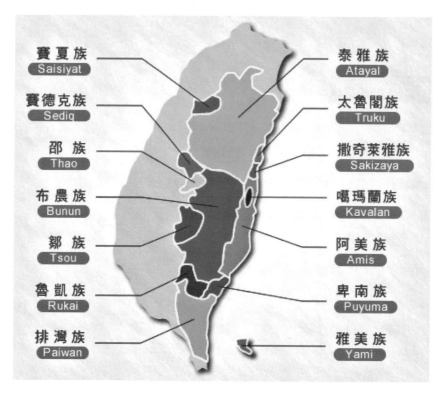

賽夏族 Saisiyat

賽德克族 Sediq

邵族 Thao

布農族 Bunun

鄒族 Tsou

魯凱族 Rukai

排灣族 Paiwan

泰雅族 Atayal

太魯閣族 Truku

撒奇萊雅族 Sakizaya

噶瑪蘭族 Kavalan

阿美族 Amis

卑南族 Puyuma

雅美族 Yami

Map 1

The current population is about 70,000. The Paiwan people are famous for their social hierarchy and material culture.[6] The difference between the nobility and commoners is represented in mythical stories (of origin), rituals, names, decorating privileges in tattooing, sculpture, and textiles (which include motifs of human figures, snakes, the sun, sacred pottery, and hunting scenes). Paiwan society is generally characterized as a house society where the symbolic components like the personal name pool and house name and material possessions like heirlooms are passed on through the first-born child. This primogeniture rule applies to both the aristocrats (*mamazangilan*) and commoners (*qatditan*). The importance attached to the continuity of the house (*umaq*) and house name is culturally emphasized regardless of social status. *Umaq* refers to the corporeality of a house, a house one is born in and, in the past, the grave, one's final destiny. The Paiwan people can trace their ancestry bilaterally and make claims accordingly, but usually they trace their lineage through ancestors of higher social status. In the past, most Paiwan societies had elaborate ancestral rituals, the most important one being *Melevep* (or *Leve-leveq-an*) that took place once every five years.[7] The concept of *lugem* (potency) plays an important role in Paiwan personhood, which, to an important extent, is related to ancestral stock. As most Paiwan personal names are gender-specific and inherited (from an ancestral name pool), they reflect the name bearers' social status in the hierarchical system. Birth order is important in that the best names go to the first-born child, who is called *vusum* ("the seed millet"). *Vusum* also refers to the nobility and this gives a sense of the importance of primogeniture rule in Paiwan society and its emphasis on social hierarchy. The data presented in this article was gathered mostly from the Taiwu Township in Pingtung County, with supplementary data from other selected areas in Pingtung. The population size of the settlements varies from several hundred to a couple of thousands.

What's in a Name? Why Do Names Matter?

Among the Austronesian-speaking Paiwan, there are six kinds of appellations which I have heard, or seen used, to identify persons among themselves. These are: a personal name and house name; a kinship term; a status title; a nickname; a Chinese and/or Japanese name (given by the government); and a Christian name. The first three consist not only of a collection of markers but also of a distinct terminological scheme, which Geertz referred to as "symbolic orders of person-definition."[8] Newly introduced names, resulting from the encounters with state forces (Japanese and Chinese) and religious denominations (mainly Catholics and Presbyterians), are unevenly incorporated into Paiwan naming practices. These names have also influenced the vernacular naming system. They are not used concurrently and their usage depends on the situation and individuals involved. In this article, I combine the personal and house names together for two reasons. First, a house name alone cannot be used to identify an individual, but it can be used by an individual to identify himself or herself with a group of people related to the same house. Second, a house name is often added to a personal name to distinguish an individual among a group of people who share the same name — a situation that arises due to the repetitive use of the same names in the community. In other words, both personal and house names represent individual identity in different contexts.

Personal names and status titles are often used to illustrate the hierarchical nature of Paiwan society and the relation between the ranked names and indigenous political dynamics. These newly introduced names are used in specific contexts and have not entered indigenous political dynamics, but their articulation with the indigenous naming system is interesting for comparative purposes. The (Austronesian) Paiwan naming system in Taiwan is similar in its origins to those of East Indonesia and the Philippines discussed elsewhere in the present book, but interacts with external norms (Japanese and Chinese) that are very different from the Western ones that influenced those naming systems. Before turning to the discussion of personal names, I shall describe the most common kin terms and status titles used in Paiwan daily life.

Kinship Terms

Among the different names mentioned above, kinship terms are the ones most often used in daily interaction. Paiwanese kinship terminology is formally known in anthropology as the "Hawaiian" type of kinship system. In this system, individuals classify their relatives essentially according to the generation these relatives occupy in relation to their own generation. In other words, one's siblings, half-siblings, cousins, and all of their spouses' siblings are grouped together under the same term, *kaka*. This excludes the case where one's spouse is related to oneself but occupies a different genealogical position in terms of generation, a case which was not uncommon in the past.[9] All uncles and aunts on either side are categorized with mother (*kina*) and father (*kama*). All children of one's siblings, cousins, and spouse (nephews and nieces of all sorts, except for the situation mentioned above) are classified with one's own children. The general term for child(ren) is *alak*, but this is often used referentially, not vocatively. Most of the time, children are called by their personal names or simply *kakelian* (the little one). In some cases, however, reciprocal terms are used between parents and children: female children are called *la kina* (or *ina*) and male children *la kama* (or *ama*) when the parents want to flatter them for having done something good or to ask a service of them. One possible explanation for this exceptional occurrence is the teknonymous principle: a person's child will be his/her grandchild's parent. For example, Muni's child (Lampau) will be her grandchild's (younger namesake Muni's) parent. So the older Muni uses her younger namesake's usage to call Lampau "la kama." Due to the reciprocal terms between grandparent and grandchild, the grandparent adopts the usage of his or her younger namesake.

In the second generation above and below the actors' own, terms become completely reciprocal. The term for grandparent and grandchild is the same, *vuvu*. These two generations and the individuals who comprise them are culturally identified. The reciprocal terminology proceeds on through the third generation and beyond, with specific terms to denote the generational difference: *kavuwan, kakiton,* and *kakavi* (fifth generation down from the ego's position). The three-generation span (self, plus two ascending or descending generations) is considered as a complete cycle in terms of terminology. It is to be noted that the reciprocal term between parent and child is not common in Oceanic societies. In general, the Paiwan people's knowledge of genealogy is confined to those whose lives they have overlapped with. There are households with four generations of living kin, and most middle-aged people's genealogical memory extends to five generations, with the exception of a few noble houses where the remembrance of selected ancestors (especially the linear first-born line) is an important part of the marriage ritual and a source of authority and status.[10]

Despite the shared terminology in denoting a vast range of relatives, there are special terms to distinguish the relative distance among them in terms of genealogical positions. For example, siblings and half-siblings are referred to as *vertik;* first (full) cousins are referred to as *sikacekel;* second cousins are referred to as *sangasangasan;* and third cousins are referred to as *pasasamusan.* In other words, people who share parents or a single parent are called *vertik;* people who share any one grandparent, excluding *vertik,* are called *sikacekel;* people who share any one great-grandparent, excluding *vertik* and *sikacekel,* are called *sangasangasan.* People who share any one great-great-grandparent, except those in the above three categories, are called *pasasamusan.* These ancestor-centered kin terms are also used referentially and seldom vocatively. The referential forms are only used to convey kinship information, never as a general means of identifying people. These terms appear in public discourse only in response to some questions with respect to which the existence of the kin tie is felt to be a relevant piece of information. For example, *sangasangasan* is the first and ideal criterion for choosing one's mate. The term was used to explain to me how endogamous marriage arrangements within the same rank were made in the past and to trace relationships between ancestors or living kin in the abstract.[11] This single ancestor-centered kin network is becoming more important as family groupings based on a single common ancestor are mobilized for various reasons in contemporary social life.

Kinship terms are often used in daily interaction, sometimes in combination with personal names, such as *"kina* Kerker." For relatives one generation junior to oneself, vocative forms do not exist. Instead, the personal name is used, with the exception mentioned above. For relatives genealogically senior to oneself, kin terms alone are sufficient; personal names (and occasionally house names) are added to specify an individual in a group setting.

Thus, in general, we can say that this system of kinship terminology defines individuals in a primarily taxonomic fashion. However, this general rule only applies to people of roughly the same status. When it comes to addressing the highest nobility or people with a status higher than oneself, prestigious personal names or the simple referential term "*vusam*" is applied instead.[12] In other words, the social norms associated with kinship are habitually overridden by culturally valued norms of naming that refer directly to social hierarchy. This substituted reference points to the particular identity quality the nobility wish to attract to themselves.

Categories of kinship terminology and names cross over and inter-relate or they are kept distinct depending on the context of usage. Politics and kinship make use of apparently fixed categories, but by manipulating them one can combine legitimacy in one sphere with that of another. Thus, kinship status becomes political status and vice-versa, though it appears that the belief is that these domains should be kept as separate kin obligations. Further, the obligations between nobility and commoners are conceptualized differently. This can also be seen through the usage of the term "*vusam*."

The term "*vusam*" refers to the first-born child and distinguishes this child from the rest of its siblings, a characteristic of systems with a rule of primogeniture. Strictly speaking, however, this term does not refer to first-born children but to the first child that survives; stillborns and early deaths are not assigned the status of *vusam*. (The practice of necronymic naming was, however, sometimes applied by giving a child the name of an earlier sibling who had died.) As its literal meaning is "seed-millet," it refers to continuity through the generations.

There is a notion that the *vusam* has special social and ritual status. This is not only demonstrated in various social arrangements, but also in naming practice.[13] The best name is reserved for the *vusam* and younger siblings consult the *vusam* in naming their descendants. Implicitly, the name order also implies a hierarchical order: the relative status of siblings is defined in terms of seniority of birth order.[14] This is what M.W. Young referred to as "normative rank."[15]

The term "*vusam*" also refers to the nobility, extending the kinship-like relation to that between the nobles and the commoners, with the nobles as the firstborn (representing house of origin) and the commoners as branching-off siblings. Social hierarchy is built into daily language usage.

Status Title

The term *"mamazangilan"* is often translated as "aristocratic nobility" in Chinese texts, and *"qatitan"* is translated as "commoner." The origin of the hierarchical division between *mamazangilan* and *qatitan* is legitimized by myth.[16] It is said that the ancestor of the chiefly Mavaliu house in Piuma emerged from the egg of a snake while commoners were descended from a dog, with the emblem of the snake being considered superior to the dog. This distinction is also shown in the daily usage of the term *"tsautsau"* "person; human being." The colloquial phrase *"tsautsau timadu"* means "s/he is a person" but also "s/he is a noble." Upon hearing a commoner's name, one's response is often *"inika tsautsau"* or "not a person," meaning "not a noble." However, even within these two categories of noble and commoner, individuals differentiate among themselves according to their individual "make-up," genealogical positions, and birth order.

Individuals constantly discriminate among themselves according to the social positions into which they were born; however, the nature of this difference needs further qualification. Synchronically, the difference between *mamazangilan* and *qatitan* is definite because each person is born into a social position; diachronically, however, the boundary of these two categories often shifts because the social position of the next generation can be manipulated through marriage. For instance, it was not uncommon for children to say to me that they had a higher status than one of their parents. Thus, the status title does not refer to a stable social group but to individuals.

The cultural preference for endogamous marriage practices among the nobles also maintains the social boundary. Due to the strict endogamous custom in the past, sexual encounters between *mamazangilan* and *qatitan* were not considered "proper" marriages.[17] A "proper" marriage (that is, one with a formal ritual celebration) was defined by an equivalent status between two parties, with some exceptions. (There were a few cases where the firstborn of a noble house decided to marry a commoner and ended up leaving the house for the second child to take over the position.) Though the notion of a proper marriage has changed, marriage negotiation remains the salient site for status competition, particularly for those whose status is relatively similar.[18] During my fieldwork in the mid-1990s, the marriage preference toward firstborns and higher-ranking partners, among others (for example, occupational preferences), was vocally articulated and inter-marriage between nobility and commoners was increasing. The Christian notion of love was sometimes used to legitimize intermarriage between people of different ranks. I have argued that this increase, paradoxically, intensifies the debates around status competition and the inflation of certain noble names, as well as their eventual devaluation.[19]

Personal Names and House Names[20]

A Paiwan name includes a personal name and a house name, such as "Pailis (personal name) a Pacikel (house name)," where normally the house name refers to the name of the house into which one is born. This can be changed when a person marries into another house, in which case the house name of the spouse is adopted. This applies to either sex. It should be noted that the Paiwan house is the most basic cultural unit in the society. It embodies the symbolic and material components that are passed on through the first-born child or *vusam*.

House Names

A house name refers to the name given to the physical structure of a particular house. A house name, however, can outlive the physical structure and it can be appropriated by different residential groups. Thus, analytically, the house-as-name and house-as-physical-structure should be distinguished. A house name should not be confused with the surname that is used in Western or Chinese societies, as house names normally can only be passed on through the first-born child of the house of origin. In Piuma I was constantly told that house names did not carry any value (indicating social status) despite the fact that some houses were considered as *vinqacan* (from the beginning of time), which justified their chiefly status. Lévi-Strauss' emphasis on the material (house-as-physical-structure) and immaterial (house-as-name) nature of house wealth is important when considering the relation of the house to both hierarchies of status or ritual power and to economic stratification.[21] Among the Paiwan, however, every house carries a house name and the inauguration and naming of a new house constitute an important social event along with the religious ceremony attached to it.

Since the firstborn (*vusum*) inherits the house property and thus the house names, a non-firstborn who marries another non-firstborn has to establish a new house and create a new house name.[22] There is a cultural emphasis on the house of origin having a higher status than the derived houses, which often have to rely on the house of origin for financial and other support. This branching-off of new households from established ones is a constant process among the Paiwan and the recognition of

interrelatedness between natal and derived houses is frequently emphasized. People might not be able to detail the exact genealogical juncture
of the branching-off but they all recognize the derivative relation among
houses.[23] The same analogy (original versus derivative) also applies to the
relationship between the nobility and commoners, though in a symbolic
sense. In practice, name-bestowing also allows the nobility to extend their
influence over the commoners. The same applies to name-giving, an act
through which the relationships between the firstborn and the rest of the
siblings are bound, recognized, and valued.

When introduced to a Paiwan from a different region, usually one
would cite the most prominent house name in the community and specify
one's relation to that house. For example, a person can say that he or
she belongs to La Patsikel (current residence), or La Leleman (house of
origin), or to La Mavaliu (associated noble house). They could also use
the house name of their ancestors if they are known in the region where
the listeners come from. This ambiguity leaves much room for maneuver,
allowing people to highlight different identities in different contexts,
such that how one defines oneself will depend upon the context and the
other party.

The strategic use of house names actually demonstrates an act of
identification in a particular context. For a politics of naming, we need to
decide which names have value and significance for whom, situationally.[24]
People often use the expression, "I am also from that house," as a qualifier
to legitimize their position when expressing opinions. Theoretically, one
can claim to belong to the houses from where all of one's ancestors came;
that is, if these ties are traceable and well maintained. In cases where an
exact link between two houses is untraceable, people express the link
through the memory of objects, such as cooking utensils or ploughs,
transmitted between the houses at marriage. Marriage payment only flows
from the groom's natal house to the bride's house, so the objects represent
an affinal kin tie through a male ancestor from other houses.

Personal Names

The social order defined by personal names is complicated. It is the most
important one, or the autonym, in Macdonald's terms (in this volume).
To me a Paiwan personal name is the answer that Paiwan people often
give to the following question "*Tima su ngadan*?" ("Who is your name?")
Among the Paiwan, one must ask "Who is your name?" and never "What
is your name?" This personified form and the elaborate ancestral rites
indicate a strong personal connection between the name bearers and
their name providers whose identity and status the name bearers come

to assume. This is also why the Paiwan people keep referring back to ancestors in naming. Names are not impersonal objects detached from one's bodily self. The personal naming system has characteristics that are significant for an understanding of the Paiwanese idea of personhood. The word "*ngadan*" is also the term for reputation in Paiwan language; thus, "*nanguaq a ngadan*" (good name) refers either to the nobility or a person of good reputation.

Personal names are drawn from an established pool of names, although there is the possibility of creating new ones. One is usually named after one's ancestors — a practice which results in the frequent duplication of names within any given group, particularly among first cousins. More importantly, names indicate familial connections and an affiliation of sorts, which in turn reveal the status of the named. A name represents who you are, what your status is, how you will be treated, and what rights you might be entitled to. In the case of Piuma today, these include the rights of decoration[25] and marriage payment.[26] A name is not just an individual marker but is embedded in complex social networks and carries significant symbolic meanings. Bien Chiang rightly argues that personal names of a set of siblings record the marriage relations of previous generations,[27] although according to my experience in Piuma, this only applies to marriages between people of similar status. In the case of marriages between people of varying social ranks, the second generation is often given names from the higher-ranking ancestors. Thus personal names are not just personal; they also reveal social relations and the cultural value attached to these relations.

Most Paiwan personal names are gender-specific. Examples are Muni, Pailis, and Tibulan for females and Lampau, Kulili, and Tanupak for males. In fact, according to Lei Shih only one out of 292 names that he collected in Su-Paiwan in the 1960s was shared by both sexes.[28] Among those 292 names, there were 190 male specific names, 99 female specific names, and two unspecified names (no information available). In Piuma, I was told that all names are gendered. In Shih's sample of 1,611 names, there are 121 names that appear only once. In all the naming events I witnessed in Piuma, newborn babies were named after someone else, though I know of a few cases outside Piuma where the newborns were given names that had never been used before to commemorate a particular event or person. Among the genealogies I collected in Piuma, there are names that appear more frequently than others in different generations. For example, names of lower rank, such as *udalan* and *lamawan*, are no longer in use. Many Paiwan names have meanings denoting natural objects, such as grass, or natural phenomena, such as thunder or bird sounds. However, the meanings of some other names are lost to the current speech community. In fact, some say that names have no specific meanings. In this case, one could say that the meanings of names are of no more import than the names themselves.

A Paiwan name is generally given not long after a baby is born by a family member or if a "better" name is sought by a person of higher rank. Most naming occasions occur privately within a family, unless one asks for a name beyond the control of one's family. Normally, when both parents come from the same rank, the first-born child is named after an ancestor of the *vusam* (firstborn); the next child is named after an ancestor of the in-marrying spouse; the remaining children's names alternate between the two. The sequence is often not followed exactly and can be discussed if special conditions occur, for example, to memorialize a newly deceased relative. If neither parent is *vusam*, then negotiation can be made between these two houses.

Specific personal names are often retained within a particular rank, such as the *mamazangilan*, and the right to give names is reserved for the *vusam* of the house where the name originated. Usually a name giver would be one's parents or grandparents, if the names are common within the family. In the case where one would like to name a child after an in-marrying ancestor whose name is "better" than the rest of the names in the family, then one has to ask permission from the current firstborn of the house where this in-marrying ancestor originated. Asking for names from a higher-ranking family member signifies an act of identification. On the other hand, it is said that high-ranking noble families that "married down" for more than three generations would lose their noble status and consequently their access to "good" names. However, if only one person married down, it does not affect the family's ability to marry at the same level or up again. This custom allows some elasticity and is often subject to manipulation.[29]

Basically, the principle of seniority (precedence) governs the relationships between the name giver and the named, linking the firstborn with the rest of the siblings through the act of name-giving and linking the nobility with commoners through the act of name-bestowing.[30] Again, the homology between the firstborn and the nobility is enacted in naming practices.

A child is often given a second personal name if its parents come from different regions. If a person is called by his first personal name by his paternal kinsmen in the village where he resides, he can be called by his second personal name in his maternal kinsmen's district. This is particularly common among the nobility among whom regional intermarriage is often practised. Following this logic, a person can have third or fourth names if his maternal and paternal grandparents also come from different regions with their own distinct name stock. Once ties are weakened, a name is often not used and it is eventually dropped.[31] A name that is not used in daily life is considered non-existent, though it remains a possibility for a subsequent naming occasion.

The relationship between the named and the person he or she is named after (name provider, in most cases, a deceased person[32]) is that of commemoration and emulation. When choosing names, people often discuss the personality and reputation of the persons with the same name. More frequently they name a child after an ancestor or a person they admire. In other cases, more than one name is given to a child, and it is only later, by common agreement, that a name best suited to the character of the child is selected. It was said that several bearers of the name Kui (a high-ranking name) showed the characteristics of drunken men. The name was quite popular at one time but is no longer so. A name can be considered "too good" for a person (in terms of ranking differences) but it can also be spoiled by a person (in terms of personal reputation).

Despite the boundary drawn between *mamazangilan* and *adidan* and the rules to maintain it, this boundary is often transgressed through various cultural mechanisms such as inter-rank marriage arrangements (buying names), adoption, appropriation of names during political struggles, and so on, to change the course of the status of future generations.[33] Thus personal names and naming do not only reflect the socio-political parameters (ranking hierarchy) but also the means to alter these parameters in times of change.

Nicknames

Nicknames are often given after one's marriage. It is said that the marrying couple has to be very careful about their behavior during the marriage feast period because it is the time when villagers discuss what kind of nickname would be given to them. In this sense, nicknames in Piuma are tied to the concept of a conjugal unit. Often only one nickname is assigned to a couple. Some of the nicknames refer to personal (physical) characteristics. Most nicknames told to me have, in one way or another, sexual connotations. For example, one middle-aged *kama* was said to be a "competent hunter," particularly good at setting up the indigenous mechanical spear (*vuluk*) to catch a wild pig (*vavui*). This statement was interpreted as referring to his numerous sexual encounters, implied metaphorically by *vuluk*. Some other nicknames describe the female's private part. Nicknames also provide information about the social relation between spouses. For instance, *Malimali* (thank you) refers to a couple with children from previous relationships (often coming from the female). *Lacen* (leftover [food]) refers to people taking things without paying for them, in this case, the bride price. "Theft" refers to couples who have had a sexual relationship before marriage. There is also a social consensus that one cannot say the nicknames directly to the persons so named, but it is considered enjoyable to talk around such names in a metaphorical way in front of them. People can comprehend the message from the stories told and play with it. Occasionally, this practice leads to conflict when the rhetoric is misused or the social relation is considered too distant to play this game. The first time I heard people talking about nicknames was at a wake after a funeral, when it is customary to gather in front of the deceased's house for a period of time to accompany the family members. Joking serves as a means for identifying the in-group circle within a community other than kinship and hierarchical principles. While it is most often done among peers, sometimes the elders can call the youth by nicknames but not the other way round.

Names Given by the State (Japanese or Chinese Names)

The first comprehensive population census in aboriginal areas was established by the Japanese Government in the early part of the twentieth century, not long after Taiwan was taken over in 1895. Like other colonial powers of the age, census taking was an important step toward statecraft, a project of legibility in Scott's terminology.[34] Household registration was further enforced for population control and management. Even though Japanese institutions, such as schools and police stations, did not reach remote settlements until the early 1930s, most people were included in the census before then and people had to go to the village nearest to them for birth registration. The household registration contained the following information: Paiwan personal name, house name, date of birth (and death if applicable), birth order, residence, marriage information, and parents' names. The personal and house names were initially pronounced using indigenous pronunciation but spelled in Katakana, the Japanese phonetic form. Thus, this Katakana form should be counted as the first transliteration of the Paiwan language (however illegible). When the military government took power in the 1930s, Shinto shrine attendance was further imposed on Japanese colonies. Japanese names in Kanji, which had nothing to do with the indigenous naming system, were also introduced to cultivate a sense of national identity and belonging, which later encouraged the colonial subjects to join the war in the Pacific, though they were never considered as "citizens" as such. The Civil Law of 1896, which emphasized the continuity of the family in the male line with only the eldest son inheriting, did not apply to colonial subjects in Taiwan. Thus, the primogeniture rule of Paiwan inheritance practices survived. This is shown on the household registration records, where female household heads prevailed and their in-marrying male spouses had to carry their house name.

The short-lived Japanese names (Kanji form) did not displace (or replace) the names used in daily life. People used their Japanese names only in official contexts and when they dealt with outsiders, although a few Japanese names found their way into the Paiwan name pool. These names are still used today, and are more or less regulated by Paiwan naming practices. Due to the close association between the *mamazangilan* and Japanese officers in some regions, these Japanese names were most often assumed by these *mamazangilan* and they carried the prestige associated with that status. Today, Japanese names are seldom used unless there is a necessity to converse in Japanese among the older generation, that is, in response to Japanese visitors or people who have also had the same Japanese colonial experience. In other words, the Japanese names are used mostly with outsiders and only occasionally (or rarely) with insiders.

After 1945, the Chinese KMT nationalist government took over Taiwan. The Japanese household registration system was maintained but Chinese characters (non-alphabetical) were used instead. The system remained roughly the same; however, information on one's profession or means of subsistence and level of education were added. (See Appendices I and II for the differences between the two systems[35]). It has now become an entertaining topic for people to retell the peculiar results of adopting Chinese surnames. In one case, a set of eight siblings carries at least four different Chinese surnames. This is because surnames were given to people randomly without tracing the relationships between households. Family members who married out of their natal house or established a new house of their own were given different surnames. In the former instance, these family members assumed their spouse's surname (either male or female); in the latter, most likely, the male household heads were given a new surname to be passed on to their descendants. The role of Paiwan house names was often seen as equivalent to that of a Chinese surname, as some early works on the Paiwan have implied. However, Paiwan house names do not presume a patrilineal bias as Chinese surnames do. The patrilineal bias of the Chinese system was not entirely imposed on the

Paiwan people. This is reflected in the case of Paiwan female household heads with Chinese surnames who retained these surnames and passed them on to their children. Among the Chinese, the father's surname is passed on to all descendants and it is changed only when a female member assumes her husband's surname upon marriage. (Currently, Chinese married women can choose whether or not they will take up her husband's surname. As for the children, in most cases they carry their father's surname unless a special agreement has been reached.) Paiwan house names are passed on only within the original house through the firstborn, and new house names are created upon non-firstborn siblings' marriages with other non-firstborn spouses. The house names of non-firstborn couples' descendants are then different from either of their parents' natal house names. In a newly established house, it is the husband's Chinese surname that is often assumed by the children.

Despite the generational differences in house names, siblings who are born to the same house share the same house name due to the cultural emphasis on the house of origin. This emphasis on the original house can also be seen through the burial practices: the cultural ideal is to be buried back in the house of origin (natal house). (In Piuma, however, commoners are less adamant about keeping this practice. On the other hand, the nobility who married into commoners' houses strongly emphasize the importance of this burial practice.) It is possible that when the Chinese naming system was first introduced, the house name was taken as the equivalent of the Chinese surname, thus applying Chinese lineal rule onto the Paiwan house name system. Based on the Chinese family law at that time, in-marrying spouses (often females) were asked to take up the surname of the household head. This resulted in Paiwan siblings taking up different Chinese surnames because of marriage with a *vusam* or another non-*vusam* male. As there was a high percentage of female household heads in Paiwan society, male siblings with different Chinese surnames became a possibility. This situation highlights the different cultural principles between the Paiwan and the Chinese: a Chinese surname functions to record the lineal descent through a male line while a Paiwan house name is a marker for a sibling set without sex discrimination. Moreover, it is passed on through a *vusam*.

Chinese names are used in all government-related matters such as schools, household registration, identity registration, and medical insurance. Paiwan names are used in family-related activities and internal kinship networks, as well as for communication within the same language group. As the state institutions encroach more upon the lives of the

Paiwan people, Chinese names have become increasingly used by the younger generation in contexts other than their local communities. In the 1990s, elders were alarmed by the degree of ignorance among the youth about their own house names. Thus, efforts were made during the Presbyterian Church Friday family meetings, which rotated among the houses of each family meeting unit, to teach children about the house name of the family where the meeting was being held.

In 1984 indigenous rights activists launched the Name Correction Movement to request the government to call the indigenous people by their chosen name — *yuan-tsu-min* (原住民), "the indigenous peoples" — instead of *shan-bao* (山胞), "mountain compatriot" and to revive the indigenous naming system.[36] Subsequently, indigenous names in Chinese characters were allowed to be adopted in official documents in 1995. However, only a few people took this option partly because the bureaucracy did not make it easy to change the names and the task to fit indigenous names into the Chinese form was enormous. Between 1995 and 2005, only 890 people (out of 460,000) changed their Chinese name to the indigenous one. Sixty-five people later reverted to their Chinese names.[37] The second wave of reverting to indigenous names was launched when the national identification card (身分證) was renewed in 2007 and it was estimated that there were more than 10,000 people took to opportunity to add indigenous name onto the new ID card. This official acknowledgement of the indigenous naming system, however, did legitimize the use of indigenous names in contexts other than the local communities. Lately, personal business cards have become very popular among the Paiwan people. Found on these cards are both the Chinese and Paiwan names (either in Romanized phonetic form or in Chinese characters), although often the Paiwan name order is reversed to accord with the Chinese one. In other words, the house name is used as an equivalent to the Chinese surname and placed in front of the personal name, as in this example: 利格拉樂。阿熄; Pasausa。Vikung. There is also a reverse influence phenomenon where the Chinese name is phonetically similar to the Paiwan name, such as 依琳 Ilin; 幕妮 Muni. Some commoners have also adopted Chinese names that are phonetically similar to Paiwan noble names, even when they are not eligible for such high-ranking names in the indigenous naming system. When confronted, these commoners could claim that it is a Chinese name and not their "real name."

The adoption of the Chinese naming system by the Paiwan people has increasingly started to show a tendency toward male-centeredness. For instance, some now carry their father's Chinese surname even when their father is an in-marrying spouse, but not the reverse. I was told that nowadays young people prefer to establish a new house of their own partly because they do not like to stay with their parents-in-law and partly because the young men in particular would like their children to have surnames of their own. This increasing "male centeredness," which characterizes the larger Han society, has had a negative impact on the female firstborns as well as the in-marrying male spouses, who increasingly feel pressured. (In fact, there is a joke about forming a local in-marrying spouse association.) These in-marrying male spouses feel they now have less authority in the family than their female counterpart and they feel less "manly" because their position (in-marrying) makes them look as though they cannot afford to raise their family on their own. These ideas seem to derive from the influence of Chinese society where in-marrying males have a less favorable position in the family. Indeed, there are a number of cases of this type of marriage, which concurs with a point made by Anthony Reid in the present volume about the increased patriarchal tendency accompanying the adoption of a surname system.

Christian Names (Catholic versus Presbyterian Practices)

Since the introduction of Christianity after World War II, Christian names have also been introduced in the Paiwan region. It has been mandatory in the Catholic Church to give a baptismal name to the baptized person. If it is an infant baptism, the name can be decided by the parents or the priest. The name is given after a particular saint or an apostle, such as Saint Paul, Saint Thomas, or Saint Joseph. This baptismal name can be changed at the time of confirmation if another saint's name is preferred. Dominican Catholics maintain this tradition of giving baptismal names in Taiwan. However, among the Paiwan Catholics, I never heard the use of Christian names in daily interaction. I discovered this naming practice among them only after I consulted the Catholic Church archives on the registration of believers, indicating that each person who became a Catholic would have a name card in the file. This file was not deleted even if the person changed his or her church affiliation. According to the Spanish priest working among the Paiwan in Pingtung, there has been an increase in the number of people adopting Chinese Catholic names (from both the New Testament and the Old Testament). The fact that the practice of being named after a deceased person is not alien to the Paiwan people and the increasing knowledge of biblical stories might have contributed to the increasing popularity of Catholic names (in Chinese form, such as 保羅, Bao Luo and 約瑟, Yue Se) among the Catholics in Paiwan.

The Presbyterian Church of England (PCE) in Paiwan has a different practice for naming, not only among the indigenous groups but also among the Chinese/Taiwanese. A Presbyterian missionary who performed baptisms in mountain churches in the early 1950s said that he had never given Christian names to those he baptized. In fact his Chinese co-workers did not have Christian names either. This probably has to do with Protestantism's emphasis on unmediated communication with the divine and consequently the emphasis on worshipping in one's native tongue. "If God speaks to each believer in the language of the heart, then His church should call them by their native names," he said. The PCE first arrived in Taiwan in 1865. At that time the Protestant mission movement had thoroughly married the idea of "vernacularization of the soul to a framework of romantic primordialism."[38] In principle local vernaculars were deemed to be the proper media for Christian proselytizing. Indeed the translation of the Bible into the vernacular has since become the first task of PCE overseas missions among groups whose languages have not been "rendered" into writing. However, some Paiwan Christians adopt Chinese names with a Christian message, such as 神恩, Shen En (God's grace) and 重生, Chong Sheng (new life or born again.) Alternatively, they simply adopt a Chinese translation of Christian names, such as 約翰, Yue Han (John.)

Even today, the choice of Christian names (in Chinese forms) among the Presbyterians (if they have Christian names) is different from that of Catholics. This difference in naming practice among different denominations can be traced to the division in the history of the Christian Church and the Puritan movement after the Reformation. Presbyterians scorned any names that might be considered as Catholic or had an association with non-scriptural saints, and considered the evocation of these names superstitious.[39] Instead, they preferred to use the Bible, especially the Old Testament, as their major name resource despite the fact that the Protestant Reformation lay great emphasis on New Testament references for its theology.[40] In no case would a Presbyterian take the name of a Catholic saint.

As seen above, the traditional Paiwan naming system has persisted despite the influence of Chinese/Christian names. While this system has been used together with foreign systems, it has never been replaced. It is arguable that the effect of the adoption of Christian names among Chinese Christians is greater than among the Paiwan people. In the Chinese naming system the generation marker disappears as a result of adopting Christian names; however, in the Paiwan naming system this marker is retained alongside foreign names.

Table 1   Sample List of Paiwan Names by Gender

Male names		*Female names*	
Tanupak	Kulili	Malevelev	Duku
Lampau	Lamayav	Muni	Tsankim
Quvulas	Sula	Galesles	Pailis
Tsmelesai	Ribun	Rezeman	Paqesan
Lutamkan	Kalavas	Jiujiul	Kereker
Langalu	Vikung	Dibulan	Awu
Kui	Tsamak	Vavauni	Wudalan
Balu	Bukilingan	Lavaus	Aselep
Takanau	Malatsmats	Batakauv	Lailai
Legeai	Gilegilav	Arai	Venen
Qalutsangal	Bangtil	Ruzim	Kai

Conclusion

In this paper, I have described six different appellations that have been used among the Paiwan people to articulate (1) the importance of the vernacular naming system in understanding Paiwan hierarchy and the ways in which that hierarchy can be subverted and negotiated through names; and 2) the possible challenge posed by the Japanese, Chinese, and Christian naming practices on the Paiwan vernacular naming system through dominant state legal regimes and religious organizations. These newly introduced names have come to be seen as a way of referring to the individual, or what Joel Kuipers refers to as a process of indexicalization,[41] and not as a vehicle for addressing or classifying people in relation to their traditional prestigious background or behaviors. However, there are signs of moving toward a male-centered pattern after 60 years of contact with the Taiwanese bureaucracy.

Some commoners even use Chinese names to defy the traditional hierarchical naming system as Chinese names are not bound by traditional naming procedures. Among the Paiwan people the answer to the question *"Tima su ngadan?"* (Who is your name?) depends to a great extent on the context, and the particular identity a person wishes to stress or highlight and on the audience one addresses. The primogeniture rule of inheritance has helped to preserve property within the house of origin, even though the contemporary legal principle that grants non-firstborn siblings a fair share of the property has undermined the authority of the *vusam*. The impact of the state legal principles on the Paiwan naming system remains to be seen.

APPENDIX 1

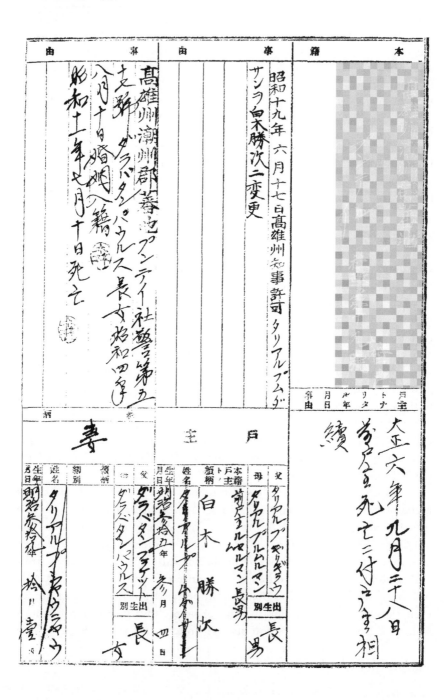

籍　別
本　籍　　寄　籍

台湾省
屏東
省縣市　省縣市
住　址

前變動		
姓名及戶長	戶長時間	及原因

本籍：屏東縣泰武鄉

教育程度／行業：農業　職位：自耕農

配偶姓名：林烏硃

戶長

父	母	與戶長關係	姓名	出生年月日
林白野ヤヤ　小ク名不　中キ牛末	林姁拉　中半才		林加再	民國陸年參月伍日　次男

本籍：屏東縣泰武鄉

山　[興泰校]　事由　[戶長 戶主]

教育程度／行業：農業　職位：自耕農

配偶姓名：林加再（妻）

父	母	親屬別	姓名	出生年月日
方白野ヤ中　末キヰ少	方梨也ポト		林烏硃	民國參年陸月茶日　次女

Notes

[1]   A.G. Morice, "Carrier Onomatology," *American Anthropologist* 35, (1933): 632–58; E.E. Evans-Prichard, "Nuer Modes of Address," in *Language in Culture and Society: A Reader in Linguistics and Anthropology*, ed. Dell Hymes (New York: Harper & Row, 1964); Claude Lévi-Strauss, *The Savage Mind* (Chicago: University of Chicago Press, 1968 [1966]); G. Jahoda, "A Note on Ashanti Names and Their Relationship to Personality," *British Journal of Psychology* 54 (1954): 192–5; Clifford Geertz, "Person, Time, and Conduct in Bali: An Essay in Cultural Analysis," in *The Interpretation of Cultures* (New York: Basic Books, 1972 [1966]). For a cross-cultural study of personal naming practices, see Richard Alford, *Naming and Identity: A Cross-Cultural Study of Personal Naming Practices* (New Haven, Connecticut: HRAF Press, 1988).

[2]   Renato Rosaldo, *Ilongot Headhunting 1883–1974: a Study in Society and History* (Stanford: Stanford University Press, 1984).

[3]   Ku Kun-hui, "The Symbolic and the Material in the Recognition of Hierarchy Among Austronesian Paiwan," *TsingHua University (Hsin-chu) Anthropological and Area Studies Paper Series* No. 1, 2006.

[4]   James C. Scott, John Tehranian and Jeremy Mathias, "The Production of Legal Identities Proper to States: The Case of the Permanent Family Surname," *Comparative Studies of Society and History* 44, 1 (2002): 4–44.

[5]   Derived from Council of Indigenous Peoples (CIP) website, http://www.apc. gov.tw/main/index_en.jsp

[6]   Shih Lei, *Su-Paiwan: An Ethnography of a Paiwan Village in Northern Paiwan* (Taipei, Nankang: Institution of Ethnology, Academia Sinica, 1956 [1971]); Chen Chi-lu, *Material Culture of the Formosan Aborigines* (Taipei: Southern Materials Center, 1988); Chiang Bien, "A New Approach to the Aristocratic System of the Paiwan, A Case Study of Ta-she," *Bulletin of Institute of Ethnology Academia Sinica* 55 (1983): 1–48.

[7]   See Bien Chiang, "House and Social Hierarchy of the Paiwan", unpublished PhD diss., Anthropology, University of Pennsylvania, 1993; Hsu Kong-ming, *The Rituals and Culture of the Paiwan in Kuralau* (Taipei: Dau-hsiang, 1994).

[8]   Clifford Geertz, "Person, Time, and Conduct in Bali: An Essay in Cultural Analysis," in *The Interpretation of Cultures* (New York: Basic Books, 1972 [1966]), p. 368.

[9]   In such cases, kin terms used to refer to the spouse's relations remain the same and they are separated from those used of one's spouse. For example, if one marries one's uncle, one would still call one's husband's parents *vuvu* (grandparents) instead of *kina* (mother) or *kama* (father.)

[10]   Cf. Chiang, "House and Social Hierarchy," and Ku, "The Symbolic and the Material in the Recognition of Hierarchy."

[11]   Even today, for marriage feast preparations, *sangasangasan* still has a dominant presence. The distribution of meat during a marriage feast period is carried out in terms of this categorical map, with slight modifications. It was said that meat should be distributed to each *pasasamusan*'s household and for

those beyond this category, meat was sent to the firstborns' house to deliver the news. It was up to the firstborn to transmit the news to other siblings.

12   Despite similarities, this situation differs from Shelly Errington's study of Lulu. Shelly Errington, *Meaning and Power in a Southeast Asian Realm* (Princeton, New Jersey: Princeton University Press, 1989), p. 192.

13   See Lei Shih, *Su-Paiwan: An Ethnography of a Paiwan Village in Northern Paiwan* (Taipei: Institution of Ethnology, Academia Sinica, 1971); Bien Chiang, *House and Social Hierarchy of the Paiwan*, unpublished PhD diss., University of Pennsylvania, 1993; Kazuko Matsuzawa, "Social and Ritual Power of Paiwan Chiefs: Oceanian Perspectives," in *Austronesian Studies Relating to Taiwan*, eds. P. Jen-kuei Lee *et al.* (Taipei, Nankang: Academia Sinica, 1995), pp. 109–40; Kong-ming Hsu, *The Rituals and Culture of the Paiwan in Kuralau* (Taipei: Dau-hsiang, 1994); Yen-ho Wu, *Eastern Paiwan in Taimali River Areas*, Institute of Ethnology, Data Collection 7 (Taipei, Nankang: Academia Sinica, 1993).

14   See also Janet Carsten and Stephen Hugh-Jones, *About the House: Lévi-Strauss and Beyond* (Cambridge: Cambridge University Press, 1995).

15   M.W. Young, "From Riches to Rags: Dismantling Hierarchy in Kalauna," *History and Anthropology* 7, 1–4 (1994): 265.

16   The relationship between the two varies from location to location, though there are also some commonalities. This relationship was often characterized as that of landlord and tenant. See Lei Shih, *Su-Paiwan*. Chiang argues that the existence of commoner landlords makes the previous argument insufficient. He then proposes that the *mamazangilan* is a special category of people functioning to mediate conflicts within and between villages. See Bien Chiang, *House and Social Hierarchy of the Paiwan*. The case of Piuma also confirms this explanation. There are commoner landowners in Piuma, such as La Leleman. The role of the nobility as peacemakers was also emphasized.

17   Children born from this kind of relationship could be incorporated into the noble's house by being offered a *muri alak* a ceremony to give full recognition to the child as part of the house and a proper name by the firstborn of that house. This privilege of granting names is not extended to the female sexual partner.

18   In other words, marriages between people of different status can be considered as proper marriages as long as the proper procedures are followed and publicly witnessed. Legally, monogamy is the norm. Christian values are sometimes deployed to explain this change.

19   Ku, "The Symbolic and the Material in the Recognition of Hierarchy."

20   House names are often suggested by elders to the new couples who establish the house. I was told that most of the names did not contain meanings (or at least meanings known to the speakers), though some do have semantic meanings denoting physical objects or the landscape, such as *sapai* (house-pit) or *gadu* (mountains.) Other house names carry social connotations. An example is *ka-umaq-an* (principal one among all the houses.)

21   Janet Carsten, and Stephen Hugh-Jones, "Introduction," in *About the House: Lévi-Strauss and Beyond*, eds. Janet Carsten and Stephen Hugh-Jones (Cambridge: Cambridge University Press, 1995), p. 51.

22   It is also possible to create more than one house in a lifetime. Often, once a firstborn has grown to maturity, the parents can leave the house to him or her and create another house (and house name) with a new partner, regardless of whether they are a firstborn, an in-marrying spouse, or a founder of the house.

23   See also Chiang, "House and Social Hierarchy," p. 185.

24   See also Debbora Battaglia, "Toward an Ethics of the Open Subject," in *Anthropological Theory Today*, ed. Henrietta L. Moore (Cambridge: Polity Press, 1999).

25   The decoration rights include personal adornment and house decoration. In contemporary Piuma, decorating with an eagle feather remains the privilege of the nobility. Traditional carvings (*sasuayan*) and the stone tablet (*saulai*) can only be installed in noble's houses. For details on personal adornment, see Ku Kun-hui, "Social Meanings of Personal Adornment among the Paiwan," in *Research Report on Music, Dance, Ritual and Folk Activities of Taiwanese Aborigine*, eds. Bien-hsiung Liu and Tai-li Hu (Taipei, Nankang: Academia Sinica, 1989), pp. 68–83.

26   This statement needs further qualification. Although today marriage payment is often paid to the bride's family, the actual amount depends upon the relative status of the houses of the bride and groom. In the case of marriage between a high-ranking male and a low-ranking female, no marriage payment was required in the past.

27   Chiang Bien, "Burial and Naming: Two Memory Mechanisms of the Paiwan," in *Time, History and Memory*, ed. Huang Yinggui (Taipei, Nankang: Institute of Ethnology, Academia Sinica, 1998), pp. 381–415.

28   Shih Lei, *Su-Paiwan*.

29   Some members of La Paqetavai were criticized for keeping high-ranking names even after marrying down (with low-ranking commoners) for two generations. They in turn sought higher-ranking mates to "rescue" the situation.

30   See also James J. Fox, "Reflections on 'Hierarchy' and 'Precedence'," *History and Anthropology* 7 (1994): 87–108.

31   In Piuma there is a woman with three names, all of which are still in constant use, indicating that the kin ties are still relatively strong. See also John Kirkpatrick, *The Marquesan Notion of the Person* (Michigan: UMI Research Press, 1983).

32   In referring to a recently deceased relative, the kin term and personal name with a past tense signifier (*anga*) are used, for example, *vuvu Pailis-anga*. Otherwise, personal names are not applied to the deceased. In the ancestral rite or five-year rite, *Maleveq*, the collective term *vuvu* is used to refer to all the ancestors.

33   Ku, "The Symbolic and the Material in the Recognition of Hierarchy."

34 Scott, Tehranian and Mathias, "The Production of Legal Identities."

35 Thanks to Hong Liju for scanning the documents.

36 Ku Kun-hui, "Rights to Recognition: Minority/Indigenous Politics in Emerging Taiwanese Nationalism," *Social Analysis* 49, 2 (2005): 99–121.

37 Democratic Progress Party (DVD document), *What is your Indigenous Names?* (Taipei: DPP Headquarter 2005).

38 Mary Margaret Steedly, "The Importance of Proper Names: Language and National Identity in Colonial Karoland," *American Ethnologist* 23, 3 (1996): 447.

39 J.M. Corkery, "Attitudes to Naming Practices by the Church in England during the 16th and 17th century," *Genealogist's Magazine* 23, 8 (1990): 293.

40 S. Wilson, *The Meaning of Naming: A Social and Cultural History of Personal Naming in Western Europe* (London: UCL Press, 1998), p. 194.

41 Kuipers, J. C, *Language, Identity, and Marginality in Indonesia. The Changing Nature of Ritual Speech on the Island of Sumba* (Cambridge: Cambridge University Press, 1998), p. 96.

CHAPTER 10

On Sense and Reference in Eastern Indonesian Personal Names: Finding Space for a Sociology of Naming

R.H. Barnes

Charles Macdonald (1999: 108) has written of necronyms among the Penan of Borneo that while Needham (1954a, 1971) considers them to be names, one could think it more correct to interpret them as titles. Many anthropologists over the decades have noted that the personal names of a given peoples are more like titles than proper names (see Barnes 1982: 211 for a survey). I have tried to address these issues in so far as they may be elucidated by the divergent positions within the philosophy of John Stuart Mill and Gottlob Frege (see below). Whereas Lévi-Strauss' suggestions concerning classification and naming provide several fruitful starting points, his conception of classification is faulty and must be emended. Between Mill's connotation and denotation and Lévi-Strauss' classification, Frege's (from a sociological point of view) not fully developed distinction between sense and reference (*Sinn und Bedeutung*) provides the logical space for a more successful exploration of both the philosophical and sociological issues of naming in real societies. Above all, Frege permits, as Mill does not, definite descriptions to be used as proper names, although, *pace* Lévi-Strauss they do not classify when they are so used. Nevertheless, in such usage they may well convey information which may be used to classify by those who know how to interpret them. I have set these issues out thoroughly elsewhere and do not have anything new to say about them. My ethnographic examples came from the Hidatsa of North Dakota and the Omaha of Nebraska and were very different from those of the Kedang

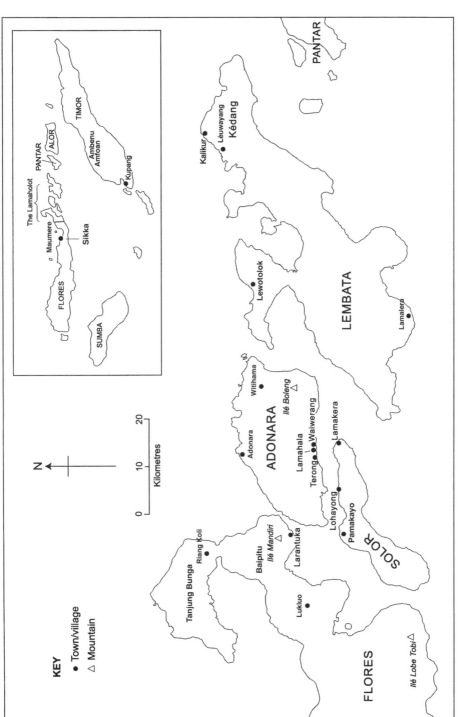

Map 1 East Flores and the Solor Islands

of Lembata and Lamaholot of Lembata, Adonara, Solor and Flores I want to consider here, but the broader issues apply anywhere (Barnes 1980, 1982, 1984: 104–23).

My position is that, unlike philosophers who seem concerned to established whether Mill is right that proper names (N.B. in propositions), as Mill claimed, do not have connotation or instead, as Frege claimed, do have sense, anthropologists do not need to resolve whether given nomenclature practices constitute proper names or titles. Instead we can use the alternatives, whether conceived in a sophisticated philosophical way or simply conceived colloquially, as standards for exploring the particular features each ethnographic instance reveals.

Kedang

Some of the many ways in which personal names have been found to be semantically meaningful have been surveyed by Alford (1988: 59–65) and Macdonald (1999). Naming practices in the Kedang and Lamaholot language areas unsurprisingly resemble in some respects those described by Pauwels (1999) for Tanimbar. Personal names in Kedang consist in a Christian or Muslim given name, a village name and (nowadays) a surname. Either the Christian or Muslim given name or the village name may be reduced to an initial for purposes of signature. The surname is always the name of the natal patrilineal clan, such as Apelabi, from Ape Labi. Those who have not converted to Catholicism or Islam will have no Christian or Muslim given name. They may also have little use for a surname, especially if they are illiterate and do not travel far from the region. For day-to-day village affairs, the surname is of little or no relevance. The village name normally consists of two components, the first being the actual village given name of the man or woman, the second being the first component of the father's village given name (compare Vroklage 1953: 448).[1] Thus Pèu Langun was named Pèu by his father Langun Wayan. When by coincidence two people have the same two names in their village name, they may be distinguished by adding that of the father's father of each (e.g. Pèu Langun Wayan). When the full name including Christian or Muslim given name, village name and surname is used (mostly in bureaucratic contexts) only the first element of the village name is used, if at all. In recent times, a very few individuals have been given no village name, but they are usually children of people from Kedang who left many years ago and are living elsewhere.

The parents choose a name for their child by preference only. Although sometimes the village name may be that of an ancestor, there is no tradition of bestowing such a name. There seems to be no tradition of choosing a name by means of augury. Names are bestowed at about the end of the period of restriction following birth. Men or women are sometimes addressed by the name of their child, although there is no system of teknonymy. Sometimes the village name, at least the version by which a person is commonly known, may deviate from the common pattern, although the proper form is remembered (Barnes 1974: 154). Rarely, the second component of the name used in daily practice may be that of the mother, for one reason or another.

Sometimes individuals change their name. Lèu Ameq was named Ameq (Ameq Laba), but he changed Ameq to Lèu. Instead of being called Lèu Laba, people referred to him as Lèu Ameq. Two brothers who were close friends of mine were named Boli Kapal and Molan Bala. Of these, Molan was the older. His father, Bala, had named him Amaq, whereas Boli he had named Kapal. *Amaq* means "skin" and Molan, not liking to be named Skin, changed it to Molan. Thereafter he was named Molan Bala. Boli was less fortunate. For years I thought that the second component in his name was the Indonesian *kapal*, which means "ship." However, Molan finally explained to me that Kapal is the Kedang word which means "thick." The two village given names of the brothers formed the phrase *amaq kapal* or "thick skin," an expression which in Kedang means much the same as the English expression "thick skinned." Om Suda Apelabi explained that such a naming pattern indicated that the parent was making a statement about some third person, in this case clearly indirectly registering a complaint.

A man in the village of Lèuwayang was named Pèu Payong, but because he was deaf and dumb, he was called Pèu Bukeq. *Bukeq* means "deaf." Thus his popular sobriquet referred to a personal characteristic, his disability. Another villager had two wives. He lived with the second, but still visited the first, with whom he had two children. She named her daughter by him Banger and her son Toang. Both *banger* and *toang* mean "wait for." She chose these names because she had to wait for her husband to come to her, whereas the second wife did not.

Many village names have meaning, as seen in the above cases. Some examples and their meanings are presented in Table 1.

Most of the above names come from the genealogy of the Ape Utung clan. A common woman's name is Daten, which means "bad." Another woman's name is "miteng" meaning "black." Generally speaking male and female village names are gender specific, but there are a few names, such as Kewa or Tutoq, which may be applied to either males or females. The stock of women's names seems no smaller than that of male names (large

Table 1

Village Names	Meaning
Ameq	Ask or invite
Pèu	Mango
Hoeq	Festival
Rian	Large (also a term of address for a grandfather or grandmother)
Utung	Small
Lèu	Village
Ledo	To walk
Hola	Exhausted
Bèyèng	Run
Laba	Chisel or fight
Laleng	Inside or disposition
Aiq	Thorn
Hering	Set down
Tamal	Tamarind
Naya	Name
Tuaq	Palmwine
Lotaq	Stack up
Maing	Tool for planting rice seedlings
Darang	Hot

in both cases), although there are some commonplace women's names such as Peni, Areq ("girl") and Inaq (term of address for an older woman, such as mother). There are many other meaningful names for men and women, but the above sample should suffice. There are no descent group specific names for either men or women.

There are no name prohibitions, and there is no special prohibition on addressing others by name. Nevertheless all males, even infants, may be addressed *amo* (actually >*amo*), which is the address term for the reference term *ame*, that is father, etc., and indeed all (older) males. A man who is sufficiently superior in age (such as a grandparent) or is a wife-giver may be addressed *bapa*. It is more polite to address an older male Amo Pèu, rather than simply as Pèu. The equivalent term for females is *inaq*, related to the reference term *ine*, "mother," etc. We have seen above that an address term for grandparents is *rian*. For a more comprehensive list of terms of address see Tables 9 and 11 in Barnes (1974: 271–2). Roughly speaking, terms of address exist only for those who are superior to ego by virtue of age or alliance. People can also be addressed *reu*, "friend." People sometimes bestow nicknames on others, but none given me, all names of renowned ancestors, ever achieved any currency. The last ruler of Kedang, whom I knew, was called Kapitan Mas. His name was Muhammad Abdulsalam Sarabiti. "Mas" was made up from the initials of his name.

There are no birth order names, although there are expressions for oldest child (>*anaq mèkèr*), middle child (>*anaq ayaq*, literally "middle child"), and youngest child (>*anaq tu* >*utuq*, literally "breast tip child"). There are no hidden names or system of double names, such as Renard-Clamagirand (1999: 31) reports for Wewewa, Sumba.[2] As elsewhere in Indonesia, one protects one's good name through proper behavior. I know of no doctrine that someone who shares the name of an ancestor also shares with him any "vital force" or any other matter (Pauwels 1999: 51). I have not encountered the notion that any child, let alone the first, receives its soul when it is given its name (Forth 1981: 75). Nor have I heard of masking names, disguising the presence of a child from the ancestors (Pauwels 1999: 55). I have not come across shortened forms of the village name as nicknames (Pauwels 1999: 55). Personal names give no indication of class position as in Toraja (Koubi 1999: 131). I have not encountered name changes for therapeutic reasons (Vroklage 1953: 449, Koubi 1999: 146–50, Tule 2004: 157); nor have I encountered ritual names (Koubi 1999: 155–61). So far as I know there are no death names (Needham 1954a, 1965, 1971) and no mourning terms (Needham 1954b, 1959). Historical records have revealed a practice of exchanging regional and personal names between rulers in order to seal an alliance, although for everyday matters such name exchanges had no practical effect (Barnes 2001: 290).

In Leuwayang, Kédang, genealogies of males are remembered which extend back around 20 to 23 generations before reaching clearly mythical figures and names of God. In Leuwayang traditional priests recite the genealogies of all living males in the village including the youngest infants

Table 2 Naming in Lèuwayang, Kédang

- Christian or Muslim given name (in some [now most] cases), village name (own plus father's or own plus father's plus father's father's), surname taken from clan name, some nicknames.
- The village given name is from a wide stock, but usually is not inherited. Most, but not all, such names indicate gender. Some, but not all, such names have a clear meaning.
- Surnames are mostly for bureaucratic use, but are increasingly important in modern Indonesian life.
- No name prohibitions. Address by name permitted.

back to God during an entire night of the annual harvest ritual (Barnes 2001: 281–2, 2005a: 369–73). The names of females are not so recited and remembered in this patrilineal society. Memory of wives and sisters of males is retrievable only a few generations into the past, except for certain historically important personalities.

Lamaholot

The depth of genealogical memory in the neighboring Lamaholot language region is extremely variable, from just a few generations even among aristocrats to extensive ranges. The genealogy that the former district head Kakang Bau provided me in Lamalera extended back only to his great-grandfather (Barnes 1996: 61). The genealogy of the rajas of Larantuka goes back around 19 generations, although there is some telescoping. The highest levels are mythical and seem to contain significant fictions intended to establish their claim to position (Dietrich 1997: 111). The Raja's agent in Riang Koli, Flores was able to recite twenty-three generations of his own genealogy for Vatter (1932: 135). The genealogy of the Rajas of Adonara goes back only to Begu Ama, murdered in 1850, and the genealogy of the Kapitan of Adonara is also short (Barnes 2005b: 32, 2005c: 15). Arakian Kamba Kéi Helu, son of a Kapitan and then Acting Raja of Adonara and brother of another Acting Raja, told me that there was so much close marriage in his family and the names were used over and over again so that it is difficult for them to remember their genealogies.

Vatter (1932: 117–8) wrote concerning the villages behind the Mandiri mountain in East Flores that,

> A child does not receive a name immediately after birth, but usually only a few years later. Then by preference an older, honorable name from the ancestors of the clan will be chosen or one gives the child the name of a recently deceased family member. On the other hand, it will never be named after a still living family member, because the name is not regarded as merely a designation, but as an important part of a living person and therefore is seen as something unique. If there have already been several children who have died in a family, then one attempts to trick the evil spirits that one holds to be guilty of the deaths by giving the children born later no name at all, but calls them "Naran-také," that is "name-not," thus "nameless;" or they let them appear to the spirits as insignificant and somewhat unworthy of their interest by giving them a derogatory name, such as "Aho-Tain," that is "dog excrement." Sometimes a person's name relates to a specific event,

which had impressed them at the time of the birth. Thus there was in Leloba a man named "Rea," which means "great war," because when he was born a violent feud broke out between Leloba and Larantuka.

Arndt (1940: 29–31) says that in East Flores a child does not receive a name immediately after its birth. After returning from hanging the child's afterbirth and navel cord in a banyan, the parents celebrate the birth festival called *hadik lala*, "set up rice gruel," actually a basket of unstamped rice rather than gruel. Female relatives come to stamp the rice. Others are forbidden to do so. The parents and their children may not eat this rice at the feast. The grandparents come and give the child a name, usually one which has been borne by an ancestor. Later this name is often exchanged for another, especially if the child constantly cries or is always sick. Often the new name is ugly, such as *Ahotaing*, dog excrement, and so on. Arndt's informant (who in all probability the same as Vatter's) assured him that the child will then cease to cry. When the child grows larger, then it assumes again its previous name. In addition to the normal name, children receive pet names.

For Lukluo, East Flores, Arndt's information is sparser. Here the name is given two or three days after the birth. The name might be that of a deceased father or that of a grandparent. Until it receives the name, the infant is called *Ludo* or *Boso*, "Master." These terms can be used later as pet names (Arndt 1940: 44).

> The first name will be changed if the child constantly cries or is sick and indeed often to an ugly name; so too in Larantuka. The ancestors whose names the children bear either do not love the child or they love it too well; therefore they allow it to die. Either they want to have it with them or they want to revenge themselves on it by killing it." (Arndt 1940: 45)

His account of name giving in Leloba is similar to that he gave for East Flores generally, which is hardly surprising. The afterbirth is hung in a *rita* tree.[3] After those who do so return, the child receives a name and the feast takes place. When a newborn child is given a name, names from the father's and from the mother's families will be recited, one of which will be given the child. If the mother's brother bestows the name, he receives an elephant tusk and returns to his sister a sarong (1940: 47, 50). The discrepancies between Vatter's and Arndt's reports can, I think, be attributed to their informants.

Table 3   Naming in East Flores (1930s)

- Name from ancestor. Each name unique to the bearer at the time. Absence of name or derogatory name to deceive evil spirits. Commemorative names.
- Grandparents give name. Therapeutic name changes.

Arndt writes of East Adonara that a child receives a name when it begins to speak. Until then a boy is called *kopong*, while a girl is called *barek*. The first child receives the name of a grandfather or grandmother. The other children receive those of other deceased relatives. If the child is later constantly sick or very frequently cries, its name will be changed either to that of another deceased relative or to a different, generally ugly, name, such as *medho*, *maida*, "bad fellow," *menaka*, "witch."[4] Twins of the same sex are welcomed, those of opposite sex not, because one of them must die. Male twins are named Kopong and Mamu, "youth"[5] or Rimo, "tiger," and Gara, "elephant." Pampus (1999) does not confirm the meanings for *rimo* and *gara*, but the genealogy of the Lamablawa Wĕtĕ clan of Witihama, Adonara contains two men named Rimo Gara. An alternative explanation of *gara* is that it is from *gĕrarā* meaning "prohibition," but we may be dealing with homonyms. Female twins would be named Barek[6] and Sédo, meaning "maiden" (Arndt 1940: 140–1). Pampus does not confirm *sédo*, but my own notes from Witihama indicate that *kopong mamu* means "youth" and *sédo barek* means "maiden."

According to Arndt in West Adonara, a baby receives its name immediately after birth. Frequent illness later is a sign that evil spirits want to torment the child with this name and that it must therefore have another name (Arndt 1940: 145). In southwest Solor, the infant is given its name either immediately after or a few days after birth, usually by agreement between the mother and father. The names of ancestors are favored. A constantly crying or sickly child will have its name changed, often to an ugly one. When an unmarried mother refuses to reveal the name of the father, the child will be given no name and instead will be called Naran Také, "nameless." There are derogatory names, nicknames, names of honor, and pet names (Arndt 1940: 192). In Wulubelolong, East Solor, an infant receives no name for about a year. During the interval a boy is called Kopong. A girl is called Ina or Késéng.[7]

In my own intensive field research in Lamalera, Lembata and Witihama, Adonara, I have been unable to confirm many of the aspects of name giving described by Vatter and Arndt. Except for a very few identifiable mistakes, I have found their reports reliable when I have been in a position to check. The discrepancies must be attributed to three factors. The first is substantial incompleteness of data on their part as well as on mine. The second is the very evident regional variation in features of language and culture within the Lamaholot language area. Another factor leading to discrepancies is incompleteness in the reports made by informants, disagreements which it is very difficult to control for its changes over decades. Not to be overlooked of course is incompleteness on the part of informants, disagreements among them, and individual variations of practice within the same locality. Nevertheless, I take the descriptions by Arndt and Vatter as very useful background to my own information, potentially supplementing it, bearing in mind that what is true for one Lamaholot community may well not be true of another. It may be borne in mind that Arndt never visited Lembata and recorded no information about it and that Vatter's useful report from Lamalera was based on a brief stay.

In recent decades in Lamalera, Lembata (which is today entirely Catholic), young children when baptized receive a saint's name. The legal identity consists of the saint's name, the village given name, and a surname derived from the patrilineal descent group. Most surnames are identical to the clan name spelled in a simplified form suitable for Indonesian, but there are exceptions. They may, for example, be shorter forms of the clan name. Within the Beliko Lolong clan, one segment has taken instead the name of the legendary village ancestor Korohama as its surname. The Dasi Langu section of Lefo Tukan clan has created for itself the surname Dasion, possibly to be interpreted as Dasi Onã, which could be viewed as an alternative name for Dasi Langu, with the same semantic implications. Adults are universally addressed Bapa, "father," or Ema, "mother," sometimes followed by the saint name. This practice allows for respectful, yet friendly, address to anyone of any station, including the youngest child. An aged person or important personage may be address *magu* from *bélé-magu*, all persons two generations older than ego or more, regardless of the nature of the relationship. Otherwise all relatives older than ego must be addressed by the appropriate relationship term. Relationship terms of address are not distinguished from terms of reference in Lamalera (see Barnes 1996: 346–54). The exception to this generalization is that persons younger than ego, except young children, are never addressed by a relationship term. Instead they are addressed by either the saint's name or the village name.

Saints' names (there may be more than one) generally take the Latin form, but in daily use may be shortened. As one of my acquaintances commented, village names, like European names, have meanings. His example was Nara Beto, meaning the troops are coming. His saint's name, the meaning of which he certainly knows, is Petrus. Some village names derive from legendary personages. Hopi Lĕfo "purchase the village" refers to a semi-historical event when it became necessary to ransom the village from intruders. The Kedang pattern of the father's name making up the second component of the village name seems not to be current today, but I have speculated that present usage of the saint's name plus the village name has replaced an older pattern similar to that in Kedang. The former *kakang* (district leader) now referred to as Mikael Molan appears in contemporary records as Molan Dasi, Dasi being his father's village name. Dasi in turn was known as Dasi Dasi, again incorporating his father's village name. His father, the last remembered figure in the genealogy of this line, was Ata Kebelake Dasi. The first two components of this name is the Lamaholot title which is equivalent to the Larantuka Malay Kakang. Dasi Dasi, whose name is embodied in the lineage name of Dasi Langu and the surname Dasion, was also known as Kakang Yosef Raja Muda. In this case, the name incorporates the saint's name followed by a title. This title Raja Muda, a sort of second raja, was given him by Raja Lorenzo Oesi Vieira Godinho of Larantuka, to whom Lamalera was subject.[8]

A man may name a son after his own father, and a woman may name a daughter after her mother, but this practice is far from invariable. Names may be derived from more distant relatives, such as a father's brother or mother's father. Some names have private significance. Some names have comical or ridiculous meanings, although not all village names have any implied additional significance. I have encountered no indication in Lamalera that children may be given no name at all for whatever reason. However, in Miku Langu section of Bedi Oná clan there was once a man bearing the name Narantaka, which has the same significance as the slightly different forms mentioned by Vatter and Arndt, namely "nameless." I never obtained an explanation for this particular instance.

Table 4 Naming in Lamalera, Lembata

- Saint's name, village given name, surnames from clan name. Saint's name may be shortened. Occasional titles.
- Older persons not addressed by village name. Younger persons addressed by saint's name or village name.
- Village names may have meaning. Village names derived from relatives.

Keraf (1978: 102, 105–6) remarks that people may not address or refer to people older than themselves by name, and that it is particularly prohibited to do so to their parents. He says that this restriction has led as a form of compensation to addressing all children, related or not, as *ama*, if male, or *ina*, if female. These terms, commonplace elsewhere in some parts of the Lamaholot language area, meaning "father" and "mother" are no longer used in everyday speech in these meanings in Lamalera except in compound expressions. The more common *bapa*, for "father," and *ema*, for "mother," have recently also become appropriate for addressing children. Keraf says that this restriction also explains why children here and throughout the Lamaholot area are generally called by the Christian names rather than the village names, since Christian names are in no way restricted (Keraf 1978: 112–4, 346–7). In Witihama, Adonara, too it is not proper to call a person by his name alone, without a title or one of the common terms for men or women, such as Ama or Ema, although Christian or Muslim names are not so restricted. As in Kedang, in Witihama the names of female ancestors further back than the grandmothers are easily forgotten. This circumstance comes about, as was explained to me, "because women change clans." At first this might seem an inadequate explanation for forgetting the names of great-grandmothers, but it must be kept in mind that the names of male ancestors are remembered for many generations because they are the bearers of and justification for clan membership, whereas women are not.

From my field research in eastern and northern Adonara, I have somewhat different features to describe than from Lamalera. For one thing, there is a substantial Muslim population on Adonara. In addition I have more legendary and historical information pertaining to Adonara, than I do for Lamalera. Many aspects of personal names on Adonara pose difficulties. For one thing, nicknames are very common. Names are frequently reused and passed down in either the male or female line. There is no simple pattern for forming village names, as in Kedang and Lamalera, (although the genealogy of the Rajas of Adonara shows a tendency in that direction). As the examples of Yosef Raja Muda and Ata Kebelake Dasi in Lamalera provide a hint, the relation between names and titles is particularly problematic. For the historian trying to reconstruct some sort of picture of the historical past of Adonara from documents and oral traditions, these and other circumstances lead to a maze of uncertainties.

The general pattern currently is that anyone will have a Christian or Muslim given name; a village name of at least two components, but sometimes more; and a surname. A person may also have a title. These titles may relate to occupation, as also on Lembata and elsewhere in Indonesia. Examples are Guru (teacher) or Mentri (Menteri, minister, official), Pater (priestly title usually reserved for Europeans), Romo (priestly title usually reserved for Indonesians), Imam (Muslim prayer leader).[9] Other titles relate to achievements such as Haji (title for a male who has made the hajj), Hajjah (title for a female who has made the hajj), Profésor, Doktor, Dokotranda (title for a woman who has a B.A.), Doktorandus (title for a man who has a B.A.), and so on. All of these titles are born by people in or from this region. Some titles, if I may call them that, have no bearing on occupation or achievement. Among these I would number Om (the Dutch for "uncle"). Nyonya (married woman) from Portuguese perhaps and Nona (young woman) from Portuguese Dona are, as in Indonesian, commonplace (Santa Maria 1967: 60, 111). Other titles relate to office, about which more later.

I have uncovered very little evidence for teknonymy in the Lamaholot language region. My only vestige of such evidence comes from the story of Ba Naruq in which the figure of Kiaq Mitĕn is referred to as Sĕleman (i.e., Sulaiman) Ema Aman, which Guru Thomas Silalahi (who narrated the story for me) interpreted as meaning "father of Sĕleman Ema," thus a form of technonym. Since in the story Kiaq Mitĕn is too young to be a father, Guru Thomas surmised that he had taken the name and title of an ancestor. Another figure, Kiaq Buraq is referred to as Bĕrahin Nogo Kakan, i.e., the elder brother of Bĕrahin Nogo. Guru Thomas interpreted this usage to mean that Kiaq Buraq had taken the name and title of an ancestor who was the elder brother of Bĕrahin Nogo. However, I have no other evidence with which to confirm or refute this interpretation, which was offered as speculation in any case (Barnes 2002: 497–8). In Lamaholot the oldest child is *anaq wĕru'i*, while the youngest is *tuhu wutŭ*. *Tuhu wutŭ* means "breast tip" (Pampus 1999).

I was assured in Witihama that names have meaning. Oma Nama's namesake Nama Raga bore an inversion of Raga Nama, "guard the ceremonial clearing." Personal names are passed down from either the father's or the mother's side or they are made up to commemorate some event. Several people were named Proklamasi to celebrate August 17th, 1945, the day that Sukarno and a small committee declared Indonesian independence. In conversation I once brought up the Kedang practice of a father giving his children names that implied some criticism of someone else and mentioned the case described above. The response I received was that it would be very difficult to do so in Witihama. It is done in animal names, but in the case of a human being, it could only be done for someone of very low status.

The example of Longa Jawa shows how names and nicknames may be intimately tied up to events. His real name was Belai Saraka, after the former Kapitan of Lamahala who stirred up various conflicts in the nineteenth century and was finally exiled to Pekalongan, Java by the Dutch in 1889 (Barnes 2001: 293–4). Longa Jawa's mother, a close relative of Belai Saraka, came from Lamahala, although he lived in Witihama. Longa is a shortened form of Pekalongan, and his nickname was a commemoration of Belai Saraka's exile. Longa Jawa was one of those along with Buang Duran killed by the army as Communists in 1965 (Barnes 2003: 22–3). Another instructive example is Arakian Kamba Kéi Helu, mentioned above. Arakian Kamba is the name of a very important Raja of Adonara in the late nineteenth and early twentieth centuries (Barnes 2005b: 6–7, esp. Photo 4, and *passim*; 2005c: 11), to whom as a member of the line of the Kapitan of Adonara he has various genealogical links via marriage. Kéi Helu is supposed to be the name of a man from the village of Adonara (his village) who went off to the Moluccas, but he has found the people in the Moluccas do not recognized the name. Arakian Kamba Kéi Helu's nickname, by which he is more commonly known, is Ama Nuen Ape. Ama is the commonplace polite term of address for a male. Nuen is related to *těnuě*, "old" and means "grandparent." *Ape* means "fire." He told me that he is called "Grandfather Fire" because his thoughts are like fire, that is to say rapid. The name alludes to his frequent role in resolving customary law problems for which he is in big demand, as I can attest.

Ama Nuen Ape's brother, who served as Acting Raja in the late 1940s and early 1950s, was called Bapa Kaya (see Barnes 2005b: 33). Bapa, meaning "father," is a commonly used component of names of various personages in the intermarried aristocratic clans of the village of Adonara and the village of Kalikur, Kedang. Among these are the last rightful Raja of Adonara Bapa Nur, whom Bapa Kaya replaced and who was the brother's son of Arakian Kamba. Another is Bapa Dia, ruler (or Rian Baraq) of Kédang, who married Arakian Kamba's daughter. Still living is Bapa Dia's son and Arakian Kamba's grandson Bapa Tenueng (N.T. Sarabiti, village name Begu). Bapa Nur's name also occurs as Bapa Nuhur, containing an interpolated *h* of no semantic import as is common in words in eastern Adonara. Nur is an Arabic name. His full Muslim name is Muhamad Nur, and his village name is Begu, an ancient name in his patriline.

Another name to be reckoned with in Witihama is Boro Tura, of which there are and have been many, especially in Lama Tokan Goran Tokan clan. It seems to have come into that clan from Balawelin clan via marriage. One of the heads of Witihama four generations above the last was named Boro Tura. His great-grandson was also named Boro Tura and was also the head of Witihama, but he was and is known as Kelaké Kéi. Pampus has *kělake* as "married man," but Arndt (1937: 21) translates it as "leader, the eldest." It is in fact a title, indicating his role as head of Witihama; incidentally though, he was also the eldest son. Kéi is his father's village name. His father was named Kéi Lebu, but known as Kéi Tokan (Barnes 2005b: 18, figure 1). I have this genealogy from Kelaké Kéi's son, who was himself the last hereditary ruler of Witihama. He signs himself Haji Muktar LK Kei, from Muktar Lebu Kelaké Kéi, although his real name is Lebu Raya after his great-grandfather. He goes by both the name Haji Muktar Kelaké Kéi and Haji Muktar Lebu Raya Kéin. He is often referred to as Haji Muktar or even Haji Lebu. By the way there are many Lebu Raya in Lamablawa Wĕtĕ clan, which has frequently intermarried with Lama Tokan Goran Tokan.

Another Boro Tura was Ahmad Boro Tura, known as Mat Boro, who was murdered by the army along with Buang Duran in 1965, because he was deemed to be a Communist. The name Boro Salan is an example of a place name being used to differentiate between people of the same name, but the example is somewhat more complicated than that. Boro Salan's real village name is Boro Tura, but his commonly used name Boro Salan means Boro [Tura] in Salan. That designation would not convey much meaning, unless the hearer knows that Salan is a literary name for Witihama. Thus Boro Salan means Boro Tura from Witihama. That would not distinguish him very well, given that there are many Boro Tura from Witihama, except that most, or all, of the rest are either Muslim's or Catholics and are commonly addressed and referred to by their Muslim or Christian given names. Boro Salan was the oldest living male in Lama Tokan Goran Tokan clan in 2000. Kiaq Salan Lamablawa is also so called to distinguish him, but I do not know his actual name. Bebe Kewa who fought the Dutch in the Hinga War (Barnes 2005b: 17–20, figure 2) was also known as Bebe Lali Salan. *Lali* is a direction term, so the name means Bebe [Kewa] at Witihama.

Table 5 Naming in Witihama, Adonara

- Christian or Muslim given name, village name of two or more components, surname, some nicknames, occasional titles.
- Village names not used for address of elder people without title. Christian or Muslim names unrestricted. Names have meaning. Commemorative names.
- Names taken from ancestors.

The founder of the Lama Tokan Goran Tokan clan, i.e., that of Haji Muktar Kelaké Kéi, was the legendary figure Jou Boli, who is supposed to have been one of seven brothers who came from the Moluccas and established the line of the Rajas of Adonara. He is sometimes said to have been the first Raja of Adonara, which is difficult to reconcile with both the sparse surviving documentary evidence and with the legend that he left the village of Adonara and eventually settled in Hinga, before this line eventually moved to the present site of Witihama. Jou or Rou is the title of a Muslim religious instructor. In the legend of the founding of the dynasty, he is named Jou Boli Ama, thus his village name is Boli Ama. In the report that has him the first Raja of Adonara he is also called Sili Lan Sengaji, although in other reports Sili Lan Sengaji is the father of Jou Boli. This designation is plainly just a series of titles. Sili is Ternatese *kaicil*, pronounced *kaicili*, the title of a prince or someone of princely descent line. *La* is an article before male names in south Sulewesi (Berg 1996: 287, Pelras 1999: 167). It appears in the name of another, even more legendary, figure associated with the village of Adonara and also with the region of Witihama, namely La Asan, generally deemed to be from Buton. The local name Lasan is deemed to derive from La Asan. Sengaji was the title often borne by leaders in the region in the sixteenth and seventeenth centuries. *Sangaji* was the title of a district head under the Sultan of Ternate (de Clercq 1890: 294); for a discussion of the influence of the Sultan of Ternate in this region during that period see Barnes (1996: 12–3). Another report has it that the leader of the expedition from the Moluccas who settled in the village of Adonara and became raja was Sili Rou (i.e., Jou) Sengaji Mamun Pati Lio. Jou Boli was also called Jou Weli Tadon, which translates "Jou down at [the village of] Adonara." Tadon is a ritual name for the village of Adonara. It appears in a report recorded by Arndt (1940: 148) about the legendary founders of the branch of Lama Tokan clan that claims to be autochthonous Kelaké Ado Pehan and Kewae Sodé Boléng. Arndt lists their sons and includes Asan Lau Tadong, i.e., Asan down [seaward] at [the village of] Adonara, in which we can see a reference to La Asan. However, in this and another respect the list results from a confusion by his informant, because La Asan could not have been the son of this pair. Tadon is not only the ritual name for the village of Adonara, but also for the island, which is known as Nusa Tadon Adonara. Keraf (1978: 6) refers to Nusa Tadon Adonara in the language of ancient texts and gives the following stanza:

> *Tero Haukoli ago koli lolo*
> Terong Haukoli decorated with lontar leaves
> *Tadon Adonara gobo toré futu*
> Tadon Adonara crowned with bamboo shoots

In the ceremonial clearing called Nama Sarabiti in the village of Adonara there is a large black, squarish, smooth stone, which is Nuba

Ama Tadon, "the ceremonial stone of Father Tadon". The temple of the clan of the Rajas of Adonara, so I was told, is called the house of Tadon and is said to be very sacred, but I could obtain no further information as to the significance of Tadon or who he was.

The difficulties in trying to identify figures whose names appear in the scant documentary evident for the history of this region may be demonstrated by reference to Suban Pulo. Suban Pulo, according to myth, was the original inhabitant of the region which includes the present Lamahala who gave permission for the first outsiders to come ashore, leading to the eventual establishment of that village. According to the myth he lived at Ilé Tobi Turu, that is the "Sleeping Tamarind Mountain" –a name which no longer has any currency (Barnes 2002: 497). A Subang Pula (obviously a scribe's error), Sengaji of Lamahala, is a signatory to a letter to the Governor-General and Council of India dated October 20, 1681 (Haan 1919: 619). This Suban Pulo cannot be the mythical figure for several reasons. The office of Raja was in Selolong (Lawang Ona) Clan, according to present memory, while those who claim patrilineal descent from Suban Pulo are in Suban Ona clan. Furthermore, 1681 is much too late a date to make a connection to a legend about a time before there was a Lamahala, since the village is mentioned in Portuguese documents in the sixteenth century. Then, too, Dutch records record the names of some Sengaji (or possible Sengaji) of Lamahala before this Suban Pulo. The fact that names are reused makes for difficulties in tracing historical figures as does the fact that they may appear in records or oral traditions identified either by name or by title or, indeed, by nickname, so an historian may not even know whether he is dealing with the same person or different persons.

Conclusion

We have been on familiar anthropological territory in this paper. Whatever the ethnographic particularities of the examples, it is unlikely that any of them will strike anthropologists as unusual. Nor should I think that they would give historians pause. By any definition of titles or personal names, the boundary between titles and names is sometimes quite fluid on Adonara. Both I and the people whose lives I study in this region are satisfied that personal names often have meaning in quite a variety of ways. Even the modern forms including the new surnames are situated only imprecisely between unique identifiers (Scott *et al.*, 2002: 35) and classifications (cp. Macdonald 1999: 111). The Indonesian and local governments have fostered the adoption of surnames for the same reasons states have done so elsewhere (Scott *et al.*, 2002: 11), primarily for taxation, voting and general population control and peace-keeping reasons. Shorn of the surname, personal names, especially village given names, often are borne by several persons. On the other hand personal names in this region do not actually classify, even when they clearly have meaning. The most that can be said of them, as in other parts of the world, is that they may well provide evidence — for example as to ancestry, descent group, and so on — which might be used to classify their bearers in various ways. But many of these meanings have little or nothing to do with classification, as is shown, for example, in the case described above of Amaq Bala and Kapal Bala, where the meaning was a semi-private comment about the behavior of a third person.

Personal names have other functions than those proper names serve in formal propositional logic. Indeed, although they can be and are used in daily speech in propositions, they are characteristically used in many other forms of utterance. It has often been observed that in these daily usages context often carries much of the burden of determining which person is intended. Where ambiguities are not entirely removed by context, other means, some of which have been described here, can be resorted to for clarity. None of these facts directly address the problems Mill and other logicians have been trying to cope with through Mill's distinction between connotation and denotation or Frege's distinction between *Sinn* and *Bedeutung*, but I should think that anthropologists generally would be more comfortable with the analogy of Frege's position that proper names have sense as well as reference, than with Mill's position that proper names, hence also personal names, have only denotation without connotation.

Notes

1   For the Keo of central Flores, the second component of the village name is the mother's personal name (Tule 2004: 155–6).

2   For comparative comments on name giving on Sumba see Onvlee (1973: 77–81).

3   For identification of this tree see Barnes (1996: 392 n 6).

4   I can confirm that *medo* or *medhon'* means "bad" in Witihama, but I cannot confirm Arndt's claim that it is specific to Witihama (Arndt 1937: 15). However, it does not appear in Pampus. Neither Arndt nor Pampus have *maida*, and I have not run across it.

5   From *kéropó* and *kémamu* with the same meanings (Pampus 1999).

6   From *kébarek* with the same meaning.

7   *Ina* means "mother" in ritual language. I have located no meaning for *késéng*.

8   For the fate of this Raja of Larantuka see Barnes (2005b).

9   Romo was explained to me as a Javanese title that used to be applied to an
     itinerant priest with no fixed station (i.e., one belonging to no order), but
     is no longer limited in that way. So I was told, it derives from Rama of the
     Ramayana, but I am in no position to attest that this interpretation is correct.
     Javanese *rama* means 1. "father, older and or higher-ranking male" and
     2. Roman Catholic Priest (Robson and Wibisono 2002). I would think that
     it is a reflex of proto-Austronesian *ama*, "father" etc., as Dempwolff (1938:
     15) interprets it (see Fernandez 1996: 159).

PART IV

"Class C":
Complex Centralized Societies

CHAPTER 11

Names and Name Changing in Early Modern Kyoto, Japan

Mary Louise Nagata

Introduction

In pre-modern Japan an individual could use a variety of names to identify himself in various ways: personal names, surnames, house names, retirement names, and death names are commonly found in pre-modern documents. Surnames could be clan names, or branches of clans named for the location where the founder lived when he established the branch. Often the split took place when a founder held a political office or some other high social status position. For this reason, patrilineal siblings could use different surnames representing different social or political statuses rather than kinship. Feudal leaders and the politically powerful also gave surnames to vassals or important allies as a sign of group membership and status. An artist or artisan who established a new technique might also change his name or use a different name when creating or performing in the new method or style, and this new name would be given to and used by later artists who learned to create or perform according to the new school or style. Names, therefore, could signify status, both within society and within one's family or household of residence.[1]

During the Tokugawa period (1600–1868), surnames tended to have political significance, identifying members of the warrior class with the lords who controlled their respective domains. Commoners who had surnames were originally prohibited from using them. This prohibition, however, was not strictly maintained and some commoner families gained or maintained use of their surnames even in the seventeenth century.

Many domains even sold the right to use a surname. In many places, the use of the surname among commoners was limited to the head of the household and his heir, so surnames represented status within a family or household as well as in society.[2] The study of names in the Japanese past relies necessarily upon documents, particularly official documents like population registers. However, documents of a less official nature suggest that the patterns and practice I discuss here also represent the vernacular system of everyday use since short versions of various officially recorded names appear in combination as nicknames even in some official documents. For example, the official journal of Takoyakushi Neighborhood refers to Hishiya Etsusuke 菱屋悦助 as Hishietsu 菱悦, forming a nickname by combining the first characters of his house name and his personal name.[3] The importance of using names to signify status combined with the playful method of turning these status names into nicknames suggests that the Japanese system is a "Class C" system which nevertheless has aspects of "Class A" and that these characteristics describe naming practices for all social statuses.[4] Finally, although China was a powerful and prestigious neighbor to Japan, the Chinese naming system does not appear to have had any great influence on Japanese naming practices.

This study investigates personal names used by commoners in Tokugawa Japan focusing particularly on the practice of changing one's personal name, sometimes several times during the life-course. Since most commoners were prohibited from using surnames, and by definition had no political status names, the personal name (autonym) was often the only name used to identify a person, particularly in most rural villages. In the city, people also used a house name that further served as a business or shop name, and some families, both in the city and in rural villages, used surnames.

Name changing was common in pre-modern Japan until 1868 when the practice was banned.[5] There are two explanations for name changing in early modern Japan commonly given in the research literature that have generally been accepted without much critical evaluation. One explanation is the rite of passage called *gempuku* commonly practised by the warrior class during the medieval and early modern periods. *Gempuku* was a coming-of-age rite traditionally held for young men at the age of 15. During the ceremony, the new adult's forelock was shaved off and he donned adult clothing for the first time. A non-kin sponsor called a naming parent (*nazuke oya*) would christen the new adult with an adult name as part of the ceremony.[6]

One problem with this explanation is whether people of non-elite classes also adopted this warrior class rite. If so, what was the meaning they attached to the rite outside of the warrior society and how common was it? Many villages were organized by age group hierarchy and *gempuku* was usually not a part of this organization. In villages using this organization, young men entered a village youth group at ages 15 to 17 and lived together in a dormitory until marriage. There were some variations in the organization, but the group was a way of socializing the young men to adult responsibilities in village society and sometimes used as a way of socializing newcomers of any age.[7]

Unfortunately, scholars have often assumed the practice of name changing shows that a village practised *gempuku* as a coming-of-age rite without critical analysis to test that assumption. If name changing were necessarily a sign of *gempuku* as a coming-of-age rite, I would expect that a majority of young men would change their names at or near the appropriate age for coming of age. I tested this assumption in my analysis of name changing practices in Nishijō, a small agricultural village in central Japan using a series of annual population registers for a 99-year period. I found that only a third (35 per cent) of the men living in the village between the ages of 15 and 20 — the typical age period reported for the *gempuku* rite with coming of age defined as around 15 to 17 — changed their names. Only by extending the age of the analysis sample to 25 did half of the young men appearing in the registers change their names. I had to conclude that, although name changing was quite common among the men of Nishijō, they probably did not practise the *gempuku* rite to celebrate coming of age.[8] After further analysis of a second village, Shimomoriya in northeastern Japan, I concluded that some form of the *gempuku* ceremony was likely used for name changes at any age to establish a fictive parent-child relationship between the namer, or naming parent called *nazuke oya*, and the named, thereby making the namer a sponsor responsible for the named.[9]

The second explanation for name changing in the research literature is name inheritance with headship succession. The principle is simple. Some families — often village elites — reserved a specific name (autonym) that the head of the family or household inherited as a headship name together with the position. Behind this name change is one of the rules in the fluid Japanese naming framework: two members of a family cannot hold the same name (autonym) at the same time. Actually, this rule was part of a taboo against name duplication, which was considered dangerous for the souls of the two people who shared names.[10] One legal reason to change one's name after the 1868 ban was this taboo.[11] Thus, the only way for the head of the house to always hold the same name was for the old head to give up the name upon retirement and the new head to forsake his former name and take the headship name.

Headship name inheritance (*katoku shūmei*) is easily found in tax and landholding records and inheritance documents.[12] However, although many new heads changed their names when they inherited, they often did not change to a specific headship name while others inherited the family headship name several years before or after becoming head. Some families showed membership in the family line by forming male names around a single character shared by all names (autonym). In Nishijō, for example, one family shared the character Kan in their headship names and headship passed from Kannojo 勘之丞 to Kanzaemon 勘左衛門 to Kankichi 勘吉. Because only part of the name was shared, two people could use these names simultaneously without breaking the duplication taboo. Thus, in Nishijō the next head, or heir, sometimes took his headship name before inheriting the position. Moreover, heir candidates who did not succeed to headship for some reason seem to have changed their names away from the family pattern.[13] Families that did not have specific headship names, however, also had some members who inherited lineal names.

In Shimomoriya membership included all male members of the family regardless of birth order or potential to succeed as head. In some families in Nishijō, however, this pattern was limited to heads of household and their heirs. Since commoners often recruited younger sons or men from outside the family to be heir through adoption or marriage, these recruited heirs would change their names (autonym) to match the lineal pattern when they became candidates as the next head. When a candidate did not succeed or when he left the family, especially if he was the eldest son or the person formerly expected to succeed to headship, he would change his name away from the lineal pattern.

Even when a family did not reserve a specific autonym for use by the head or when it did not have a specific naming pattern, some heirs inherited an autonym used by a former head. Analysis of the population registers of both Nishijō and Shimomoriya revealed that the person with the weakest claim to headship succession — either because he was a younger son or he was recruited from outside the family — was the most likely to inherit a name. When this is combined with the earlier finding that name changing used the *gempuku* rite to establish a sponsor for the named person even when coming of age was not an issue, then the use of name changes to assimilate outsiders into the family and community becomes clearer. An outsider adopted by the family to be heir was in the weakest position within both the family and community. By having a naming ceremony and giving him the autonym of a family ancestor, the family both gave him a sponsor to assist in his assimilation and announced their support, or at least acceptance, of him to the community.[14] Moreover, since the reasons for the taboo against duplication was the belief that the life force of the soul was attached to the name, headship name inheritance implies that the new head also gained a spiritual connection to all former heads who used the name. Presumably this would include the hope that the new head would also benefit from their experience. This would also be yet another reason for an adopted outsider to inherit a name (autonym) used by former heads as a way to impose the influence of former users of the name.

This study represents my fourth analysis of names and name changing in early modern Japan. The previous studies focused on rural villages in two different regions of Japan, both separately and in comparison. However, my interest in the practice came from notations of name changes recorded in the labor documents of Kyoto businesses. This study, therefore, addresses name changing in the city of Kyoto. I expect name changes in Kyoto to be different from the patterns I found in Nishijō and Shimomoriya. Kyoto is a city and it had an annual population turnover of 20 per cent, largely from migration whereas the village populations were more stable.[15] While I found that name changing in rural villages included a mechanism to assimilate outsiders into village society by establishing sponsors for them, I do not expect to find that name changing was used to establish sponsors to assimilate outsiders into a community where migration was common. Instead of community political factors behind name changing, I expect that business factors were more important because many families were businesses and members of families that were not businesses were nevertheless employed by families that were.

For data I used series of population registers from three neighborhoods in the city. Two neighborhoods, Takoyakushi and Seidō, were quite affluent with many businesses having live-in employees. The third neighborhood, Sujikaibashi, was a poorer neighborhood where many employees of the silk textile industry lived and whose registers included an investigation of households in need of assistance in 1861. In addition to the population registers, I used miscellaneous qualitative documents regarding inheritance from various Kyoto businesses, including the Fukui family collection of the Kyoto measures guild as well as administrative documents at the neighborhood level. These documents provide information regarding name changes and name inheritance that the population registers cannot provide and they are an important part of the investigation. On the other hand, the population registers also reveal who was most likely to change his or her name and when such a change was most likely to occur.

The population registers of early modern Kyoto were compiled by neighborhood officials in each neighborhood separately, so gaining a comprehensive view of the city is impossible without collecting the registers for all or most of the neighborhoods. Nevertheless, a comparison of three very different neighborhoods provides three samples of residents in rather different circumstances and social statuses in Kyoto. Moreover, these registers were compiled for the same authorities suggesting uniformity in data form, thus making them easy to compare.

The Kyoto registers were compiled annually in the ninth month of the lunar calendar. The registers list each resident as a member of a specific household and indicate the person's relation to the household head. Each household is identified by house name or profession and the name of the head. A few households are identified by the surname instead of the house name and these households tended to belong to medical doctors. I primarily used registers compiled after 1843 because previous registers did not record age.

The Takoyakushi Neighborhood document collection also includes the official journals of neighborhood officials for three years that coincide with the population register data for that neighborhood. These journals provide the official record of important events in the neighborhood, including the details of one headship succession by retirement that included name inheritance as part of the process. Kyoto neighborhoods had their own administrative organizations represented by the neighborhood officials and their own laws or rules in a form of local autonomy. I also included the laws of Takoyakushi Neighborhood since they are representative of many neighborhood laws and they mention name changing.[16]

In short, I have documents providing quantitative data from the population registers and qualitative data from various sources to address the ways in which name changes were understood, particularly the relation of name changing to inheritance. I will begin with name inheritance and headship succession in the next section. Then I will address the relation of name changes to employment. Both of these analyses use a combination of qualitative and quantitative data. The population registers provide a broad view of how common the practice was, who specifically changed their names and when they did so. In the concluding discussion I will also introduce name changes that do not fit the above categories.

Name Inheritance and Headship Succession

In rural villages, name inheritance for headship succession was most common when the heir was in a weak position to claim headship because he was not the eldest son, a son, or a member of the patriline, or because he came from outside the community. For example, adopted sons were more likely than other heirs to inherit a name (autonym) used by previous heads and this practice was most likely when the adopted son came from outside the village community or did not enter the family as a son-in-law married to a daughter.[17]

In family businesses, however, headship name inheritance seems to have been relatively common. One possible reason for a business to reserve a specific name for exclusive use by the head is that the licensing, contracts, guild memberships, and other requirements for operating and maintaining a business in Tokugawa Japan were all in the name of the business defined as the combination of the house name called *yagō* and the autonym used by the head of the house when he gained the license for that business. Moreover, legal documents often refer to headship succession of a business as inheritance of the headship name. The Fukui family provides a concrete example.

The position of head of the measures guild, together with the responsibility of standardizing the measures of western Japan, was part of the monopoly license given to the individual carpenter, Fukui Sakuzaemon, to manufacture the measures that would serve as the standard. At that time, the carpenter was also given the right to use the surname Fukui, which was also the name of the village from which he came, and Sakuzaemon was his autonym. The license was given to Fukui Sakuzaemon, so in one sense, as long as the head of the family was called Fukui Sakuzaemon, it could maintain this license and the privileges that accompanied the position as well as all of the contracts necessary to fulfill the responsibilities of the position without re-negotiating each time there was a new head. In another sense, however, this position required a certain amount of skill since the current Sakuzaemon needed to be a qualified carpenter and manufacturer who could maintain the required standards and also manage the business. Moreover, a large business had many employees and branches dependent upon the survival of the whole for their individual survival and leaving these responsibilities to the chances of fertility and genetics could be quite risky. Inheritance of a specific headship name also meant that each head could use the same name, no matter who he was before he inherited it. The best candidate for an heir from a business perspective may not necessarily be the best candidate from an inheritance perspective, but the name allowed the family and business to proclaim their support for the new head regardless of his previous background. Name inheritance may also have included the hope that former holders of the name would influence the new head.

The Fukui family collection includes documents regarding seven successions to the headship of the Fukui family and business. In each case the former head — the current Fukui Sakuzaemon — wrote *notes verbales* addressed to the Nakai magistrate stating that he was ill and no longer able to fulfill his official duties. In these *notes verbales* Fukui Sakuzaemon designated his intended heir claiming that the heir had completed the necessary apprenticeships and that he was undergoing final training by assisting Sakuzaemon in his headship duties. In some instances there were also wills or other contracts with the new heir specifying other conditions of the succession process. When the heir became the new head, he also generally swore an oath when he officially inherited the name Fukui Sakuzaemon.

Although sons were the preferred heirs to keep the business in the family, this was not always possible or practical for fulfilling the role of the next head. For instance, the current Fukui Sakuzaemon might not have any sons, or his sons might be too young to fulfill the necessary qualifications and duties of the head of the business, or outside pressures might require Sakuzaemon to recruit another heir. Indeed, headship passed to the current Sakuzaemon's son in only two of the seven successions in the data.[18]

Name inheritance is frequently mentioned in these documents as part of the succession process. In *notes verbales* written by Fukui Ukyō to the Nakai magistrate in 1725, Ukyō identifies the inheritance of the name Sakuzaemon with inheritance of the duty attached to the position of head of the Fukui family. He writes, "I thank you for passing the duty of the measures held by my parent Sakuzaemon to me. With this I wish to change my name to Sakuzaemon."[19] Each of the new Sakuzaemons swore an oath to the magistrate making promises regarding the business and position of the Fukui house in manufacturing standard measures to be marketed at established prices. The opening of the oath, however, refers to headship succession as "taking the ancestral name of my good father Sakuzaemon." In 1761 "good father" is covered with a slip of paper with "adoptive father" written on it and several later oaths use this phrasing again, showing how common it was for the new head to have been the adoptive rather than the natural son and heir of the former head.[20] This identification of name inheritance with headship succession is even more explicit in other documents referring to this process. In 1761 Shimizu Heibei, another member of the measures guild, wrote to a third member about the choice of Sakuzaemon's heir. The document begins: "Fukui Sakuzaemon is ill and he has no son. I (Shimizu Heibei) received a request from Sakuzaemon that, as he has no heir to his name, he requests you to support master Hikoshichi for inheriting his (Sakuzaemon's) name…"[21]

There are some documents in the Fukui collection that refer to inheritance and succession in other, possibly related, families such as the Shimizu family that prominently featured in some of the documents above. In 1723 Shimizu Heizō wrote a *notes verbales* to the magistrate: "I am ill and, as my nephew Heiroku has been assisting me these past seven years, I request that my name be passed to him."[22] These various examples from the Fukui collection clearly refer to headship succession as name inheritance. Moreover, many of these successions were not cases of father-to-son primogeniture, but cases of passing on to nephews or other heirs recruited from outside the family through adoption. The village evidence suggests that the need for flexibility in the choice of an heir to family businesses to ensure a capable head may have been a factor in using specific headship names and identifying headship succession with name inheritance.[23]

Business name inheritance was not limited to the carpenter's guild. Moreover, name inheritance was not reserved for heirs with weak claims to inheritance as suggested by the village analysis.[24] The Takoyakushi neighborhood data collection includes the official journal written by a neighborhood official in 1853.[25] On the eleventh day of the ninth month the official, Fujikawa Genbei, records that "Kondaya Jinbei has passed headship to his son Hisatarō and Hisatarō is now to be called Jinbei." Shōbei from the main house of Kondaya also signed this record.[26] This is a case of name inheritance with headship succession by the eldest son. The population registers of Takoyakushi neighborhood also confirm that Hisatarō was Jinbei's son since he appears in the household from the beginning of the data series in 1843 when he was recorded as aged 12. The 1853 register also includes a notation that Jinbei has retired from headship taking the retirement name Kōyū and that Hisatarō is now head and that he has changed his name to Jinbei. The business name used the house name with the personal name of the head. Incidentally, Fujikawa Genbei is identified in the population registers by his house name Harimaya Genbei. The registers indicate that Kondaya Jinbei took his turn as neighborhood elder in 1841, but he used his surname Yashiro when he recorded the neighborhood journal. Moreover, even though the use of surnames was purportedly limited to the warrior class elite, these families with surnames — Yashiro, Fujikawa, Shimizu, and Fukui — were artisans and merchants and, therefore, commoners.

While the qualitative evidence suggests that name inheritance was an integral part of the headship succession process, analysis of the population registers for Seidō neighborhood reveals it was not necessary to the process. In 50 years of annual registration from 1818 to 1868 (1867 is missing from the series), I identified 25 cases of headship succession, and name inheritance was practised in 13 cases. Successions that took place with the retirement of the former head usually included name inheritance, whereas the death of the former head often did not induce a name change.[27] Examination of the name changes recorded in the population registers for all three neighborhoods in the data set for 1843–62 reveals eight cases of name changes at inheritance out of 10 successions. Of these, six involved name inheritance where the new head took the name of the former head, who also took a retirement name. So it looks as though name inheritance was important, especially when there was time to plan the succession process, but it was not a necessary part of the process. Instead, name inheritance was likely a final sign of support and agreement from the wider family and business hierarchy for the new head. Heirs who took over upon the death of the former head often did so in an emergency, sometimes as a temporary measure until a better candidate appeared.

Name Changes and Employment

Further investigation of the population registers reveals 119 name changes recorded for these three neighborhoods during the analysis period 1843–62. Obviously, most of these changes were not related to headship succession since only eight changes took place with succession, with another four changes by the retiring former heads. Further investigation reveals that 73 name changes in the registers were made by servants employed by households and businesses in the neighborhoods and 68 name changes were made by young people aged 16 to 20. There are several ways to look at this pattern.

These name changes may have been part of coming of age in Kyoto. Certainly more than half of the name changes took place at the right age for coming of age. Moreover, Takoyakushi neighborhood laws also mention *gempuku*, if only to note that residents of the neighborhood were not to give or require gifts when changing to the headship name, *gempuku*, or other happy events.[28] If all the young men changed their name once in the registers during this five-year age period, the probability would be 0.20. However, the probability that a young man would change his name at that time was 0.085, whereas I would expect a rite of passage to be slightly more common.

Research using the documents of major businesses of the Tokugawa period has produced the following scenario of the service career path. Male servants would begin as apprentices at 12 years old, running errands and helping out with various household tasks while completing the apprenticeship.[29] Then, at around age 17 the young apprentice would graduate to become a *tedai* (a skilled or management employee of a business) and start earning a wage while working in the business. At this point the employee would change his personal name, receiving a new one as a sign of his new status.[30]

In the career scenario, the servant who made the transition from apprentice to *tedai* changed his name in the *gempuku* rite. The population registers necessarily recorded name changes since they were official changes in identity. Examination of the Seidō and Takoyakushi registers reveals that 39 male servants in the Seidō registers and 37 male servants in the Takoyakushi registers changed their names. Households in Sujikaibashi did not employ servants. Did these name changes represent coming of age or a change of status? This is a difficult question to answer, but I argue for change of status with the new name representing membership in a new group — the employer's house.

Live-in employment in Kyoto at this time was a life-cycle phenomenon and largely limited to young men aged 13 to 27 and women aged 15 to 23. Servants changed their names throughout the age period of life-cycle service as shown in Table 1, but particularly around age 19.[31] However, age 19 was also the average and most common age for transition from apprentice to *tedai*. Moreover, a relatively small proportion of male servants changed their names at the peak ages of 16 to 20. This means that only a few servants of the appropriate age changed their names and name changing was not a coming-of-age rite that all servants performed.

Examination of status provides a different picture (see Table 2) and also reveals that the relation between name changing and the transition from apprentice to skilled *tedai* could vary by employer. All 39 of the servants that changed their names in the Seidō data entered the data as apprentices, 21 of them entered at ages 10 to 14. Most of the servants changing their names in Seidō were still apprentices and 44 per cent of them became *tedai* in the data after they changed their names. In Takoyakushi, most servants changed their names when or after they became *tedai* and 77 per cent of them made the transition in the data. Turning this around, however, 80 per cent of the apprentices that became *tedai* in Seidō changed their names within a couple of years of the transition.

Since many servants migrated to the city from rural villages, becoming a full-fledged trained employee also meant a change in social status from peasant to merchant or artisan and a name change could be a reflection of the change in social status. Examination of the birth provinces of

Table 1   Servant Age at Name Change in Seidō and Takoyakushi, 1843–68

Age	Seidō	Takoyakushi	Total
11–15	6	0	6
16	0	0	0
17	5	5	10
18	7	8	15
19	13	13	26
20	2	7	9
21–25	6	3	9
26–31	3	3	
Total Changes	39	39	78
Total Male Servants 16–20	71	135	206

Note: The Takoyakushi numbers include two female servants.

Table 2   Servant Status and Name Changes in Seidō and Takoyakushi

Status	Seidō	Takoyakushi	Total
Apprentices	280	251	531
Tedai	45	119	164
Apprentice-*tedai* transitions	21	44	65
Transition + name change	17	30	47
Total male servant name changes	39	37	76
Name changes as apprentice	33	6	39
Name changes as *tedai*	6	31	37

people who changed their names, however, reveals little difference in the probability of name changing by birth province. Finally, while there were many servants who changed their names without making the transition to *tedai*, most of those who made the transition in the data also changed their names, suggesting that these two changes were indeed linked.

One last comment is that some of the servants apparently changed their names due to family issues having no relation to their status in the employer's household. One servant, for example, inherited his birth family's headship name while in service. In the end, we cannot say definitively why they changed their names at one time and not another, but the name changes were likely related to the service career as well as other status issues. In any case, the promotion to skilled employee thesis seems to work better as an explanation for these name changes than the coming-of-age thesis and fits with the overall role of names signifying status in the family or in society as well as group membership.

Two female servants also changed their names in the Takoyakushi registers. There is no explanation in the research literature for female name changes and female employees did not have labels for different statuses within the employment hierarchy except for the distinction between nannies and maids. The population registers, labor contracts, and documents from the Fukui data, however, also suggest status as an explanation.

From 1819 until 1831 the Fukui family was embroiled in a complex dispute over headship succession. The Sakuzaemon of 1819 was in debt and he arranged for headship to pass to Kanshichirō, the son of his greatest creditor. Kanshichirō married Sakuzaemon's niece, underwent the necessary apprenticeships and training, and succeeded to headship, thus becoming the new Sakuzaemon in 1820 with the former Sakuzaemon changing his name to Sō'uemon. At the time of this process, Sō'uemon had a mistress who incredibly was party to the adoption agreements and other aspects of the succession process. She signed various documents until the final settlement of the case in 1833 after Sō'uemon's death. During this process, the mistress also changed her name and description several times. She first appears as Iwa, a relative of Sakuzaemon. In some later documents she appears as a servant called Sayo while in one document she is identified as a servant called Mitsu. She seems to have changed her name every time she changed employers or households. At the same time, when she lived independently or with her "spouse," she was always identified as Iwa.[32]

In fact, many labor contracts for female employees of Kyoto businesses note name changes at the time of employment although this is not recorded in the population registers and there does not seem to be any specific name an employer would use for a majority of female servants. The question of female name changes is a topic for further research, but this evidence also connects name changes to changes in status.

Conclusion

A survey of name changing practices in early modern Kyoto reveals several aspects of name changing and, therefore, of naming. Many family businesses reserved specific autonyms inherited along with the position for use by the heads of the family that were. Since headship succession in family businesses often took place with the retirement rather than the death of the former head, name inheritance meant that the former head also took a retirement name. Many elderly men and women also entered lay Buddhist orders in retirement and took another Buddhist name reflecting this status as a lay monk or nun. Name changes were also related to status changes while employed in service, particularly when young men who had entered service in their early teens acquired the necessary skills to be employed as skilled or management employees in the business rather than just as servants or apprentices.

As an example of the system working, suppose a young man with the autonym Shinsuke was employed by Harimaya. When Shinsuke became *tedai*, he changed his name to Zenbei. He no longer used the name Shinsuke. Later, Zenbei left Harimaya and established his household as Harimaya Zenbei. He retained the house name of his employer since he had become a member of Harimaya when he became *tedai*. Suppose that his birth family had the use of a surname, Nakano. Zenbei could call himself either Harimaya Zenbei or Nakano Zenbei. He retained the Nakano surname as long as he was still heir to his family line. Perhaps a couple of years later he decided to marry an heiress, the daughter of Maruya Jinuemon. So he entered her house and changed his autonym to Jinbei, or maybe he just remained Zenbei until he succeeded to head-ship, when he became Maruya Jinuemon and his father-in-law changed his name to Myōren, a Buddhist name. Having succeeded to headship of Maruya, the new Jinuemon could no longer use the surname Nakano because he was no longer a member of the Nakano family line and candidate for next head.

All of these name changes were related to changes in status within the family and within society. In this respect, name changing in the city was similar to name changing in rural villages. The majority of people changing their names in the data were in their late teens suggesting that coming of age could have been part of the practice, but name changing was not overly common in the general population. Employment as either servants or apprentices was also common at these ages, and most of the servants who changed their names also changed status to skilled employees of a business, providing a much stronger connection to status than to age.

Another way to understand name changes and status is to think of names or name types as representing group membership. An heir recruited from outside the family line, which could continue through either sons or daughters, changed his name to show that he joined the line. A servant changed his name to show that he joined the employer's house. An elderly man changed to a Buddhist name after retirement to show he had left the world and joined a religious order.

Unlike rural villages, the urban population was fluid with a regular population turnover of 20 per cent and name changing was not part of the assimilation process for outsiders to the community. The use of name inheritance in family businesses to assimilate outsiders to the family and establish mentors for adopted heirs that needed training or oversight was, however, useful for maintaining capable people as heirs. Moreover, the religious belief that duplication — while dangerous when two people held the same name at the same time — could allow the spirit of former users of a name to influence later users of that name, was yet another reason to continue name inheritance in family businesses, especially when recruiting capable heirs from outside the family.

All of these changes point to names, even personal ones, as signifying status. Since status changed over time, names also changed. These names were held sequentially, not in parallel as shown in the example above of Shinsuke who became Zenbei and then Jinuemon. At the same time, many people also used surnames and house names that identified them as members of larger social groups by family, business, and residence. There has not been room in this study to address these other name types in detail, so here I will only say that these names were used in parallel, but they could also change as group membership changed. In the example above, Zenbei shared the use of the house name Harimaya with other members of the house and he could also use his surname Nakano as long as he remained the heir, but he abandoned Harimaya for Maruya and also lost the use of the surname Nakano when he joined a different family line. Religious belief was also an integral part of the system as people changed their names both to avoid duplication within a household or family and to consciously duplicate names held by important ascendants to gain the influence and benefit of their abilities and experience.

These factors together suggest that early modern Japan had a complex "Class C" naming system described as a "titles system" where names have a strong relation to status.[33] This system changed in 1868 with the new Meiji Regime as all Japanese were required to declare a surname that would henceforth denote kinship, and individuals were prohibited from changing their names, with some exceptions. These exceptions were notably related to the religious aspect of names and name changing. After 1868 a person could change his personal name if someone else in the local community had the exact same name, if he felt that a long run of bad luck was attached to the name, or for name inheritance in some families. The process also continued in professional names in the arts such as stage names or pen names. The decision of the Meiji Government may have been an effort to strengthen and simplify the administrative control of the population by the central government. At the same time, the practices of Western imperialist nations also undoubtedly influenced the new system since gaining their respect as a modern nation had become a political necessity. So for nearly the first time in Japanese history, the Japanese naming system changed under the influence of powerful outsiders.

Notes

1   Herbert Plutschow, *Japan's Name Culture: The Significance of Names in a Religious, Political and Social Context* (Kent, CT: Japan Library, 1995).

2   Mary Louise Nagata, "Name Changing Patterns and the Stem Family in Early Modern Japan: Shimomoriya," in *The Stem Family in Eurasian Perspective: Revisiting House Societies, 17th–20th centuries*, eds. Antoinette Fauve-Chamoux and Emiko Ochiai (Bern, CH: Peter Lang, 2009), pp. 361–77.

3   Takoyakushi chō, Yashiro Jinbei Yaku Chū, "Nikki," *Takoyakushi Neighborhood Journal*, 1/1/1841–3/2/1842, Takoyakushi chō Collection D2, Kyoto City Library of Historical Documents. Dates in Japanese documents follow the lunar calendar. Note that Japanese names always list the personal name last.

4   See Charles J-H Macdonald, "Toward a Classification of Naming Systems in Insular Southeast Asia," this volume.

5   Takagi Tadashi, "Meiji Minpō Shikkō Mae ni Okeru Shūmei," in *Kantō Tanki Daigaku Kiyō* 2 (1981): 27–30.

6   Ōtō Osamu, *Kinsei Nōmin To Ie, Mura, Kokka* (Tokyo: Yoshikawa Kōbunkan, 1996), p. 124; Plutschow, *Japan's Name Culture*, pp. 5–7, 47–58, 169–76.

7   Kimura Isono, "Nōmin no Issho," in *Seikatsu Shi*, vol. 2, eds. Morisue Yoshiaki *et al.* (Tokyo: Yamakawa Shuppansha, 1981), pp. 224–8; Ōtō, *Kinsei Nōmin To Ie*, pp. 124–30.

8   Mary Louise Nagata, "Why Did You Change Your Name? Name Changing Patterns and the Life Course in Early Modern Japan," *History of the Family: An International Quarterly* 4, 3 (1998): 315–38.

9   Mary Louise Nagata, "Balancing Family Strategies with Individual Choice: Name Changing in Early Modern Japan," *Japan Review* 11 (1999): 145–66.

10 Plutschow, *Japan's Name Culture*, pp. 5–7, 47–58, 169–76; Harada Toshiaki, "Kaimei ni Tsuite," *Minzoku* 4, 1 (1928): 51–72.

11 Takagi, "Meiji Minpō Shikkō Mae ni Okeru Shūmei," pp. 27–30.

12 Takagi, "Meiji Minpō Shikkō Mae ni Okeru Shūmei," pp. 27–30; Ōtō, *Kinsei Nōmin To Ie*, pp. 232–4.

13 Nagata, "Why Did You Change Your Name?", pp. 333–4.

14 Nagata, "Balancing Family Strategies with Individual Choice: Name Changing in Early Modern Japan," *Japan Review* 11, (1999): 145–66.

15 Mary Louise Nagata, "Migrations et Enterprise à Kyoto au Début de l'époque Moderne," in *Entreprises en Movement: Migrants, Pratiques Entrepreneuriales et Diversités Culturelles dans le Monde, XVe–XXe siècle*, eds. Corine Maite and Manuela Martini (Valenciennes: Presses Universitaires de Valenciennes, 2007), pp. 149–66.

16 Kyoto Shi Rekishi Shiryōkan, ed., *Kyōto Machi Shikimoku Shūsei* [Compilation of the Laws of Kyoto Neighborhoods] (Kyoto: Kyoto City Library of Historical Documents, 1999).

17 Nagata, "Balancing Family Strategies with Individual Choice," pp. 156–9; Nagata, "Name Changing Patterns and the Stem Family," pp. 291–319.

18 Mary Louise Nagata, "Headship and Succession in Early Modern Kyoto: The Role of Women," *Continuity and Change* 19, 1 (2004): 91–2.

19 Sakuzaemon's son Fukui Ukyō [to Nakai Shusui Sama], "Osore Nagara Kōjō Sho Mōshi Age Sōrō," *Notes Verbales* 8/1725, Fukui Collection, Kyoto City Library of Historical Documents, No. 414.

20 Fukui Sakuzaemon [to Nakai Shusui Dono], "Kishōmon Maegaki", Oath preface, 5/28/1761, Fukui Collection, Kyoto City Library of Historical Documents, No. 1554.

21 Shimizu Heibei [to Tsukokuya Jinbei Dono], "Issatsu," Agreement 2/1761, Fukui Collection, Kyoto City Library of Historical Documents, No. 1636.

22 Shimizu Heizō [to Obugyō Sama], "Osore Nagara Motte Kōjō Sho Negae Age Tatematsuri Sōrō," Request to magistrate 2/1723, Fukui Collection, Kyoto City Library of Historical Documents, No. 1537.

23 Nagata, "Name Changing Patterns and the Stem Family," pp. 361–77; Nagata, "Balancing Family Strategies with Individual Choice," pp. 159–62.

24 Nagata, "Balancing Family Strategies with Individual Choice," pp. 159–62.

25 Takoyakushi chō, Fujikawa Genbei, "Nikki," *Takoyakushi Neighborhood Journal*, Kaei 6 (1853) 8/5 to Kaei 7 (1854) 1, Takoyakushi chō Collection D5, Kyoto City Library of Historical Documents.

26 Fujikawa Genbei, "Nikki," 1853, Takoyakushi chō Collection D5, 5.

27 Mary Louise Nagata, "Inheritance in Stem-Family Businesses in Early Modern Kyoto, Japan" (paper presented at the Social Science History Association meeting, Chicago, 2001). This research was subsequently absorbed into a later article, "Headship and Succession in Early Modern Kyoto: The Role of Women," *Continuity and Change* 19, 1 (2004): 73–104, but the published article did not include the names analysis.

28 Kyoto Shi Rekishi Shiryōkan, ed., *Kyōto Machi Shikimoku Shūsei* [Compilation of the Laws of Kyoto Neighborhoods] (Kyoto: Kyoto City Library of Historical Documents, 1999), 145.

29 Nakano Takashi, *Shōka Dōzokudan no Kenkyū*, vol. 1 (Tokyo: Miraisha, 1978); Ogura Eiichirō, *Ōmi Shōnin no Keiei* (Kyoto: Sanburaito Shuppan, 1988); Mary Louise Nagata, *Labor Contracts and Labor Relations in Early Modern Central Japan* (London and New York: Curzon-Routledge, 2005).

30 Nagata, *Labor Contracts and Labor Relations*, pp. 31–8.

31 Note that I extend the data period to 1868 to make use of all available data.

32 Mary Louise Nagata, "Mistress or Wife? Fukui Sakuzaemon vs. Iwa, 1819–1833," *Continuity and Change* 18, 2 (2003): 287–309.

33 Charles J-H Macdonald, "Toward a Classification of Naming Systems in Insular Southeast Asia," this volume.

CHAPTER 12

Personal Identity Complex and Name Changes among the Sinhalese in Sri Lanka

M. W. Amarasiri de Silva

Introduction

The use of names among the Sinhalese as markers of personal identity has a historic basis in caste. Today, names are still important among the Sinhalese as indicators of the caste of a person, although this no longer applies to all names and castes as much as it did in traditional times.[1] At present, traditional "high-caste" names are preferred, and names indicating "low-caste" status are disappearing. This situation would appear to indicate the diminishing significance of caste as a determinant of social status and the emergence of a class system where one's name is seen as a status reflector rather than as a caste identifier. However, this paper argues that caste, as a structural entity among the Sinhalese, has not diminished in significance. Rather, it has assumed a new role in modern Sinhalese society vis-à-vis class. Today, names reflect the intersection of the residual effect of caste and the modern manifestations of class structure.

In the traditional period, an individual was considered a member of a group where caste provided the overarching boundary; personal status was subsumed within a group status, which was defined by kinship and caste. The need for any change in personal status, therefore, never arose. However, castes as status groups have been subject to change over a long period. For instance, rearrangements of the hierarchy of castes and of subdivisions within a single caste were reported during the British Period.[2]

Although caste is viewed as a structural entity with an assumed hierarchy, occasionally in traditional times individuals did change their social status by moving into castes that were regarded as being of a higher level. Such instances of individual mobility within the traditional caste system were facilitated by name changes, and names functioned as identifiers of an individual's caste, village of origin or residence (the village of origin and residence were often coterminous), and occupation.[3]

The Sinhalese have changed their names through newspaper notifications for several decades now, as this has been the easiest way of fulfilling a legal requirement that name changes be made public. Name changes in newspaper notifications are of two types: personal or first name changes, and family name changes.

Classification of Sinhalese Names

Among the Sinhalese, family names are passed from one generation to the next and used as distinctive identifiers of family and kinship groups. In the traditional period, there were two kinds of family names: the *patabendi* (honorific) names and non-*patabendi* or ordinary names. Traditionally, *patabendi* names were conferred by the kings for conspicuous military exploits.[4] During the Kandyan Kingdom period (1474–1815),[5] *patabendi* names were found in the dominant *radala* Goigama caste families who constituted the landed aristocracy.[6] The *patabendi* names were later treated as patronymics and used as family names by the descendants of the conferee. As Pieris notes, "Scions of a man honoured with a *patabendi* title such as 'Suriyasekera Mudiyanse' would convert it into a patronymic by adding the suffix '*lage*' (belonging to or descending from) and call themselves Suriyasekera Mudiyanselage, 'descendants from Suriyasekera Mudiyanse.'"[7] Referring to this process of converting *patabendi* titles into patronymics, Obeyesekere concludes that it "has resulted in a spread of *patabendi* titles in Kandyan society."[8] Since such patronymics were widely used by affluent families in the Kandyan provinces, who were largely Goigama, they were generally thought of as a prerogative of the Goigama caste, particularly the *radala* Goigama sub-caste.

Although we do not have much information about patronymics used by castes other than the Goigama during or prior to the Kandyan era, different castes have folk stories referring to the conferring of honorific names on their ancestors by kings and provincial rulers. This practice was evident during the times of colonial rulers, who granted *patabendi* names to the local and regional officials they appointed. Obeyesekere, however, states that "with the three streams of foreign conquest, the prohibition against assuming patronymics and titles associated with rank was lifted, and there was a mass 'usurpation' of these honorifics particularly among the dominant Goigama and a few of the Karava caste."[9] The presence or absence of a *patabendi* name identifies a person in terms of his/her class status within the caste. Generally, those who did not have a *patabendi* name were considered lower in the caste hierarchy than those who had such a name. Lately, however, *patabendi* names have been used to distinguish one's origins, whether upcountry or low country,[10] and sometimes one's religious affiliation.

Another important category of names is known as *vasagama* names, or names indicating the place of origin. During the Kandyan period, ordinary Goigama people who did not use *patabendi* names had *vasagama* names. The *vasagama* name indicates a person's hamlet or village of origin. As each hamlet or village consists of several kin groups, *vasagama* names usually have nametags to identify the particular line of succession. For example, the name Pahala Medagama Gamage Jinadasa, mentioned in Obeyesekere, has three distinct components.[11] Jinadasa is the individual's personal name. The first two words, Pahala Medagama, refer to his place of origin or *vasagama*. Finally, Jinadasa of Pahala Medagama belongs to the particular line of succession named Gamage. Thus, the *vasagama* indicates the hamlet of origin of the forefathers of the person concerned and his line of succession.

The people without *patabendi* or *vasagama* names were the "low castes" in the Kandyan Kingdom. While some of them were identified with a *Ge* name or "house name," such as Ihala Gedera "house located at the upper elevation" or Pahala Gedera "house located at the lower elevation," others were identified with their father's name, for example, Ukkuwage Puncha "Puncha, the son of Ukkuwa."[12] Yalman observes that ordinary Goigama people, as opposed to the aristocratic Goigama, were considered to be of a "low caste" because their forefathers had been serfs and did not have title names. "These serfs were no longer bound by feudal (*rajakariya*) laws, but 'respectable' people would not intermarry or interdine with them. Their 'lowness' was evident in their names, for they were distinguished from other Goigama — so it was claimed — by their lack of ancient titles and *vasagama* names. They had been the 'working people' (*vada karayo*) like the low castes."[13]

In traditional villages, however, "low castes" such as the potters or the washermen were identified by particular family (*Ge*) and personal names, which was one of the ways of segregating people into different castes, and putting them in social positions relative to the "higher castes" in the villages. Although the "low-caste" people may not have liked the way in which they had been identified and labeled as being people without *vasagama* and honorifics, they could not do much to prevent the continuation of such a system of naming, for it was regulated by the "high-caste" people. The registrars of births and deaths, who registered the newborn children, were often Goigama people in Kandyan upcountry villages and had the discretion to name the children of "low-caste" parents in accordance with the traditional, Kandyan system.[14] Even when parents wanted to name their children differently to alleviate the social stigma attached to "low-caste" names, they could not bypass the registrars who followed the old tradition.

Although traditionally the naming system had an importance for symbolic identity and a meaning required for stratification and interaction, in modern society social identity denoted by names does not necessarily correspond to the assumed social roles and status of people. Since traditional *Ge* (house or family) names and personal names, particularly those considered to be "low-caste," are now regarded as a barrier for socialization, the *vasagama*, honorifics and patronymics of the "high castes" are being emulated and widely used. As a result, these *vasagama* have lost their traditional social meaning, which had been associated with demonstrated leadership and proprietorship.

Although the name of an individual has become less of a status marker in present-day Sri Lankan society, the traditional values of the caste system persist in many different ways, thus fostering the hierarchy and perpetuating the stigma attached to low-caste people. Name changes are a necessary and an accepted form of eliminating the lingering notion of the caste-related lowness of a person in modern society, but are not a sufficient condition for upward mobility.

Ways of Changing Name among the Sinhalese

Before the popularity of using newspaper announcements as a means of making a name change public and consequently assuming high-status names, there were other ways by which Sinhalese changed their names. In traditional society, low-caste but powerful persons who aspired to assume social prestige practised hypogamy, or marriage into a "higher caste." For example, Yalman describes how an ordinary Goigama man named Dehi Gaha Pitiya Kalu Banda of Terutenna, who did not have a title name, married into an aristocratic family and adopted the aristocratic title (*radala*) of his wife, Nissanka Mudiyanselage Tun Amunu Gedera, a name that was later also assumed by almost all of his kinsmen. Yalman further notes, "There were some 'low' Goigama who had grown rich and thereupon changed their place of residence and successfully assumed aristocratic titles."[15]

Obeyesekere reports another way of changing one's name and assuming a title name (honorifics and patronymics).[16] According to him, in Hinidumpattuwa, the rich and powerful people who were emancipated from the ordinary caste and kin groups formed new social bonds with similarly powerful and rich families of the same caste in the region. These groups were called *pelantiya*. They were distinguished from the ordinary caste members by their distinct honorifics and patronymics, the form and meaning of which often resembled title names (*patabendi nam*), which had been bestowed upon the ancestors of the family by the kings in the Kandyan Kingdom.

This paper focuses on how the present-day Sinhalese use newspaper advertisements as a way of changing their names, a method that has become increasingly popular in the last few decades. The increase in the number of name changes has been quite dramatic. In the year before economic liberalization policies were introduced in 1977, only 484 people announced changes in their names in newspapers. Two decades later, this number increased to around 4,000 per year during the period 1993 to 1995 as shown in Figure 1.

Given this background, it is pertinent to ask why people change their names. In Obeyesekere's words:

> (Can we say that) usurpation of honorifics … is an emulation of a position of power, prestige and authority by persons who were traditionally debarred from such positions? Is it because people want to do away with names that associate with caste status? Alternatively, is it because the traditional naming system has become obsolete and it is given a new meaning in the modern class society?[17]

This paper attempts to answer some of these questions by analyzing newspaper announcements of name changes in the present context of class and caste mobility among the Sinhalese. In doing so, this study investigates whether the name changes have actually contributed to any change in caste status for those who changed their names; or whether such changes of name facilitated merging into the wider society in modern times in a free and equal manner by alleviating the derogatory and stigmatizing connotations of traditional names.

Materials and Methods

The data for this study consists mainly of notifications of name changes in Sinhala newspapers from 1993 to 1995.[18] These were compared with notifications published in 1976, just before economic liberalization policies were introduced, in an effort to account for the significant increase in these notifications after these policies were implemented.[19] The following variables were chosen for analysis after an initial review of the notifications:

1. Type of name change (first name or family name)
2. Initiator of name change (individual or family)
3. Gender of the advertiser (if an individual initiated the name change)
4. Names used (by families/individuals) prior to the proposed name change
5. Caste indicated in the previous name
6. Assumed (new) name and the caste indicated by this name
7. District of residence
8. Date of notification

The castes associated with names were identified through discussions with key informants from different geographical locations where name changes were reported. Frequency distributions were then obtained using caste, district, initiator of name change, and gender as controlling variables.

Findings

From 1993 to 1995, a total of 12,063 notifications of name changes or an average of 4,021 per year was published in those Sinhala newspapers

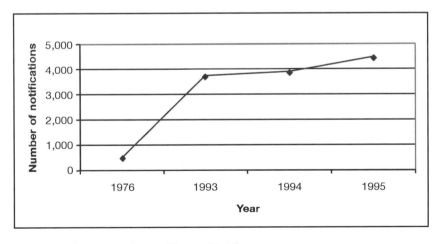

Figure 1 Increase in Name Change Notifications

surveyed. By comparison, the notifications published in 1976 totaled only 484, or about one-ninth of the average annual number of notifications published in the period from 1993 to 1995 (see Figure 1). The marked rise in the number of notifications in the later years suggests the increased significance of name changes as a form of individual and class mobility and a mechanism of destigmatizing one's family name.

In addition, it suggests that names have become increasingly recognized as a marker of an individual's social status in the wider society. (Henceforth, title names, that is, honorifics and patronymics, *vasagama* names, and *Ge* names, will all be considered under one category as family names for convenience).

Table 1   Type of Name Change Implied in Notifications

	Who changed the name			
Type of name change	*Individual*	*Whole Family*	*No information*	*Total*
Only family name changed	2,386 (19.0%)	1,767 (14.1%)	55 (.4%)	4,208 (33.5%)
Only first name changed	3,588 (28.6%)	0 (.0%)	0 (.0%)	3,588 (28.6%)
Both first and family name changed	3,304 (26.4%)	1,425 (11.4%)	9 (.1%)	4,738 (37.8%)
Type of name change not identifiable	3 (.0%)		10 (.1%)	13 (.1%)
Total	9,281 (74.0%)	3,192 (25.5%)	74 (.6%)	12,537 (100.0%)

Of the total 12,547 notifications in Table 1, 28.6 per cent were changes of first (personal) names only; 33.5 per cent were changes of family names only. Of the total number of cases, 25.5 per cent related to changes of family name for a whole family, 19.0 per cent to changes of family name for an individual only and 26.4 per cent to changes of family and first name for an individual. The proportion of cases involving a change in first name only fell from about 30 per cent in 1976 to around 28 per cent in 1993/95, while change in family name only has increased from 20 per cent in 1976 to 35 per cent in 1995.

If the adoption of new family names is equated with an entirely new caste status, then about 71 per cent of those who assumed new family names have changed their caste status from a "low caste" to that of Goigama or *radala* Goigama. At this rate, the average number of families assuming Goigama caste status every year amounts to about 800 families, or approximately 4,000 persons if we assume that a family consists of five members. In addition, there are about 1,400 individuals assuming Goigama caste names each year. This accounts for a considerable portion of the increase in the number of people in the Goigama caste, despite the fact that traditional values attached to the patronymics, honorifics, and *vasagama* names of the Goigama are being "pejorated," as Obeyesekere notes.[20]

The individuals who changed their family names were predominantly male (about 70 per cent). Though we do not have information on their age and relative social status, it is likely that these individuals were young males who aspired to move up the social ladder through employment and marriage.[21] As in any social context in Sri Lanka, those aspiring to change are mainly young males. However, the percentage of females among those changing their family name increased from 22.5 per cent in 1976 to 33.3 per cent in 1995, indicating that females of the non-Goigama castes are also increasingly becoming socially mobile and aspiring to change their social status. This may be a sign of improvement in the quality of life of these "low-caste" women, who are traditionally poor and less educated.

Table 2 shows the geographical distribution of family name changes announced by individuals and families. The higher percentages were found in urban areas such as Colombo (13 per cent) and Gampaha (12 per cent), as well as in districts in the traditional Kandyan territories. These territories include Kurunegala, Kandy, Ratnapura, Kegalle, Anuradhapura, and Badulla, and account for about 50 per cent of the total. The districts in the south, though very populous, have relatively few notifications of family name changes.

Districts with a large percentage of Tamils among their population, such as Vavuniya, Jaffna, and Trincomalee, had only a few notifications, while others like Batticaloa and Mannar did not have any, suggesting that, among the Tamils and Muslims, the family name does not seem to have any particular social prestige or caste connotations attached to it. It is possible, however, that such notifications were published in Tamil newspapers, which were not included in this study. It is worth mentioning that notifications by Tamils accounted for 6.5 per cent of the total, of which about 80 per cent sought Sinhala family names, mostly of the Goigama caste. Of these, the majority (28 per cent) were from Colombo, while Ratnapura (11 per cent), Gampaha (9 per cent), Kalutara (8 per cent), and Kandy (8 per cent) reported a considerable number of Tamils seeking Sinhala Goigama names.[22]

Table 2 Distribution of Family Name Changes by District

District	Number of name change notifications	Percentage of notifications
Colombo	1,193	13.3
Kurunegala	1,092	12.2
Gampaha	1,079	12.1
Kandy	775	8.7
Ratnapura	754	8.4
Kegalle	714	8.0
Anuradhapura	508	5.7
Badulla	449	5.0
Matara	316	3.5
Galle	290	3.2
Kalutara	280	3.1
Matale	256	2.9
Puttalam	204	2.3
Hambantota	180	2.0
Nuwaraeliya	132	1.5
Polonnaruwa	125	1.4
Monaragala	119	1.3
Ampara	60	0.7
Trincomalee	16	0.2
Vavuniya	7	0.1
Jaffna	2	0.0
District not mentioned	395	4.4
Total	8,946	100

It is interesting to note that 85 per cent of all Tamils seeking name changes in the four years under review published their notifications between 1993 and 1995, compared to only 15 per cent in 1976. An increase in the number of Tamils changing their names to Sinhala names may have been due to the 1983 communal riots and the subsequent civil unrest, the war in the northern districts and the mass exodus of internally displaced persons in the 1990s.[23] Names are an explicit symbolic expressions of ethnicity. Name changes would have facilitated avoiding public identification of Tamil ethnicity, especially in urban work places, business circles, and residential areas — the focus of communal riots in 1983. Most of the politically neutral Tamils living in the said districts would have preferred ethnically neutral English names, while those who were closely linked with the Sinhalese would have preferred Sinhalese names.

Table 3 Assumed Caste Positions Identified through Changed Names Given in Notifications by Original Tamil Name Holders

Assumed caste or ethnic group depicted in the new name	Frequency	Percentage
Goigama	356	43.7
Unidentified castes	225	27.6
Retained Tamil Identity	82	10.1
Muslim	66	8.0
Acaste	33	4.0
Karava	33	4.0
Burgher	16	2.0
Durava	4	0.5
Total	815	100.0

Patterns of Family Name Changes

Table 4 presents the frequency distribution of family name changes by Goigama caste persons who notified name changes through the newspapers. The data shows that Goigama people made about 28 per cent of the name changes. About 60 per cent of these notifications did not indicate any caste change, but modified names by modernizing them. The second largest category (21.4 per cent) was those who assumed *radala* Goigama names. There were a few, largely females, who assumed Muslim names after marrying Muslim persons.

Table 4 Changed Caste Status Implied in Notifications by Goigama Caste Persons

Assumed caste status	Number of notifications	Percentage of notifications
Goigama unchanged (name modernized)	2,012	59.8
Radala Goigama	720	21.4
Not identified	558	16.7
Muslim name	48	1.4
Karava	17	0.5
Durava	5	0.1
Acaste	4	0.1
Total	3,364	100

The name changes by Goigama persons adopted two broad methods: a) modernizing family names by rearranging them to follow the English/

Western style and b) assuming traditional title names and honorifics. The examples presented in Table 5 illustrate these name changes.

Table 5 Patterns of Name Changes among the Goigama

Original name	Changed name	Comments
Yapa Mudiyanselage Yahapathami	Yapa Mudiyanselage Ranjit Priyantha Yapa	The name has been modernized and it has assumed an upper-class status. Adding a traditional "high-caste" name tag, such as Yapa, is a modern way of making the name look elegant. When the name is initialized, the traditional family name "Yapa" can be written as Y.M.R.P. Yapa. This makes the family name or the kinship line more prominent. If the old name were written in the same way, it would be Y.M. Yahapathami. The status difference between the two names Y.M. Yahapathami and Y.M.R.P Yapa is quite marked.
Udagama Liyanage Alice Noona	Udagama Liyanage Asoka Udagama or U.L.A. Udagama	The change of personal name is not obvious as it is written with initials — the way most Sinhalese write their names nowadays. (This is also a practice adopted by the "low castes" when they change their names, which will be discussed later.) This name change represents a complete reversal of the way names were presented in traditional times. If this name were written traditionally with initials, it would be U.L. Alice Noona. The Westernized, modern way of writing the name is U.L.A. Udagama.
P.M. Sarlis Appuhami (from Colombo)	Charles Sirigunatileke	The first name has been modernized and the traditional Appuhami name has been dropped. A modern acaste and high-class family name has been adopted. The two names Sarlis and Appuhami are considered old-fashioned names of traditional villagers.

Table 5 *continued*

Original name	Changed name	Comments
Dan Watta Liyanage Kamalawathi	Illeperumage Dona Kamalawathi Ariya Wijenayake	The family name Liyanage is a Goigama succession line found in the low country. The assumed name Wijenayake connotes "high caste" and high-class status. When Kamalawathi is changed to Dona Kamalawathi, it shifts from an ordinary first name to a low-country aristocratic first name.
Jayawardene Mudalige Arumawathie	Jayawardene Mudalige Aruna Jayawardene	The traditional name has been modernized by using part of the family name as a tag at the end of the name. When written with initials the two names look different and portray two different social statuses. J.M. Anumawathie is very much a village name, while J.M.A. Jayawardene looks elitist.
K.H. Heen Banda	Sumit Attanayake	The ordinary Goigama name has been changed to a modern Goigama name. Being a resident of Colombo the person so named preferred Sumit to Heen Banda, with the colorful family name, Attanayake. (Attanayake was the name under which Rohana Wijeweera, the slain JVP leader, sought refuge during his last few years of underworld politics.)
Ukku Bandage Ram Banda	Wanninayake Mudiyanselage Ranjith Bandara Wanninayake	As pointed out by Leach, most villagers in Anuradhapura do not have *vasagama* names. Although they are Goigama, they do not have titles or prestigious *vasagama*. They follow the tradition of using the father's name as an identifier of the son, as in the case of Ukku Bandage Ram Banda (Ram Banda, the son of Ukku Banda). Many name changes of ordinary Goigama in the Anuradhapura district are of this type.

Table 5   *continued*

Original name	Changed name	Comments
Kiri Menikage Karunadasa	Karunadasa Mudiyanse	Sometimes, especially when a child is born to an unmarried woman, the child is named after the mother, as in Kiri Menikage Karunadasa. This name was changed to a title name with Mudiyanse, a "high-caste" honorific.
Wijetunga Mudiyanselage Sarath Bandara or W.M. Sarath Bandara	Sarath Bandara Wijetunga or S.B. Wijetunge	This is a classic example of a modernized Goigama name, where the family name has assumed only part of the traditional title name. In this change, it is clear that S.B. Wijetunge assumes higher social status than W.M. Sarath Bandara.

Non-Goigama Name Changes

Among all the name changes, family name changes among the non-Goigama castes were the most frequent. Of the total number of people who changed their names, 64 per cent were Sinhalese from non-Goigama castes and, of these, the non-Goigama from the Bathgama, Naketi, Dura, Hena, and Vahumpura castes were important (see Table 6). The Bathgama and Dura castes,[24] which were traditionally concentrated in the Kandyan districts, are now dispersed in other districts as well, as revealed in the notifications (see Table 7).

As shown in Table 7, Bathgama caste persons, who were traditionally confined to the Kandyan territories, now live in many other districts. Among the Bathgama persons who changed their family names, about 40 per cent came from districts outside the traditional Kandyan territories. Similarly, Dura caste persons were also traditionally found in the Kandyan territories, but only about 12 per cent of those who have changed their names came from districts outside the traditional Kandyan territories, indicating their lower geographical mobility. This indicates that the Bathgama caste has been more dynamic than the Dura caste as they (the Bathgama) have been moving out of their traditional villages in the past several decades. It is interesting to note that Dura and Bathgama residents in the low-country districts have assumed low-country family names of the Goigama, Karava, and Salagama[26]. For example, in Galle district, about 13 per cent of Dura caste persons have assumed Karava and Salagama names, 9 and 4 per cent respectively.

Table 6   Percentage Distribution of Non-Goigama Caste Applicants

Original caste of applicants	Number of applicants	Percentage of applicants
Bathgama	1,528	20.3
Naketi	1,304	17.3
Hena	1,019	13.5
Dura	915	12.1
Acaste	863	11.5
Vahumpura	734	9.7
Achari	457	6.1
Karava	284	3.8
Salagama	139	1.8
Kumbal	138	1.8
Patti	43	0.6
Durava	35	0.5
Panna	17	0.2
Burgher	17	0.2
Galladu	9	0.1
Gattara	8	0.1
Hunu	8	0.1
Rodi	7	0.1
Malay	7	0.1
Total	7,532	100.0

Name changes by non-Goigama persons seem to display a pattern that is quite distinct from that used by the Goigama who changed their names. The most widely seen practice among the "low castes" in Kandyan/ up country districts is the de-stigmatizing of family names with derogatory connotations by assuming new family names that resemble those of the Goigama caste. Omitting traditional family names that denote caste status and assuming new *Ge* (house or family) names is a trend among the "low castes." Although the new *Ge* names resemble Goigama family names, they are not traditional Goigama family names. The invention of new family names without caste connotations can be seen in many name changes that were reported. Such new family names are identified in this study as acaste names or names without a caste connotation. Examples of these patterns of name changes are presented below.

(a)   Upasaka Panikkiyalage Somasiri was changed to Udadeniye Pathiranage Somasiri. In the assumed name, Panikkiyalage has been omitted for its obvious caste connotation. As in some of the Goigama name

Table 7[25]

District	Näketi	Kumbal	Salagama	Hena	Patti	Bathgama	Karava	Vahumpura	Durava	Dura	Achari	Acaste	Total
Colombo	5.1%	8.0%	9.5%	8.0%		7.8%	20.3%	8.2%	11.1%	3.80%	9.20%	9.7%	13.5%
Kurunegala	8.5%	4.0%		14.3%	18.2%	10.8%	6.8%	9.6%	11.1%	16.20%	3.40%	1.4%	11.8%
Gampaha	1.7%		9.5%	6.9%		19.0%	8.5%	5.5%	11.1%	1.6%	6.9%	2.8%	10.4%
Kandy	9.8%			9.0%	45.4%	10.8%	5.1%	7.5%	11.1%	11.4%	9.2%	18.1%	8.8%
Ratnapura	9.4%	56.0%	19.0%	22.9%		10.0%	3.4%	24.0%	11.1%	9.2%	28.7%	13.2%	8.7%
Kegalle	3.8%	8.0%		6.9%	18.2%	16.5%	3.4%	6.2%		5.9%	4.6%	7.6%	7.2%
Anuradhapura	9.8%			1.7%		6.9%	5.0%	1.4%		3.8%	5.7%	4.9%	6.0%
Badulla	12.0%			1.1%		2.2%	5.1%	7.5%		32.4%	3.4%	7.6%	4.9%
Matara	10.7%	4.0%	14.3%	12.6%	18.2%	1.3%	8.5%	2.1%	22.3%	1.1%	9.3%	0.7%	3.6%
Kalutara	0.4%	8.0%	4.8%	3.4%		1.3%	3.4%	5.5%		0.7%	3.5%	2.8%	3.2%
Matale	6.4%			2.3%		2.6%	1.7%	2.1%		4.3%	2.3%	13.7%	3.1%
Galle	1.7%	8.0%	14.3%	6.3%		0.9%	18.6%	10.1%	22.2%	1.6%	4.7%	1.4%	3.1%
Hambantota	3.8%			1.7%		1.3%	3.4%	2.1%		1.6%	4.6%	2.1%	2.8%
Putralam			4.8%	1.10%		2.1%	1.7%	0.7%		0.5%	3.4%		2.3%
Monaragala	7.7%		10.0%			0.9%		4.1%		1.1%		5.6%	1.9%
Nuwaraeliya	4.7%		4.8%	0.6%		1.7%	1.70%	1.30%	11.1%	2.7%	1.1%	3.50%	1.7%
Polonnaruwa	1.3%	4.0%		0.6%		2.6%		2.10%		1.6%		2.80%	1.6%
Ampara	2.6%			0.6%		0.9%	3.40%			0.5%		1.40%	0.7%
Trincomalee	0.4%					0.4%						0.70%	0.2%
Missing	0.2%		9.0%										4.5%
Total	100.0%	100.0%	100.0%	100.0%	100.0%	100.0%	100.0%	100.0%	100.0%	100.0%	100.0%	100.0%	100.0%

changes, the initials are retained in this case: U.P. Somasiri is used in public correspondence. The difference between the two names is striking. The first one means "the son of the pious Panikkiya, the drummer of Udadeniya." The meaning of the second name is "of the house of Udadeniye Pathirana" or "of the Udadeniye Pathirana line of succession."

(b) Ranhili Pedige was changed to Ranasinghege. In this example, the whole family has adopted the Ranasinghege family name. Pedige is a well-known traditional family name of the Bathgama caste in some districts. This family replaced its traditional name with Ranasinghege, which is not a recognized Goigama name indicating a line of succession. Although many Goigama people, particularly those from the low country, use Ranasinghe as a prestigious family name, they seldom use it as a name for a particular line of succession, unlike the name Gamage.

(c) Assuming new family names that are widely used by a particular caste is another way of changing family names. Many name changes by Dura caste persons involved assuming the name Pathiranage, while Rajapaksage and Nuwarapaksage were names preferred by Bathgama caste persons. Judging by the notifications, these seem to be the recognized modern family names of the Dura and Bathgama castes.

(d) Rankiralaya Nandoris alias Wijepala was changed to Ratnayakage Sunil Senanayake. The name should have been changed to Ratnayake Mudiyanselage Sunil Senanayake Ratnayake or R.M.S.S. Ratnayake to modernize it and make the change of caste into a Goigama. However, this person did not do so. Being a person from a traditional village in Ratnapura, he may have thought that his fellow villagers, neighbors and kinsfolk might react badly to such a drastic name change that indicates a change of caste. The name change adopted by Wijepala would eliminate the traditional low-caste connotations without assuming a "higher-caste" status. Although Ratnayake is a well-known Goigama name, there is no accepted line of succession called Rathnayakage among the Goigama. It is interesting to note that this name was not changed to Ratnayake Mudiyanselage, which is a widely used title name among the Goigama.

(e) Many "low castes" changed part of their traditional name to make it prestigious. For example, Weledurayalayegedera Pina "Pina, the son of the *duraya*, the drummer, residing in the house by the paddy field" was changed to Mangala Gamage Chandrasena Welagedera. The omission of "*durayaleye*" from the traditional name resulted in the name "Welagedera," which is a prestigious Kandyan Goigama

name. Other examples are Welekumburegedera to Welagedera;
Hewahakuruge to Hewage; and Bambaranda Badalge to Bambarande.

(f) The assumption of completely different titles and *vasagama* names
that have no relationship whatsoever to traditional names was
also found in the notifications. This type of name change matches
Obeyesekere's observation of the pejoration of Goigama honorifics
and patronymics. Some examples are presented in Table 8.

Table 8 The Assumption of Completely Different Titles and *Vasagama* Names,
which Have No Relationship Whatsoever to Traditional Names

Original name	Changed name	Comments
Hapan Pedige Pina	Gemunu Abhayawardene	Complete change of the traditional family name and the traditional first name.
Hewa Pedige Palitha	Palitha Hewa Pathirana	Complete change into a modern name with a change of family name into one that resembles a Goigama name. Many Pedige names have been changed over to Pathirana as here.
Hawadi Durage Gunawathi	Dissanayake Mudiyanselage Chandra Ratnayake	Complete change to a Goigama high-class name and a change to a modern first name.
Alutgedera Ukkuamma	Nakat Walauve Gedera Seeta Kumarihami	This person assumed the name of a *walauva* "manor house" and the personal name Kumarihami, which is traditionally used by *radala* Goigama, while retaining her traditional Nakati caste name, Nakat Gedera.
Sudu Hakuru Norbert	Norbert Wijesinghe	English names are being used as first names among "low-caste" persons. This has been a practice in order to avoid adopting caste-bound first names. However, when the family name is changed to a Goigama "high-caste" one, retaining the English first name, it sounds very much a modern high-class name, as in this case.

Table 8   *continued*

Original name	Changed name	Comments
Horatal Pedige Allen (from Colombo)	Harischandra Liyanage Allen Ratnayake	This is a good example of a name change by assuming a modernized, upper-class Goigama name.
Suduwa Devage Leslie Tennyson Fernando	Sirimannage Leslie Tennyson Sirimanne	It seems that this name had been changed earlier to look like a Karava name, but the bearer was not satisfied with that social status; hence the change to a high-class Goigama name.
Medawewegedara Peiris (from Nuwaraeliya)	Medawewegedara Peiris Nihal Medawewa	This is a good example of how people modernize "low-caste" names to look like "high-caste" aristocracy, but without changing the original *Ge* name. Here part of the *Ge* name, Medawewa, is used as a *vasagama*. This new *vasagama* sounds like a Goigama upper-class name. Many traditional *vasagama* names in the Anuradhapura area end with the suffix *wewa* "tank," as in Mahadivulwewa. However, this person was from Nuwaraeliya where tank irrigation is not well known.

(g)   Some people created non-traditional family names that identify their caste; however, unlike traditional family names, these created names are not derogatory. Some examples are presented in Table 9.

Table 9   Non-traditional Family Names

Original name	Changed name	Comments
Wedanchari Nakatige	Peter Wansakkarage	This name is a non-existent "Goigama type" name.
Matara Badalge (potter caste of Matara)	Matara Bandarage (Bandarage is a Goigama name.)	This name is a non-existent "Goigama type" name.

Table 9 *continued*

Original name	Changed name	Comments
Badahela Badde Vidanayalaye Peris Appu	Deva Bandu Kumaratungalage Peris Chandradasa	Here the obvious caste connotations in the *vasagama* have been omitted, and Appu has been dropped, although it was a popular Goigama name several decades ago. The new name is acaste but resembles a high-class name.
R.P.D. Jayalath Noona (from Narammala)	Rajapaksege Vinita Rajapakse	This person from Narammala has an obvious caste connotation in her name. However, the new name, Vinita, a recent name with a modern outlook, together with the changed *vasagama* from R.P.D. to Rajapaksage makes the name different. Rajapaksage in this particular area is of the same caste as R.P.D., but it is a modern way of identifying upper-class status within the caste.

(h) Among changes in the family names, one notable feature is the retention of the initials or the coining of a family name to suit the initials. This is particularly true among the "low castes." Such changes give no indication that the family name has been changed. Some examples of this type of name change are presented below.

Table 10 Examples of the Retention of Initials in the Family Name

Original name	Changed name	Comments
Etugal Pedige Piyatilleke	Epa Patiranage Piyatilleke	When written with the initials (E.P. Piyatilleke), this name looks unchanged. Thus villagers, close associates, and kinsfolk of the bearer would not know that the name has been changed.
Nuwarapaksa Pedige Turin Ratnayake	Nawaratne Patiranage Turin Ratnayake	In both the original and changed versions, the name is written as N.P. Turin Ratnayake.

Table 10   *continued*

Original name	Changed name	Comments
Hewage Charles	Hettiarachchige Charles	Despite the change, the name can still be written as H.G. Charles.
Karuna Pedige Wijeratne	Kumara Pathiranage Wijeratne	Can be written as K.P. Wijeratne. Another example of Pedige being changed to Pathiranage, a Goigama-like family name.
Kaludevage (in Kalutara)	Kulasuriyage	This is a change of family name by a whole family in Kalutara. Kaludevage has a caste connotation. Pedige and Devage are family name tags of traditional Bathgama caste names. The Karava use Kaludevage as well, in the Aluthgama and Kalutara areas. Kulasuriya is a Karava middle-class name, and it is socially recognized as a "better name" in the Karava caste. The initials K.G. are seen in the new name. Adding a "*ge*" to Kulasuriya makes it a unique and non-Karava name.
Mananalage Gedera Puncha	Maha Gedara Dharmaratne	This is an acaste name. The initials remain the same — M.G.
Rantilake Pedige Kiri Banda	Rajapakse Patirannehelage Kiri Banda	Pathirannehelage is a Goigama family name. This person had a Goigama first name "Kiri Banda" that became appropriate with the new family name.
Hapan Pedige Sobana	Haputantri Palithage Sumit Samantha Somaratne	In this name, an attempt has been made to retain the traditional initials, H.P.S. Consequently, a new *vasagama* name, Palithage, has been coined. Palitha is usually a first name, but here it has been used as a *vasagama*.

Table 10   *continued*

Original name	Changed name	Comments
Horatal Pedige Chara	Hewa Patiranage Charlis	Chara is a mutation of the English name Charles, which is often used in villages as a first name for "low-caste" people. However, Charlis is a popular name among the traditional low-country Sinhalese. Sometimes it is fully Anglicized to Charles to make it exceptional. Here the first name as well as the *vasagama* has been changed to make the name look modern.

Family name changes among the "low castes" can be categorized into three types. The most common is the assumption of obvious Goigama family names and "Goigama-like" family names. Such changes accounted for 64 per cent of all the name changes reported in the newspaper notifications (see Table 11). The acaste names comprised about 21 per cent of the total newly assumed family names. Those who changed their traditional family names did not assume caste names other than Goigama or Goigama-like

Table 11   Frequency Distribution of Assumed Caste Status by non-Goigama Castes

Assumed caste	Frequency	Percentage
Goigama	4,670	64.2
Acaste	1,529	21.0
Karava	443	6.1
Bathgama	96	1.3
Hena	95	1.3
Vahumpura	86	1.2
Achari	76	1.0
Naketi	67	0.9
Dura	62	0.9
Durava	57	0.8
Salagama	43	0.6
Burgher	24	0.3
Patti	11	0.2
Kumbal	9	0.1
Galladu	6	0.1
Panna	5	0.1
Total	7,279	100.0

names, except in cases where non-Goigama castes regionally predominate. An example is the assumption of Karava names in the coastal districts and Bathgama popular caste names in Kegalle and Rambukkana areas.

Conclusion

Sinhalese name changes need to be understood in the context of a caste-class mix and also of a change in culture, values and norms in contemporary Sri Lanka.[27] After independence from the British in 1948, the most important change in Sinhalese culture was the development of a national or public sphere where a common identity was sought and parochial differences were ignored. This development was seen in the formation of a national identity and was manifested in the areas of music, dance, and dressing. For example, certain caste-bound cultural practices such as Kandyan dancing have become part of the national culture. The way in which people of different castes now wear the upcountry ceremonial dress at their wedding is another example. Such attire, often rented from studios where the wedding photographs are taken, was originally worn only by the *radala* Goigama. In Kandyan areas and in cities in the low country, such as Colombo and Galle, couples who wish to portray the glamour of "Kandyanness" often use this attire at their weddings regardless of their caste. Like changing their name, this practice has helped them to avoid the connotations of caste.

This paper has argued that, among the Sinhalese, the tradition of naming has moved away from the parochial confines of the local onomastic system to a widely accepted system where local distinctions such as kinship, lineage, and caste distinctions are not recognized or implied in names. The change is partly due to a paradigm shift in personal identity structures from a kinship-based local situation to a public sphere where local differences are not recognized but where prestige and class matter.[28] In the traditional period, names were used to classify people within their local social matrix along caste lines, through residence, kin group, or line of succession. Now the name has assumed a new role, as an index of contextualizing a person along class lines using prestige and power as determining factors. Thus, names that denote prestige and power are retained, while those that are derogatory and indicative of lowness are replaced with prestigious or value neutral ones.

It is not certain if a change of family name indeed changes one's caste status, but, when a whole family changes its family name and adopts one of a different caste, it is possible that its caste status also changes. However, in cases where individuals adopt acaste names, it is hard to say, without recourse to other facts, that they had aspired to change their caste status. A considerable number of name changes were to acaste names. The majority of people who changed their names to acaste names did so in order to eliminate lower social status attached to their traditional names, thus enabling them to socialize in the wider society or public sphere, especially outside their villages of origin. They did not want to assume Goigama names, nor were they concerned about changing their caste status.

In this study, the individuals who changed their names to Goigama-like names comprised a large percentage of the total number of family name changes. However, we cannot say that such individuals completely severed their relationships with their family and kinsfolk in the villages and that they assumed an entirely new caste status. Although these individuals have changed their family names to resemble Goigama names, they stay connected to their families and marry within the caste. These examples show that some family name changes and the assumption of "high-caste" names are not necessarily about changing caste status. The family name changes by the Goigama show that the majority did not intend to change their caste status. Rather, they assumed title names of *radala* Goigama or opted to modernize their traditional names. These changes show that people who changed their names were more concerned with the social and class status expressed through their names.

Overall, findings of this study on Sinhalese names have shown that family names are considered a marker of social status. The significance of the name as a status marker is seen more widely among the Sinhalese than in any other ethnic group in the country. Individual mobility in today's society may have established the preconditions for name changes. Increased urbanization, relocation programs involving the mass mobilization of people, educational opportunities and employment outside one's village, and problems associated with prospective marriages are some of the factors that may have precipitated the increase in name changes. It is argued here that name changes are associated with achieving higher social status rather than changing caste status. Name changes are also seen as an attempt by individuals to prevent their names from being used as an identifier of caste. The change of family name can be seen as an attempt by the individuals to minimize the effects of caste connotations in their dealings within a class-based society. Nevertheless, while caste may be losing its symbolic significance at the individual level, it does not necessarily mean that the same can be said of caste at regional levels or in political arenas where it is known to play a vital role.

Acknowledgements

The University of Peradeniya provided funds for this study (Grant No. RG/96/10/A). Mr. K.B.S. Wanninayake coordinated the collection of data at the archives in Colombo. Miss Ajanta Peiris, Miss Sujatha Mallawa Arachchi, and Mr. Bandara collected the data. The Department of Archives granted permission to browse through old newspapers. Several scholars and colleagues reviewed and provided valuable comments on an earlier draft of this paper. Particular mention must be made of Professors Katharine S. Bjork, Charles Macdonald, Zheng Yangwen and P.W.S. de Silva. I thank them all.

Notes

1. "Traditional times" in this paper does not refer to a particular time period because, when viewing name changes, "traditional times" reflects individual family situations in particular historical periods, and it is specific to the family. Therefore, the historical period referred to as "traditional times" is amorphous and refers to a broad period for each family when its forbears did not change their structure of names.

2. Michael Roberts, *Caste Conflict and Elite Formation: The Rise of a Karava Elite in Sri Lanka, 1500–1931* (Cambridge: Cambridge University Press, 1982); and Nur Yalman, "The Flexibility of Caste Principles in a Kandyan Community," in *Aspects of Caste in South India, Ceylon and North-west Pakistan*, ed. E.R Leach (Cambridge: Cambridge University Press, 1960), pp. 78–112.

3. Yalman, "The Flexibility of Caste Principles in a Kandyan Community," p. 88.

4. Ralph Pieris, *Sinhalese Social Organisation* (Colombo: University of Ceylon Press, 1956).

5. The year of the foundation of the Kandyan Kingdom is controversial [or 'dubious' or 'uncertain']. According to T.B.H. Abeyasinghe, the Kandyan Kingdom was founded in 1474. See T.B.H. Abeyasinghe, "The Kingdom of Kandy: Foundations and Foreign Relations to 1638," in *History of Sri Lanka*, Vol. II, ed. K.M. de Silva (Peradeniya: University of Peradeniya, 1995), pp. 123–61.

6. Goigama is the majority caste in Sri Lanka. Within this caste are sub-castes such as the *radala*, which constituted the landed aristocracy in the past.

7. Pieris, *Sinhalese Social Organisation*, p. 173.

8. Obeyesekere, *Land Tenure in Village Ceylon: A Sociological and Historical Study* (Cambridge: Cambridge University Press, 1967), p. 224.

9. Ibid., p. 225.

10. The division of upcountry and low country in Sri Lanka has a social significance. The low country areas were under the colonial rule since 1505, and underwent many changes as a result. Adoption of Christianity, Catholicism and European names and cultures are some such changes. The upcountry areas

were under the rule of the Sinhalese kings until they were captured by the British in 1815. Most of the patronymics were originated in the upcountry areas that were conferred by the kings.

11   Ibid., p. 15.

12   Names such as Puncha and Ukkuwa are "low-caste" names.

13   The definition given by Yalman in this quotation is used throughout this paper to denote caste status as "low-caste." Therefore, it is used with inverted commas throughout the paper. Yalman, "The Flexibility of Caste Principles in a Kandyan Community," p. 88.

14   This system changed particularly after the 1960s when village-level officials were appointed on the basis of their educational qualifications rather than of their traditional family status, authority and ownership of land. The Grama Sevaka Niladharis replaced the Arachchis (village headmen) during this period. However, in certain villages even in 1980s, the registrars of births, deaths and marriages, who were Goigama *radala*, were of the view that low-caste persons should be named according to the old tradition.

15   Yalman, "The Flexibility of Caste Principles in a Kandyan Community," p. 88.

16   Obeyesekere, *Land Tenure in Village Ceylon: A Sociological and Historical Study*, pp. 224–6.

17   Ibid., p. 226.

18   The Sinhala newspapers that were covered in this research include *Jantha*, *Dinamina*, *Divaina*, *Lak Janatha*, and *Lankadeepa*. It is believed that these newspapers are representative of the Sinhala newspapers published during this period in Sri Lanka.

19   It is widely believed that economic liberalization policies introduced after 1977 have resulted in the upward mobility of individuals. Self-employment and other income sources have increased as a result (Central Bank Reports). This comparison could serve as a test of the hypothesis that the opening up of the economy provided opportunities for involvement in wider society, creating the backdrop for name changes.

20   Obeyesekere, *Land Tenure in Village Ceylon: A Sociological and Historical Study*, p. 226.

21   In interviews with Registrars of Births, Deaths, and Marriages, it was mentioned that individuals who wish to change their names have to make an application personally, and the majority of applicants are in the age category of 20–30 years.

22   According to the census of 2001, the percentage of Tamils (both Sri Lankan and Indian Tamils) in these districts were 10.9 per cent in Ratnapura, 3.6 in Gampaha, 3.9 per cent in Kalutara and 12.2 per cent in Kandy.

23   However, the actual timing of the increase in the adoption by Tamils of Sinhala names cannot be ascertained from the present data, which is restricted to particular limited periods.

24   Dura caste in Kandyan areas is different from Durava caste in the low country.

25   Castes that accounted for less than 5 per cent of the name change notifications are not included in this table.

26   Karava and Salagama are castes that are found predominantly in the low country.

27   A new group of non-caste-based political entrepreneurs has emerged and gained influence in India over the past 20 years as observed by Anirudh Krishna, and this is somewhat similar to the processes seen in Sri Lanka. See Krishna, Anirudh, "What is happening to Caste? A View from Some North Indian Villages," *Journal of Asian Studies* 62, 4 (2003): 1171–93.

28   For example, although it is important to know Jinadasa's kinship group and lineage in the context of the village, when Jinadasa moves out of that local context, such details become irrelevant. In the delocalized context, the factors that play an important role are class and prestige.

CHAPTER 13

Naming and Chinese Muslim Identities: Boundary-making, Negotiation, and Hybridity in Malaysia[1]

Hew Wai Weng 丘偉榮

Setting the Context: Chinese Muslims in Malaysia

Chinese Muslims are an intermediate minority community in Malaysia. According to the latest census, there are only 57,000 Chinese Muslims in Malaysia, which is 0.25 per cent of the country's total population, 0.41 per cent of the total Muslim population, and 1 per cent of the total Chinese population. In Malaysia, Malays are defined as Muslims according to the Federal Constitution, while the Chinese are mostly non-Muslim. Chinese Muslims are, therefore, a minority group within the two majority communities in the country: a Chinese minority among Malay Muslims and a Muslim minority within the non-Muslim Chinese population. The equivalence of ethnicity to religion is common in Malaysia where the stereotype that "Muslim equals to Malay" (that is, "Conversion to Islam = Conversion to Malay," "Islamic name = Malay name," and "Islamic festival = Malay festival") is deeply rooted in Malaysian society. Islam is not only a religion for the Malays but also one of the main constitutional criteria for defining their identity. In contrast, Islam is a "negative marker" for the Chinese. If a Chinese converts to Islam, his "Chineseness" is always questioned. For instance, not eating pork is a positive marker for Muslims but a negative marker for the Chinese. Therefore, a Chinese who does not consume pork is suspected of being a Muslim (Long 1988).

Racialized politics and the bureaucratization of Islam have demarcated the boundaries of Chinese Muslims and caused them a dilemma where their identity is concerned. In the past, there were cases where the application of Chinese Muslims for low-cost housing was rejected by the Malaysian Chinese Association (MCA) because they were considered to be Muslim. It was the United Malays National Organization (UMNO) that initially referred such applications to the MCA simply because they considered the applicants to be Chinese (Lim 1980). [2] Islam has been used as a tool to mark and control the boundary between the Chinese and the Malays in the racialized politics of Malaysia. Chinese Muslims stand between this boundary, and have to negotiate their identities in both public and private spheres.

Most Chinese Muslims in Malaysia are converts. Many of them convert to Islam because of marriage to Malay or Muslim partners; the rest are driven either by their interest in Islam, influence of friends, or economic purposes. Some of them may have multiple reasons for converting. For example, a Chinese who might have been familiar with Islam for a long time might convert after marrying a Muslim. However, it should be noted that there are complexities within the Chinese convert community because of their different backgrounds such as gender, socio-economic status, education background, and area of residence. These factors have implications on their adjustment when it comes to their identity and cultural interaction after conversion. Some Chinese converted to Islam during the 1970s for economic reasons, after the implementation of the National Economic Policy which favors the Bumiputra. Most of these Chinese were working-class males with low education levels. They converted in order to avail of privileges that were reserved for the Bumiputra, such as licenses, loans, lands, and low-cost housing. However, after they realized that conversion to Islam did not guarantee entitlement to Bumiputra privileges, fewer Chinese have converted to Islam for economic reasons. Nowadays, many converts are from the well-educated, higher income groups and they are sincere in their conversion as compared to the converts in the 1970s (Ma 1996).

Departing from the stereotypical view that "conversion to Islam is the same as conversion to being Malay" (*Masuk Islam itu Masuk Melayu*), some Chinese Muslims today struggle to project their "Chinese Muslim" identity by adopting Chinese surnames, organizing a Chinese Muslim Association, building a Chinese-style mosque, and having Chinese *halal* restaurants. They feel that there is no contradiction in following Islamic teachings and practising Chinese culture at the same time.[3] This paper focuses on how the Malaysian authorities constrain the ways in which

Chinese Muslims identify themselves, and how they negotiate their identities in the cultural and historical context of Malaysian society. Naming,
as an avenue of identity-making and contestation, offers an interesting
reflection of the situation.

Names and Identities: What's in a Name?

The naming system adopted by the Malaysians from different ethnic and
religious backgrounds has a social and political context. Besides their use
as identity markers for ethnicity, religion, and gender in daily life, names
are also used to define boundaries in administrative affairs, especially to
identify whether a person is a Bumiputra and thus eligible for the privileges accruing to that status, or a Muslim and hence covered by Islamic
laws. Chinese names in Malaysia (mostly non-Muslim) always begin with
an inherited Chinese surname followed by a Chinese given name. For
example, in the name Tan Zhi Ming, Tan is the inherited surname and
Zhi Ming is the given name. The translation of Chinese Malaysian names
in Roman form is usually based on the pronunciation used in the person's
Chinese dialect; thus, it can reflect one's dialect identity. However, in
Taiwan, China, and Singapore, the representation of Chinese names has
been standardized by using the Mandarin pronunciation; in Hong Kong,
it is usually based on the Cantonese pronunciation.

Malay Muslim names are usually based on the naming form of Arab
Muslims, which begin with a given Islamic name, followed by *bin* "son
of" or *binti* "daughter of," and then the name of one's father. For example,
in the name Amirul bin Azahar, Amirul is the given name and Azahar
is the bearer's father's name). There are two major differences between
Chinese and Malay names. Chinese names always have a surname, but
Malay names do not. In addition, Malay Muslims usually adopt Islamic
names which usually originate from Arab, Turkish, and Persian traditions
(Mak 2000: 17) but Chinese seldom adopt such names. Therefore, there
is a general perception that a Chinese who converts to Islam has to change
his/her original Chinese name to a new so-called Malay name.

In his article, "The Innovation of 'Islamic Names,'" A. Muhammad
challenges the meaning of Islamic names.[4] He argues that, the concept of
an "Islamic name" is not just a false concept but an innovation that has
no basis in the Qur'an. He questions whether the so-called Islamic names,
such as Muhammad, Ali, and Khadija are merely Arabic names. He adds
that since Islam is a universal faith which does not distinguish between
cultures, races, or colors, the act of changing one's name does not make
him or her a Muslim; rather, it alienates that person from the universality

of Islam. A. Muhammad's argument may be right conceptually, but in practice, naming is not a natural or neutral matter. It has cultural, historical, and political implications within a society, especially in the Malaysian society where a variety of issues are always intertwined with ethnicity and religion and where naming has been used as a form of ethnic and religious control in administrative affairs.

A change of name reflects a change of ethnic and religious identity, as well as of social and political status. For example, many Greeks gave their children Hellenic names or changed their Christian names, like John and Paul, to Hellenic names like Pericles and Themistocles, in order to project their Greek identity during the development of Greek nationalism in the eighteenth century (Friedman 1994: 121). Besides, changing one's names is often associated with upward social mobility. For example, several Hollywood stars with ethnic roots in Eastern and Southern Europe adopted Anglo-Saxon sounding stage names. For example, Bernic Schwartz changed his name to Tony Curtis; Issur Danielovith to Kirk Douglas, and Dino Crocetti to Dean Martin (Hirschman 2003: 20; citing from Baltzell 1966: 47).

Culture and identity awareness can also be shaped through naming, depending on certain contexts and situations in a society. For example, around the year 1945, many Muslims living in Sumatra's Tapanuli turned to their own clan names instead of using Islamic names only: Mansur became Mansur Lubis and Tahir became Tahir Situmarong, as a negative response to Malay nationalism. When it became a liability to be known as Malay, many Batak Muslims reassessed their identities and returned to their Batak clan names. In those days, reversion to clan names meant that the persons concerned had given up their Malay culture and identity, and they had returned to their roots, that is, the Batak clan (Ariffin 1993: 82–3). Another example is the major difference between the naming system adopted by Muslims in Malaysia and Indonesia. For the most part, Malay Muslims in Malaysia use full Arab Muslim names, but Javanese Muslims maintain their customary names. Perhaps this is indicative of different Islamization processes (Mak 2002: 77, 86).[5] To keep their Indian identity, some Indian Muslims in Malaysia continue to use "a/l" (*anak lelaki* "son of") or "a/p" (*anak perempuan* "daughter of"), rather than "*bin/binti*" in their identity cards (Nagata 1993: 527).

The term "Baba" refers to a creole community in Malaysia made up of Malay and Chinese cultures. Although the Baba adopted many aspects of the Malay culture, most of them did not convert to Islam and kept their traditional folk beliefs. In the Baba community, Chinese names are used because such a name confirms one's Chinese status. Most Babas do not use their name as a symbol of their Baba identity since it does not distinguish them from non-Baba Chinese. The relationship between a Baba's name and his identity is most clearly illustrated in the case of some Babas who were arrested together with their Malay friends for not fasting during the Muslim fasting month. Their fluency in Malay and inability to speak Chinese did nothing to help them convince the officers that they were Chinese and not Malays. It was the Chinese name on their identity cards that persuaded religious officials that they were not Malay (Tan 1988:106). The case of the Hui in Malaysia is different. In China, the Hui are a Muslim community, but most of the descendants of the Hui in Malaysia have lost their identity and have been assimilated either into the Malay Muslim or Chinese non-Muslim community. Very few have retained their Hui identity. Those who become Malay Muslims only have Muslim names, such as Amirul bin Azahar, while those assimilated into the Chinese community have only Chinese names, like Ma Zhi Ming. Those who retain their Hui identity have a combination of both Islamic and Chinese names, such as Amirul Ma Zhi Ming. This combination reflects the unique Hui identity.

Conversion to Islam and the Changing of Name

In Malaysia, conversion to Islam is a public, not a private affair. It changes the convert's status to a Muslim who is bound by Islamic law. Converts also need to go through a bureaucratic procedure at the religious department, including a change of name, which is not required by law but always encouraged and advised by the authorities. Although not required by Islamic teaching, changing one's name after conversion to Islam has been seen as justifiable because it facilitates identification in a multi-ethnic and religious society such as Malaysia. One religious officer suggested that Chinese converts to Islam should change their names to avoid being confused with non-Muslim Chinese. Most of the time, religious officers in Malaysia advise the convert to adopt an Islamic name that ends "bin/binti Abdullah." At the last stage of administration procedure, Muslim converts will be given an Islamic card (where their Islamic name will be officially displayed) by the religious departments. After that, they will be encouraged or advised to change their religious information and name in their identity cards.

At the federal level, the Malaysia Islamic Development Department or Jabatan Kemajuan Islam Malaysia (JAKIM) and the National Registration Department (NRD) represent religious and secular authority, respectively. Each one has a role in the naming of converts. There are two main documents that deal with naming policy for converts. The first document is the JPN.0.b/90(4), a letter which was issued in 1981 by the NRD to each state religious department (Ku 1997). The second document is the Naming Guideline for Converts, published by JAKIM in 1998. However, in the last few decades, some changes with regard to the naming patterns have been allowed. For example, whether or not converts use "bin/binti Abdullah" now depends on the policies adopted by religious authorities in the different states of the country.

The 1981 Policy of the National Registration Department

In 1981, a letter was sent by the National Registration Department (NRD) to all state religious departments to regulate the naming procedures for converts (Ku 1997). According to this document, the original family name should be written after the Islamic name in the identity card. For instance, if Tan Ah Chiap converted to Islam and he chose Abdul Rahim as his Islamic name, then his name should be written as Abdul Rahim Tan bin Abdullah. Furthermore, the use of "alias" was prohibited. Thus, a name like Abdul Rahim @ Tan Ah Chiap was not allowed. The NRD's reason for keeping the family name was to show that the person was a new convert, and not a Malay or Bumiputra (Ku 1997). Consequently, the convert was prohibited from enjoying Malay privileges under the constitution. However, if a male convert married a Malay or Muslim Bumiputra, their children were allowed to adopt a full Malay or Islamic name and drop the original family name. Such children were considered to be Malays or Bumiputra, and they were allowed to enjoy privileges accorded to Malays.[6] In the case of the *orang asli* "indigenous people" and Bumiputra converts, the original and family names could be dropped if they agreed to adopt a new Islamic name. This was because conversion to Islam did not change their status as Bumiputra which, under the constitution, allowed them to enjoy Malay privileges.

The 1998 Policy of the Malaysia Islamic Development Department

The Naming Guideline for New Converts published in 1998 by the Malaysia Islamic Development Department (JAKIM) under the Prime Minister's Department outlined two types of naming policies for converts, one for Bumiputra converts and for non-Bumiputra converts. In general, the guideline was similar to the 1981 letter issued by the NRD described above. According to the Guideline, all converts had to adopt a new Muslim name ending with "bin/binti Abdullah" for administrative purposes. However, the policies for Bumiputra and non-Bumiputra converts differed. Bumiputra converts, like Sabahans, Sarawakians, and *orang asli* were allowed to adopt full Islamic names. However, non-Bumiputra converts, like Chinese and Indian converts, had to retain their surnames. Moreover, they were not allowed to adopt full Islamic names. For instance, if a Chinese convert called Tan Zhi Ming converted to Islam and assumed the Arab-Islamic name Amirul, then his name should be Amirul Tan bin Abdullah. He is prohibited from using the name Amirul Muhammad, which is a full Arab-Islamic name. Compared to the 1981 NRD letter, the 1998 JAKIM guideline is more flexible. Under the latter, Tan Zhi Ming would have more choices, such as Amirul Tan Zhi Ming, Amirul bin Tan Abdullah, Amirul Tan bin Abdullah, Ahmad bin Abdullah Tan, or Amirul Arif bin Tan. However, he would still be prohibted from adopting a full Arab-Islamic name.

The situation was the same for Indian converts. For instance, if an Indian named Balakrishnan a/l Maniam converted, he could adopt names like Tajuddin Balakrishnan bin Abdullah, Balakrishnan bin Abdullah, Tajuddin bin Maniam, or Tajuddin bin Abdullah Balakrishnan. Like the Chinese convert, he was not allowed to use Tajuddin bin Abdullah, a full Arab-Islamic name. It should be noted that the use of "a/l" (*anak lelaki* "son of") or "a/p" (*anak perempuan* "daughter of") was changed to "*bin/binti*" in the naming system for Indian converts.

The Muslim/Non-Muslim Boundary

The following discussion will reveal that naming in Malaysia is not just an ethnic and religious identity marker, but is used by the state to control social boundaries. Besides using an Islamic name to signal their Muslim identity, converts are always advised to adopt an Islamic name with a religious meaning. Muslim identification is important because the Islamic bureaucracy in Malaysia has made Islam a public identity. A Muslim is constrained by the duties and legislations enforced by the Islamic authorities in the inheritance of wealth, marriage, burial, and other affairs. Therefore, names not only reflect a Muslim's religious identity; it also reflects his status in the legal and administrative system. The converts to other religions such as Buddhism, Christianity, and Hinduism, sometimes adopt religious names as well; but, this is not an administrative process and it does not have a major impact on their public life.

According to the 1998 JAKIM Naming Guideline for New Converts, the standardization of naming for converts is important for the following reasons:

(a)   When a convert dies, it is easy to recognize the dead person, as well as handle the burial, inheritance of wealth, and other related matters

(b)   It prevents the new converts from leaving the religion

(c)   Identification for their religious belief

In the past, there were many court cases in order to determine whether a dead person was a Muslim or not, and consequently whether the body should be buried in the Islamic way.[7] To avoid this problem, religious officials suggested that converts change their names immediately after conversion, so that their Muslim identity could be shown easily in their identity card. While the majority of the Chinese Muslims recognized the rationale for adopting an Islamic name or at least changing the religious information in their identity cards, they were unhappy with the choice of names that were available to them. Thus, after the introduction of MyKad, the new identity card with the chip technology, some Chinese Muslims argued that they only needed to change their religious information on this card and that there was no longer any need for them to change their names since their Muslim identity would already be shown on the MyKad.[8]

The Bumiputra/Non-Bumiputra Divide

If a change of name is recommended for identification purposes in the case of Muslim converts, why were converts, especially those who are not Bumiputra, not allowed to adopt a full Arab-Islamic name? It should be noted that a name is not just a religious identity marker; it also indicates who should be given privileges within the context of the racialized politics of Malaysia and who should not. As clearly stated in the 1981 NRD letter, non-Bumiputra converts, including Chinese converts, had to keep their surname. They were also not allowed to adopt a full Arab-Islamic name. This policy was made to emphasize that the new converts were not Malays or Bumiputra; hence, they were not eligible for any Bumiputra privileges. However, if they married Malays and other Bumiputra Muslims, their children could adopt a full Arab-Islamic name and be considered as Bumiputra.

Some officials contend that certain Chinese converted to Islam because they wanted to gain access to the special privileges given to people with Bumiputra status during the 1970s, after the implementation of the National Economic Policy. These officials said that if a Chinese convert used an Arab-Islamic name for administrative matters, they could not determine whether the person was Malay or Chinese. Thus, the naming policy was needed to protect Malay rights from being abused by the new converts. In other words, the naming policy was used to prevent the converts from becoming Malay and, thus, Bumiputra. Although Chinese converts may have fulfilled the social-cultural definition of being a Malay as stated in the constitution, the government has not officially regarded them as such since 1981.[9] This is because the government has used the name appearing in the identity card as the only basis for determining whether one is Malay or not. As evidence, Lim (1983: 232) notes two cases in the 1970s. In one case, a Chinese convert tried to apply for a fund meant only for Bumiputra. The convert was not given the funds because he had a Chinese surname in his identity card although he spoke fluent Malay and adopted a Malay lifestyle. In contrast, a convert who could not speak good Malay but who had only an Islamic name in his identity card succeeded in applying for a loan from the Amanah Saham Nasional, a share purchase scheme open only to Bumiputra. Therefore, one's name is the sole determinant of one's "Malayness" and consequently, one's accessibility to certain privileges.

However, Bumiputra converts, such as Kadazan and Iban converts, are allowed to have only Arab-Islamic names because such names do not change their Bumiputra status which was granted to them by the constitution. We may conclude, therefore, that the naming system has been used by the authorities as a form of ethnic and religious control by delineating the Muslims from the non-Muslims, the Malays from the non-Malays, and the Bumiputra from non Bumiputra for the politics of identification. There is no certificate to verify Bumiputra status. Instead, it is only the indication of one's name and ethnicity in the official documents which determines whether or not one is a Bumiputra. In particular, a Chinese convert has to adopt an Islamic name to show his/her "Muslimness," but he is prohibited from adopting a full Arab-Islamic name to ensure that he will not be treated as a Malay.

Criticism of the Naming Policy

Much criticism has been directed toward the naming policy described above, particularly the use of "bin/binti Abdullah." Some people have complained that such names sound too much like the father's name is Abdullah. Some say that it distinguishes the converts from other Muslims and make them feel like "second-class Muslims." Some have even claimed that the changing of one's name after conversion is not a religious demand but merely a bureaucratic procedure. On the other hand, some see it as a move by the authorities to assimilate Chinese converts into the Malay community. According to Ann (2003), however, for most Chinese, the change of name is an attempt to change their identity and the loss of one's Chinese family name is one of the main reasons why conversion to Islam has always been resisted by the converts' parents.

Nowadays, there have been a few changes in the naming policy; consequently, it has become more flexible than before. Some Chinese Muslims say that with the introduction of MyKad converts are now allowed by the NRD to adopt any name. In fact, they are even allowed to retain their original name, that is, not to adopt an Islamic name. However, the NRD has no naming policy of its own at present and that it leaves the decision on this matter to religious departments. Moreover, since religious affairs are under state control (Norani 2003), different state religious departments may have different policies. Some religious departments, such as the Federal Territory Religious Department (Jabatan Agama Islam Wilayah Persekutuan, or JAWI), follow the JAKIM guideline, while others do not. For example, the Selangor State Religious Department or Jabatan Agama Islam Selangor (JAIS) has its own naming policy which is more flexible than other religious departments. According to a JAIS Chinese Muslim officer, any name is allowed, including a full Chinese name as an Islamic name.

There are inconsistencies in the implementation of the naming policy among the different state religious departments and the NRD, which sometimes confuse the converts. It has been suggested that a unified standard naming guideline is needed to solve the naming problems for the converts and their next generation. This indicates that the current naming policy is uncertain, unclear, and inconsistent. Its implementation depends mostly on the situation, officer justification, and the preferences of the convert. Therefore, Chinese Muslims still have space to negotiate their identities through naming although they are constrained by government policy.

Identity Negotiation through Names

The change of a name reflects many changes — ethnic immigration and conflict, cultural integration and exchange, religious practice, and inheritance of collective memory. Naming indicates one's ethnic and religious identity; therefore, a name change also reflects a change in one's identity. For example, the Siamese community in Malaysia was once asked to adopt the naming system with "a/l" or "a/p" in their birth certificates. The community, which traditionally uses surnames, was unhappy with this practice and they voiced their grievances in Parliament. Subsequently, the ruling was changed and now the Siamese can use their surnames when registering their children's births (Abdul Rahman 2000: 31). The refusal of the Siamese community to change their naming system reflects their unwillingness to give up their Siamese identity.

Mixed-marriage parents can be creative when naming their children as a form of identity negotiation. For example, in his case study of Singapore, Mak (2000: 43) cited the example of a mixed marriage where the husband was a Sikh and the wife was Chinese. The child of this couple could be given a hybrid name — a combination of a Chinese and a Sikh name — like Getha Mei Kaur. Getha is a Sikh name; Mei is a Chinese name; and Kaur is a Sikh female indicator. Although constrained by the official naming policy as discussed earlier, Chinese Muslims in Malaysia can also be creative in using their names as religious and ethnic identity markers to project their identity, whether to retain their Chineseness, to emphasize their Muslimness, or to project both identities together. For a Chinese Muslim, choosing a name means choosing an identity. The choice depends on a variety of factors which may shift according to the situation. The following discussion will show the dynamics and complexity of identities among Chinese Muslims arising from the adoption of different naming systems. It should be noted, however, that all names used as example are fictitious.

During my fieldwork for this research, I noted that most Chinese Muslims have names containing both Chinese surnames and Islamic names. Such names usually end with "bin/binti Abdullah." Examples are Mohamad Yusof Yap, Sulaiman Soo bin Abdullah, and Marlena Tan binti Abdullah. Very few Chinese Muslims have purely Arab-Islamic names, such as Sulaiman Abdullah. A convert may have a Malay name with an Islamic name, such as Puteh Noraini bin Abdullah (Puteh is a traditional Malay name); however, these are mostly people who converted before 1981.

A Chinese convert named Salehuddin Lim bin Abdullah, whose original name was Lim Khai Hock, reported that he initially planned to adopt a full Arab-Islamic name, Salehuddin bin Abdullah, because his religious identity was very important identity for him. However, he finally chose to maintain his Chinese surname (Lim) to prove to his family and friends that he was still a Chinese despite his conversion to Islam. He considered this to be a form of *dakwah* "preaching of religion." It showed the universality of Islam and proved that conversion to Islam does not reduce one's "Chineseness."

There are other converts who refuse to use the names "bin/binti Abdullah" and to adopt Islamic names with their original Chinese names. Some examples are Tan Ee Siang who changed his name to Azlan Tan Ee Siang and Yong Siu Ling who adopted the name Maswani Yong Siu

Ling. These names are similar to those used by Chinese Christians and Hui Muslims in China. Converts who adopt such names argue that there is no reason for them to use "bin/binti Abdullah" because it is not their father's name. Furthermore, they argue that Islamic teaching does not require them to change their name after conversion.

Another convert, Lim Wan Seng, who has an Islamic name (Lim bin Abdullah) in his Islamic card, never changed his name in his identity card or on his business card.[10] When asked by Muslim friends why he does not have an Islamic name, he explains that his Chinese name (Lim Wan Seng) is also his Muslim name because it has good meaning. Besides, he adds, according to Islamic teaching, there is no requirement to change one's name after conversion. We may say that this move is an effort to maintain his Chineseness and resist assimilation into the Malay community.

Another interesting case is that of a Chinese Muslim couple who converted to Islam after their marriage but who did not go through any administrative conversion procedures at the Religious Department. They maintained that conversion is their promise to God; therefore, a formal registration process was neither important nor necessary. Thus, they did not change their names in their identity cards. They merely adopted an Islamic name without changing their original names (for example, from Soo Zhi Tong to Harith Soo Zhi Tong) to introduce themselves as Muslim to the others. This situation shows that the official conversion procedure can be ignored if a convert believes that conversion is merely a personal matter and it has nothing to do with the authorities.

The choice of names for one's children also indicates whether or not a Chinese Muslim prefers to perpetuate his "Chineseness" in the next generation. In the past, it was believed that the next generation of Chinese converts would lose their Chinese identity, and that this would be followed by the loss of their Chinese surnames and the Chinese language. This was especially true among those who married Malays. However, some recent cases revealed in my research show that there is an effort to pass on the Chinese identity to children through the continued use of Chinese surnames. There were a few Chinese Muslim men who married Malay or Indian Muslim women who kept their Chinese surname and passed it on to their children. They also sent their children to Chinese-language primary schools. Moreover, their children have names like Aminah Hakim Tan bin Rashid Hakim Tan on their birth certificates and identity cards (Aminah is a given Islamic name; Rashid is her father's name; and Tan is her Chinese surname.) In addition, such children would also have a Chinese full name, such Aminah Hakim Tan Le Lian, when they go to Chinese school.

A Chinese Muslim man married to a Malay woman reported that a hospital official had tried to register his newborn son's identity as Malay in the birth certificate because he (the father) had an Islamic name. The father argued with the official and explained that the baby should be registered as a Chinese since his father was Chinese. Besides, he added, an Islamic name was not the same as a Malay name. He stressed that although his son adopts a Muslim name (for example, calling himself Kamal Lim bin Mustapa), he still maintained his Chinese surname (Lim).

Another Chinese Muslim reported that he was prohibited by a government official from passing his Chinese family name on to his child. Initially, he planned to appeal his case, but his wife convinced him to keep the Malay name in the official document so that their child could access Bumiputra privileges in the future. In private, however, he passed on his family name and gave a full Chinese name to his child in order to preserve the child's Chinese identity in daily life.

In another case, a Chinese Muslim man married to a Malay woman said that he would pass his Chinese surname to his children with a full Chinese name and an Islamic name. For example, the child's name would be Rashid Tan Chi Meng bin Azahar Tan. It would consist of a Chinese surname (Tan); a full Chinese name (Chi Meng); and an Islamic name (Rashid). This man was aware that if they gave up their Chinese surname his children would enjoy Bumiputra status, but for him maintaining the Chinese identity was more important than having this status.

Unlike in the past, more and more Chinese Muslims now pass their Chinese surnames on to their children. This suggests that these converts are more concerned with maintaining their Chinese identity than accessing the Bumiputra privileges. Some converts give their children a name with both Islamic and Chinese names but omit "bin/binti Abdullah," so that Tan Zhi Fern might become Zarina Tan Zhi Fern. Other converts say they will choose a "more universal" and "less Malay" name for their children, like Sarah, Maria, Adam, Jefri, and Daniel, which are also Christian names. A Chinese female convert married to a Malay man said that although their children have only Islamic names, they have been given Chinese names based on the translation of their Muslim names' pronunciation by their teachers in Chinese primary school. In fact, their children's friends call them by their Chinese names.

The resulting flexible and hybrid identitites arising from the naming practices of Chinese Muslims indicate that the next generation of Chinese Muslims will not necessarily be fully assimilated into the Malay community. Further research into this situation is needed.

Flexible Names, Flexible Identities

Research has shown that identity is not fixed, but fluid. This is the case with Chinese Muslim names as ethnic and religious markers, which can shift when the situation and actors change. Chinese Muslims have the choice of emphasizing their Islamic names, Chinese names, or both depending on a variety of factors, for example, whether it concerns their public or private identities, whether it is a situation at home or at work, or whether they interacting with the Malays, Chinese, or other Chinese Muslims. This flexibility may be seen in the case of a Hui Muslim lecturer at a local university. He described his situation as follows: "I have two names. My Chinese friends call me Ma Jin (Chinese name), and my Muslim friends call me Ibrahim (Islamic name)." Another example is a Chinese Muslim man married to a Malay woman. He said, "My Chinese family and friends call me by my Chinese name, while my Malay family and friends greet me with my Islamic name. I am used to it. In my business card, my Islamic name is stated along with my Chinese name, without the "bin/binti." In addition, my Islamic name is Adam, which is also recognized as a Christian name; therefore, people do not know whether or not I am a Muslim unless I disclose my religious identity."

Some Chinese Muslims use different names in their identity cards, Islamic cards and business cards. Their names also vary according to the people with whom they are interacting. For instance, one Chinese Muslim introduces himself as Azahar Lee. He has an official Islamic name Mohd Azahar Helmi Lee bin Abdullah on his Islamic card, but his identity card still bears his original name, that is, Lim Boon Wei, and his business card gives his name as Mohd Azahar Helmi @ Lee Boon Wei. Another Chinese Muslim does not use his Chinese surname on his staff identity card at the Malaysian Islamic Understanding Institute. On this card his name is given as Muhammad Fuad bin Abdullah, but on his committee member's card in the Malaysian Chinese Muslim Association, he includes his Chinese surname, Muhammad Fuad Lim bin Abdullah. At the same time, on his business card, his Islamic name, Muhammad Fuad Abdullah, is written in both Latin and Arabic forms along with his full Chinese name in Chinese characters. This case clearly shows that a Chinese Muslim may have varied identities which are manifested in the different names used for different organizations and situations.

One Chinese Muslim gave his son a full Arab-Islamic name and this name appears in the son's identity card. He reportedly did this so that the son would be able to enjoy Bumiputra privileges. However, his son also has a full Chinese name which is used in his Chinese school in order to preserve his Chineseness. In my fieldwork, I found that more and more Chinese Muslims introduce themselves by their Islamic names followed by their Chinese surnames in order to project both their Chinese and Islamic identities. Examples are such names as Marlena Chin, Amin Tan, Yusof Lam, and Maria Lee Siew Fong.

Hybrid Names, Hybrid Identities

In the 1970s, some Chinese converts used their Islamic names to identify themselves as Malays and thus gain access to Bumiputra privileges. However, nowadays Chinese converts believe that they no longer need to change their name and adopt an Islamic name after conversion, as long as their names carry a good meaning. They prefer to keep their Chinese identity although they have converted to Islam. However, such naming practices, whether they involve a full Arab-Islamic name or a full Chinese name, are generally not allowed by government and religious department policies. Therefore, most Chinese Muslims have names which contain both their Islamic names and Chinese surnames followed by "bin/binti Abdullah," such as Amirul Tan bin Abdullah. There are Chinese Muslims who question the use of "bin/binti Abdullah," since it is not a religious requirement and it conflicts with the inheritance of the Chinese surname. Instead, they prefer the naming system adopted by the Hui Muslims in China, as in Amirul Tan Zhi Meng. Nowadays, Chinese Muslims can choose the names they want to put on their Islamic cards and identity cards as a result of the government's loosening of the naming policy.

I have observed that conversion to Islam among the Chinese has created a few new naming forms which combine both Chinese and Malay Muslim naming practices in Malaysia. We may call these names "hybrid" or "mixed" names. For example, a Chinese Muslim's son may have the name Rashid Tan Chi Ming bin Azahar Tan. This long and complex name contains his Chinese surname (Tan), full given Chinese name (Chi Ming), his father's Islamic name (Azahar), and his own given Islamic name (Rashid). It is neither a fully Chinese nor Malay name. It is the name of a Chinese Muslim which has resulted from the negotiation between identities as defined by the authorities and one's daily activities.

These hybrid names are a result of the official policy that prohibits Chinese converts from adopting a full Islamic name or maintaining a full Chinese name. Consequently, these names are used by the Chinese converts to represent and project their Chinese Muslim identities and to challenge the constitutional and official definition which equates Malays with Muslims. These hybrid names make the identity of the Chinese

Muslims ambivalent, shifting between Malay and Chinese. A respondent in Mandal's study (2001: 147) said that "Chinese companies with Malay names create confusion, as 'we cannot differentiate the ones that are Malay from those that are Chinese.'" It seems, therefore, that using Chinese Muslim names that combine both naming systems make it difficult for Malaysians to identify a person's ethnicity through his/her name.

Today, Chinese Muslims increasingly feel comfortable using their hybrid names. This is a manifestation of their resistance to re-assimilation into the non-Muslim Chinese community and to total assimilation into the Malay Muslim community. With these hybrid names, they have found a way to project their uniqueness within the Malaysian population. This paper has discussed how the identities of the Chinese Muslims are represented, constructed, and negotiated through naming, and how their unique identity would be lost if they only use Malay Muslim or Chinese names.

Conclusion

Naming, as a process of identity-making and contestation, has cultural, historical, and political significance within a society. In the context of Malaysia's ethnic politics and Islamic bureaucracy, naming has been used to establish the boundaries between Muslims and non-Muslims and between Bumiputra and non-Bumiputra. A name determines whether a person is considered to be Malay and thus eligible for Bumiputra privileges. Moreover, a name also determines whether or not a person is to be treated as a Muslim and thus covered by Islamic laws. Nevertheless, although guidelines have been established by the authorities, Chinese Muslims have had the freedom to represent their identities through various naming practices in their daily life. The various naming forms they have used show the complexity of the community and their flexible identities, depending on their "audiences." Their choices of names for their children also reflect the attempt to pass on their "Chineseness" to the next generation. Nowadays, more and more Chinese Muslims have adopted "hybrid" names which contain both Chinese and Islamic elements. These names are the result of the official policies that prohibit them from adopting full Islamic or Chinese names, as well as, the interaction between the two "vernacular" naming systems. However, it should be noted that Chinese Muslims use these names to establish their identity within the Malaysian population and to challenge the state's policy which equates Malays with Muslims. From the above discussion, we may conclude that naming can be a form of state control, but it can also be used by a community to negotiate and project a unique identity.

Notes

1   This article is derived from a chapter in my MPhil thesis, "The Cultural
     and Historical Context of Chinese Muslims Identities: Boundary-making,
     Negotiation and Hybridity in Malaysia," supervised by Dr. Sumit K. Mandal
     and Norani Othman, at the Institute of Malaysian and International Studies
     (IKMAS), National University of Malaysia (UKM). All names used as
     examples in this paper are pseudonyms.

2   The Malaysian Chinese Association (MCA) and the United Malays National
     Organization (UMNO) are both political parties representing the Chinese
     and Malays respectively, in the ruling coalition of Malaysia.

3   The reasons why some Chinese Muslims have become more concerned about
     keeping their Chinese identity are discussed in my thesis. They include: (1)
     the government does not consider them to be Malays; (2) they hope to be
     recognized by their Chinese family and by Chinese society; (3) it is a form
     of *dakwah* or "preaching of religion" to manifest the universality of Islam,
     indicating that cultural identity is not lost after conversion to Islam; (4) it
     is an indication that converts today are better educated and more sincere in
     their conversion than· was the case in the 1970s; (5) it reflects globalization
     and the influence of Muslim from China.

4   A. Muhammad, "The Innovation of 'Islamic Names,'" http://www.submission.
     org/muslim-names.html.

5   One informant in my research mentioned that after the Islamic resurgence in
     Malaysia in the 1970s, more Malays adopted full Arab-Islamic names. Very
     few persisted in using traditional Malay names such as Mimi, Intan, Awang,
     Delima, and Puteh. However, there were some Malays who deliberately resisted
     using their Arabic or Islamic name in opposition to the "Arabization" of
     Islam in Malaysia.

6   Given that both Malay and Chinese societies are patrilineal, the children of
     female converts who marry Malay and Muslim Bumiputra normally follow
     the father's identity and naming system.

7   In the 1980s and 1990s, there were many disputes between the religious
     department and the families of the deceased as to how the corpses of Chinese
     Muslims who converted without informing their family should be dealt with.
     Some cases were even brought to courts, involving political party intervention
     and media coverage.

8   In MyKad, the term "Islam" is indicated for Muslims only. There is no such
     indication for non-Muslims. There were some objections to this policy because
     it split Malaysians into Muslims and non-Muslims. By indicating only the
     Islamic identity in the MyKad, the significance of the Muslim identity in
     public affairs is highlighted.

9   According to the Constitution of Malaysia, a Malay is defined as a person who
     believes in Islam, speaks the Malay language and adopts Malay customs.

10   The Islamic card is an official card issued by the religious departments to the
     convert, after a convert has gone through the religious conversion procedures.

BIBLIOGRAPHY

Documents

"Inherited Family Firms and Management Practices: The Case for Modernising the UK's Inheritance Tax", Policy Analysis, Centre for Economic Performance, LSE, 2006. http://cep.lse.ac.uk/briefings

Kyōto Muromachi dōri Nijō Sagaru Takoyakushi Chō "Shūmon Ninbetsu Aratame Chō." [Takoyakushi Neighbourhood South of the Corner of Muromachi and Nijō Streets in Kyōto Religious and Population Investigation Registers 1843–1857].

Kyōto Ogawa dōri Sanjō Agaru Seidō Chō "Shūmon Ninbetsu Aratame Chō" [Seido Neighborhood North of the Corner of Ogawa and Sanjo Streets in Kyoto city: Religious and Population Investigation Registers 1818–67, 1868 (unpublished)].

Kyōto Ōmiya dōri Teranouchi Sujichigaibashi Chō "Shūmon Ninbetsu Aratame Chō" Sujikaibashi Neighborhood at the Corner of Omiya and Teranouchi Streets: Religious and Population Investigation Registers 1843–5, 1848–51, 1856–7, 1860, 1862 (unpublished)].

Kyōto Shi Rekishi Shiryōkan. *Kyō Masu za Fukui ke Monjo I* [The Documents of the Fukui Family of the Measures Guild]. Kyoto: Kyōto Shi Rekishi Shiryōkan [Kyoto City Library Historical Documents], 2001.

Kyōto Machi Shikimoku Shūsei [Compilation of the Laws of Kyoto Neighborhoods]. Kyoto: Kyōto Shi Rekishi Shiryōkan [Kyoto City Library of Historical Documents], 1999.

_____. Takoyakushi chō, Yashiro Jinbei Yaku Chū. "Nikki" *Takoyakushi Neighborhood Journal*, 1/1/1841–3/2/1842. Takoyakushi chō Collection D2, Kyoto: Kyōto Shi Rekishi Shiryōkan [Kyoto City Library Historical Documents].

Moritani, Katsuhisa *et al. Fukui ke Kyūzō: Kyō Masu za Kankei Shiryō Chōsa Hōkoku sho* [Stores of the Fukui Family: Report on Investigation of Data Relating to the Kyoto Measures Guild]. Kyoto: Unpublished report held at the Kyoto Shi Rekishi Shiryōkan (Kyoto City Library Historical Documents), 1998.

Subvlevacion de Tayabas y Cuestion Sobre al Apellido de Los Indios. University of Santo Tomas Archives, tomo 6, folletos tomo 115.

Books and Articles

Abdul Rahman Embong. *The Culture and Practice of Pluralism in Post-Independence Malaysia.* IKMAS Working Paper Series No. 18. Bangi: IKMAS, Universiti Kebangsaan Malaysia, 2000.

305

Abella, Domingo. "Introduction." In *Catalogo Alfabetico de Apellidos*. Manila: Philippine National Archives, 1973.

Ai, San. "Daizu" [The Dai Nationality]. In *Zhongguoren de Xingming* [Surnames and Names of China's People], ed. Zhang Lianfang. Beijing: Shehui kexue, 1992, pp. 317–24.

Akiyama, Kunizō. *Kinsei Kyōto Machigumi Hattatsu Shi* [History of the Development of Neighborhood Groups in Early Modern Kyoto]. Kyoto: Hōsei Daigaku Shuppan Kyoku, 1980.

Alford, Richard D. *Naming and Identity: A Cross-Cultural Study of Personal Naming Practices*. New Haven: HRAF Press, 1988.

Allerton, D.J. "The Linguistic and Sociolinguistic Status of Proper Names — What Are They and Who Do They Belong To." *Journal of Pragmatics* 11, 1 (1987): 61–92.

Alleton, Viviane. *Les Chinois et la Passion des Noms*. Paris: Aubier, 1993.

Ann, Wan Seng. "Kenapa Dakwah di Kalangan Masyarakat Cina Gagal." *Bulletin PERKIM* 11 (2003): 4.

Antoun, Richard T. "On the Significance of Names in an Arab Village." *Ethnology* 7 (1968): 158–70.

Ariffin Omar. *Bangsa Melayu: Malay Concepts of Democracy and Community, 1940–50*. New York: Oxford University Press, 1993.

Arndt, Paul. *Grammatik der Solor-Sprache*. Ende, Flores: Arnoldus Drukkerij, 1937.

──────. *Soziale Verhältnisse auf Ost-Flores, Adonare und Solor*. Munster i.W.: Verlag der Aschendorffschen Verlagsbuchhandlung, 1940.

Asuncion, Diosdado. *Ang Kasaysayan ng mga Pangalan, Palayaw at Apelyido sa Pilipinas: Ilang Komentaryo*. Diliman College of Social Sciences and Philosophy Professorial Chair papers Series. Quezon City: University of the Philippines, 1997.

Baltzell, E. Digby. *The Protestant Establishment: Aristoracy and Caste in America*. New York: Vintage Books, 1966.

Barnes, R.H. *Kédang: A Study of the Collective Thought of an Eastern Indonesian People*. Oxford: The Clarendon Press, 1974.

──────. "Hidatsa Personal Names: An Interpretation." *Plains Anthropologist* 25, 90 (1980): 311–31.

──────. "Personal Names and Social Classification." In *Semantic Anthropology*, ed. David Parkin, A.S.A. Monograph 22. London: Academic Press, 1982, pp. 211–26.

──────. *Two Crows Denies It: A History of Controversy in Omaha Sociology*. Lincoln, Nebraska: University of Nebraska Press, 1984.

──────. *Sea Hunters of Indonesia: Fishers and Weavers of Lamalera*. Oxford: Clarendon Press, 1996.

──────. "Alliance and Warfare in an Eastern Indonesian Principality: Kédang in the Last Half of the Nineteenth Century." *Bijdragen tot de Taal-, Land- en Volkenkunde* 157, 2 (2001): 271–311.

──────. "Ba Naruq: an Eastern Indonesian Narrative." *Anthropos* 97 (2002): 495–504.

_____. "Fransiskus/Usman Buang Duran: Catholic, Muslim, Communist." *Bijdragen tot de Taal-, Land- en Volkenkunde* 159, 1 (2003): 1–29.

_____. "A Ritual Resurgence in Eastern Indonesia." *Anthropos* 100 (2005a): 359–77.

_____. "Hongi Hinga and its Implications: A War of Colonial Consolidation in the Timor Residency in 1904." *Bijdragen tot de Taal-, Land- en Volkenkunde* 161, 1 (2005b): 1–39.

_____. "The Murder of Sengaji Begu: A Turning Point in Dutch Involvement in the Solor Archipelago." *Masyarakat Indonesia* 31, 1 (2005c): 1–17.

Barth, Fredrick. "Introduction." In *Ethnic Groups and Boundaries: The Social Organization of Cultural Difference*, ed. Fredrik Barth. London: George Allen & Unwin, 1969, pp. 9–38.

Barthélémy, T. "Noms Patronymiques et Noms de Terre dans la Noblesse Française (XVIIIe–XXe Siècles)." In *Le Patronyme: Histoire, Anthropologie, Société*, eds. Guy Brunet *et al.* Paris: CNRS, 2001, pp. 61–79.

Battaglia, Debbora. "Toward an Ethics of the Open Subject." In *Anthropological Theory Today*, ed. Henrietta L. Moore. Cambridge: Polity Press, 1999, pp. 114–50.

Bayly, C.A. *Rulers, Townsmen and Bazaars: North Indian Society in the Age of British Expansion, 1770–1870*. Cambridge: Cambridge University Press, 1983.

Bean, S.S. "Ethnology and the Study of Proper Names." *Anthropological Linguistics* 22 (1980): 305–16.

Benjamin, Geoffrey. "Temiar Personal Names." *Bijdragen tot de Taal-, Land- en Volkenkunde* 124 (1968), 99–134.

_____. "On Being Tribal in the Malay World." In *Tribal Communities in the Malay World: Historical, Cultural and Social Perspectives*, eds. G. Benjamin and C. Chou. Singapore: Institute of Southeast Asian Studies, 2002, pp. 7–76.

_____. "'Indigeny-Exogeny': The Fundamental Social Dimension?" Unpublished manuscript, 2003.

Benjamin, G., and Cynthia Chou., eds. *Tribal Communities in the Malay World: Historical, Cultural and Social Perspectives*. Singapore: Institute of Southeast Asian Studies, 2002.

Berg, René van den. *Muna-English Dictionary*. In collaboration with La Ode Sidu. Leiden: Koninklijk Instituut voor Taal-, Land- en Volkenkunde, 1996.

Bloch, Maurice E.F. *How We Think They Think: Anthropological Approaches to Cognition, Memory and Literary*. Boulder: Westview Press, 1998.

Bourdieu, Pierre. *Distinction: A Social Critique of the Judgment of Taste*. Cambridge: Harvard University Press, 1984.

Brassett, Philip R. and Cecilia Brassett. "Diachronic and Synchronic Overview of the Tujia Language of Central South China." *International Journal of the Sociology of Language* 173 (2005): 75–97.

Brewer, Jeffrey D. "Bimanese Personal Names: Meaning and Use." *Ethnology* 20, 3 (1981): 203–15.

Bruck, Gabriele vom, and Barbara Bodenhorn. "Entangled in Histories: An Introduction to the Anthropology of Names and Naming." In *The Anthropology of Names and Naming*, eds. Barbara Bodenhorn and Gabriele vom Bruck. Cambridge: Cambridge University Press, 2006, pp. 1–30.

Calendariong Maanghang, *Iglesia Filipina Independiente Calendar*. Various years.

Carsten, Janet, and Stephen Hugh-Jones. "Introduction." In *About the House*, eds. Janet Carsten and Stephen Hugh-Jones. Cambridge: Cambridge University Press, 1995, pp. 1–46.

Catalogo Alfabetico de Apellidos. Manila: Philippine National Archives, 1973.

Charles, Lucienne Hoerr. "Drama in First-Naming Ceremonies." *Journal of American Folklore* 64, (1951): 11–35.

Chen, Chi-lu. *Material Culture of the Formosan Aborigines*. Taipei: Southern Materials Center, 1988.

Chen, Meiwen. *Cong Mingming Tan Guangxi Tianlin Pangu Yao Ren de Goucheng Yu Shengming de Laiyuan* [The Formation of the Pangu Yao People of Tianlin, Guangxi, and the Origin of Life as Seen from the Perspective of Naming Practices]. Taipei: Tangshan, 2003.

Chiang, Bien. "A New Approach to the Aristocratic System of the Paiwan: A Case Study of Ta-she." *Bulletin of Institute of Ethnology Academia Sinica* 55 (1983): 1–48.

————. "House and Social Hierarchy of the Paiwan." PhD diss., University of Pennsylvania, 1993.

————. "Burial and Naming: Two Memory Mechanisms of the Paiwan." In *Time, History and Memory*, ed. Huang Yinggui. Taipei (Nankang): Institute of Ethnology, Academia Sinica, 1998, pp. 381–415.

Chirino, Pedro. *The Philippines in 1600*. Translated by Ramon Echevarria. Manila: Historical Conservation Society, 1969.

Clercq, F.S.A. de, *Bijdragen tot de Kennis der Residentie Ternate*. Leiden: Brill, 1890.

Colin, Francisco. "Native Races and Their Customs" (excerpt from *Labor Evangelica*). In *The Philippine Islands* 40, eds. Emma Blair and James Robertson. Cleveland: AH Clark, 1903–09, pp. 58–62.

Corkery, J.M. "Attitudes to Naming Practices by the Church in England during the 16th and 17th century." *Genealogist's Magazine* 23, 8 (1990): 292.

Crawley, Ernest, with Thedore Besterman. *The Mystic Rose: A Study of Primitive Marriage and of Primitive Thought in its Bearing on Marriage* 2. London: Methuen, 1927 [1902].

Cullinane, Michael. "The Changing Nature of the Cebu Urban Elite in the 19th Century." In *Philippine Social History: Global Trade and Local Transformations*, eds. A.W. McCoy and C. de Jesus. Sydney: Allen & Unwin for ASAA, and Manila: Ateneo de Manila University Press, 1982, pp. 251–96.

————. "Accounting for Souls." In *Population and History: The Demographic Origins of the Modern Philippines*, eds. Daniel Doeppers and Peter Xenos. Madison: University of Wisconsin Center for Southeast Asian Studies, and Quezon City: Ateneo de Manila University Press, 1998, pp. 281–346.

Dauzat, Albert. *Les Noms de Famille de France.* Paris: Payot, 1945.

de Veyra, Santiago. "Conspiracy Against the Spaniards." In *The Philippine Islands*, 7 eds. Emma Blair and James Robertson, 100. Cleveland: AH Clark, 1903–09.

Delaporte, Y. "Des Noms Silencieux. Le Système Anthroponymique des Sourds Français." *L'Homme* 146 (1998): 7–45.

Democratic Progress Party. *What is Your Indigenous Names?* DVD. Taipei: DPP Headquarter 2005.

Dempwolff, Otto. *Vergleichende Lautlehre des Austronesischen Wortschatzes,* 3 (Beiheft zur Zeitschrift für Eingeborenen-Sprachen Number 19). Berlin: D. Reimer, 1938.

Dietrich, Stefan. *Kota Rénya, 'Die Stadt der Köningin': Religion, Identität und Wandel in einer Ostindonesischen Kleinstadt.* Stuttgart: Habilitationsschrift Universität München, 1997.

Doeppers, Daniel, and Peter Xenos, eds. *Population and History: The Demographic Origins of the Modern Philippines.* Quezon City: Ateneo de Manila University Press, 1998 and Madison: University of Wisconsin CSEAS, 1998.

Dorian, Nancy C. "A Substitute Name System in the Scottish Highlands." *American Anthropologist* 72 (1970): 303–19.

Dumont, Louis. *Homo Hierarchicus: The Caste System and its Implications.* Translated from the French by Mark Sainsbury. London: Weidenfeld & Nicolson, 1970).

Dutton, George. "Crossing Oceans, Crossing Boundaries: The Remarkable life of Philiphê Binh (1759–1832)." In *Viet Nam: Borderless Histories,* eds. Nhung Tuyet Tran and Anthony Reid. Madison: University of Wisconsin Press, 2006, pp. 219–55.

Ebrey, Patricia. "Surnames and Han Chinese Identity." In *Negotiating Ethnicities in China and Taiwan,* ed. Melissa J. Brown, China Research Monograph No. 46. Berkeley: Institute of East Asian Studies, University of California, 1996, pp. 19–36.

Eder, J. "Naming Practices and the Definition of Affines among the Batak of the Philippines." *Ethnology* 14, 1 (1975): 59–70.

Ellen, Roy. "Semantic Anarchy and Ordered Social Practice in Nuaulu Personal Naming." *Bijdragen tot de Taal-, Land- en Volkenkunde* 139, 1 (1983): 18–45.

End, T.V.D. *Gereformeerde Zending op Sumba,* 1859–1972: een Bronnenpublicatie. Alphen aan den Rijn: Aska, 1987.

English, Leo James. *Tagalog-English Dictionary.* Quezon City: Congregation of the Most Holy Redeemer, 1986.

Errington, Sherry. *Meaning and Power in a Southeast Asian Realm.* Princeton, NJ: Princeton University Press, 1989.

Evans-Prichard, E.E. "Nuer Modes of Address." In *Language in Culture and Society: A Reader in Linguistics and Anthropology,* ed. Dell Hymes. New York: Happer & Row, 1964, pp. 221–7.

Falla, Jonathan. *True Love and Bartholomew: Rebels on the Burmese Border.* Cambridge: Cambridge University Press, 1991.

Faure, David. *China and Capitalism: A History of Business Enterprise in Modern China*. Hong Kong: Hong Kong University Press, 2006.

Fenner, Bruce. *Cebu under the Spanish Flag, 1521–1896: An Economic and Social History*. Cebu: San Carlos Publications, 1985.

Fernandez, Inyo Yos. *Relasi Historis Kekerabatan Bahasa Flores: Kajian Linguistik Historis Komparatif terhadap Sembilan Bahasa di Flores*. Ende, Flores: Penerbit Nusa Indah, 1996.

Fiskesjö, Magnus. Wa Field-Notes (1995; 1996–98; 2006).

————. "Ximeng Wa Dictionary." Unpublished manuscript file, 1996–2006.

————. "On the 'Raw' and the 'Cooked' Barbarians of Imperial China." *Inner Asia* 1, 2 (1999): 139–68.

————. "The Fate of Sacrifice and the Making of Wa History." PhD diss., Chicago: University of Chicago, 2000.

————. "The Barbarian Borderland and the Chinese Imagination — Travelers in Wa country." *Inner Asia* 4, 1 (2002): 81–99.

————. "Rescuing the Empire: Chinese Nation-building in the Twentieth Century." Special issue on nation building and ethnic minorities in East and Southeast Asia. *European Journal of East Asian Studies* 5, 1 (2006): 15–44.

————. "Renaming the Barbarians: Ethnonymy, Civilization and Modernity in China and Southeast Asia." Unpublished manuscript.

————. "Both kin and anti-kin: On the ambiguous status of the 'slave' in Wa society." Unpublished manuscript.

Forth, Gregory L. *Rindi: An Ethnographic Study of a Traditional Domain in Eastern Sumba*. The Hague: Martinus Nijhoff, 1981.

————. "Blood, Milk and Coconuts: A Study of Intra-Cultural Variation." *Man*, n.s., 18, 4 (1983): 654–68.

Fox, James J. "Reflections on 'Hierarchy' and 'Precedence'." *History and Anthropology* 7 (1994): 87–108.

————. "The Transformation of Progenitor Lines of Origin: Patterns of Precedence in Eastern Indonesia." In *Origins, Ancestry and Alliance*, eds. J. Fox and Clifford Sather. Canberra: The Australian National University, 1996, pp. 130–53.

Friedman, Jonathan. *Cultural Identity and Global Process*. London: SAGE, 1994.

————. *System, Structure, and Contradiction in the Evolution of "Asiatic" Social Formations*. 2nd ed. Walnut Creek: Altamira, 1998.

Geddes, W.R. *The Land Dayaks of Sarawak: A Report on a Social Economic Survey of the Land Dayaks of Sarawak Presented to the Colonial Social Science Research Council*. London: Her Majesty's Stationery Office, 1954.

Geertz, Clifford. *The Interpretation of Cultures*. New York: Basic Books, 1973.

————. "Person, Time, and Conduct in Bali: An Essay in Cultural Analysis." In *The Interpretation of Cultures*. New York: Basic Books, 1972 [1966].

————. "'From the Native's Point of View': On the Nature of Anthropological Understanding." In *Local Knowledge: Further Essays in Interpretive Anthropology*. New York: Basic Books, 1983.

Geertz, Hildred, and Clifford Geertz. "Teknonymy in Bali: Parenthood, Age-grading and Genealogical Amnesia." *Journal of the Royal Anthropological Institute of Great Britain and Ireland* 94, 2 (1964): 94–108.

Geirnaert-Martin, D. *The Woven Land of Laboya: Socio-Cosmic Ideas and Values in West Sumba, Eastern Indonesia.* Leiden: Leiden University, 1992.

Gemelli Careri. Giovanni Francesco, *A Voyage to the Philippines.* Manila: Filipiniana Book Guild, 1963.

Ghani, Abdul. *Nama-nama Melayu Islam.* Shah Alam: Karisma Publication Sdn. Bhd., 2003.

Haan, F. de, ed. *Dagh-Register gehouden int Casteel Batavia vant Passerende daer ter Plaetse als over Geheel Nederlandts-India. Anno 1681.* The Hague: Nijhoff, 1919.

Hall, Stuart. "New Ethnicities." In *Stuart Hall: Critical Dialogues in Cultural Studies,* eds. David Morley and Chen Kuan-Hsing. London: Routledge, pp. 441–9.

Harada, Toshiaki. "Kaimei ni Tsuite" [Regarding Name Changing]. *Minzoku* [Ethnicity], 4, 1 (1928): 51–72.

Hareven, Tamara. *Families, History, and Social Change: Life-Course and Cross-Cultural Perspectives.* Boulder, CO: Westview Press, 2000.

Haripranata, H., *Ceritera Sejarah Gereja Katolik Sumba dan Sumbawa.* Ende, S. N.: Arnoldus, 1984.

Harrell, Stevan, ed. *Perspectives on the Yi of Southwest China.* Berkeley: University of California Press, 2001.

He, Jiren. "Lahuzu" [The Lahu Nationality]. In *Zhongguoren de Xingming* [Surnames and Names of China's People], ed. Zhang Lianfang. Beijing: Shehui kexue, 1992, pp. 343–53.

Hefright, Brook. "Language ideologies and linguistic practice among the Bai." Paper presented at the Society for East Asian Anthropology conference, Taipei, Taiwan, July 5, 2009.

Herman, John E. "Empire in the Southwest: Early Qing Reforms to the Native Chieftain System." *Journal of Asian Studies* 56, 1 (1997): 47–74.

Herrmans, Isabell. "Representing Unpredictability: An Analysis of a Curing Ritual among the East Kalimantan Luangan." *Journal of Ritual Studies* 18, 1 (2004): 50–61.

Hew, Wai Weng. "The Cultural and Historical Context of Chinese Muslims Identities: Boundary-making, Negotiation and Hybridity in Malaysia", Masters thesis, Institute of Malaysian and International Studies (IKMAS), National University of Malaysia (UKM), 2005.

Hewison, Kevin. *Bankers and Bureaucrats: Capital and the Role of the State in Thailand.* New Haven: Yale University Southeast Studies, 1989.

Hirschman, Charles. "The Rise and Fall of the Concept of Race." Paper presented at the annual meeting of the Population Association of America in Minneapolis MN, May 1–3, 2003.

Hoskins, J. *Biographical Objects: How Things Tell the Stories of People's Lives.* New York: Routledge, 1998.

Hou, Tijun. *Shuo Xing Jie Ming.* Beijing: Dandai shijie chubanshe, 2004.

Hou, Xudong. "Zhongguo Gudai Renmin de Shiyong Jiqi Yiyi: Zunbei, Tongshu yu Zeren." *Lishi Yanjiu* 297, 5 (2005): 3–21.

Hsu, Kong-ming. *The Rituals and Culture of the Paiwan in Kuralau*. Taipei: Dauhsiang, 1994.

Huaxia Funu Mingren Cidian Bianweihui. *Huaxia Funu Mingren Cidian*. Beijing: Huaxia chubanshe, 1988.

Hudson, Alfred, and Judith Hudson. "The Ma'anyan of Paju Epat." In *Essays on Borneo Societies* (Hull Monographs on South-East Asia No. 7), ed. Victor T. King. Oxford: Oxford University Press, 1978, pp. 215–32.

Ileto, Reynaldo. *Pasyon and Revolution: Popular Movements in the Philippines, 1840–1910*. Manila: Ateneo de Manila University Press, 1979.

Jabatan Kemajuan Islam Malaysia. *Garis Panduan Penamaan Saudara Baru*. Kuala Lumpur: Jabatan Kemajuan Islam Malaysia, 1998.

Jabatan Perangkaan Malaysia. *Banci Penduduk dan Perumahan Malaysia 2000: Taburan Penduduk dan Ciri-ciri Asas Demografi*. Kuala Lumpur: Jabatan Perangkaan Malaysia, 2001.

Jahoda, G. "A Note on Ashanti Names and Their Relationship to Personality." *British Journal of Psychology* 54 (1954): 192–5.

Ji, Xiuqing. *Zhongguo Renming Tanxi*. Beijing: Zhongguo guangbodianshi chubanshe, 1993.

Jones, Robert B. *Karen Linguistic Studies*. Berkeley and Los Angeles: University of California Press, 1961.

Jones, R., and Nigel Phillips. "Personal Names in Malaysia and Indonesia." In *Name Studies*, eds. E. Eichler *et al*. New York: Walter de Gruyter, 1995, pp. 902–4.

Kautz, Charles. "Bansag and Apelyido: Problems of Comparison in Changing Tagalog Social Organizations." In *Studies in Philippine Anthropology*, ed. Mario Zamora. Quezon City: Alemar Phoenix Publishers, 1967, pp. 397–418.

Keane, Webb. *Signs of Recognition: Powers and Hazards of Representation in an Indonesian Society*. Berkeley: University of California Press, 1997.

Keraf, Gregorius. *Morfologi Dialek Lamalera*. Ende, Flores: Arnoldus, 1978.

King Vajiravudh's royal birthday speech of 1914 and King Vajiravudh's essay, "Priap nam sakun kap chusae," as cited and translated in Walter Vella, *Chaiyo: King Vajiravudh and the Development of Thai Nationalism*. Honolulu: University of Hawaii Press, 1978, pp. 129–31.

King, Victor. "Introduction." In *Essays on Borneo Societies* (Hull Monographs on South-East Asia), ed. Victor T. King. Oxford: Oxford University Press, 1978, pp. 1–36.

Kimura, Isono. "Nōmin no Issho" [The Life Course of Peasants]. In *Seikatsu Shi*. [Lifestyle History]. 2nd ed., vol. 2, eds. Morisue Yoshiaki *et al*. Tokyo: Yamakawa Shuppansha, 1981, pp. 224–8.

Kirkpatrick, John. *The Marquesan Notion of the Person*. Ann Arbor MI: UMI Research Press, 1983.

"Korean Name", in Wikipedia: The Free Encyclopedia, 2007. http://en.wikipedia.org/wiki/Korean_name

Koubi, Jeannine. "Noms et Classe Sociale chez les Toradja de Sulawesi." In *D'un Nom à L'autre en Asie du Sud-Est: Approches Ethnologiques*, eds. Josiane Massard-Vincent and Simonne Pauwels. Paris: Karthala, 1999, pp. 129–264.

Krishna, Anirudh. "What is Happening to Caste? A View from Some North Indian Villages." *The Journal of Asian Studies*, 62, 4 (2003): 1171–93.

Ku, Kun-hui. "Social Meanings of Personal Adornment among the Paiwan." In *Research Report on Music, Dance, Ritual and Folk Activities of Taiwanese Aborigines*. Taipei (Nankang): Academia Sinica, 1989, pp. 68–83.

_____. "Rights to Recognition: Minority/Indigenous Politics in Emerging Taiwanese Nationalism." *Social Analysis* 49, 2 (2005): 99–121.

_____. *The Symbolic and the Material in the Recognition of Hierarchy Among Austronesian Paiwan*. Tsing Hua Anthropological and Area Studies Series No. 1. Hsin-chu: Institute of Anthropology, National Tsing Hua University, 2006.

Ku Md. Ali Bin Hj. Ku Ramli. *Dakwah kepada Saudara Baru: Satu Kajian Mengenai Pendekatan Dalam Aspek Bimbingan dan Kebajikan*. Tesis Ijazah sarjana Pengajian Islam, Fakulti Pengajian Islam, UKM, 1997.

Kuipers, J.C. *Language, Identity, and Marginality in Indonesia: The Changing Nature of Ritual Speech on the Island of Sumba*. Cambridge: Cambridge University Press, 1998.

Kuo, Eddie, and Bjorn Jernudd, "Balancing Macro- and Micro-sociolinguistic Perspectives in Language Management: The Case of Singapore", In *Babel or Behemoth: Language Trends in Asia*, eds. Jennifer Lindsay and Tan Ying Ying. Singapore: Asia Research Institute, 2003, pp. 103–23.

Larkin, John. The *Pampangans: Colonial Society in a Philippine Province*. Quezon City: New Day, 1993.

Leach, Edmund R. *Pul Eliya a Village in Ceylon: A Study of Land Tenure and Kinship*. Cambridge: Cambridge University Press, 1961.

Lehman, F.K. "Kayah Society as a Function of the Shan-Burman-Karen Context." In *Contemporary Change in Traditional Societies*, ed. J. Steward. Urbana: University of Illinois Press, 1961, pp. 1–104.

_____. "Who are the Karen, and If So, Why? Karen Ethnohistory and a Formal Theory of Ethnicity." In *Ethnic Adaptation and Identity: The Karen on the Thai Frontier with Burma*, ed. C.F. Keyes. Philadelphia: Institute for the Study of Human Issues, 1979, pp. 215–53.

Lévi-Strauss, Claude. *La Pensée Sauvage*. Paris: Plon, 1962.

_____. *The Savage Mind*. London: Weidenfeld and Nicholson, 1966 and Chicago: University of Chicago Press, 1968.

Li, Daoyong. "Wazu" [The Wa nationality]. In *Zhongguoren de Xingming* [Surnames and Names of China's People], ed. Zhang Lianfang. Beijing: Shehui kexue, 1992, pp. 334–42.

Li, Tanya. *Malays in Singapore: Culture, Economy, and Ideology*. Singapore: Oxford University Press, 1989.

Lieberson, S. *A Matter of Taste: How Names, Fashions, and Culture Change*. New Haven: Yale University Press, 2000.

Lim, Hin Fui. "Kajian di Kelang: Sebab-sebab Orang Cina Memeluk Agama Islam." *Widya* 34 (1980): 56–9.

_____. *Kajian Tentang Identiti dan Pertubuhan Pemeluk-pemeluk Agam Islam di Pulau Pinang.* Masters thesis. Universiti Sains Malaysia, Pinang. 1983.

Lintner, Bertil. *The Rise and Fall of the Communist Party of Burma (CPB).* Ithaca, NY: Cornell University Southeast Asia Program, 1990.

Liu, Xiaoyan. *Best Chinese Names: Your Guide to Auspicious Names.* Trans. Wu Jingyu. Singapore: Asiapac Books, 1999.

Löfgren, Orvar, ed. *Hej, det är från Försäkringskassan: Informaliseringen av Sverige.* Stockholm: Natur och kultur, 1988.

Long, Litt Woon. *Alone with my Halal Chicken: The Chinese Muslim Converts and Ethnic Bipolarization in Malaysia. Mag.* (Unpublished PhD thesis). Oslo: University of Oslo, 1988.

Lowie, Robert H. *Primitive Society.* London: George Routledge and Sons, 1921.

Luo, Zhiji. "Ximeng Wazu Xingshi Diaocha Baogao" [Report on Investigations of Clan Names of the Wa Nationality at Ximeng]. In *Wazu Shehui Lishi Diaocha* [Investigations of the Society and History of the Wa Nationality]. Vol. 4. Kunming: Yunnan renmin chubanshe, 1986, pp. 20–50.

_____. *Wazu Shehui Lishi yu Wenhua* [The Society, History and Culture of the Wa Nationality]. Beijing: Zhongyang minzu daxue, 1995.

Lyons, C. *Definiteness.* Cambridge and New York: Cambridge University Press, 1999.

Ma, Rosey. *Difficulties Faced by Chinese Muslim Converts in Malaysia.* Tesis Sarjana. Kuala Lumpur: Universiti Islam Antarabangsa, 1996.

_____. *Chinese Muslims in Malaysia: History and Development.* (CAPAS Southeast Asia Research Paper no. 62 July 2003). Taipei: Center for Asia-Pacific Area Studies, Academia Sinica, 2003.

Ma, Yong. "Zhongguo Xingshi Zhidu de Yange." In *Zhongguo Wenhua Yanjiu Jikan,* Shanghai: Fudan daxue chubanshe, 1985, pp. 1–17.

Macdonald, Charles. "De L'anonymat au Renom: Systèmes du Nom Personnel dans Quelques Sociétés d'Asie du Sud-Est (Notes Comparatives)", in *D'un Nom à L'autre en Asie du Sud-Est: Approches Ethnologiques,* eds. Josiane Massard-Vincent and Simonne Pauwels. Paris: Karthala, 1999, pp. 105–28.

_____. "Personal Names as an Index of National Integration: Local Naming Practices and State-produced Legal Identities." *Pilipinas* 42 (March 2004): 61–75.

_____. "Can Personal Names be Translated?" *IIAS Newsletter* 36 (2005): 14.

_____. "Inuit personal names. A unique system? Or the needle in the haystack." Paper presented at the 15th International Inuit Studies Conference. Paris, 26–28 October 2006. Proceedings of the 15th International Inuit Studies Conference, Collignon, B. and Therrien, M., in press.

Mak, Lau-Fong. *The Rules of the Name Game in Insular Southeast Asian Societies.* PROSEA Research Paper No. 35. Taipei: Program for Southeast Asian Area Studies (PROSEA), Academia Sinica, 2000.

_____. *Islamization in Southeast Asia.* Taipei: Asia-Pacific Research Programme Academic Sinica. 2002.

Mandal, S.K. "Boundaries and Beyond: Wither the Cultural Bases for Political Community in Malaysia?" In *The Politics of Multi-Culturalism: Pluralism and Citizenship in Malaysia, Singapore, and Indonesia,* ed. Robert Hefner. Hawaii: University of Hawaii Press, 2001, pp. 141–64.

Mandelbaum, David G. *Society in India* University of California Press, 1970.

Marlowe, David. "In the Mosaic: The Cognitive and Structural Aspects of Karen-Other Relationships." In *Ethnic Adaptation and Identity: The Karen on the Thai Frontier with Burma,* ed. C.F. Keyes. Philadelphia: Institute for the Study of Human Issues, 1979, pp. 165–214.

Marshall, Harry I. *The Karen People of Burma: A Study in Anthropology and Ethnology.* Columbus: Ohio State University, 1922.

Massard-Vincent, Josiane. "Noms et Appellations chez les Malais Péninsulaires." In *D'un Nom à l'autre en Asie du Sud-Est,* eds. J. Massard-Vincent and S. Pauwels. Paris: Karthala, 1999, pp. 193–226.

Matsuzawa, Kazuko. "Social and Ritual Power of Paiwan Chiefs: Oceanian Perspectives." In *Austronesian Studies Relating to Taiwan,* eds. P. Jen-kuei Lee *et al.* Taipei: Academia Sinica, 1995, pp. 109–37.

Mauss, Marcel. "A Category of the Human Mind: The Notion of Person; The Notion of Self." In *The Category of the Person,* eds. Michael Carrithers, Steven Collins, and Steven Lukes. Cambridge: Cambridge University Press, 1985 [1938], pp. 1–25.

Maxwell, A. "Kadayan Personal Names and Naming." *Naming Systems.Proceedings of the American Ethnological Society 1980,* ed. E. Tooker. Washington DC: The American Ethnological Society, 1984, pp. 25–39.

Maybury-Lewis, David. "Name, Person, and Ideology in Central Brazil." In *1980 Proceedings of the American Ethnological Society,* ed. Elizabeth H. Tooker. Washington: American Ethnological Society, 1984, pp. 1–10.

McCoy, Alfred W. "A Queen Dies Slowly: The Rise and Decline of Iloilo City." In *Philippine Social History: Global Trade and Local Transformations,* eds. A.W. McCoy and Ed. C. de Jesus. Sydney: Allen & Unwin for ASAA, 1982, pp. 314–6.

_____, ed. *An Anarchy of Families: State and Family in the Philippines.* Madison: University of Wisconsin Center for Southeast Asian Studies, 1993.

McKinley, Robert, "Cain and Abel on the Malay Peninsula." In *Siblingship in Oceania: Studies in the Meaning of Kin Relations,* ed. Mac Marshall. Lanham: University Press of America, 1983, pp. 335–87.

_____. "The Philosophy of Kinship: A Reply to Schneider's Critique of the Study of Kinship." In *The Cultural Analysis of Kinship: The Legacy of David M. Schneider,* eds. Richard Feinberg and Martin Ottenheimer. Urbana: University of Illinois Press, 2001, pp. 131–67.

Mertz, E. "A Cape Breton System of Personal Names: Pragmatic and Semantic Change." *Semiotica* 44, 1–2 (1983): 55–74.

Mill, J.S. *A System of Logic, Ratiocinative and Inductive; Being a Connected View of the Principles of Evidence and the Methods of Scientific Investigation.* New York: Harper & Brothers, 1870.

Miller, Nathan. "Some Aspects of the Name in Culture-History." *American Journal of Sociology* 32, 4 (1927): 585–600.

Mitchell, D. "Tragedy in Sumba: Why Neighbours Hacked Each Other to Death in a Remote Part of Indonesia." *Inside Indonesia* (1999): 58–9.

Molino, Jean. "Le Nom Propre dans la Langue." *Langages* 66 (1982): 5–20.

Morice, A.G. "Carrier Onomatology," *American Anthropologist* 35 (1933): 632–58.

Muhammad, A. "Innovation of 'Islamic Names'", Submitters Perspective: Monthly Bulletin of the International Community of Submitters. Masjid Tucson. http://www.masjidtucson.org/publications/books/SP/1999/sep/page1.html.

Murdock, George Peter. *Social Structure.* New York: The MacMillan Company, 1949.

Nagata, Judith. "Religion and Ethnicity among the Indian Muslims of Malaya." In *India Communities in Southeast*, eds. K.S. Sandhu and A. Mani. Singapore: ISEAS, 1993, pp. 513–40.

Nagata, Mary Louise. "Why Did You Change Your Name? Name Changing Patterns and the Life Course in Early Modern Japan." *History of the Family: An International Quarterly* 4, 3 (1998): 315–38.

————. "Name Changing Patterns and the Stem Family in Early Modern Japan: Shimomoriya." In *The Stem family in Eurasian Perspective: Revisiting House Societies, 17th–20th centuries*, eds. Antoinette Fauve-Chamoux and Emiko Ochiai (Bern, CH: Peter Lang, 2009), pp. 361–77.

————. "Balancing Family Strategies with Individual Choice: Name Changing in Early Modern Japan." *Japan Review*, 11 (1999): 145–66.

————. "Mistress or Wife? Fukui Sakuzaemon vs. Iwa, 1819–1833." *Continuity and Change* 18, 2 (2003): 287–309.

————. "Headship and Succession in Early Modern Kyoto: the Role of Women." *Continuity and Change* 19, 1 (2004): 73–104.

————. *Labor Contracts and Labor Relations in Early Modern Central Japan.* London and New York: Routledge-Curzon Press, 2005.

Nakano, Takashi. *Shōka Dōzokudan no Kenkyū* [Research on Merchant Federations]. I. Tokyo: Miraisha, 1978.

Nari, Bilige [Bilik, Naran]. *Xingming* [Naming]. Beijing: Zhongyang minzu daxue, 2000.

Needham, Rodney. "The System of Teknonyms and Death-Names of the Penan." *Southwestern Journal of Anthropology* 10, 1954a: 416–31.

————. "A Penan Mourning-Usage." *Bijdragen tot de Taal-, Land- en Volkenkunde* 110, (1954b): 263–7.

————. "Mourning-Terms." *Bijdragen tot de Taal-, Land- en Volkenkunde* 115, 1 (1959): 58–89.

————. "Death-names and Solidarity in Penan Society." *Bijdragen tot de Taal-, Land- en Volkenkunde* 121, 1 (1965): 58–76.

_____. "Penan Friendship-Names." In *The Translation of Culture*, ed. T.O. Beidelman. London: Tavistock, 1971, pp. 203–30.

Nicolaisen, Ida. "Ancestral Names and Government Names: Assessing Self and Social Identity among the Punan Bah of Central Borneo." *KVHAA Konferenser* 42, (1998): 361–82.

Noceda, Juan de, and Pedro de Sanlucar. *Vocabulario de la Lengua Tagala*. Manila: Imp. De Ramirez y Giraudier, 1860.

Obeyesekere, Gananath. *Land Tenure in Village Ceylon: A Sociological and Historical Study*. Cambridge: Cambridge University Press, 1967.

Ogura, Eiichirō. *Ōmi Shōnin no Keiei* [The business Practices of the Omi Merchants]. Kyoto: Sanburaito Shuppan, 1988.

Omar, Ariffin. *Bangsa Melayu: Malay Concepts of Democracy and Community, 1940–1950*. New York: Oxford University Press. 1993.

Onvlee, L. "Palatalisatie in Eenige Soembaneesche Dialecten", in *Feestbundel Tegenover het 150 jarig Bestaan van het Bataviaasch Genootschaap*, Deel II. Batavia: Bataviaasch Genootschaap, 1930, pp. 234–45.

_____. *Cultuur als Antwoord*. Verhandelingen van het Koninklijk Instituut voor Taal-, Land- en Volkenkund 66. The Hague: Nijhoff, 1973.

_____. "On the Significance of Livestock in Sumba." In *The Flow of Life: Essays on Eastern Indonesia*, ed. J.J. Fox. Cambridge MA: Harvard University Press, 1980.

Othman, Norani. "Islamization and Democratization in Malaysia in Regional and Global Contexts." In *Challenging Authoritatianism in Southeast Asia: Comparing Indonesia and Malaysia,* eds. Ariel Heryanto and Sumit K. Mandal. London: Routledge Curzon, 2003, pp. 117–41.

Ōtō, Osamu. *Kinsei Nōmin to Ie, Mura, Kokka* [Early Modern Peasants and Family, Village, Nation]. Tokyo: Yoshikawa Kōbunkan, 1996.

Owen, Norman. "Life, Death and the Sacraments in a Nineteenth Century Bikol Parish." In *Population and History: The Demographic Origins of the Modern Philippines*, eds. Daniel Doeppers and Peter Xenos. Quezon City: Ateneo de Manila University Press, 1998, pp. 225–52.

"Pakistan Telephone Directory: Karachi", 2006. http://www.karachiplus.com/teledir

Pampus, Karl-Heinz. *Koda Kiwã: Dreisprachiges Wörterbuch des Lamaholot (Dialekt von Lewolema) Lamaholot–Indonesisch–Deutsch* (Deutsche Morgenländiche Gesellschaft). Stuttgart: Franz Steiner Verlag, 1999.

Panganiban, Jose Villa. *English-Tagalog Vocabulary*. Manila: University Publishing, 1946.

_____. *Fundamental Tagalog*. Manila: Philippine Educational Company, 1939.

Parkin, David. "Politics of Naming among the Giriama." In *Social Anthropology and the Politics of Language*, ed. Ralph Grillo. London: Routledge, 1989, pp. 61–89.

Parsons, Elsie Clews. "Teknonymy." *American Journal of Sociology* 19, 5 (1914): 649–50.

—————. "Avoidance in Melanesia." *Journal of American Folklore* 29 (1916): 282–92.

Pauwels, Simonne. "Nom et Renom à Hursu (Tanimbar, Indonésie de l'Est)." In *D'un Nom à L'autre en Asie du Sud-Est: Approches Ethnologiques*, eds. Josiane Massard-Vincent and Simonne Pauwels. Paris: Karthala, 1999, pp. 45–60.

—————. "La Nomination, les Ancêtres et la Renommée à Hursu, Village de L'archipel de Tanimbar, Indonésie de l'Est." In *D'un Nom à L'autre en Asie du Sud-Est: Approches Ethnologiques*, eds. J. Massard-Vincent and S. Pauwels. Paris: Karthala, 1999, pp. 45–60.

Pelras, Christian. "Le Sytème de Dénomination Individuelle des Bugis." *D'un Nom à L'autre en Asie du Sud-Est: Approches Ethnologiques*, eds. J. Massard-Vincent and S. Pauwels. Paris: Karthala, 1999, pp. 165–92.

Penny, David H. "Growth of 'Economic Mindedness' Among Small Farmers in North Sumatra, Indonesia." In *Subsistence Agriculture and Economic Development*, ed. C.R. Wharton. Chicago: Aldine Publishing Co., 1969, pp. 152–61.

Philips, C.H. "India and Pakistan." In *Handbook of Oriental History*, ed. C.H. Philips. London: Royal Historical Society, 1951, pp. 51–5.

Pieris, Ralph. *Sinhalese Social Organisation*. Colombo: University of Ceylon Press, 1956.

Plutschow, Herbert. *Japan's Name Culture: The Significance of Names in a Religious, Political and Social Context*. Richmond, Surrey: Japan Library, 1995.

Pongpaichit, Pasuk, and Chris Baker. *Thaksin: The Business of Politics in Thailand*. Chiang Mai: Silkworm Books, 2004.

Proschan, Frank. "Who are the 'Khaa'?", in *Proceedings of the 6th International Conference on Thai Studies* (Chieng Mai, Thailand, 14–17 October 1996), Vol. 4, pt 1, pp. 391–414.

Radcliffe-Brown, A.R. "On Joking Relationships." *Africa* 13, 3 (1940): 195–210.

—————. *The Andaman Islanders*. New York: The Free Press, 1964.

Rafael, Vicente. *Contracting Colonialism: Translation and Christian Conversion in Tagalog Society under Early Spanish Rule*. Quezon City: Ateneo de Manila University, 1988.

Rajah, Ananda. "Implications of Traditional Karen Land Use Systems for the Introduction of New Cropping Systems: Some Observations from Ban Hua Lao, Huai Thung Choa, Northern Thailand", *Mountain Research and Development* 3 (special issue), 4 (1983): 352–6.

—————. "ʔau? Ma Xae: Domestic Ritual and the Ideology of Kinship among the Sgaw Karen of Palokhi, Northern Thailand", *Mankind* (now *The Australian Journal of Anthropology*) 14 (special issue), 4 (1984): 348–56.

—————. "Remaining Karen: a Study of Cultural Reproduction and the Maintenance of Identity." PhD diss., The Australian National University, 1986.

—————. "Commensalism as Practical Symbol and Symbolic Practice among the Sgaw Karen of Northern Thailand." *Southeast Asian Journal of Social Science* 17, 1 (1989): 70–87.

_____. "Ethnicity, Nationalism and the Nation-state: The Karen in Burma and Thailand." In *Ethnic Groups across National Boundaries in Mainland Southeast Asia*, ed. Gehan Wijeyewardene. Singapore: Institute of Southeast Asian Studies, 1990, pp. 102–33.

_____. "Transformations of Karen Myths of Origin and Relations of Power." In *Patterns and Illusions: Thai History and Thought*, 2nd ed., eds. Gehan Wijeyewardene and E.C. Chapman. Canberra: The Richard Davis Fund and the Department of Anthropology, Research School of Pacific Studies, The Australian National University, 1993, pp. 237–76.

_____. Review of *True Love and Bartholomew: Rebels on the Burmese Border* by Jonathan Falla. *Man*, n.s., 29, 1 (1994): 198–9.

_____. "A 'Nation of Intent' in Burma: Karen Ethno-nationalism, Nationalism and Narrations of Nation." *The Pacific Review* 15, 4 (2002): 517–37.

Reaney, P.H. *The Origin of English Surnames*. London: Routledge and Kegan Paul, 1967.

Renard-Clamagirand, B. *Marobo, une Société Ema de Timor*. Paris: SELAF, 1982.

_____. "Le Nom Wewewa: Jeu et Enjeu (Sumba, Indonésie de l'Est)." In *D'un Nom à L'autre en Asie du Sud-Est: Approches Ethnologiques*, eds. J. Massard-Vincent and S. Pauwels. Paris: Karthala, 1999, pp. 27–44.

Rivers, W.H.R. *The History of Melanesian Society*. Vol. 2. Cambridge: Cambridge University Press, 1914.

Roberts, Michael. *Caste Conflict and Elite Formation: The Rise of a Karava Elite in Sri Lanka, 1500–1931*. Cambridge: Cambridge University Press, 1982.

Robson, Stuart, and Wibisono Singgih. *Javanese-English Dictionary*. Hong Kong: Periplus, 2002.

Rosaldo, Renato. *Ilongot Headhunting 1883–1974: A Study in Society and History*. Stanford: Stanford University Press, 1984.

_____. "Ilongot Naming: the Play of Associations." In *Naming Systems: 1980 Proceedings of the American Ethnological Society*, ed. Elizabeth H. Tooker. Washington: American Ethnological Society, 1984, pp. 11–24.

Rousseau, Jérôme. "The Kayan." In *Essays on Borneo Societies* (Hull Monographs on South-East Asia), ed. Victor T. King. Oxford: Oxford University Press, 1978, pp. 78–91.

Santa Maria, Luigi. *I Prestiti Portoghesi nel Malese-Indonesiano*. Serie Orientalistica Vol. 4. Napoli: Instituto Orientale di Napoli, 1967.

Santos, Jose P. *Ang Tatlong Napabantog na "Tulisan" sa Pilipinas*. Gerona: n.p., 1936.

Scott, James C. *Seeing like a State: How Certain Schemes to Improve the Human Condition Have Failed*. New Haven: Yale University Press, 1998.

Scott, James C. *et al.* "The Production of Legal Identities Proper to States: The Case of the Permanent Family Surname." *Comparative Studies of Society and History* 44, 1 (2002): 4–44.

Shamsul, A.B. "Debating about Identity in Malaysia: A Discourse Analysis." In *Mediating Identities in a Changing Malaysia*, ed. Zawami Ibrahim. Kyoto: Kyoto University, Center for Southeast Asian Studies, 1996, pp. 8–31.

Shih, Lei. *Su-Paiwan: An Ethnography of A Paiwan Village in Northern Paiwan.* Taipei: Institution of Ethnology, Academia Sinica, 1956 [1971].

Sillander, Kenneth. *Acting Authoritatively: How Authority Is Expressed among the Bentian of Indonesian Borneo.* Helsinki: Swedish School of Social Science Publications No. 17, University of Helsinki Press, 2004.

Smeaton, Donald. *The Loyal Karens of Burma.* London: Kegan Paul, Trench and Co., 1887.

Smith, Martin. *Burma: The Insurgency and the Politics of Ethnicity.* Dhaka: University Press, 1999.

Smith, Zadie. *White Teeth: A Novel.* New York: Random House, 2000.

Spence, Jonathan D. *The Question of Hu.* New York: Random House, 1989.

Steedly, Mary Margaret. "The Importance of Proper Names: Language and National Identity in Colonial Karoland." *American Ethnologist* 23, 3 (1996): 447–75.

Steinmetz, S.R. *Ethnologische Studien zur Ersten Entwicklung der Strafe.* Vol. 2. Leiden and Leipzig: Van Doesburgh, 1894.

Stokhof, W.A.L. "Names and Naming in Ateita and Environment (Woisika, Alor)." *Lingua* 61, 2 and 3 (1983): 179–207.

Sturgeon, Janet C. *Border Landscapes: The Politics of Akha Land Use in China and Thailand.* Seattle: University of Washington Press, 2005.

Suehiro, Akira. *Capital Accumulation in Thailand, 1855–1985.* Tokyo: Centre for East Asian Cultural Studies, 1989.

Sumner, W.G. and Keller, A.G. *The Science of Society.* Vol. 3. New Haven: Yale University Press, 1929.

Takagi, Tadashi. "Meiji Minpō Shikkō Mae ni Okeru Shūmei" [Name Inheritance before the Enactment of the Meiji Civil Law]. *Kantō Tanki Daigaku Kiyō* 2 (1981): 27–30.

Tan, Antonio. *The Chinese Mestizos and the Formation of the Filipino Nationality.* Manila: Kaisa Para sa Kaunlaran, 1994.

Tan, Chee Beng. *The Baba of Melaka: Culture Identity of a Chinese Peranakan Community in Malaysia.* Petaling Jaya: Pelanduk Publications, 1988.

————. "A Note on the Orang Yunnan in Terengganu." *Archipel* 42 (1991): 93–120.

Tan, Michael. "Monosyllabic Surnames." *Philippine Daily Inquirer.* November 11, 2005.

————. "Wanted: Pinoy Names." Pinoy Kasi, Philippine Daily Inquirer, Manila. http://www.pinoykasi.homestead.com/files/2002articles/03282002_Wanted_Pinoy_names...1/19/2006

————."Monosyllabic Surnames." Pinoy Kasi, Philippine Daily Inquirer, Manila. http://www.pinoykasi.homestead.com/files/2001articles/07192001_Monosyllabic.htm...1/19/2006

Tani, Naoki. *Nakai ke Daiku Shihai no Kenkyū* [Research on the Nakai Family Control over Carpenters]. Tokyo: Shibunkaku Shuppan, 1992.

Tapp, Nicholas. *Sovereignty and Rebellion: The White Hmong of Northern Thailand.* Rev. ed. Bangkok: White Lotus, 2005.

Thomson, D.F. "Names and Naming in the Wik Monkan Tribe." *The Journal of the Royal Anthropological Institute of Great Britain and Ireland* 76 (1946): 157–68.

Tonkin, Elizabeth. "Jealousy Names, Civilised names: Anthroponymy of the Jlao Kru of Liberia." *Man*, n.s., 15 (1980) 4: 653–64

Tsing, Anna Lowenhaupt. *In the Realm of the Diamond Queen: Marginality in an Out-of-the-Way Place*. Princeton, NJ: Princeton University Press, 1993.

Tule, Philipus. *Longing for the House of God: Dwelling in the House of the Ancestors*. Studia Instituti Anthropos. Vol. 50. Fribourg, Switzerland: Academic Press, 2004.

Turkoz, Meltem. *The Social Life of the State's Gantasy: Memories and Documents on Turkey's 1934 Surname Law*. PhD diss., University of Pennsylvania, 2004.

Turner, Terence. "Production, Exploitation and Social Consciousness in the 'Peripheral Situation'." *Social Analysis* 19 (1986): 91–119.

―――. "Ethno-ethnohistory: Myth and History in Native South American Representations of Contact with Western Society." In *Rethinking History and Myth: Indigenous South American Perspectives on the Past*, ed. Jonathan D. Hill. Urbana: University of Illinois Press, 1988, pp. 235–81.

Tylor, Edward. "On a Method of Investigating the Development of Institutions; Applied to Laws of Marriage and Descent." *Journal of the Royal Anthropological Institute of Great Britain and Ireland* 18 (1889): 245–72.

Uhlenbeck, E.M. "Systematic Features of Javanese Personal Names." *Word* 25, 3 (1969): 321–35.

Utami, Ayu. *Saman. A Novel*. Translated by Pamela Allen. Jakarta/Singapore: Equinox Publishing, 2005.

Vatter, Ernst. *Ata Kiwan: Unbekannte Bergvolker in Tropischen Holland*. Leipzig: Bibliographisches Institut AG, 1932.

Vella, Walter. *Chaiyo: King Vajiravudh and the Development of Thai Nationalism*. Honolulu: University of Hawaii Press, 1978.

Vroklage, B.A.G. *Ethnographie der Belu in Zentral-Timor*. 3 vols. Leiden: Brill, 1953.

Wang, Quangen. *Zhongguo Renming Wenhua*. Beijing: Tuanjie chubanshe, 2000.

Hutagalung, Waldemar. *Poestaha Taringot toe Tarombo ni Halak Batak* Laguboti: Zendingsdrukkerij, 1926.

Watkins, Justin. "The Wa System of Personal Names." Wa Dictionary Project, SOAS, London. http://mercury.soas.ac.uk/wadict/wa_naming.html.

―――. "Draft comprehensive chart of personal names." Wa Dictionary Project, SOAS, London. http://mercury.soas.ac.uk/wadict/wa_naming_chart.html.

―――. "Writing of the Wa Language." Wa Dictionary Project, SOAS, London. http://mercury.soas.ac.uk/wadict/wa_orthography.html.

―――. "Maps of the Greater Wa-speaking Area." Wa Dictionary Project, SOAS, London. http://mercury.soas.ac.uk/wadict/wa_maps.html.

Watson, Rubie. "The Named and the Nameless: Gender and Person in Chinese Society." *American Ethnologist* 13, 4 (1986): 619–31.

Weber, Max. *Economy and Society*, Vol. 1. Eds G. Roth and C. Wittich. Berkeley: University of California Press, 1978.

Weinstock, Joseph. "Kaharingan and the Luangan Dayaks: Religion and Identity in Central East Borneo." PhD diss., Cornell University, 1983.

Werbner, Phina, and Tariq Madood. eds. *Debating Cultural Hybridity: Multi-cultural Identities and the Politics of Anti-racism*. London: Zed Books, 1997.

Wickberg, Edgar. *The Chinese in Philippine Life, 1850–1898*. New Haven: Yale University Press, 1965. Reprinted, Manila: Ateneo de Manila Press, 2000.

―――――. *The Chinese Mestizo in Philippine History*. Manila: Kaisa para sa Kaunlaran, 2001.

Wilken, G.A. *Handleiding voor de Vergelijkende Volkenkunde van Nederlandsch-Indie*. Leiden: Brill, 1893.

Wilson, S. *The Meaning of Naming: A Social and Cultural History of Personal Naming in Western Europe*. London: UCL Press, 1998.

Wolters, W. "The Making of Civil Society in Historical Perspective." In *Civil Society: In Search of Transition*, ed. H.A.I.A. Schulte-Nordholt. Yogyakarta: Pustaka Pelajar, 2002.

Wu, Yen-ho. *Eastern Paiwan in Taimali River Areas*. Institute of Ethnology Data Collection 7. Taipei (Nankang): Academia Sinica, 1993.

Xiao, Yaotian. *Zhongguo Renming de Yanjiu*. Penang: Penang jiaoyu chubanshe, 1970.

Xiao, Zegong and Gao Dengzhi, "Wazu Xingshi de Xingcheng" [The Formation of Wa Surnames]. In *Wazu Minjian Gushi Jicheng* (Collected Wa Nationality Folktales), eds. Shang Zhonghao *et al*. Kunming: Yunnan minzu, 1990, pp. 18–91.

Xu, Jianshun, and Xian Xin. *Mingming: Zhongguo Xingming Wenhua de Aomiao*. Beijing: Zhongguo shuju, 1999.

Yahya, Y. *Ganti Nama*. Jakarta: Yayasan Tunas Bangsa, 1987.

Yalman, Nur. "The Flexibility of Caste Principles in a Kandyan Community", In *Aspects of Caste in South India, Ceylon and North-west Pakistan*, ed. E.R. Leach. Cambridge University Press, 1960, pp. 78–112.

Yasuoka, Shigeaki. "Edo Kōki — Meiji Zenki no Nishijin Hatagyō no Dōkō" [Main Trends of the Nishijin Textile Industry in the 19th Century] *Shakai Kagaku* 23 (1997): 1–23.

Yin, Shaoting. *People and Forests: Yunnan Swidden Agriculture in Human-Ecological Perspective*. Translated by Magnus Fiskesjö. Kunming: Yunnan Education, 2001.

Young, M.W. "From Riches to Rags: Dismantling Hierarchy in Kalauna." *History and Anthropology* 7, 1–4 (1994): 263–78.

Ypes, W.K.H. *Bijdrage tot de Kennis van de Stamverwantschap, de Inheemsche Rechtsgemeenschappen en het Grondenrecht der Toba- en Dairibataks*. The Hague: Nijhoff for Adatrechtstichting, 1932.

Yuan, Yuliu. *Zhongguo Xingmingxue* [The Study of Chinese Surnames and Given Names. Beijing: Guangming ribao, 1994.

Zaide, Gregorio. *Philippine Political and Cultural History*. Vol. 2. Manila: Philippine Education Company, 1956.

Zhang, Lianfang, ed. *Zhongguoren de Xingming* [Surnames and Names of China's People]. Beijing: Shehui kexue, 1992.

Zhao, Furong. *Zhongguo Wazu Wenhua* [China's Wa Culture]. Beijing: Minzu, 2005.

Zonabend, F. "Nom." In *Dictionaire de l'ethnologie et de l'anthropologie*, eds. P. Bonte and M. Izard. Paris: PUF/Quadrige, 2002.

CONTRIBUTORS

Robert Barnes

R.H. Barnes is Professor of Social Anthropology at the Institute of Social and Cultural Anthropology, University of Oxford. He specializes in Eastern Indonesia. His publications include *Kédang: A Study of the Collective Thought of an Eastern Indonesian People*, Oxford: Clarendon Press (1974), *Sea Hunters of Indonesia: Fishers and Weavers of Lamalera*, Oxford: Clarendon Press (1996), and many articles on topics related to the region.

Magnus Fiskesjö

Magnus Fiskesjö teaches anthropology and Asian studies at Cornell University. An anthropologist and archaeologist educated in Sweden, China, and the US, his research is mainly in China and Southeast Asia. Since the mid-1990s he has done field research in the Wa country on the China-Burma border, initially for his dissertation at the University of Chicago, "The Fate of Sacrifice and the Making of Wa History" (2000). He is the translator of *People and Forests: Yunnan Swidden Agriculture in Human-Ecological Perspective*, written by the Chinese anthropologist Yin Shaoting (2001). Having served from 2000 to 2005 as the director of the Museum of Far Eastern Antiquities in Stockholm, Sweden, he also writes on museums and global cultural heritage issues, including the co-authored bilingual volume *China Before China: Johan Gunnar Andersson, Ding Wenjiang, and the Discovery of China's Prehistory* (2004), with Chen Xingcan.

Francis Alvarez Gealogo

Francis Alvarez Gealogo is an Associate Professor of History at the Ateneo de Manila University. His research interests include Philippine social and demographic history; history of social movements; and the history of the Aglipayan movement. He served as editor of the *Diliman Review* while at the University of the Philippines. His articles were published in the *Philippine Social Sciences Review*, the *Diliman Review*, *Social Science Information*, *Philippine Studies*, the *Journal of History (Philippines)*, and contributed entries for the *Philippine Social Science Encyclopedia* for which he served as co-editor of the History volume. He is the present Managing Editor of *Philippine Studies*.

Hew Wai Weng 丘偉榮

Hew Wai Weng 丘偉榮 is a PhD student in the Department of Political and Social Change, Research School of Pacific and Asian Studies (RSPAS), at the Australian National University. His research topic is "Contesting Chinese and Islamic Identities in Malaysia and Indonesia: The Case of Chinese Muslims." Wai-Weng obtained his MPhil from Institute of Malaysian and International Studies (IKMAS), National University of Malaysia (UKM). He was an associate researcher at a Center for Opinion Research and a journalist for a local Chinese publication in Malaysia.

Ku Kun-hui 顧坤惠

Ku Kun-hui 顧坤惠 is an Associate Professor at the Institute of Anthropology, National Tsing Hua University, Taiwan and an Adjunct Research Professor at the Department of Anthropology, University of Western Ontario, Canada. She was educated in Taiwan (NTU), Canada (UWO) and the UK (Cambridge), and was a former Harvard-Yenching visiting scholar (2005–6). She specializes in Austronesian Taiwan, especially the Paiwan people among whom she has conducted fieldwork since 1987. She publishes both in English and in Chinese in the area of indigenous rights and nationalism, material cultures, voting and democracy, naming and hierarchy, Christian conversion and so on. Her research interests include religion and modernity, material and symbolic cultures, historical anthropology, and the anthropology of law.

Joel Kuipers

Joel Kuipers is Professor of Anthropology at George Washington University. Since 1978, he has conducted ethnographic and linguistic fieldwork in Indonesia, focusing on the relationship between language and systems of authority. He was written two books (*Power and Performance*, University of Pennsylvania, 1990, and *Language, Identity and Marginality in Indonesia*, 1998, Cambridge University Press) and many articles about Sumba.

Charles J-H Macdonald

Charles J-H Macdonald is a social anthropologist and Southeast Asianist. He holds a PhD and a *Doctorat d'Etat* from the Sorbonne and has done extensive fieldwork in the Philippines (mostly on Palawan), Indonesia, and south-central Vietnam among the Raglai. He is a research fellow

Emeritus (Directeur de Recherche Emerite) at the French National Center for Scientific Research (CNRS) and is attached to the Université de la Méditerranée in Marseilles (France). His more recent interests include, besides naming practices, the anthropology of suicide, Austronesian lexicography, anthropological theory, and anarchy. He has written several articles on these topics and has recently published a book on suicide, *Uncultural Behavior: An Anthropological Investigation of Suicide in the Southern Philippines* (University of Hawaii Press, 2006). He has published numerous books and articles, mostly in French, on mythology, social structure, religion and rituals, kinship, Palawan and Raglai ethnography, and various other topics.

Mary Louise Nagata

Mary Louise Nagata received her PhD from University of Hawai'i at Mānoa in 1996. She then joined the EurAsia Project on Population and Family History as a post-doctoral research fellow at the International Research Center for Japanese Studies in Kyoto, Japan under the leadership of Professor Hayami Akira. She was elected *membre associé* of the Ecole des Hautes Etudes en Sciences Sociales, Centre de Recherche Historiques (EHESS/CRH) in 1999 after she moved to Geneva, Switzerland. She is currently Assistant Professor of Asian History at Francis Marion University in Florence, South Carolina.

Ananda Rajah

Until his untimely death in January 2007, Ananda Rajah was an Associate Professor in the Department of Sociology, National University of Singapore. He carried out anthropological research on the Karen in northern Thailand and Burma, examining ethnicity, ethnic conflict and the nation-state and the anthropology and sociology of religion. He was awarded the Eighth Royal Anthropological Institute Fellowship in Urgent Anthropology at the University of Durham, United Kingdom, in 2003.

Anthony Reid

Anthony Reid is an historian of Southeast Asia, now again at the Australian National University, after periods as founding Director of the Asia Research Institute at the National University of Singapore (2002–7), and before that at UCLA, ANU, and the University of Malaya. His books include *The Contest for North Sumatra: Atjeh, the Netherlands and Britain, 1858–1898* (1969); *The Indonesian National Revolution* (1974); *The Blood of the People: Revolution and the End of Traditional Rule in Northern Sumatra* (1979); *Southeast Asia in the Age of Commerce, 1450–1680* (2 vols.

1988–93); *Charting the Shape of Early Modern Southeast Asia* (1999); *An Indonesian Frontier: Acehnese and Other Histories of Sumatra* (2004); and *Imperial Alchemy: Nationalism and Political Identity in Southeast Asia* (2009).

Kenneth Sillander

Kenneth Sillander is an Academy of Finland Postdoctoral Researcher based at the Swedish School of Social Science, University of Helsinki. He received his doctoral degree in social anthropology from the University of Helsinki in 2004. He has conducted ethnographic research in Indonesia on the Bentian people of East Kalimantan and published articles on Bentian ethnicity, social organization, and ritual. He is currently preparing two edited volumes: one on solidarity among swidden cultivators and hunter-gatherers in Southeast Asia, and another on ancestors in Borneo societies.

M.W. Amarasiri de Silva

M.W. Amarasiri de Silva is Professor of Sociology at the University of Peradeniya, Sri Lanka. He holds a PhD in anthropology and an MSc in Rural Development Planning, and has written widely on fishing communities, health and social sciences, social change, reproductive health, adolescence, and sexuality and poverty in Sri Lanka. He has been a fellow, advisor, team leader and consultant in many national and international programs and projects on health and social sciences, poverty, social change and social reconstruction. His current interests are the social impact of planned change, effects of the war and natural disasters, and social reconstruction in the war and disaster affected areas, and social and cultural change in Sri Lanka.

Zheng Yangwen 鄭揚文

Zheng Yangwen 鄭揚文 received her PhD from the University of Cambridge (King's College) in 2001. She taught/researched at the University of Pennsylvania (2002–4) and National University of Singapore (Asia Research Institute 2004–6) before joining the University of Manchester in 2007. Her major publications include *The Social Life of Opium in China* (Cambridge University Press, 2005, with the Italian translation published by UTET in 2007 and Korean translation published by ECO-LIVRES in 2009). She co-edited *Negotiating Asymmetry: China's Place in Asia* (with Anthony Reid. NUS Press and University of Hawaii Press, 2009), *The Body in Asia* (with Bryan S. Turner. Berghahn Books, 2009), and *The Cold War in Asia: The Battle for Hearts and Minds* (with Hong Liu and Michael Szonyi. Brill USA, 2010).

INDEX

acaste names, 284
Africa, East, 63
Amanah Saham Nasional, 296
apelyido (surname), 39, 41
   use of, Chinese mestizos, 31–2
Arabic-Islamic names, 9–10, 23, 290,
   294–5, 298, 302
Asia, 1, 16, 23, 25, 28, 30
   Northeast, 4, 22
   South, 7, 16, 21
   Southeast, 2, 7, 9, 15, 21–3,
      29–30, 63, 77, 87, 96, 129,
      144
Asian kin system
   relational titles of, 2
Aung San, General, 130
Australia, 13
autonym, 78, 247, 251
   added names of Weyewa, 88
   Bentian, 106–8
   example of complex, 87
   Hursu *versus* Palawan, 81
   in Palawan, 80
   morphology of, 78–9
   multi-type, 81
   Palokhi, related to events, 132
   relinquished, Palokhi, 135
   restriction in public usage of
      Bentian, 107
   restrictions on use of, 79
   to define communities, 155

Baba community, 291–2
baptismal names

by Lamaholot, 233
by Paiwan Catholics, 215
by Paiwan Presbyerians, 216
in Philippines pre-1849, 25, 41–2
use of, in England, 22
Batak
   Muslims, 11, 291
   names, 10–1
   Philippines, 80, 86, 96
   Sumatra, 10–1, 291
ba zi, 64–5
bansag, 39–40
barangays, 41
bemo naming
   by Sumbanese, 193–5
Benjamin, Geoffrey, 85, 113–4, 120,
   143–5, 149
benren (autochthonous people), 163–4
Big Wa, 152, 154
binyag, 38, *see also* baptismal names
birth order and names/naming, 2, 8,
   25, 80, 92, 94
   among the Bentian, 103, 106, 117
   among the Wa, 154, 156–9
   in Central Indonesia, 90–1
   in China, 64, 66
   in Eastern Indonesia, 227, 231–2
   in Karen naming, 130, 132, 136
   in Kyoto, 248, 255–6, 258
   in Malaysia, 300
   in Malaysia-Borneo, 85, 88
   in Sumba, 182, 185, 190
   in Taiwan (Paiwan), 201, 204–5,
      211
   in the Philippines, 41, 44, 85, 88